# WILD FICTIONS

## ALSO BY AMITAV GHOSH

*The Glass Palace*

*The Hungry Tide*

*Jungle Nama: A Story of the Sundarban*

*The Living Mountain: A Fable for Our Times*

*Mahaparbat: Ek Kahani Hamare Daur Ki*

*Smoke and Ashes: A Writer's Journey Through Opium's Hidden Histories*

# WILD FICTIONS

*Essays*

AMITAV GHOSH

FOURTH ESTATE · *New Delhi*

First published in India by Fourth Estate 2025
An imprint of HarperCollins *Publishers*
4th Floor, Tower A, Building No. 10, DLF Cyber City,
DLF Phase II, Gurugram, Haryana – 122002
www.harpercollins.co.in

2 4 6 8 10 9 7 5 3 1



P-ISBN: 978-93-6569-100-9
E-ISBN: 978-93-6569-330-0



Typeset in 12/16 Dante MT at
Manipal Technologies Limited, Manipal

Printed and bound at
Replika Press Pvt. Ltd.

FSC
www.fsc.org
MIX
Paper | Supporting responsible forestry
FSC™ C016779

This book is produced from independently certified FSC® paper to ensure responsible forest management.

*To Sukanta and Supriya Chaudhuri*

# Contents


| | | |
|---|---|---|
| | *Introduction* | ix |
| | **Climate Change and Environment** | |
| One | The Great Uprooting: Migration and Displacement in an Age of Planetary Crisis | 5 |
| Two | Storm of Consequences | 29 |
| Three | Cyclone Nargis | 34 |
| Four | Folly in the Sundarbans? | 38 |
| Five | The Town by the Sea | 45 |
| Six | A Tragic Predicament | 71 |
| | **Witnesses** | |
| Seven | Santanu Das and the First World War | 85 |
| Eight | *Abhi Le Baghdad* | 93 |
| Nine | At 'Home and the World' in Iraq, 1915–17 | 123 |
| Ten | Shared Sorrows: Indians and Armenians in the Prison Camps of Ras al-'Ain, 1916–18 | 143 |
| Eleven | Of Fanás and Forecastles: The Indian Ocean and Some Lost Languages of the Age of Sail | 169 |
| Twelve | Wordless Pasts: The Indian Exodus from Burma and the Writing of *The Glass Palace* | 191 |

## Travel and Discovery


Thirteen Confessions of a Xenophile 215

Fourteen The Mountains Are High and the Emperor Is Far Away 227

Fifteen The Spice Islands 239


## Narratives


Sixteen The Well-Travelled Banyan 263

Seventeen 11 September 2001 267

Eighteen Wild Fictions 272


## Conversations


Nineteen *Provincializing Europe*: A Correspondence 299

Twenty Imperial Denial 337

Twenty-one Storytelling and the Spectrum of the Past 347

Twenty-two Shashi Tharoor's *An Era of Darkness* 361

Twenty-three Priya Satia's *Time's Monster* 370


## Presentations


Twenty-four The Making of *In an Antique Land*: India, Egypt and the Cairo Geniza 383

Twenty-five Computers and Spinning Wheels 405

Twenty-six The Way of A.K. Ramanujan 418

*Afterword* 427

*Notes* 433

# Introduction

The pieces in this collection are about a wide variety of subjects, yet there is one thread that runs through most of them: of bearing witness to a rupture in time, of chronicling the passing of an era that began 300 years ago, in the eighteenth century. This was, of course, the period that saw the birth of modernity and industrial civilization, in which, under the leadership of the British empire, the West tightened its grip over most of the world, culminating ultimately in the emergence of the US as the planet's sole superpower. Starting with the collapse of the Soviet Union, the 'unipolar moment' peaked at the turn of the millennium and then ran into a series of profound shocks that began in 2001.

In the summer of 2001, I was scheduled to deliver a lecture in Colombo in memory of Neelan Tiruchelvam, the eminent Sri Lankan lawyer who had emerged in the course of the country's long civil war as the most prominent liberal voice within the Tamil community. As a voice of moderation, Tiruchelvam was a target for extremists, particularly the Liberation Tigers of Tamil Eelam (LTTE), and his life ended tragically in a gruesome car bombing on 29 July 1999.

My talk was scheduled for the second anniversary of Tiruchelvam's death, but five days before that, on 24 July 2001, the LTTE carried out what was then the boldest and most spectacular act of terrorism the world had seen: fourteen suicide commandos attacked Colombo's international airport, killing seven soldiers and destroying or damaging twenty-six aircraft, including several fighter jets.

The following day, pictures of the airport with burnt and crippled planes strewn across the runways appeared on TV and computer screens around the world. The next few days passed in great uncertainty for me because I did not know whether I would be able to travel to Colombo or not. I was determined to go, if at all possible, because I felt that this was a time when it was urgently necessary to remember a man like Neelan Tiruchelvam. Fortunately, flights resumed soon, and I was able to travel to Colombo as planned. I remember vividly the spectacle that greeted me when my plane landed: burnt-out shells of planes and helicopters were littered everywhere, and some of them had even melted into the tarmac. The airport was not new to me. I had lived in Colombo as a child in the 1960s, when Sri Lanka was the most 'advanced' nation in the Indian subcontinent, with the highest literacy rates, the best health services and so on. To look around that airport, with its charred wreckage, was to know that the teleology that had sustained modernity, with its promises of never-ending growth and progress, was a delusion.

Six weeks later, on 11 September 2001, I was in Brooklyn with my family. It was an important day for us because it was the beginning of the school year, and our ten-year-old daughter, Lila, was joining a new school, one that happened to face the World Trade Center from across the East River and Lower Manhattan. Early that morning, my wife dropped Lila off and then went to her workplace, so when the attacks began, she was a long way away, in midtown Manhattan. I was at home with our eight-year-old son, Nayan, so when the city's schools began to shut down, we set off together to bring Lila home. I held Nayan's hand all the way because it would have been easy for us to be separated by the streams of people now pouring over the Brooklyn Bridge. The crowds included many people who worked in the financial districts of Manhattan; their expensive business clothes were coated in grey dust and they were walking as if in a daze, stupefied by what they had seen. They were the lucky ones; later that day, we would find out that our friend and neighbour Frank de Martini was among the missing.

When we finally found Lila in the crowded foyer of her school, the first words she uttered were: 'I saw it all through the windows of my history class.' This turned out to be true: my daughter and her classmates had seen the attacks on the twin towers through a schoolroom window.

Unlike Lila, and many other New Yorkers, I did not behold the attacks of 9/11 with my own eyes. Yet on that day, I felt that I was watching another turn in a cycle of history that I had witnessed from many different angles—in India, the US and the Middle East. Twenty years earlier, as a doctoral student in anthropology, I had done my fieldwork in a couple of villages in Egypt's Beheira province. I had been back several times since then and had observed many ominous portents (as described in 'The Making of *In an Antique Land*'). Now it was as if this history had followed me to New York and detonated on my doorstep with devastating force. This uncanny feeling deepened when I learnt that Mohamed Atta, the leader of the 9/11 attack teams, hailed from the same region where I had done my fieldwork in Egypt; indeed, his ancestral village was closely connected with the places where I had worked. It was then that I understood that the world was now entering a 'time of monsters', as Antonio Gramsci once put it, when an old era was dying and a new one was struggling to be born. But the monsters that Gramsci had in mind were political creatures—fascists. What is distinctive about our time is that its monsters also consist of weather events that would have been thought of as improbable or freakish in Gramsci's lifetime: supercharged storms, megadroughts, catastrophic rain bombs and the like. Back then, these monsters would have been considered 'natural' phenomena or acts of God. But knowing what we now know about anthropogenic greenhouse gas emissions and their role in intensifying climate disasters, it is no longer possible to cling to the fiction of there being a strict division between the natural and the political: wildfires, rain bombs and the like are also deeply political creatures in that they are the by-products of historical processes that have hugely benefited a small minority of human beings at the expense of the great majority of the world's population. The same could be said about the policies and administrative actions through which landscapes have come to be divided between the 'natural' and the 'social': this is indeed the theme of the essay from which the title of this collection—*Wild Fictions*—is taken.

For me, the third millennium had dawned with the launching of a new project that would ultimately become *The Hungry Tide*. The novel is set in the Sundarbans, and it was while doing the background research for the book that I began to think seriously about climate change and environmental disasters. Indeed, the novel's climactic scenes occur during a cyclone that sends a great wall of water surging through the mangrove forest.

*The Hungry Tide* was published in the summer of 2004. On 25 December that year, I arrived in Kolkata on a family visit. The next morning, still sleepy and jet-lagged, I opened my computer, only to be jolted awake by horrifying images of a tsunami that was triggered by an undersea earthquake centred off the west coast of

Sumatra. The Sundarbans was one of the areas that was swamped by the great wave. Although the wave in *The Hungry Tide* is not a tsunami but a cyclonic storm surge, it still felt as though a scene that had played out in my head, over and over again, had suddenly been actualized in the real world. The thought of this was so unsettling that I felt compelled to travel to one of the worst-affected areas, the Nicobar Islands.

Eight months later, when Hurricane Katrina struck New Orleans, I was in Mauritius on a research trip. Watching the disaster unfold from the perspective of a small island nation was weirdly illuminating. Mauritius happens to be located in a notorious 'cyclone alley' and is frequently hit by powerful storms. Yet cyclone-related deaths are very rare on the island, because the population has grown extremely proficient in coping with major storms. My Mauritian friends (as I describe in 'Cyclone Nargis') were astounded to observe the utter ineptitude of the world's sole hyperpower—long vaunted as the most advanced nation on Earth—in dealing with the aftermath of Hurricane Katrina. I was reminded of 'The Overcrowded Barracoon', V.S. Naipaul's essay on Mauritius in which he depicts the island as backward, overpopulated and teetering on the brink of collapse. Always implicit in Naipaul's judgements are comparisons with the affluent countries of the West, which in his thinking represent the highest standards of good governance. Now it was as if the heavens themselves had intervened to prove him wrong. The stunning incompetence with which Hurricane Katrina was handled suggested that over many years of neoliberal governance, the capabilities of the American state had been massively eroded. Hurricane Katrina was not primarily an environmental disaster; rather, it was an example of what Christian Parenti calls a 'catastrophic convergence'—a collision between a climatic event and social and historical factors, like crumbling infrastructure, poverty, patterns of terraforming, governmental neglect and structural racism.

To me, this seemed like yet another sign that the era of Euro-centred modernity was ending and that the West could no longer be thought of as setting the standards for good governance and political sagacity. This impression would be confirmed again and again over the following years, with the US repeatedly seeking to demonstrate its omnipotence as the world's sole hyperpower. But every one of the projects that it undertook during this time—for example, the occupations of Afghanistan and Iraq—ended in failure, ultimately rebounding on the West.

A good example is the so-called European migrant crisis that began after the intensification of the Syrian civil war in 2011. As tens of thousands of refugees from Syria, Afghanistan and Iraq poured into Germany and other European countries, migration became an explosive political issue, destabilizing governments and contributing substantially to Britain's exit from the European Union. The Western media described the migrants who were then arriving in Europe as being from war-torn nations in the Middle East and Africa, but pictures of the exodus told a somewhat different story, for they invariably included many people who were clearly from the Indian subcontinent.

What was driving these youthful subcontinental migrants to undertake difficult, dangerous (and expensive) journeys across the Balkans and the Mediterranean? Being unable to find any convincing explanations in the media, I decided to make my own inquiries: in 2017, I travelled around Italy, visiting the country's holding facilities for migrants and interviewing recently arrived refugees and asylum seekers. This was an education in itself, and it partly inspired my 2019 novel *Gun Island*. Later I decided to write a non-fiction account of what I had learnt during my travels in Italy: the result was 'The Great Uprooting: Migration and Displacement in an Age of Planetary Crisis'. Since then, the issue of migration has continued to roil politics in the West, leading to an upsurge in support for demagogues and right-wing movements. Driving the ascendancy of these neo-fascist movements is a myth of victimhood, in which affluent countries are seen as the aggrieved parties, resisting invasions by black and brown foreigners. Yet the fact is that the preconditions for these mass migrations were created by none other than the West itself, with the multiple invasions and regime-change operations that it launched across the world while revelling in the delirium of the unipolar moment.

The Cold War ended so abruptly and in such a fashion that the American political class came to be convinced that the US had achieved absolute and permanent geopolitical supremacy and that its paramountcy would never again be challenged. In this period, the hubris of the US, and indeed of the collective West, was such as to surpass anything that existed even in the glory days of European imperialism. American politicians and pundits, along with their epigones in Europe and the Anglosphere, decided that they had a duty to impose their will wherever they wanted for whatever reason. The result was a swath of destruction that stretched from Afghanistan and Pakistan to Iraq, Syria, Yemen and Libya.

NATO's bombing of Libya is a particularly egregious example of the short-sightedness of Western actions in this period. Libya was host to hundreds of thousands of Asian and African migrants: after the government collapsed and the country descended into civil war, these workers had nowhere to go except across the Mediterranean. Did none of NATO's leaders, with all the collective wisdom of their pundits and think tanks, see this coming? Their pronouncements from that time—recall Hillary Clinton gloating after the death of Muammar Gaddafi: 'We came, we saw, he died'—suggest that they did not. The minds of Western leaders appear to have been so addled by their hubris that they believed their actions would never have any consequences.

One effect of this hubris was to create a conviction among Western political elites that they were right about everything, and that alternative points of view were either wrong or misbegotten or dishonourably motivated. I had personal experience of this in the lead-up to the Iraq War in 2003, when I found myself locked in an argument with a prominent editor who seemed genuinely convinced that the US was benevolent and altruistic, the only such empire in history. (My attempts to point out that every European empire, going back to the Portuguese, had harboured this delusion were met with short shrift.)

Unpleasant though this experience was, it had a fruitful outcome for me: I lost interest in writing for the mainstream media. From then on, when I wrote short pieces, it was either for my own blog or for talks that I had been invited to deliver at various venues. I invested a lot of work in these pieces, yet it did not occur to me to publish them, because I thought of them as belonging to a different genre from essays or articles. Yet when I went through the presentations that had accumulated in my archives over the years, I was surprised to find that many of them also held their own as texts, so I am glad that they are finally being committed to print.

In order to write about this time of monsters, I have had to overhaul my accustomed modes of thinking by expanding my interests and by delving into subjects like climate science, geology, botany and much else. This was how I came to learn that this time had already come to be known by many names, like the 'Anthropocene', the 'Capitalocene', the 'Technocene', the 'Thanatozoic' and so on (my personal favourite is Donna Haraway's play on the name of a monster, 'Chthulucene').

This proliferation of names is an indication of the diversity and breadth of the disciplines that are now engaged in addressing the subject. Joining in these engagements has been greatly rewarding for me because it has resulted in many absorbing conversations, encounters and collaborations with scholars whose fields of work are very different from mine: historians, scientists, philosophers and many others. They, like me, are eager to venture beyond the accustomed boundaries of their disciplines and discover new ways of thinking. One indication of the degree to which academics are now seeking to broaden their horizons is the fact that I was recently invited to deliver, in quick succession, keynote addresses to two vastly different groups of academic specialists: one was the annual conference of the American Geophysical Union, the world's largest gathering of climate scientists, and the other was the annual meeting of the Modern Language Association, the world's biggest convocation of literary critics!

The penultimate section of this collection, 'Conversations', is a product of some of these collaborations: one is a forum on the Ibis Trilogy that was organized and published in *The American Historical Review*, and the other is a forum on my book *The Great Derangement: Climate Change and the Unthinkable*, published in *The Journal of Asian Studies*. Also included in this section is an email exchange that I had with Dipesh Chakrabarty many years ago, which was published by the *Radical History Review* in 2002. Since then, Dipesh has become a pioneer in thinking about this age of monsters, and our engagements with each other have continued to be a source of inspiration for me.

In the course of this journey, I have acquired many debts, some of which cannot be allowed to pass unacknowledged. I would particularly like to thank Julia Adeney Thomas, Alan Thomas, Udayan Mitra, Shatarupa Ghoshal, Rahul Srivastava, Aaron Lobo, Dipesh Chakrabarty, Santanu Das, Debjani Ganguly, Giorgio Agamben, Ginevra Bompiani, Madhumita Mazumdar, Ahona Ghosh and Suhana Dipona Basu.

My greatest debt, as always, is to my wife, Deborah Baker, and our children, Lila and Nayan: without their support and forbearance, these pieces would never have been written.

# CLIMATE CHANGE AND ENVIRONMENT

'The Town by the Sea' was written in the immediate aftermath of the 2004 tsunami, which had a catastrophic impact on the Nicobar Islands. The tsunami was not, of course, in any way connected with global warming, but like many other disasters of our time it created conditions that were ripe for exploitation by 'disaster capitalism'.[1] One of the worst hit places was Great Nicobar Island, where the population lived mainly on the southern and western coasts. After the tsunami, the survivors were moved to other locations, where they were accommodated in makeshift camps: this was intended as a temporary measure, to tide them over until the sites of their original homes were fit for reclamation. Yet, twenty years later, the evacuees still remain in those camps: they have not been allowed to rebuild their ancestral villages even though they have long been pleading with the authorities to be allowed to do so. This is because the current BJP government and its crony businessmen have other plans for that land: they intend to build a massive container port on Great Nicobar Island, with a township for 350,000 people, hotels and resorts for tourists, and a military base.[2] In the process, close to a million old-growth trees will be cut down and the habitats of innumerable endemic species will be destroyed. The indigenous Shompen people, who have very little contact with the outside world, will almost certainly perish. This is nothing other than ecocide on a monstrous scale combined with a blatantly colonial land grab, with its accompanying implications of a genocide of indigenous peoples.

Equally shocking is the refusal to learn. The most obvious lesson of the 2004 tsunami, is that building seashore settlements in tectonically active regions, like the one in which the Nicobar Islands are located, is to create the conditions for future disasters.

The stretch of ocean that surrounds the Nicobar Islands faces many other challenges as well (like those discussed in 'Storm of Consequences', an article I wrote in collaboration with the marine biologist Aaron Lobo). Two of the most significant challenges are intensifying cyclones and the rise in the sea level. It is nothing less than a certainty that the container port the government intends to build will one day be swept away either by a tsunami or a cyclonic storm surge. By then, of course, the disaster capitalists will be long gone from the scene, having pocketed their profits. In the meantime, an entire rainforest—a globally recognized biodiversity hotspot—will have been destroyed with all the life that it supports, and the Shompen and Great Nicobarese people will have paid a terrible price, all for nothing.

# ONE

# The Great Uprooting: Migration and Displacement in an Age of Planetary Crisis

## 1.

Much, if not most, of my work is about migrants and displaced people, so it is scarcely surprising that the so-called European 'migration crisis' of 2014–16 caught my attention. Like millions of others around the world, I was riveted by media reports about the refugees who were then making their way to Europe via the Mediterranean and the Balkans.

At a certain point, as I followed the coverage, I noticed something that I couldn't quite make sense of. The European media were more or less unanimous in claiming that the refugees were from war-torn or economically devastated countries in Africa and the Middle East—Eritrea, Somalia, Syria, Iraq, Afghanistan and so on. But when

I looked closely at photographs and television footage, I saw many faces that were unmistakably from the Indian subcontinent. Indeed a large number seemed to be from the part of the world where my own origins lie—Bengal.[1]

On looking deeper into the matter I learnt from official UN statistics that Bangladesh was near the top of the list of the countries of origin of the migrants and refugees.[2] This was completely at odds with the media narrative about refugees fleeing from war-torn and economically devastated countries. There are, of course, many simmering political conflicts in Bangladesh—as indeed there are in every South Asian country—but the level of violence there does not even begin to approach that of, say, Syria or Afghanistan or Eritrea.[3] Nor can it be said that Bangladesh's economy is in dire straits: the country has actually been one of the better performers globally for the last few years; its growth rate surpassed India's in 2018. It is a fact also that according to some social indicators Bangladesh has outdone India: average life expectancy in the country is now seventy-two years, as opposed to sixty-eight years in India and sixty-six in Pakistan. Indeed Bangladesh's performance has been so impressive that a leading economist recently commented that the country is 'on a path that would have been unimaginable just two decades ago: toward becoming an Asian success story'.[4]

Having long been immersed in the credentialled discourse on climate change, it was perhaps inevitable that I should begin to wonder whether the exodus from the Indian subcontinent was somehow related to global warming. The fact that many of the migrants were from Bangladesh seemed to support this idea.[5] As is well known, the Bengal Delta is extremely vulnerable to climatic disruptions and it is projected that tens of millions of Bangladeshis will be displaced by sea-level rise in the coming decades.[6]

Given all this, it seemed natural to assume that climate change was somehow, invisibly, pushing people out of Bangladesh. Why else would so many young men—the migrants were indeed overwhelmingly male and young—be undertaking dangerous journeys across West Asia and North Africa to Europe?

Such answers as I was able to find in the media tended to be formulaic: it was often said, for instance, that the migrants had set off in search of 'a better life'. To me this seemed to beg many questions: What is a good life? How is that life imagined? What are the images and promises that give shape to the idea of a better life? On examination it turned out that the phrase 'better life' was just another meaningless marketing slogan.[7]

Media reports rarely probe into the motivations of migrants in any depth. This may be because the journalists who write about 'the migration crisis' are largely Western and their interests tend to be focused on matters of policy, public welfare and so on. Moreover, and most crucially, very few of these journalists are familiar with the languages of the migrants. It struck me that this might be a barrier to understanding some aspects of this phenomenon.

Because of the circumstances of my birth and education, I happen to speak three languages that are widely spoken among migrant communities: Bengali, Hindi/Urdu and Egyptian Arabic. This might, I thought, provide a different perspective (and I am now convinced that this is indeed the case), so in 2017 I decided to spend some time in Italy to see what I could learn—from the migrants themselves, and from the people who work with them.[8] The concern that was uppermost in my mind at that time was climate change. Was it possible, I asked myself, that the European migrant crisis marked the beginning of a long-predicted era of mass 'climate migration'?[9]

**2.**

In recent years, phrases like 'climate migration' and 'climate-related migration' have become mantras to conjure with, especially when it comes to attracting funding from Western aid and development agencies. The anthropologist Camelia Dewan has described at length how Bangladeshi 'development brokers' make use of the concept of climate migration as a 'masala' to add spice to their project proposals, knowing that it is a sure way of stimulating the appetites of Western donors.[10] To foreground climate change as the primary driver of migration, Dewan argues, is to ignore a whole range of other causal factors such as the building of embankments and the introduction of shrimp farming, which has had devastating effects on the ecology of the Bengal Delta. She writes, '[The] recasting of migrants in Bangladesh and other regions of the world as "climate refugees" ignores how migration was, and continues to be, a central part of agrarian lives where causes of migration are multifaceted and contradictory, as are the motivations of those who move.'[11]

In fact, as Jason Cons, another anthropologist, has shown, what Western donors are mainly concerned with is reducing the outflow of migrants from poor countries because migration has become a politically explosive issue in their home countries. Cons quotes a British development professional: 'This is where the UK redlines. We can't handle 165 million Bangladeshis showing up on the UK's shores.'[12]

There can be no question that increasing numbers of people are migrating, either overseas or within their own countries, as is happening on a large scale in India and Bangladesh. But to imagine that this is happening primarily because of environmental factors is to succumb to a form of reasoning that Mike Hulme, a founder of the Tyndall Centre for Climate Change Research, has described as 'climate reductionism', which, in his definition, is a process of 'isolating climate as the (primary) determinant of past, present and future systems behavior and response'.[13] In other words, to think of climate change as the principal cause of contemporary migration is to ignore a great variety of historical, social and technological factors that are acting as accelerants of global population flows.

The Bengali migrants I spoke with in Italy insisted, almost without exception, that environmental changes were only one of many factors that had shaped their decision to leave.[14] Of the other factors, those that were cited most often were land disputes, family difficulties, religious conflicts and political problems.

But as I listened to the migrants' stories, it became obvious that the more easily identifiable factors sometimes obscured certain motivating forces that were also formative yet difficult to identify. One such was the power of example, or the desire to emulate friends, neighbours and relatives who had already made the journey.[15]

This is perhaps particularly important in relation to Bangladesh, which has a long history of sending young men overseas. Maritime trade was a critical vector in this: for centuries, Bengali men supplied much of the labour for sailships and steamers. Some of these sailors—or lascars, as they were called—settled in Britain and other countries, including the US.[16] Because of the money they sent home these migrants came to be greatly admired in their villages. In other words, successful migrants became, as it were, objects of mimesis in every stratum of society.[17]

Mimesis has probably always played an important part in the movements of people. In the nineteenth century, for instance, many migratory journeys from Europe to Australia and the Americas were prompted by the example of friends and relatives. But today we are in an age in which the mimetic urge has become a gold mine for new, very powerful technologies. The different forms of social media, for example, are programmed precisely on mimetic principles. As Geoff Shullenberger points out in an illuminating account of the genesis of Facebook: 'Social media platforms perpetually enjoin users, through various means, to enter the iterative chain of mimesis: to signal their desires to other users, eliciting further desires in the process.'[18] It is worth recalling that the seed money for Facebook came from Peter Thiel, a disciple of the leading contemporary theorist of mimesis, René Girard. Indeed Thiel credits Girard's theories with having inspired his interest in this technology (it is no small irony that Thiel has become a leading supporter of various right-wing movements that are fiercely opposed to migration).

In exploiting the mimetic urge, social media has given a new strength and urgency to the desires that it generates. Moreover, such is the power of social media that it has ensured that no one, anywhere, is excluded from these desires. Even in the remotest corners of the world, social media is now accessible to anyone who has the means to buy a device that is available in many inexpensive iterations: the smartphone, which provides even the illiterate a means of accessing the internet through voice-recognition technology.[19]

Cellphones have also hugely accelerated the circulation of images, thereby greatly expanding the influence of the advertising industry, which is expressly dedicated to the production of mimetic desire. This in turn has brought about a homogenization of desire on a scale never before seen, extending across the planet and into the deepest reaches of the human soul. Today, with very few exceptions, people everywhere, on every continent, nurture the same aspirations and cravings, most of which are centred on commodities.

This cannot but have profound consequences. Let us imagine, for example, a boy in a Bengal village who spends most of his day working in his father's rice fields. The conditions are difficult because he is on his feet through the day under a burning sun, often standing in ankle-deep mud. Changing weather patterns are making things still worse because daytime temperatures now sometimes go up almost to 50 degrees and the rains, increasingly, don't come on time. The boy's family does, however, happen to possess a cellphone, which they charge with a solar panel. Through WhatsApp they are linked to a couple of relatives who have already sold up and left. On the screen of their phone they see advertisements for fine clothes, refrigerators and other goods; they also see pictures of their relatives taken on the streets of prosperous Western cities.

Does the boy's uprooting begin with climate events? Or does it begin with the images he sees on that tiny screen? Is it a coincidence that climate events and consumer culture have begun to impact his life at the same time? Or are they perhaps both symptoms of the same thing: an ever-increasing acceleration of economy and technology, production and consumption?

The transformative powers of devices like computers and smartphones have long been recognized. Such devices are not merely tools that humans use to achieve certain ends. To use them is to inevitably interact with them, and this process is known to bring about certain neurological changes in human 'mind-bodies', especially among the young and impressionable.[20]

All of this is well known, yet when the effects of virtual reality on human consciousness are discussed, it is almost always in relation to affluent and semi-affluent countries. The very subject conjures up images of Palo Alto, Shanghai and Osaka, and of unsociable teenagers skulking in rooms filled with expensive gear.

In my view this picture is deeply misleading. The digital revolution has broken the long-standing links between affluence, education and technical ability. In India and in many other poor countries, there are large numbers of people whose virtual abilities are completely disproportionate to their formal education and material circumstances. Even in remote villages young people are exposed to digital technologies quite early and many become adept at using the internet.[21] Although they may not be immersed in the virtual world in the way of teenagers in, say, Palo Alto or Osaka, the impact on them may be just as great, or even greater, precisely because of the vast difference between their lived reality and what they see on the screen.

This in turn raises another question: What is the nature of the migrant's agency in these circumstances? Take the case of the boy in the Bengal village: Is his decision to migrate wholly his own or is it, to some degree, the product of his interactions with the 'cognitive assemblage' that manifests itself in his handheld device? If that is the case, then to what degree are young migrants responsible for their decision to move?[22]

Today there is widespread awareness of the ethical and philosophical dilemmas that arise when humans interact with self-guided machines—autonomous weapons like killer drones, for instance.[23] If we are unwilling to accept that the same dilemmas may arise also at the other end of the human and technological spectrum—that is, in relation to poor people in the Global South—it is perhaps because we are unable to acknowledge the true scale of the disruptions that have been set in motion by the technologies of our time.[24]

**3.**

To return to that boy in a Bengal village: his predicament is not wholly imaginary. Across Italy I met many young Bengali migrants who had grown up in such villages. Many of them had come to Italy through Libya, where they had been subjected to beatings, abuse and torture. They all spoke of being 'sold' by labour contractors, of being deprived of food and water, of being denied wages and of the constant threat of robbery by roadside gangs.

These accounts are so saturated with stories of savagery that it is easy to think of those experiences as being somehow extrinsic to our own time of accelerated communication; they are taken to be symptoms of the growing gulf between the Global South and the Global North. Yet, far from being throwbacks, these journeys are inseparable from contemporary technologies.[25]

Cellphones, for instance, are a pervasive presence on the migrants' persons and within their accounts of their travels. Every link in the chain of movement depends on them: it is through them that migrants receive money from home and make payments to the agents who arrange their itineraries; their mobile devices are the compasses that guide them on their long overland treks; they are the sources that provide vital information about entry points, shelters and assistance. When migrants confront danger, their first move is to reach for their phones to summon help; it is through them that they distract themselves from the rigours of the road, stay in constant touch with their cohorts and chronicle their movements for their friends and relatives.

Similarly, cellphones and social media are indispensable also for the clandestine networks that arrange migrant passages.[26] The internet makes every element of their business safer and more anonymous, from recruiting and publicizing their services to procuring forged documents for the migrants. 'The cellphone is an essential instrument for traffickers,' notes a prominent Italian anti-mafia official. 'They are not like other organized criminals who stay away from telephonic communications.'[27]

No wonder then that cellphones have become iconic of the present wave of migration in the same way that bundles and battered suitcases were in earlier times.[28] Far from expanding the distance between poor and rich countries, in certain very important respects information technology has actually shrunk that gulf.

Yet the presence of this technology is rarely explicitly identified, neither by the narrator nor by the listener—and the reason for this is that the cellphone has become a part of our 'technological unconscious'. In other words, these devices and technologies are now so deeply embedded in our unconscious cognitive processes that we take them for granted in the same way that we do the presence of electricity or cars. Like all formative technologies, this one too has become invisible.[29]

But every now and then a detail surfaces to remind us of this ubiquitous presence. Here, for example, is a story that I was told by a twenty-something Bangladeshi migrant who had spent several years in Libya: I'll call him Palash. One day when Palash and some others were walking back from a day's work on the outskirts of Tripoli, they were ambushed by a gang of Kalashnikov-carrying Libyans. The only thing of value that Palash had on him was his cellphone; he managed to kick it into the sand, praying that it would not ring or light up with a notification.

When the gangsters asked him to hand over his valuables, he gave them his money and told them he had nothing else, not even a cellphone. The gangsters didn't believe him and made him strip naked, and then bent him over so that they could probe his rectum with sticks to see if he had hidden something in there. Finding nothing, they beat him and stabbed him in the arm, but he still didn't tell them that the phone was lying in the sand nearby. They left him lying by the road, bleeding profusely—and the first thing he did, even before binding his wounds or putting on his clothes, was retrieve his cellphone. To him it was almost as valuable as life itself.

It might be asked: If the migrants are indeed adept at dealing with information technology, then why are they not able to acquire more realistic impressions of the current conditions in Europe? Why do they not understand that they will probably never find regular employment in Greece or Italy, and might well have to eke out a living selling trinkets on the street while being preyed upon by gangs, predatory employers and even the police?

This is where the interactive aspect of the cyber world becomes crucial. It is widely acknowledged today that the information provided to us by the internet and social media is to a large extent shaped by our own desires, presuppositions and networks. As a result, such information often has the effect of buttressing our prejudices and expectations, leading us to lend credence to 'fake news'. I suspect that this is precisely what happened to many of the migrants I met. What they saw of Europe on the net was shaped by their own expectations and by feedback from their social networks: they ended up seeing what they wanted to see. In effect they, like so many of us, are victims of wish-fulfilment fantasies based on 'fake news'.

As an illustration here is a story told to two Italian reporters by a Pakistani 'connection man' based in Italy:

> Every time I go home to Pakistan, I meet many people. One day a close friend from my schooldays comes to see me. 'Help my son to go to Italy,' he begs me. 'It's not a good time,' I tell him. He falls silent. 'What does your son do?' I ask. 'He has a medical testing laboratory. He manages it and is doing well.' I look him in the eyes: 'Let him remain here then; it's much better, believe me. Try to convince your son.' The next day my friend comes back with tears in his eyes. He tells me that he has conveyed my words to his son but the boy is desperate and wants to leave at all costs. If he can't leave, he will shoot himself in the head with a pistol. My friend explains that he would prefer to lose the cost of the journey than lose his son. He does not want to have that on his conscience. The boy has to go. So then I tell him that I will think of a way of changing the boy's mind and I go to meet him at his medical laboratory. It is big and clean, in a nice locality. My friend's son is wearing a white tunic, and everyone calls him 'Doctor' even though he is only a technician. I talk with him briefly because he is busy. I tell him what I said to his father. I try to make him change his mind, tell him about what he will find there and what he will lose. I explain to him that in Italy he will never have what he has in Pakistan. That he is making a mistake. But there is

nothing to be done: he wants to leave and try his luck, and thinks of nothing but Italy.

I warned them, the father and the son. I was honest with them, but it was as if I were talking to the deaf. Very well then. So on to Italy. The son arrives. I see him again after two years; he is working in the black economy, on the fields, and is often hungry. He tells me that I was right, that he regrets not having listened to me. That he would have done much better to remain in Pakistan, that this is not the land of opportunity. But it is too late.[30]

## 4.

Many of the migrants I spoke to had courted extreme danger in making their way to Europe. Some had been shot at while trying to cross borders; some had almost drowned when their boats capsized in the Mediterranean; one had come close to being run over as he tried to enter Greece by clinging to the undercarriage of an eighteen-wheel truck.

The element of risk in these journeys is so great that it is not easy to understand why any sane person would jeopardize their life in this fashion. The only explanation that suggests itself is desperation: the implication is that the migrants have been pushed to such extremes that they have no other option.

Desperation, as the scenes following the recent American withdrawal from Afghanistan have demonstrated yet again, is indeed often the prime factor that compels people to flee from war zones. Some of the catastrophic impacts of global warming, such as droughts, wildfires and sea-level rise can also leave people no choice but to relocate: their moves too are effectively driven by desperation. But those explanations can scarcely be applied to the journeys of young men, in the prime of their lives, who leave relatively peaceful countries like Bangladesh, Senegal and Morocco. The very fact that they are able to raise the funds required for these journeys indicates that they are not entirely without options.[31] Why, then, do they expose themselves to life-threatening risks?

This was a question I often asked the migrants I met in Italy. Their answers varied but were also similar in that they made me realize that my question was founded on mistaken assumptions: risk is not a measurable quantity but, rather, a perception that depends on age, material circumstances and life experience (or the lack of it). Here again social media and the internet play an important part.

Much of the information that circles back to prospective migrants comes from friends and relatives who have already reached their destinations. In their accounts, the perils of the journey are usually downplayed as only rarely posing life-threatening risks. Or as mere obstacles that can be overcome with courage and determination.

A boy growing up in a village where many slightly older youths have already departed may draw heart from his friends' accounts of their travels. But the example of their passages will also create inducements of other kinds: the pride that older villagers take in their migrant kin and the comforts afforded by remittances from abroad may convince the boy that he would be failing in his own duties to his family if he did not undertake a similar crossing himself. In this way: 'Over time a culture of migration establishes itself, and migration becomes a social norm or even a modern rite of passage in which staying at home is associated with failure and a lack of ambition.'[32] In other words, in a village where many others have already left, not to do so for fear of the risks appears as nothing other than cowardice.

But such decisions are very rarely taken by individuals. Refugees and migrants almost always travel in cohorts consisting, usually, of close friends and relatives.[33] This too creates a sense of security by, as it were, distributing the risks.

The very fact that a machinery of transcontinental movement exists invisibly—like an escalator that starts to move the moment you step on it—is sometimes enough to carry people away, almost independently of their volition. This is something new in the history of human movement. In the words of two specialists on migration: 'What we are witnessing is not just the story of traditional migrant smuggling on a larger scale. Rather we are witnessing a paradigm shift'.[34]

In Italy I met several young Bengali and Punjabi migrants who had run away from home after quarrelling with their families; they had almost inadvertently stepped on a migratory conveyor belt that had carried them all the way to Italy. One such journey was that of a fourteen-year-old Pakistani boy who had fought with his father and run off to the local railway station. In another era he might have spent a few weeks with relatives in another city before returning to his parents. But this being the age that it is, he had fallen in with a group that was starting a long overland journey across Iran and Turkey to Europe. After surviving many close brushes with death on the borders of Turkey, he had ended up in Rome.

I also met several former farmers from Pakistan whose lands had been swamped by the Jhelum floods of 2014.[35] In the past they might have moved to a different town or tried to rebuild their lives after the floods had receded. But such is the present time that they too decided to set off for Europe instead; to them that step did not seem at all drastic, which is a measure of the degree to which these journeys are now seen as normal and not at all out of the ordinary.

It is, of course, not unusual for migrants to develop apprehensions on the road. But very few are able to abort their passages, usually because they are prevented by their guides, or their cohorts of fellow migrants. But generally the consideration that keeps them from turning back is, simply, pride, or the fear of being regarded as a quitter or coward.

In speaking to migrants, I often had to remind myself that most of them were of an age when it comes almost naturally to court dangers of a certain kind, as, for instance, 'extreme adventurers' do when they toboggan down the slopes of active volcanoes or rappel through canyons. Indeed, for a certain kind of person danger is not a deterrent but an incentive.

Conversely, in some societies, the willingness to brave certain dangers has long been regarded as a necessary step towards adulthood: thus, since ancient times, ordeals of various kinds have regularly served as life-cycle rituals.[36] Today, in those parts of the world where it has become commonplace for young people to make difficult overseas journeys, migration is sometimes viewed through a similar prism, as a step towards being recognized as a fully fledged adult, capable of supporting a family.[37]

These analogies may sound far-fetched, or even frivolous, in relation to migration. But consider the case of Davide, a Cameroonian who succeeded in migrating to Europe by scaling the heavily armoured fences that surround the city of Ceuta on the coast of Morocco. Along with Melilla, Ceuta is one of two Spanish enclaves in Africa; migrants who manage to set foot in either city must, by law, be treated as though they have stepped on European soil. Both cities are surrounded by trenches and several layers of fences topped with razor wire; they are also guarded by large contingents of Spanish and Moroccan soldiers, armed with all the most advanced equipment.

Davide, who left Cameroon in September 2013 at the age of twenty-five, was interviewed in Madrid in 2018 by David Kestenbaum of National Public Radio.[38] In Kestenbaum's words: 'Davide describes the whole thing almost as if he were a kid setting out on an adventure … Unlike a lot of people trying to get from Africa to Europe, he said he wasn't persecuted back home. He wasn't starving. He wasn't fleeing violence. He was just curious about the world and excited to see it.'

Davide's journey took him from Cameroon to Algeria, and it was there that he learnt that instead of crossing the Mediterranean he could also reach Europe by climbing the fences that surround Ceuta and Melilla. So Davide travelled to Morocco and joined the large throngs of would-be migrants from all over Africa who camp near the two cities and periodically attempt to cross over.

'At the beginning,' says Davide, 'my opinion was, well, you know, I'm a pretty brave guy, and … I like challenges. I thought I would do it in one try. I'm going to take it on with a lot of optimism, because that's the type of person I am. I usually do things the first time I try them.'

Davide's first attempt to cross the fences was encouraging because he managed to get past a trench and even reached the third barrier. 'I don't know how to express it, but it was something strange. I was thinking, I'm going to do it. Then I thought, I can't do it. And then I was doing it, so I said, well, this is how it's done. I'm doing it. I'm doing it. But I don't know how to express it. That's the truth.'

Here Kestenbaum interjects: 'Did it feel like a crazy sport?'

'Yeah,' answers Davide, 'exactly! That's exactly what it is. The way you put it. It was a weird sport.'

But Davide's first attempt failed, as did many others. A year went by and doubt began to creep in. 'Why am I doing this? What good is this? ... I thought about just abandoning everything, and I would cry.'

But it was the fences that held him there. 'It's something more than a fence. I know it may seem silly but there is something mystical in this fence. I've seen people who, when they get in front of the fence, they can't move … There must be a spirit inside the fence that tries to prevent things. It's really something very powerful. It's not just a fence.'

After two years of failed attempts, Davide finally succeeded in crossing over. But his joy did not last long. 'When I realized that I had made it, it was like a vacuum. That's the truth. When we are in

Morocco, we think that whenever I manage to get there, I'm going to be very happy. But once you make it you don't feel anything. The feeling ends.'

Davide's experience is a reminder that the idea of the ordeal has always held a certain fascination for human beings. This is why for many migrants their journeys become the defining moments of their lives. This is, in a way, the strangest aspect of their plight: in Europe they are confronted with the political rationality of a certain kind of liberalism that confers its sympathy only on victims. So in dealing with the state, and when talking to activists, they learn to present themselves as victims, as objects without agency, propelled solely by external forces.[39] Yet in their own eyes, as in the eyes of their families back home, they are heroes who have taken their destinies into their hands and endured terrible ordeals.[40] No wonder then that many of them say that the worst part of their journeys consists not of their time on the road or at sea, but rather of the months and years they spend languishing in European migrant camps. In those camps there is nothing to do but wait and sleep: it is little consolation that you are fed and housed and given allowances; it is the waiting and the idleness that break the spirit.

**5.**

Listening to the migrants' stories, I was often struck by the similarities with the journeys I had long been writing about—the voyages of nineteenth-century indentured workers ('coolies').[41] Some of the parallels were uncanny: coolies too had been mainly young and overwhelmingly male; then too 'dalals' and other middlemen ('duffadars' and 'mahajans'—recruiters and contractors) had been essential cogs in the machinery of transportation; and then again debt and money-lending had been vital to the oiling of the machine.[42] There were startling parallels also in the circumstances under which the coolies had travelled; they too had been policed and preyed upon by brutal guards and overseers ('maistris'); they too had been crammed into confined spaces and had had to subsist on meagre rations. Beatings and whippings, seeing their own die before their eyes—all of this would have been familiar to the passengers of the fictional schooner of my Ibis Trilogy.

Similar also was the strength of the ties that linked the new migrants to those they left behind. Today, on entering the formal European reception system, migrants and refugees receive a daily subsistence allowance as well as a weekly stipend for phone calls: the total adds up to around 150 euros a month. Many migrants, including teenage boys, send most of this money home; often their families have no other means of support, having beggared themselves in order to pay for their sons' journeys. It is impossible not to be moved by the sacrifices some of the young migrants make to support their families back home. Similarly, under the indenture too, coolies would scrimp and save in plantations halfway around the world to be able to send something back to their villages in India.

And as with the transportation of indentured workers, this chain of movement runs upon wheels that are powered by profits. Then, as now, trafficking in human beings was an immensely lucrative form of commerce. The difference—and it is a crucial one—is that the system of indentured labour, like slavery before it, was managed and controlled by Western colonial powers. The migration flows of today, in contrast, function outside state control, and the profits that accrue from them do not go to agents who are approved by states.[43] And the profits are such that the machinery of movement is now capable of sustaining itself by creating its own markets: this business has now overtaken drugs as the world's biggest clandestine business.[44] The system has taken on its own life, outside the control of any established authority.

Contemporary communications technology is the critical factor that has allowed this traffic to escape state control. It is responsible also for another key distinction between the indenture system and the mass movements of today: since the nineteenth century, there has been a complete reversal in the control and flow of information.

During the indenture, especially in its early years, the workers knew nothing of the systems they were surrendering themselves to. They often had no idea of where they were going and the conditions that awaited them there, nor did they know much about the laws and regulations that colonial states had created to manage their transportation.

The colonial state, on the other hand, knew everything about them. It recorded in obsessive detail where they came from and which castes and tribes they belonged to. Even their bodies were studied with close attention, and special notice was taken of scars and other marks of identification. It was the state that decided where, when and how they would travel; on their arrival again it was the state that allotted them to their masters. The entire machinery was created and managed by colonial states.

This asymmetry of information has now been completely reversed. Most contemporary migrants initiate their own journeys, with their own means and networks, and by the time they arrive they are completely conversant with the relevant laws and regulations of the host country: they know their rights, they know how much money they are entitled to under law, they know everything about the immigration system, including the grounds that are most likely to gain them acceptance—for example, persecution on the basis of politics, religion, sexual orientation or gender identity.

The state, on the other hand, knows very little about them: it has only the haziest idea of who they are, where they are coming from and what their motivations are. Vanishingly few European civil servants are equipped to distinguish between, say, a Syrian and an Egyptian, or a Bangladeshi Muslim and a Bengali Hindu from India.[45]

This reversed asymmetry forms a stark contrast between this transplantation of peoples and those that preceded it: the coolie trade, like slavery, was set up for the production of certain goods, like sugar cane, tobacco, coffee, cotton, tea, rubber. These goods were intended for markets that were thousands of kilometres away, in the colonizers' home countries. It was the desires and appetites of the metropolis that moved people between continents so that they could churn out ever-growing floods of saleable merchandise. In this dispensation, slaves and coolies were producers, not consumers; they could never aspire to the desires of their masters.

But the young migrants I met had not transported themselves across continents so they could become cogs in some giant machine that produces things they themselves cannot aspire to possess. To the contrary, just as much as anyone else, they want those very things—smartphones, computers, cars. And how could they not? Since childhood, the most attractive images that they had beheld were not of the rivers and fields that surrounded them but of objects like these. And the cravings stoked by those images had inducted them into a global citizenry of desire—and therein lay the rub, for it was only upon arriving in Europe that it had dawned on many of them that they were the victims of a fantasy; their dreams of a life like that of people in advertisements were no more likely to be fulfilled in Italy than in the countries that they had left behind.

Such being the circumstances, it is hardly surprising that many migrants become disillusioned and despairing. For many of them, the conditions are not much better than what they left behind—except that at home, no matter what they lacked materially, they had, at least, had the consolations of family and community.

Disillusionment and disappointment can even affect refugees who have fled from war zones: 'My life,' a Syrian refugee in Germany told a researcher in 2015, 'I think it's finished. Because really, I had [a] great life in Syria.'[46]

**6.**

Visual imagery has played a very important part in forming our ideas about the recent waves of migration across the Balkans and the Mediterranean. It is hard to think of images that are as arresting and as viscerally powerful as those of crowds of migrants marching over mountains or of drowning people being pulled from the sea. Such indeed is the power of those images that these journeys have come to be thought of as being, in some way, primitive or atavistic. This is why many Westerners are still surprised, shocked even, to learn that many migrants possess cellphones and are adept at using them.[47] At the height of the migration crisis, some European countries even passed laws that required migrants and refugees to surrender their cellphones.[48]

No one has been more eloquent on the subject of migrants and cellphones than Donald Trump. In a speech in December 2015, Trump posed a series of questions: 'First of all, why are people in a migration having cellphones? Sort of strange. Who's paying for these cellphones? Where are they coming from? Who are they calling? Can you imagine? Many, many, many cellphones. Why, where do they get cellphones?'[49]

These questions are an indication of how profoundly the phenomenon of contemporary migration has been misunderstood. Cellphones and cyber technology are not anomalies in the context of these voyages: to the contrary they play a critical part in enabling them.[50] Of course, there are many other factors in the background: it goes without saying that migration is an extremely complex, multidimensional phenomenon in which wars, political conflicts, state collapse, climate change, poverty and inequality may all play a part. But it remains true that today cyber technology is a crucial enabling factor in the movement of large numbers of people. Far from being primitive or atavistic, these migrations have been empowered by the very same technology that allows goods and capital to flow seamlessly around the globe.

Consider Syria, for example: the refugees who fled the country in 2016 were, of course, displaced by war; that conflict in turn emerged out of a long period of drought that may have been caused or intensified by anthropogenic climate change.[51] But it was cellphone technology that was responsible for the rapidity with which news of a minor change in German immigration policy was disseminated, and for the sheer speed and scale of the exodus that followed.[52] Does this diminish the suffering of those refugees? Absolutely not; their suffering is no different from that which refugees have endured for centuries.

When people see a picture of a boatload of migrants marooned at sea, they tend to interpret the image as a disjunction in time—they see it as a confrontation of the primitive and the modern, the backward and the advanced. From this arises the misconception that is increasingly prevalent on the right—that a barrier, or a wall, can be built to keep these two temporal dimensions apart. But those images also give rise to a similar misconception on the left—that the flow of migrants can be stemmed by creating 'growth' in their countries of origin. The truth is that in a digitally interconnected world, growth can itself be a factor that motivates people to move by broadening their desires and aspirations. Thus do some middle-class, and even affluent, young Bangladeshis dream of escaping from crowded Dhaka and making a life in Finland, 'a quiet and empty country' with 'large fields and empty spaces'.[53]

It needs to be recognized that the forces that are shaping the flow of people today are no different from those that are driving the relentless acceleration in processes of production, consumption and distribution. Those who are concerned that mass migration may bring about the breakdown of communities—and I must add here that there are some legitimate reasons for these anxieties in my view—must understand that there is a fundamental contradiction between growth and the preservation of community. It is an illusion to imagine that the best way to preserve communities is by excluding other humans: the only way this can be done is by abandoning the prevalent paradigms of perpetual and ever-accelerating growth.

**7.**

The journeys of the migrants of our era represent the upending of a project that began in the sixteenth century, when European imperial powers launched the most cruel and violent demographic intervention that the world has ever known: in the service of economic expansion, they began to transport people between continents on a massive scale, ultimately changing the demographic profile of the planet. But even as they were de- and re-populating continents, European colonial governments were careful to preserve the racial and ethnic composition of their own metropolitan territories in Europe. All this was done under rigorous state control, which was exercised through a wide range of technologies ranging from armaments to the management of information.

Today all the systems that made these massive demographic interventions possible have achieved what we might call 'escape velocity', in the sense that they are increasingly beyond the control of the state. The flow of people between continents may be only the most visible aspect of the state's diminishing powers but it presents Europe with a mirror in which to see the unravelling of some of its most important institutions and projects.

It is no coincidence that this great uprooting of people is occurring at the same time that the impacts of climate change are intensifying. The relationship between the two is so close that to ask if contemporary migrations are a consequence of climate change is, I think, to ask the wrong question. Climate change and migration are, in fact, two cognate aspects of the same thing, in that both are effects of the ever-increasing growth and acceleration of processes of production, consumption and circulation. In this sense the dynamic that is driving the other uprootings that we are now witnessing—of trees, animals, plants, glaciers and so on—is no different from that which is driving the movements of humans. This is another respect in which human history has once again converged with the history of the Earth.[54]

(First published in *The Massachusetts Review*, vol. 62, no. 4, Winter 2021)

# TWO
# Storm of Consequences

The Bay of Bengal's basin contains some of the most populous regions of the Earth. No less than a quarter of the world's population is concentrated in the eight countries that border the Bay.[1] Approximately 200 million people live along the Bay's coasts, and of these a large proportion are partially or wholly dependent on its fisheries.[2]

For these men and women, the Bay can provide no more than a meagre living: 61 per cent of India's fisherfolk already live below the poverty line. Yet the numbers dependent on fisheries are only likely to grow in the years to come, partly because of climate change. In southern India, drought and water scarcity have already induced tens of thousands of farmers to join the fishing fleet.[3] Rising sea levels are also likely to drive many displaced people into the fishing industry.

But the fisheries of the Bay of Bengal have been under pressure for decades and are now severely depleted.[4] Many once-abundant species have all but disappeared. Particularly badly affected are the species at the top of the food chain. The Bay was once feared by sailors for its man-eating sharks; they are now rare in these waters. Other apex predators like grouper, croaker and rays have also been gravely hit. Catches now consist mainly of species like sardines, which are at the bottom of the marine food web.[5]

Good intentions have played no small part in creating the current situation. In the 1960s, Western aid agencies encouraged the growth of trawling in India so that fishermen could profit from the demand for prawns in foreign markets. This led to a 'pink gold rush', in which prawns were trawled by dragging fine mesh nets along the seafloor. But in addition to hauls of 'pink gold' these nets also scooped up whole seafloor ecosystems as well as vulnerable species like turtles, dolphins, sea snakes, rays and sharks. These were once called 'bycatch' and were largely discarded. Today the collateral damage of the trawling industry is processed and sold to the fast-growing poultry and aquaculture enterprises of the region.[6] In effect the processes that sustain the Bay of Bengal's fisheries are being destroyed in order to produce dirt-cheap chicken- and fish-feed.

The aid that flowed in after the massive tsunami of 2004 also had certain unintended consequences.[7] It led to the modernization and expansion of the small-scale fisheries sector, which generated an illusory boom followed by a bust.

In recent decades the governments of the seven nations that surround the Bay of Bengal have striven to expand and encourage their fisheries. Unfortunately, these efforts have often ignored questions of long-term sustainability. Although attempts have been made to regulate fishing in the Bay, they have been largely ineffective.

In the 1980s and '90s, fisheries expanded into new grounds and began to target different species, and for a while there was an increase in catches. But catch rates began to decline in the late 1990s and trawlers were forced to move farther and farther from their home waters. This in turn has created a little-noticed grid of conflict. In 2015, Sri Lankan authorities claimed to have spotted 40,544 Indian trawlers in Sri Lanka's territorial waters.[8] Seventy trawlers were seized and 450 fishermen were arrested. More than a hundred deaths have been reported.[9] Conversely, many Sri Lankan tuna fishermen have been arrested in India. On the other side of the subcontinent, large numbers of Indian fishermen are regularly detained in Pakistan: 220 of them were released in December 2016 as a goodwill gesture.

In Burma, until a ban was imposed in 2014, the catch collected by foreign fishing boats was one hundred times greater than that of local fishermen.[10] In the troubled Arakan region, where 43 per cent of the population is dependent on fisheries, catches have declined so steeply that many families are mired in debt.[11] Conflicts over fisheries and other resources are a significant, but largely unnoticed, aspect of the explosive tensions here.

The Mergui Archipelago on the Thai–Burma border is one of the more secluded parts of the Bay. In the late nineteenth century, an English fisheries officer described this area as being literally alive with fish. Today, while the archipelago's sparsely populated islands remain pristinely beautiful, some of its underwater landscapes present scenes of utter devastation. Fish stocks have been decimated by methods that include cyanide poisoning. The region was once famous for its coral reefs; these have been ravaged by dynamite fishing and climate change-induced bleaching. Yet the exploitation of these waters continues unchecked. At night, specially equipped, long-armed boats materialize around the islands and shine high-powered green lights into the water to attract plankton and the squid that follow in their wake. After nightfall, a glow that is bright enough to be visible from outer space hangs above the archipelago like a miasmic fog.[12] These squid boats, some of which are probably crewed by men who have been trafficked like slaves, help to make Thailand the world's largest exporter of squid—at least for the time being.[13]

At the same time, the Bay's ecosystems are also being disrupted by other environmental pressures. Several large rivers carrying vast quantities of untreated sewage, plastic, industrial waste and effluent from the agriculture and aquaculture industries empty into the Bay.[14] The impact of this pollution will be catastrophic. The high load of organic pollutants coupled with the diminution of the fish that keep them in control could lead to massive plankton blooms, further reducing the water's oxygen content.

In December 2016, a multinational team of scientists reported an alarming finding—a very large 'dead zone' has appeared in the Bay. Other than sulphur-oxidizing bacteria and marine worms, few creatures can live in these oxygen-depleted waters.[15] This zone already spans some 60,000 sq km and appears to be growing.[16] It is now at a point where a further reduction in its oxygen content could have the effect of stripping the water of nitrogen, a key nutrient. This transition could be triggered either by accretions of pollution or by changes in the monsoons, a predicted effect of global warming.

What is unfolding in the Bay is a 'catastrophic convergence' of flawed policy, economic overexploitation, unsustainable forms of waste management and climate change impacts that are intensifying in unpredictable ways. The scientists who identified the Bay's dead zone warn that this stretch of water is approaching a tipping point that will have serious repercussions for the planet's oceans and the global nitrogen cycle.

Should the Bay's fisheries collapse, there will also be very grave human consequences, including intensified conflict and mass displacement. If millions of people lose their livelihoods, then we can be sure that the resultant churning of populations will create huge new streams of migration across the Bay, the Indian Ocean and, indeed, the planet. Recent refugee flows in the region suggest that such a process may have already begun.

(Co-written with Aaron Savio Lobo. First published in *The Guardian*, 31 January 2017.

Aaron Lobo has a PhD in marine conservation science from the University of Cambridge. He currently heads the Marine Programme at the Wildlife Conservation Society, India.)

# THREE
## Cyclone Nargis

THE word 'cyclone' was coined in Calcutta in the 1840s by an eccentric Englishman named Henry Piddington. Inspired by the great British meteorologist Sir William Reid, Piddington became one of the earliest storm-chasers, besotted with a phenomenon that he once likened to a 'beautiful meteorite'. His elegant coinage was originally intended as a generic name for all revolving weather events, but is now applied mainly to the storms of the Indian Ocean region, like Cyclone Nargis, which struck Burma with deadly effect in early May 2008.

Piddington was among the first to recognize that a cyclone wreaks most of its damage not through wind but through water, by means of the devastating wave that is known as a 'storm surge'. In 1853, when the British colonial authorities were planning an elaborate new port on the outer edge of Bengal's mangrove forests, he issued an unambiguous warning: 'Everyone and everything must be prepared to see a day when, in the midst of the horrors of a hurricane, they will find a terrific mass of salt water rolling in …' His warning was neglected and Port Canning was built, only to be obliterated by a cyclonic surge in 1867.

The phenomenon of the storm surge has been extensively researched since Piddington's day, yet few public-response systems have drawn the obvious lessons. To this day, the warnings that accompany a storm's approach typically say nothing about moving to higher ground: their prescription is usually to seek shelter indoors. As a result, people tend to hunker down in the strongest structure within reach—only to find themselves trapped when the surge comes sweeping through.

But even if they were fully warned, where would these people go? The delta regions of Burma and Bengal are flat and swampy, with very few elevations: to move millions quickly is not an easy task even for a technologically advanced country, as Hurricane Katrina showed.

Yet for the rapidly growing countries that surround the Bay of Bengal, there is an increasing urgency to find a way to protect themselves. They have experienced some of the world's most devastating storms. The Hooghly cyclone of 1737, for example, almost erased the infant settlement of Calcutta and was once considered the worst disaster in human history: the surge that accompanied it is reckoned to have reached a height of 40 feet (as opposed to the 12 foot wave generated by Cyclone Nargis).

There are no reliable casualty estimates of that storm, but two other Bengal cyclones are known to have killed some 300,000 people each: the Backerganj cyclone of 1876 and the Bhola cyclone of 1970, both in what is now Bangladesh. Even as recently as 1991, a storm surge killed more than 100,000 people in Bangladesh. Nor are the energies of the Bay of Bengal exhausted by its all-too-frequent cyclones; there is also the extremely unstable fault line that produced the Boxing Day tsunami of 2004, which took some 230,000 lives. If global warming does bring an increase in cyclonic activity, there can be no doubt that the Bay's heavily populated coastline will be among the most vulnerable regions of the world.

Natural phenomena like tsunamis and cyclones have no respect for national boundaries—in fact they follow trajectories that seem almost to mock the vanities of nation-states. Cyclone Nargis, for example, had she stayed on her original path, would very likely have hit either India or Bangladesh; it was only in the last stretch of her journey that she veered off towards the Irrawaddy Delta.

Nation-states tend to see their interests as being confined within their own borders. But the reality is that the people who live around the Bay of Bengal have a strong mutual interest that they do not share with their compatriots in the hinterlands: they are joined by the furies (and, let it be said also, the blessings) of that body of water. Clearly they have a common interest in working together to mitigate the effects of natural disasters, for example, by designing inexpensive elevated shelters that are appropriate to the terrain, cooperating to preserve the mangrove forests that are the best natural safeguards against surges and creating a joint rapid-response force familiar with local conditions.

However, doing so would require these governments to first acknowledge a basic and ever-more evident truth of the human condition, which is that in dealing with nature's fury, no nation is an island. This is where national pride gets in the way, for this acknowledgement entails a humility that does not come easily: a glaring example was the Bush administration's rejection of the offers of foreign aid that poured in after Hurricane Katrina. It was as if the world's generosity were an affront.

Recent experience has demonstrated in spectacular ways that rich, technologically advanced nations are not invulnerable to extreme weather. What has also been established, but more quietly, is that a nation need not be wealthy or technologically advanced to be well prepared for natural disasters.

A case in point is Mauritius, a small Indian Ocean island in a zone that meteorologists call a 'cyclone factory'. The islanders have evolved a sophisticated system of precautions, combining a network of cyclone shelters with education (including regular drills), a good early warning mechanism and the mandatory closing of businesses and schools when a storm threatens. It's been a remarkable success: Cyclone Gamede of 2007, a monster of a storm that set global meteorological records for rainfall, killed only two people on the island.

I happened to be in Mauritius when Hurricane Katrina struck. I still remember the open-mouthed disbelief with which people there watched the events unfolding in Louisiana. Mauritius is a country that has learnt, through trial and experience, that early warnings alone are not enough; preparation also demands public education and political will. In an age when extreme weather events are clearly increasing in frequency, the world would do well to learn from it.

(First published in *The New York Times*, 10 May 2008)

# FOUR
# Folly in the Sundarbans?

In 2003, the Sahara India Pariwar business group submitted an ambitious plan to the Government of West Bengal, proposing the creation of an enormous new tourism complex in the Sundarbans. Although the details of the plan have not been made available to the public, the broad outlines are described on Sahara Pariwar's website. The project will include many different kinds of accommodation, including '5-star floating hotels, high-speed boathouses, land-based huts, luxury cottages' and an 'eco-village'. Landing jetties are to be built and the project is to be serviced by hovercraft and helicopters. 'Exclusive, beautiful virgin beaches' are to be created and hundreds of kilometres of waterways developed. The facilities will include 'a casino, spa, health, shopping and meditation centres, restaurant complexes and a mini golf course', and tourists will be offered a choice of 'aqua sports', including scuba diving. The total cost of the project will be somewhere in the region of Rs 6 billion (155 million USD). In short, an industrial house that has no special expertise in ecological matters is proposing a massive intervention in an area that is a designated World Heritage Site and Biosphere Reserve.

The precise status of the project is not clear. For a while, to the dismay of environmentalists everywhere, it was thought that the West Bengal government had already given the project the go-ahead. But recent statements issuing from the Writers' Building suggest that the authorities are currently re-evaluating Sahara Pariwar's proposal. This is a welcome development, not least because it provides an opportunity for a public discussion of the project and its merits.

To begin with, it is worth asking whether the project is feasible even on its own terms. How realistic, for instance, is the idea of converting a stretch of the Sundarbans into an arena for water sports and a haven for beach lovers? This is an area of mudflats and mangrove islands. There are no 'pristine beaches', nor any coral gardens. The Ganges–Brahmaputra river system carries *eight times* as much silt as the Amazon, and the waters of this region are thick with suspended particulate matter. This is not an environment that is appropriate for snorkelling or scuba diving. In the water, visibility is so low that snorkellers and scuba divers would scarcely be able to see beyond their masks. What is more, these waters are populated by estuarine sharks and marine crocodiles. A substantial number of villagers and fishermen fall prey to these animals every year. Snorkellers and divers would face many dangers, and in the event of fatalities the Sahara Pariwar and the West Bengal government would be liable to litigation.

Even swimming is extremely hazardous in the Sundarbans. The collision of river and sea in this region creates powerful currents, undertows and whirlpools. Drownings are commonplace and boats are often swamped by the swirling water. Swimmers who accidentally ingest water would face another kind of hazard. Consider, for example, the experience of an American woman who visited the Sundarbans in the 1970s. She dipped her finger in the river and touched it briefly to her tongue to test its salinity. Within a short while she developed crippling intestinal convulsions and had to be rushed to hospital. Bacteria and parasites are not the least among the many life forms that flourish in the waters of the Sundarbans.

The location Sahara Pariwar has chosen for its project lies athwart the entrance to the Hooghly river, in the vicinity of Sagar Island. This spot has the advantage of commanding direct access to the Bay of Bengal while also being easily accessible from Kolkata. But when the weather is taken into account, these apparent pluses are quickly revealed to be an uncompounded tally of minuses. A quick glance at a map is all it takes to see that the chosen location is directly exposed to the weather systems of the Bay of Bengal. What would happen if the complex were to find itself in the path of an incoming cyclone?

The Bay of Bengal is one of the most active cyclonic regions in the world: two of the most devastating hurricanes in human history were visited upon the coast of Bengal in 1737 and 1970. Each of these cyclones claimed over 300,000 lives, a greater toll than Hiroshima and Nagasaki combined. The toll might have been higher still if not for the Sundarbans. The mangrove forests have historically absorbed the first shock of incoming cyclones; they are the barrier that protects the hinterland. This is why the people who live in this region have generally been wary of creating settlements that abut directly on the sea.

That this region will be hit by another devastating storm is a near certainty in this era of global warming. Much of the destruction caused by cyclones is the result of 'storm surges'—the massive tidal waves that precede an incoming storm. What would happen to Sahara's 'floating hotel', with its restaurants, helipads, shopping arcades, meditation centres, etc., if it were to be hit by a 15 metre tidal wave and 200 kmph winds? Suffice it to say that the damage would be enormous and many lives would be lost. And what of the casualties? There are no advanced medical facilities in the Sundarbans; where would survivors be treated? Tourists who are harmed or injured are almost certain to initiate litigation. Who will be liable for damages: Sahara Pariwar or the Government of India?

And what of the question of insurance, which appears to have been ignored by the government and Sahara Pariwar alike? The 'floating hotel' will need to be insured, like any seagoing vessel. Considering the pattern of cyclonic activity in the region, no reputable firm is likely to provide insurance for this project. Even if one were to, the premiums alone would make the project unprofitable. In the absence of insurance, the government will be fully liable for all damages. If indeed a major catastrophe were to occur here, the entire tourism industry in India would suffer a crippling blow to its reputation. The risk is simply not worth it.

Sahara Pariwar claims that it will open 'virgin' areas to tourists. But the islands of the Sundarbans are not 'virgin' in any sense. The Indian part of the Sundarbans supports a population of close to 4 million people—equivalent to the entire population of New Zealand. The Sundarbans are an archipelago of islands, large and small. Many, if not most, of the islands have been populated at some time or the other. In fact, several islands were forcibly depopulated in order to make room for Project Tiger. In 1979, the Left Front government evicted tens of thousands of refugee settlers, mainly Dalits, from the island of Morichjhãpi. The cost in lives is still unaccounted, but it is likely that thousands were killed. The eviction was justified on ecological grounds: the authorities claimed that the island of Morichjhãpi had to be preserved as a forest reserve. It is scarcely conceivable that a government run by the same Left Front is now thinking of handing over a substantial part of the Sundarbans to an industrial house like Sahara Pariwar. It runs contrary to every tenet of the Front's professed ideology.

Sahara Pariwar's project would turn large stretches of this very forest, soaked in the blood of evicted refugees, into a playground for the affluent. Although forgotten elsewhere, in the Sundarbans the memory of Morichjhāpi is still vividly alive. Would it be surprising then if the people there took this project to be an affront to their memories and a deliberate provocation? And if indeed there were to be protests and disturbances, how would the government ensure the safety of the tourist complex? Piracies and water-borne dacoities are daily occurrences in the Sundarbans, yet the government is powerless to prevent these crimes. To monitor the winding waterways of the Sundarbans is no easy matter, and the police presence in the region is minimal anyway. How will the authorities provide security to tourists in a region where the machinery of state has not so much withered as never been properly implanted?

It is clear then that even within its own terms, this project is misconceived. Its chances of profitability are so slim as to suggest that some other intention lurks behind the stated motives for embarking on it. Certain other business houses are also said to be interested in expanding into the Sundarbans, and this may well have something to do with recent rumours concerning the possible discovery of oil in the region.

But what would happen if a large-scale tourist project were to actually take shape in the Sundarbans? What, for example, would be the impact on the ecosystem?

It needs to be noted first that Sahara Pariwar's project has not been subjected to a rigorous environmental-impact appraisal. However, several independent groups have conducted preliminary studies and their conclusions suggest that the effects may be disastrous.

For instance, the floating hotel is sure to disturb the patterns of sedimentation in its vicinity. The consequences are impossible to predict. It is quite conceivable that the structures will affect the flow of silt out of the Hooghly into the Bay of Bengal. This in turn will lead to greater siltation upriver and it might even cause a blockage in the river-mouth.

The floating hotel and its satellite structures will also disgorge a large quantity of sewage and waste into the surrounding waters, including grease, oil and detergents. The increased level of contaminants is certain to have an impact on the crabs and fish that live in these waters. Already, very high levels of mercury have been detected in the catch that is brought to Kolkata's markets. A sharp rise in pollution could have a potentially devastating effect on the food supply of the entire region.

The pollutants would not be restricted to sewage and waste: there would be light and noise pollution as well. The hotel's lights would disorient certain species. Olive ridley turtles, for instance, would not be able to find their way back to their nesting places.

The Sahara project also envisages the deployment of a large number of speedboats and other high-powered watercraft, possibly even jet skis. Fast-moving craft such as these pose a great danger to marine mammals, particularly to such endangered species as the Irrawaddy dolphin (*Orcaella brevirostris*). The high-pitched sound produced by speedboats disrupts their echo-location systems, often resulting in casualties. In January 2000, I myself came upon the carcass of an Irrawaddy dolphin on the banks of the Matla river. A huge hole had been gouged in its head, probably by a propeller. A surge in traffic in these waters will result in many more such casualties.

Historically the waters of the Sundarbans were home to great numbers of whales and dolphins. British naturalists of the nineteenth century reported the area to be 'teeming' with marine mammals. Very few of these animals are seen in these waters today. The fate of these species is unknown because there has been no major census or survey. There is limited expertise in this field in India, and the Sundarbans being a border region, foreign researchers have not been allowed to conduct surveys for reasons of security. For all we know the cetacean population of this region has already dwindled catastrophically. It would be nothing less than an outrage if an area that has been closed to zoologists should now be thrown open to tourist developers.

Tourism is the world's largest industry and one of India's most important revenue earners. Clearly every part of the country will have to reach an accommodation with this industry—it would be idle to pretend otherwise. There is no reason why tourists should be excluded from the Sundarbans, so long as their presence causes no harm to the ecology or to the people who live there. But if tourism is to develop here, it should be on the model of other ecologically sensitive areas, such as the Galapagos Islands, where the industry is held to very high standards. The Sundarabans deserve no less, and it is the duty of the Government of India and the Government of West Bengal to ensure that this unique ecosystem and its inhabitants, both animal and human, receive their due.

Sahara Pariwar is not the first to conceive of a grandiose plan for this region. In the early nineteenth century the British dreamt of creating a port on the Matla river that would replace Kolkata and be a rival to Bombay and Singapore. In 1854, Henry Piddington, a pioneering British meteorologist, wrote an open letter to Lord Dalhousie, begging him to reconsider the project. In his letter, Piddington warned that in the event of a 'cyclone' (a word he invented) the new port would probably be swept away. Lord Dalhousie, secure on his proconsular throne, paid no attention to this lonely voice. The port was built and took its name from Lord Canning. But Henry Piddington was soon vindicated: Port Canning was swamped by a storm in 1867 and formally abandoned by the British five years later.

Over the last few months, due to the efforts of a small group of concerned people, many letters have been sent to the chief minister of West Bengal asking him to re-examine Sahara Pariwar's project. It falls to him now, as a democratically elected leader, to show better judgement than did his lordly predecessors in the Writers' Building.

(First published in *Outlook*, 18 October 2004)

# FIVE
# The Town by the Sea

The Andaman and Nicobar Islands are one of those quadrants of the globe where political and geological fault lines run on parallel courses. Politically the islands are a Union Territory, governed directly from New Delhi, but geologically they stand just beyond the edge of the Indian tectonic plate. Stretching across 700 kilometres of the Bay of Bengal, they are held aloft by a range of undersea mountains that stands guard over the abyssal deep of the Sunda Trench. Of the 572 islands, only thirty-six are inhabited: 'the Andamans' is the name given to the northern part of the archipelago, while 'the Nicobars' lie to the south. At their uppermost point, the Andamans are just a short distance from Burma's Coco Islands, infamous for their prisons, while the southernmost edge of the Nicobars is only a couple of hundred kilometres from the Sumatran region of Aceh. This part of the chain is so positioned that the tsunami of 26 December 2004 hit it just minutes after devastating the coastline of northern Sumatra.

Despite the hundreds of kilometres of water that separate the Andamans from the Indian mainland, many of the relief camps that had been set up in Port Blair, the islands' capital city, had the appearance of miniaturized portraits of the nation. Only a small percentage of their inmates was indigenous to the islands; the others were settlers from different parts of the mainland: Bengal, Orissa, Punjab, Andhra Pradesh and Uttar Pradesh. If this came as a surprise, it was only because the identity of the islands—and indeed the alibi for the present form of their rule—lay in an administrative conception of the 'primitive' that dated back to the British Raj. The idea that these islands are somehow synonymous with backwardness is energetically promoted in Port Blair. Hoardings depicting naked 'primitives' line the streets, and I even heard of a sign that instructed onlookers to 'Love Your Primitive Tribe'. In most parts of the mainland, such images would long since have been defaced or torn down for the sheer offensiveness of their depictions. Not so on these islands, however, which are more a projection of India than a part of its body politic; as with many colonies, they represent a distended and compressed version of the mother country in its weaknesses and strengths, its aspirations and failings. During the two weeks that followed the tsunami, both the fault lines that underlie the islands seemed suddenly to have been set in motion: it was as if the deep time of geology had collided with the hurried history of an emergent nation.

The mainland settlers in the camps were almost unanimous in describing themselves as having come to the islands in search of land and opportunity. Listening to their stories, it was easy to believe that most of them found what they were looking for: here, in this far-flung chain of islands, tens of thousands of settlers had been able to make their way out of poverty and into the ranks of the country's expanding middle class. But on the morning of 26 December, this hard-won betterment became a potent source of vulnerability. For to be middle-class is to be kept afloat by a life raft of paper: identity cards, licences, ration cards, school certificates, cheque books, certificates of life insurance and receipts for fixed deposits. It was the particular nature of this disaster that it targeted not just the physical being of the victims but also the proof of the survivors' identities. An earthquake would have left remnants to rummage through; floods and hurricanes would have given survivors time to safeguard essential documents on their person. The tsunami, in the suddenness of its onslaught, allowed for no preparations: not only did it destroy the survivors' homes and decimate their families, but it also robbed them of all the evidentiary traces of their place in the world.

On 1 January 2005, I went to visit the Nirmala School Camp in Port Blair. The camp, like the school in which it was housed, was run by the Catholic Church and presided over by a mild-mannered young priest by the name of Father Johnson. On the morning of my visit, Father Johnson was at the centre of an angry altercation. The refugees had spent the last three days waiting anxiously in the camp, and in that time no one had asked them where they wanted to go or when; none of them had any idea of what was to become of them. The sense of being adrift had brought them to the end of their tether. The issue was neither deprivation nor hardship—there was enough food, and they had all the clothes they needed; it was the uncertainty that was intolerable. In the absence of any other figure of authority, they had laid siege to Father Johnson: When would they be allowed to move on? Where would they be going?

Father Johnson could give them no answers for he was, in his own way, just as helpless as they were. The officials in charge of the relief effort had told him nothing about their plans for the refugees. Now time was running out: the schools in which the camps were located were to re-open on 3 January. Father Johnson had no idea how his school would function with more than 1,600 refugees camping on the grounds.

Realizing at last that Father Johnson knew no more than they did, the inmates reduced their demands to a single, modest query: Could they be provided with some paper and a few pens? No sooner had this request been met than another uproar broke out. Those who'd been given possession of pens and paper now became the centre of the siege. Crowding together, people began to push and jostle, clamouring to have their names written down. Identity was now no more than a matter of assertion, and nothing seemed to matter more than being able to create a trail of paper. On this depended the eventual reclamation of a life.

Standing on the edge of the crowd was a stocky thirty-year-old man by the name of Obed Tara. He was, he told me, from the island of Car Nicobar, and a member of an indigenous group whose affiliations, in language and ethnicity, lie with the Malay peoples to the east. But he himself was a Naik in the 10th Madras Regiment of the Indian Army and was fluent in Hindi. On 10 December, he had set off from Kolkata, where his unit was currently stationed, in order to travel to Car Nicobar. Like most Nicobarese people, he was a Christian, a member of the Anglican Church of North India, and he'd been looking forward to celebrating Christmas at home. But this year there had been something else to look forward to as well: he was to be married on the first day of the New Year (the very day of our conversation).

On 26 December, despite the celebrations and merry-making of the night before, Obed Tara, like most members of his extended family, rose early in order to attend the Boxing Day service at their church. Their house was in the seafront settlement of Malacca, just a few hundred metres from the water. Their neighbourhood was the commercial heart of the township, and their house was surrounded by shops and godowns. They were themselves a part of the market's bustle; they owned a Maruti Omni and operated a long-distance phone booth in their house. In other words, theirs was a family that had been swept into the middle class by the commercial opportunities of the last decade.

That morning, as the family was gathering outside the house, the ground began to heave with a violence none of them had experienced before; it shook so hard that it was impossible to stand still and they were forced to throw themselves on the ground. Then the earth cracked and fountains of mud-brown water came geysering out of these fissures. Like all the islanders, Obed Tara was accustomed to tremors in the earth, but neither he nor anyone else there had ever seen anything like this. It took a while before the ground was still enough to regain a footing. No sooner had he risen to his feet than he heard a wild, roaring sound. Looking seawards, he saw a wall of water advancing towards his house. Gathering his relatives, he began to run inland. When he looked back, his house and the neighbourhood in which it stood had vanished under the waves; two elderly members of the family were lost and everything they possessed was gone: the car, the phone booth, the house. The family spent a couple of nights in the island's interior and afterwards the elders deputed him to go to Port Blair to see what he could secure for them by way of relief and supplies.

By the time Obed Tara finished telling me this story, there was a catch in his voice and he was swallowing convulsively to keep from sobbing. I asked him, 'Why don't you go to the army offices and tell them who you are? I am sure they will do what they can to help you.'

He shook his head, as if to indicate that he had considered and dismissed this thought many times over. 'The sea took my uniform, my ration card, my service card, my tribal papers; it took everything,' he said. 'I can't prove who I am. Why should they believe me?'

He led me to the far side of the camp, where another group of islanders was sitting patiently under a tent. They too had lost everything; their entire village had disappeared under the sea; salt water had invaded their fields and taken away their orchards. They could not contemplate going back, they said; the stench of death was everywhere; the water sources had been contaminated and would not be usable for years.

The leader of the group was a man by the name of Sylvester Solomon. A one-time serviceman in the Navy, he had retired some years ago. He too had lost all his papers; he had no idea how he would claim his pension again. Worse still, the bank that had the custody of his family's money had also been swept away, along with all its records.

I told him that by law the bank was obliged to return his money, and he smiled as if at a child. I wanted to persuade him of the truth of what I'd said, but when I looked into his eyes, I knew that in his place I too would not have the energy or the courage to take on the struggles that would be required to reclaim my life's savings from that bank.

In the same camp, I encountered a Sikh woman by the name of Paramjeet Kaur. Noticing my notebook, she said, 'Are you taking names too? Here, write mine down ...' She was a woman of determined aspect, dressed in a dun-coloured salwar-kameez. She had come to the islands some thirty years earlier, by dint of marriage. Her husband was a Sikh from Campbell Bay, a settlement on the southernmost tip of the Nicobar island chain, less than a couple of hundred kilometres from northern Sumatra. Like many others in the settlement, her husband belonged to a family that had been given a grant of land in recognition of service to the army (to distribute land in this way is a tradition that goes back to the British Indian Army and its efforts to engage the loyalties of Indian 'sepoys'). But Paramjeet Kaur's in-laws came to the Nicobar Islands well after Independence, in 1969, at a time when agricultural land had become scarce on the mainland. They were given 15 bighas of land and a plot to build a residence. The settlement that grew around them was as varied as the regiments of the Indian Army: there were Marathis, Malayalis, Jharkhandis and people from Uttar Pradesh and Bihar.

'There was nothing there but jungle then,' said Paramjeet Kaur. 'We cleared it with our own hands and we laid out orchards of areca and coconut. With God's blessing we prospered, and built a cement house with three rooms and a veranda.'

The strip of land that was zoned for residential plots lay right on the seafront, providing the settlers with fine ocean views. It was no mere accident then that placed Paramjeet Kaur's house in the path of the tsunami of 26 December: its location was determined by an ordering of space that owed more to Europe than to its immediate surroundings. The sea poses little danger to the smiling corniches of the French Riviera or the coastline of Italy: the land-encircled Mediterranean is not subject to the play of tides and it does not give birth to tropical storms. The Indian Ocean and the Bay of Bengal, on the other hand, are fecund in the breeding of cyclones, especially the latter. This may be the reason why a certain wariness of the sea can be seen in the lineaments of the ancient harbour cities of southern Asia, such as Mrauk-U and Malacca. They were often situated in upriver locations, at a cautious distance from open water. In recent times, however, the pattern seems to have been reversed: it could almost be stated as a rule that the more modern and prosperous a settlement, the more likely it is to hug the water. On the island of Car Nicobar, for example, the Indian Air Force base was built a few dozen metres from the water's edge, and it was so laid out that the more senior the servicemen, the closer they were to the sea. Although it is true that no one could have anticipated the tsunami, the choice of location is still surprising. Cyclones, frequent in this region, are also associated with surges of water that rise to heights of 10–15 metres and their effect would have been similar. Surely the planners were not unaware of this? But, of course, it is all too easy to be wise after the event. Given the choice between a view of the beach and a plot in the mosquito-infested interior, what would anyone have chosen before 26 December 2004?

On the morning of that day, Paramjeet Kaur and her family were inside their sea-facing house when the earthquake struck. The ground unfurled under their feet like a sheet waving in the wind, and no sooner had the shaking stopped than they heard a noise 'like the sound of a helicopter'. Paramjeet Kaur's husband, Pavitter Singh, looked outside and saw a wall of water speeding towards them. 'The sea has split apart (*samundar phat gaya*),' he shouted, 'run, run.' There was no time to gather documents or jewellery; everyone who stopped to do so was killed. Paramjeet Kaur and her family ran for 2 kilometres without looking back and were just able to save themselves.

'But for what?'

Thirty years of labour had been washed away in an instant: everything they had accumulated was gone; their land was sown with salt. 'When we were young, we had the energy to cut the jungle and reclaim the land. We laid out fields and orchards and we did well. But at my age, how can I start again? Where will I begin?'

'What will you do then?' I asked.

'We will go back to Punjab, where we have family. The government must give us land there; that is our demand.'

In other camps I met office workers from Uttar Pradesh, fishermen from coastal Andhra and construction labourers from Bengal. They had all built good lives for themselves on the islands—but now, having lost their homes, their relatives and even their identities, they were intent on returning to the mainland, no matter what.

'If nothing else,' one of them said to me, 'we will live in slums beside the railway tracks. But never again by the sea.'

How do we quantify the help needed to rebuild these ruined lives? The question is answered easily enough if we pose it not in the abstract but in relation to ourselves. To put ourselves in the place of these victims is to realize that all the help in the world would not be adequate. Sufficiency is not a concept that is applicable here: potentially there is no limit to the amount of relief that can be used.

This is the assumption that motivates ordinary people to open their purses, even though they know that governments and big companies have already contributed a great deal. It is also why no disaster assistance group has ever been known to say 'we have to raise exactly this much and no more'. But when it comes to the disbursement of these funds the assumptions seem to undergo a drastic change, and nowhere more so than in out-of-the-way places.

In the Andaman and Nicobar Islands, although the manpower and machinery for the relief effort were supplied largely by the armed forces, overall authority was concentrated in the hands of a small clutch of senior civil servants in Port Blair. No matter the sense of crisis elsewhere, the attitude of Port Blair's officialdom was one of disdainful self-sufficiency. On more than one occasion, I heard them dismissing offers of help as unnecessary and misdirected. Supplies were available aplenty, they said; in fact, they had more on their hands than could be distributed and there was a danger that perishable materials would rot on the airstrips.

This argument was, of course, entirely circular: logically speaking, bottlenecks of distribution imply a need for *more* help, not less. But for the mandarins of Port Blair, the relief effort was a zero-sum game in which they were the referees.

Were supplies really available aplenty throughout the islands? The tale told in the relief camps was, of course, the opposite of that which echoed out of the lairs of officialdom. Most of the refugees had to wait several days before they were evacuated. Forgotten in their far-flung islands, they listened to radio broadcasts that told them their nation was rushing aid to Sri Lanka and had refused all outside help as unnecessary: for the thirsty and hungry, there was little consolation in the thought that these measures might help their country establish itself as a superpower. In Campbell Bay, according to several reports, refugees were moved to such fury by the indifference of local officials that they assaulted an officer who was found ushering in the New

Year with a feast. Accounts of this incident, confirmed by several sources in the coast guards and police, were characteristically denied by the civil authorities.

In Port Blair, relief camps were the main sources of aid and sustenance for the refugees. These were all maintained by private initiatives: they were staffed by volunteers from local youth groups, religious foundations and so on, and their supplies were provided by local shopkeepers, businessmen and citizens' organizations. I met with the organizers of several relief camps and they were unanimous in stating that they had received no aid whatsoever from the government apart from some water. They knew that people on the mainland were eager to help and that a great deal of money had been raised. None of these funds had reached them, though; presumably they had met the same bottlenecks of distribution as the supplies that were lying piled on the runways. That it was possible for the people of a small town like Port Blair to provide relief to so many refugees was the bright side of this dismal story; it was proof, if any were needed, that the development of civil society in India had far outpaced the institutions of state and the personnel who staff them.

The attitude of the armed forces was not the same as that of civilian authorities. At all levels of the chain of command, from Lt. Gen. B.S. Thakur, the commanding officer in Port Blair, to the jawans who were combing through the ruins of Car Nicobar, there was an urgency, a diligence and an openness that was in striking contrast to the stance of the civilian personnel. Indeed, the feats performed by some units spoke of an exemplary dedication to duty. Consider, for example, the case of Wing Commander B.S.K. Kumar, a helicopter pilot at the Car Nicobar air base. On 26 December, he was asleep when the earthquake first made itself felt—his quarters were a mere 30 metres from the sea. Not only did he manage to outrun the tsunami with his wife and child, but he was also airborne within ten minutes of the first wave. In the course of the day, he winched up some sixty stranded people and evacuated another 240. His colleague Wing Commander Maheshwari woke too late to escape the wave. As the waters rose, he was forced to retreat to the roof of his building with his wife and daughter. Along with twenty-nine other people, he fought for his footing on the roof until all were swept off. He managed to make his way to land but was separated from his wife and child—two hours passed before they were found, clinging to the trunk of a tree. Of the thirty people on that roof, only six survived. Yet, despite the ordeal, Wing Commander Maheshwari flew several sorties that day.

Considering the diligence of the armed forces and the enthusiasm and generosity of ordinary citizens, how is the attitude of the islands' civilian administration to be accounted for? The answer is simple: a lack of democracy. As a Union Territory, the Andaman and Nicobar Islands have no legislature and thus no elected representatives with any clout apart from a single Member of Parliament. Elsewhere in India, in any crisis, officials have to answer to representatives at many levels. A failure to act would result in their being hounded by legislators and harried by trade unions, student groups and the like. As Amartya Sen has shown in his work on famines, these mechanisms are essential to the proper distribution of resources in any situation of extreme scarcity; in effect the political system serves as a means by which demands are articulated. The media similarly serves to create flows of information. These were precisely the mechanisms that were absent on the Andaman and Nicobar Islands: there were no elected representatives to speak for the people and the media had been excluded from large swathes of the territory. It was not for no reason that on the mainland, where these mechanisms did exist, the attitude of administrators in the affected districts was more sensitive to the needs of the victims; the officials there were substantially more open to the oversight of the press and to offers of help from other parts of the country.

It is common for civil servants to complain of the perils of political interference: the situation on the islands is proof that in the absence of vigorous oversight many (though certainly not all) officials will revert to the indifference and inertia that are the natural condition of any bureaucracy.

Clearly the central government was aware that there was a problem, for the relief operation was restructured on 2 January, reportedly at the personal intervention of Sonia Gandhi. Moreover, several senior members of the ruling party were dispatched to the outlying islands, not just for token visits but to make sure that the supplies were properly distributed. These are welcome first steps, but it is essential that the central government moves quickly to create a more responsive and efficient disaster relief operation in this region, not just for the management of this catastrophe but for the long term. For if anything can be said with any certainty it is that this tsunami will not be the last seismic upheaval to shake the Andaman and Nicobar Islands. In 1991, after lying dormant for 200 years, the volcano of Barren Island, off the coast of the Andamans, became active again; there are reports that it erupted around the time of the earthquake of 26 December. On 14 September 2002, there was a magnitude 6.5 earthquake near Diglipur in North Andaman Island; there were also unconfirmed reports of a minor eruption in the same area.

The signs are clear—no one can say the Earth has not provided warnings of its intent.

In Port Blair I found the tsunami's effects on the outlying islands could only be guessed at. The refugees in the camps spoke of apocalyptic devastation and tens of thousands dead; the authorities' estimates were much more modest. There were few, if any, reliable independent assessments, for the civil authorities had decided that no journalists or other 'outsiders' were to be allowed to travel to the outlying islands. The reasons given were those of the battlefield: too many resources would be spent on their protection. But there was no battle underway on the islands and the dangers of the tsunami were long past. Public ferry and steamer services linking Port Blair to the outer islands were in operation and had plenty of room for paying passengers. And yet journalists, Indian and foreign, were forcibly dragged off these ships at the behest of the authorities.

On 1 January 2005, there was an unexpected parting in this curtain of exclusion. The reason was that a couple of senior members of the ruling party had come to Port Blair with the intent of travelling farther afield. It was quickly made known that an Air Force plane would be provided to take the ministers and a retinue of journalists to the island of Car Nicobar the next day. This island, which is positioned halfway between the Andaman and Nicobar chains, is home to some 30,000 people. It also houses an air base, which makes it something of a hub in relation to the more southerly islands.

Hoping to get on this plane, I duly presented myself at the airport, only to find that a great many others had arrived with the same expectation. As always in such situations, there was considerable confusion about who would be allowed to get on. After the ministers had boarded, a minor melee ensued at the foot of the ramp that led to the plane's capacious belly. Knowing that I stood little chance of prevailing in this contest, I had almost resigned myself to being left behind, when a young man in a blue uniform tapped my elbow and pointed across the airfield. 'You want to go to Car Nicobar? That plane over there is carrying relief supplies. Just go and sit down. No one will say anything.'

I sought no explanation for this unsolicited act of consideration: it seemed typical of the general goodwill of the military personnel I had encountered on the islands. As if on tiptoe I walked across the tarmac, up the ramp and into the plane. It was a twin-engine Soviet-era AN-26, rusty but dependable, and its capacious fuselage was lined with folding benches. The round portholes that lined its sides were like eyes that had grown rheumy with age; time had sandpapered the panes of glass so they were almost opaque. The cargo area was packed with mattresses, folding beds, cases of mineral water and sacks of food, all covered with a net of webbing. There were some half a dozen men inside, sitting on the benches with their feet planted askew beside the mass of supplies. I seated myself in the only available space, next to a short, portly man with thick glasses and well-oiled, curly hair. He was dressed in a stiffly ironed brown safari suit and he had an air of irascibility that spoke of a surfeit of time spent filing papers and running offices. He was muttering angrily when I came aboard, 'What do those people care? What have they ever done to help anyone?' Of all the people on that plane, he was perhaps the last I would have chosen to sit beside: I was keen to make myself as inconspicuous as possible, while he seemed determined to draw attention to himself. It was only a matter of minutes, I thought, before the airmen evicted him. Inexplicably, they did not.

When the engines started up, my neighbour turned his attention to me. 'These big people think they are so great, but what help have they given?' I assumed this to be a general expression of disgust, of the kind that is heard on every train and bus in the country. But then he added suddenly, 'Let them go through what I have gone through. Let them suffer, then they will see ...'

This hit me with the force of a shock: his well-laundered safari suit, his air of almost comical self-importance, his irascibility—nothing about him suggested victimhood. But I understood now why the airmen had ignored his rants; they knew something about him that I did not and this was their way of showing compassion.

Meanwhile the tirade continued. 'If those politicians had suffered as I have, what would they do? This is the question I want to ask.'

I winced to think of my first response to his mutterings. 'What exactly has happened?' I asked. 'Tell me.'

He did not want his name used, so I shall call him the 'Director'. This indeed was his official title: he had been posted to the island of Car Nicobar in 1991, as Director of the island's Malaria Research Centre, and had lived there ever since. He was originally from Puri in Orissa and had been trained at Berhampur University. During his time in Car Nicobar he had married and had two children: a son who was now thirteen and a ten-year-old daughter. His home was in Malacca—the seafront township I'd heard about in the camps—and his office was just a few minutes' walk from where he lived. In this office he had accumulated a great wealth of epidemiological knowledge. Car Nicobar had once been rife with malaria, he told me. On an island with a population of just 30,000, the annual incidence had been as high as 3,810, even as recently as 1989. But during his tenure he had succeeded in bringing the rate down to a fraction of this number. It was clear, from the readiness with which he quoted the figures, that he was immensely—and justly—proud of what he had achieved on the island.

On 25 December 2004, the Director was in Port Blair, on his way to New Delhi. Since he was travelling for official reasons, he had left his family in Malacca. He spent the night in the Haddo Circuit House, which stands close to the water. On the morning of the 26th, he was woken by the shaking of his bed. He stepped off to find the floor heaving and realized that an earthquake had hit the town. As he was running out of the building, his mobile phone rang. Glancing quickly at the screen, he saw that his wife was calling from Malacca. He guessed that the earthquake had struck Car Nicobar too, but he was not unduly alarmed. Tremors were frequently felt on the island so he thought his wife would be able to cope. The guest house, meanwhile, was still shaking and there was no time to talk. He rejected the call and ran outside; he would phone back later, he decided, once the tremors stopped. He waited out the earthquake in the open and when the ground was still at last, he hit the call button on his phone. There was no answer and he wondered if the network was down. But he had little time to think about the matter because a strange phenomenon was manifesting itself before him: the water in the harbour was rising, very rapidly, and the anchored ships seemed to be swirling about in the grip of an unseen hand. Along with everyone else he ran to higher ground.

The islands of the Andaman chain rise steeply out of the sea, and the harbour and waterfront of Port Blair are sheltered by a network of winding fjords and inlets. Such is the lay of the land that the turbulence that radiated from the earthquake's epicentre manifested itself here not as an onrushing wall of water, but as a surge in the water level. Although this caused a good deal of alarm, the damage was not severe.

It was not long before it occurred to the Director that the incoming swell in Port Blair's harbour might have taken a different form elsewhere. The Nicobar Islands do not have the high elevations of their northern neighbours, the Andamans. They are low-lying islands for the most part, and some, like Car Nicobar, stand no more than a few metres above sea level at their highest point. Already anxious, the Director became frantic when news of the tsunami trickled down to the waterfront from the naval offices farther up the slope.

The Director knew of a government office in Car Nicobar that had a satellite phone. He dialled the number again and again, but it was either busy or there was no answer. When at last he got through, the voice at the other end told him, with some reluctance, that Malacca had been badly hit. It was known that there were some survivors, but as for his family, there was no word.

The Director kept calling, and in the afternoon he learnt that his thirteen-year-old son had been found clinging to the rafters of a church, some 200 metres behind their house. Arrangements were made to bring the boy to the phone and the Director was able to speak to him directly later that night. His son told him that the family had been in the bedroom when the earthquake started. A short while later, a terrifying sound from the direction of the sea had driven the three of them into the drawing room. The boy had kept running, right into the kitchen. The house was built of wood on a concrete foundation. When the wave hit, the house dissolved into splinters and the boy was carried away as if on a wind. Flailing his arms, he succeeded in grabbing hold of something that seemed to be fixed to the earth. Through wave after wave he managed to maintain his grip. When the water receded, he saw that he was holding on to the only upright structure within a radius of several hundred metres: of the township there was nothing left but a deep crust of wreckage.

'And your mother and sister?' the Director asked.

'Baba, they just disappeared …' And now for the first time, the boy began to sob, and the Director's heart broke because he knew his son was crying because he thought he would be scolded and blamed for what had happened.

'I was strict with him, sir. I am a strict man; that is my nature. But I must say he is a brave boy, a very brave boy,' the Director said, his voice trailing off.

Having spent thirteen years on the island, the Director was well acquainted with the local administration and the officers on the air base. Through their intervention he was able to get on a flight the very next day. He spent the day searching through the rubble; he found many possessions, but no trace of his daughter or his wife. He came back to Port Blair with his son the same evening and the two of them moved in with some friends. Every day since then he'd been trying to go back to find out what had become of his wife and daughter, but the flights had been closed—until this one.

'Tell me,' he said, his voice becoming uncharacteristically soft. 'What do you think? Is there any hope?'

It took me a moment to collect my wits. 'Of course there is hope,' I said. 'There is always hope. They could have been swept ashore on another part of the island.'

He nodded. 'We will see. I hope I will find out today, in Malacca.'

With some hesitation I asked if it would be all right if I came with him. He answered with a prompt nod. 'You can come.'

I had the impression that he had been dreading the lonely search that lay ahead and would be glad for some company. 'All right then,' I said. 'I will.'

At the airfield in Car Nicobar, the Director arranged a ride for us on a yellow construction truck that had been set to the task of distributing relief supplies. The truck went bouncing down the runway before turning off into a narrow road that led into a forest. Once the airstrip was behind us it was as though we had been transported to some long-ago land, unspoiled and untouched. The road wound through a dense tropical jungle, dotted at intervals with groves of slender areca palms and huts mounted on stilts. Some of these had metamorphosed into makeshift camps, sprouting awnings of plastic and tarpaulin. It was clear that the island's interior was sparsely inhabited, with the population being concentrated along the seafront.

Earlier, while the plane was making its descent, I had had a panoramic, if blurred, view of the island in the crisp morning sunlight. No more than a few kilometres across, it was flat and low, and its interior was covered by a dense canopy of greenery. A turquoise halo surrounded its shores where a fringe of sand had once formed an almost continuous length of beach—this was now still mainly underwater. I saw to my surprise that many thick coconut palms were still standing, even on the edge of the water. Relatively few palms had been flattened; most remained upright and in full possession of their greenery. As for the forest, the canopy seemed almost undisturbed. All trace of habitation, on the other hand, had been obliterated: the foundations of many buildings could be clearly seen on the ground, but of the structures they had once supported, nothing remained.

It was evident from above that the tsunami had been peculiarly selective in the manner of its destruction. Had the island been hit by a major cyclone, not a frond would have survived on the coconut palms and the forest canopy would have been denuded. Most human dwellings, on the other hand, would have retained their walls even if they lost their roofs. Not so in this instance: the villages along the shore were not merely damaged—they had been erased. It was as if the island had been hit by a weapon devised to cause the maximum possible damage to life and property, while leaving nature largely unharmed.

We came to an intersection that was flanked by low, whitewashed buildings. This was the administrative centre of the island, the Director explained; the settlement of Malacca lay a good distance away and we would have to walk from here. After getting off the truck, we came to the District Library, a structure of surprising size and solidity: like the surrounding office buildings, it was unharmed. A medical camp, manned by the Indo-Tibetan Border Police, had sprung up on its grounds, under the shade of a spreading, moss-twined padauk tree. The Director spotted a doctor sitting in a tent. He darted away and slipped under the tent's blue flap. 'Doctor, have you heard anything about my family?' he said. 'I've come because I heard some survivors had been found …'

The doctor's face froze, and after a moment's silence, he said in a tone that was non-committal and yet not discouraging, 'No news has reached me—I've not heard anything …'

We continued on our way, past the airy bungalows of the island's top officials, with their well-tended gardens. Soon we came upon two men sitting by the roadside with an odd assortment of salvaged goods. 'That's mine,' said the Director, pointing to a lampstand of turned wood. 'I paid a lot for it; it's made of padauk wood.' There was no rancour in his voice, nor did he seem to want to reclaim the object. We walked on.

A few steps ahead the road dipped towards a large clearing fringed by thick coconut palms. As with many small-town maidans, there was a plaster bust of Mahatma Gandhi standing in its centre. So far on our journey from the airport we had seen no outward sign of the damage caused by the tsunami, but now we had arrived at the periphery of the band of destruction. Mounds of splintered planks and other building materials lay scattered across the clearing, and the red-white-and-green fence that surrounded the bust of Mahatma Gandhi was swathed in refuse and dead coconut fronds. Everywhere evidence of the tsunami's incursion could be seen in pools of water that had turned rank over the last few days.

At the far end of the maidan, a fire was blazing among the coconut palms. The warehouse that supplied the island with cooking gas had stood at that spot. The tsunami had swept the warehouse away, leaving the cylinders exposed to the sun, and a fire had ensued. Every few minutes the ground shook to the blast of exploding cylinders.

Oblivious to the fire, the Director stepped away to accost a passer-by who was wheeling a loaded bicycle. Over his shoulder, he said to me, 'This is Michael; he worked in my office.' Michael was a sturdy, grizzled Nicobarese, dressed in green shorts and a grey shirt. Laying his hands on the bicycle's handlebars, the Director said in Hindi, 'Michael, listen—has there been any news of Madam? You know what she looks like. Have you seen any trace of her?'

Michael dropped his eyes, as if in embarrassment, and answered with a tiny shake of his head. Lowering his voice, the Director continued, 'And have you heard anyone speak of a girl roaming in the jungle?' When this too failed to elicit an answer, he went on, 'Michael,

I need your help. Bring some men and come. I need to dig through the rubble to see if I can find anything.' Even as he was speaking, his attention shifted to the contents of the plastic bags that were hanging from the handlebars. Flinching, he let go immediately. 'Michael!' he cried. 'What is all this stuff you've picked up! You should know better than to take things from over there—they may be contaminated.'

Michael hung his head and wheeled his bicycle silently away.

'They're all looting,' said the Director, shaking his head. 'I've heard the bazaar in Port Blair has received three sackfuls of gold from the islands ...'

In the clump of burning palm trees, yet another gas cylinder exploded. It was close enough that we could feel the rattle of the blast in the debris under our feet; a shard of metal struck an onlooker, fortunately without injury. Oblivious to the flames, the Director hurried towards a spot where a mound of mangled household objects lay piled, having been pushed through the screen of coconut palms like dough through a sieve.

'Look, that's mine,' said the Director, pointing to a blue Aristocrat suitcase made of moulded plastic. It had been hacked open with a sharp-bladed instrument and its contents were gone. The Director picked it up and shook it. 'I saw it the last time I was here,' he said. 'It was already empty. Everything had been looted.' His eyes moved over to a steel trunk lying nearby. 'That's mine too. Go and look.' Stepping over, I saw that the trunk's lock had been forced open. On the side, written in large black letters, were the Director's name and designation.

'You see,' the Director said, as if in vindication. 'Everything I've been telling you is true. These things were all mine.'

A short distance away a wooden cabinet lay overturned, and heaps of paper could be seen spilling out of its belly. The Director beckoned to me. 'See? There are all the records from my office. Thirteen years of research: all gone.' We went to kneel beside the cabinet and I saw that the papers were mimeographed data sheets, with the letterhead of the Malaria Research Centre printed on top.

Somewhere among the papers I spotted some old photographs. It was a matter of great relief to me to come upon a few retrievable mementoes, and I was quick to draw the Director's attention to the pictures. On examination it turned out that most of the pictures had been defaced by the water, but I found one where he, the Director, could be seen standing in a group of people. I held it out to him and he took it with an indifferent shrug. 'That photo was taken at the air base, I remember.' He let go and it fluttered into a puddle of stinking water.

'Don't you want to keep it?' I asked in astonishment.

'No,' he said simply. 'It means nothing. These are just work pictures.'

Then suddenly his eyes lit up. 'Look,' he said, 'my slides …' A drawer had come open, shaking loose several decks of white-rimmed photographic slides. Most were sodden with water, but some were dry and had preserved their images. To my untrained eyes, the pictures appeared to be of bacteria, hugely magnified by the lens of a microscope. The Director sorted quickly through the slides and chose a dozen or so. Close at hand there lay a roll of unused plastic bags that had been washed out of a drowned shop and dried by the sun. Peeling off one of these bags, he placed the slides carefully inside before fastening his fingers on them.

'Your home must have been nearby?' I said.

'No,' came the answer. 'The wave carried these things right out of the town. My house is still a kilometre away, over there.'

I had imagined that his possessions were bunched together because his house had stood nearby: this was an indication of how little I understood of the power of the surge. Its strength was such that it had tossed the Director's house aside, picked up his belongings and punched them through a kilometre of dense habitation.

The location the Director had pointed to was on the far side of the burning coconut palms; it was evident that to get there we would have to pass quite close to the fire, which was now spreading rapidly. We set off almost at a run, and soon came to a point where our path was blocked by a fallen tree. He clambered over, hanging on to his slides, and I followed. The fire was now less than 100 metres to our right, and as I was climbing over, there was another explosion, followed by a crackling, whooshing sound. I dropped to the ground and shut my eyes. When I looked up, the Director was still standing, regarding me with puzzled impatience. 'Come on, come on—that's where we have to go: over there.'

When I got to my feet, I had my first glimpse of the seafront where the town of Malacca had once stood, till now largely screened off from view by the coconut palms. On a stretch of land a couple of kilometres long, there were only five structures still standing: the staring, skull-like shell of a school that had lost all its doors and windows; a single neatly whitewashed bungalow in the distance; an arched gateway that had the words 'Rajiv Gandhi Memorial Park' painted on it; a small miraculously unharmed Murugan temple right beside the sea; and, lastly, the skeleton of a church with a row of parallel arches rising from the rubble like the bleached ribs of a dead animal. This was the structure that had saved the life of the Director's son. The palms along the seafront were undamaged and upright, their fronds intact, but the other trees on the site had lost all their leaves and a couple had buses, cars and sheets of corrugated iron wrapped around their trunks. If not for the tree trunks and the waving palms, the first visual analogy to suggest itself would have been Hiroshima after the bomb: the resemblance lay not just in the destruction but also in the discernible directionality of the blast. But there the similarity ended, for the sky here was a cloudless blue and no wisps of smoke rose from the ruins.

The Director led the way across the debris as if he were following a route imprinted in memory, a familiar map of streets and lanes. Despite a stiff breeze blowing in from the sea, the odour of death flowed over the site, not evenly but in whirls and eddies, sometimes growing so strong that it indicated the presence of a yet-undiscovered body. Stray dogs rooting in the ruins looked up as if amazed at the sight of human beings who were still ambient and on their feet.

We came to a point where a rectangular platform of concrete shone brightly under the sun. The Director stepped up to it and placed his feet in the middle. 'This was my house,' he said. 'Only the foundation was concrete. The rest was wood. My wife used to say that she had moved from a white house to a log cabin. You see, she was from an affluent family; she grew up in a bungalow with an air conditioner. She used to teach English in a school here, but she always wanted to leave. I applied many times, but the transfer never came.' He paused, thinking back. For much of the time that we had been together, his voice had carried a note of sharp but undirected annoyance; now it softened. 'There was so much she could have achieved,' he said. 'I was never able to give her the opportunity.'

I reached out to touch his arm, but he shook my hand away brusquely; perhaps he was not the type of man who takes kindly to expressions of sympathy; I could tell from his demeanour that he was accustomed to adversity and had invented many rules for dealing with it. The emotion he felt for his family had rarely been expressed; he had hoarded it inside himself in the way a squirrel gathers food for the winter. Loathe to spend it in his hectic middle years, he had put it away to be savoured when there was a greater sense of ease in his life, when his battles were past and he could give this hoarded love his full attention. He had never dreamt—and who could?—that one bright December day, soon after dawn, it would be stolen, still unsavoured, by the sea.

I began to walk towards the gently lapping waves, no more than 100 metres away. The Director took fright at this and called me back. 'Don't go that way; the tide is coming in. It's time to leave.'

I turned to follow him. As we headed towards the blazing palms, he stopped to point to a yellow paintbox peeping out of the rubble. 'That belonged to Vineeta, my daughter,' he said, and the flatness of his voice was harder to listen to than an outburst would have been. 'She loved to paint; she was very good at it. She was even given a prize, from Hyderabad.'

I expected him to stoop to pick up the box, but instead he turned away and marched on, gripping his bag of slides. 'Wait!' I cried. 'Don't you want to take the box?'

'No,' he said vehemently, shaking his head. 'What good will it do? What will it give back?' He stopped to look at me over the rim of his glasses. 'Do you know what happened the last time I was here? Someone had found my daughter's schoolbag and saved it for me. It was handed to me, like a card. It was the worst thing I could have seen. It was unbearable.'

He started to walk off again. Unable to restrain myself, I called out after him, 'Are you sure you don't want it—the paintbox?'

Without looking around, he said, 'Yes, I am sure.'

I stood amazed as he set off towards the blazing fire, with his slides still folded in his grip. How was it possible that the only memento he had chosen to retrieve were those magnified images? As a husband, a father, a human being, it was impossible not to wonder: What would I have done? What would I have felt? What would I have chosen to keep of the past? The truth is nobody can know, except in the extremity of that moment, and then the choice is not a choice at all but an expression of the innermost sovereignty of the self, which decides because nothing now remains to cloud its vision. In the manner of his choosing there was not a particle of hesitation, not the faintest glimmer of a doubt. Was it perhaps that in this moment of utter desolation there was some comfort in the knowledge of an impersonal effort? Could it be that he was seeking refuge in the one aspect of his existence that could not be erased by an act of nature? Or was there some consolation in the very lack of immediacy? Did the worth of those slides lie precisely in their exclusion from the unendurable pain of his loss? Whatever the reason, it was plain his mind had fixed upon a set of objects that derived their meaning from the part of his life that was lived in thought and contemplation.

There are times when words appear futile, and to no one more so than a writer. At these moments it seems that nothing is of value other than to act and to intervene in the course of events; to think, to reflect, to write seem trivial and wasteful. But the life of the mind takes many forms, and some time after the day had passed I understood that in the manner of his choosing, the Director had mounted the most singular, the most powerful defence of it that I would ever witness.

(First published in *The Hindu*, 11–13 January 2005)

# SIX

# A Tragic Predicament

'Trees were my teachers,' wrote the German poet Friedrich Hölderlin, and if there is any place on Earth that could say the same of itself, it is Ternate, a tiny island in the archipelago that was once known as the Moluccas or Spice Islands. It is now part of the province of North Maluku, in the far eastern reaches of Indonesia. The seas here are dotted with volcanic islands and Ternate is one such; the surface of the island is nothing but the gently sloping cone of a volcano, Mt Gamalama, which rises from the seafloor to a height of over 5,000 feet.

Ternate is a place that would, by most reckonings, be considered very far removed from the pathways of history. But the island was, in fact, a driver of global history for many centuries, as will be evident to anyone who sets eyes on the innumerable colonial forts that line its shores. The reason for this was a uniquely valuable tree that happened to grow on Ternate and the islands around it: *Syzygium aromaticum*, the tree that produces the clove. This spice, which was once immensely valuable, made Ternate prosperous and powerful for hundreds of years. But in the sixteenth century, at the beginning of the era of European colonization, Ternate's 'tree of life' also brought disaster upon the islanders. Various groups of European colonizers fought over Ternate and its surrounding islands in the course of a bloody struggle to establish a monopoly over the trade in cloves. The Dutch eventually prevailed, and in the seventeenth century they turned the island into a colony and decreed that henceforth cloves would only be grown on another island, in the southern Moluccas. The people of Ternate were forced, by the terms of a Dutch-enforced treaty, to 'extirpate' every clove tree on their island. The tree that had been Ternate's teacher would not return to the slopes of Mt Gamalama until the next century, when cloves were already being cultivated elsewhere and had drastically declined in value.

Today Ternate is a sleepy, quiet place, notable mainly for the ruins of the early Portuguese and Dutch forts that line its shores. But despite its remoteness from the great centres of contemporary trade, Ternate is by no means a laggard in globalization. Indonesia is one of the fastest-growing economies in the world and evidence of this is visible everywhere on the island: in the great mass of vehicles, large and small, that throng its streets, and in the fast-rising buildings that dot its villages. Indeed there is no better proof of Indonesia's rapid acceleration than its ability to deliver an abundance of goods and services to this distant corner of its territories.

But Ternate's landscape possesses an additional marker of this era of acceleration. This too is etched upon its landscape by the island's tree of destiny. Across the island, clove trees are dying; in orchard after orchard they stand in drooping clumps, their branches leafless, their trunks ashen. On the slopes of the volcano, clusters of dead trees can be seen, their leaden colours contrasting vividly with the greenery.

The farmers who tend to the trees are unanimous about the cause of the trees' demise: the climate has changed in recent years, they say;

there is less rain and it falls more erratically. This in turn has led to the spread of blights and disease. The lack of rain has been accompanied by another unprecedented phenomenon: wildfires. In March 2016, a fire raged for three days on the slopes of Mt Gamalama. Forest fires of this intensity are new to the islanders' experience.

The ongoing changes in the world's climate have thus placed the people of Ternate once again on the leading edge of history: the trees that guided their first steps in the world are now dying before their eyes as they watch helplessly.

This is a tragic predicament, considering that Ternate's volcanic environment created an especially intimate, sacralized relationship between the island's ecology and its people, who have long seen themselves as custodians of their closely interconnected world. And of none of Ternate's people is this more true than the descendants of the dynasty of sultans that has presided over the island since the fourteenth century. Some members of this dynasty still live on the island, and during my visit in 2016, I was able to interview one of them, a prince who is the son of the late ruler and the current occupant of the sultan's palace.

We sat in a courtyard that faced Mt Gamalama, so it was inevitable that our conversation should touch upon the dying clove trees that I had seen on the volcano's slopes. Like so many others on the island, the prince attributed the death of the trees to climate change—this was, for him, a deeply troubling matter since these trees had sustained his family's fortunes for 700 years.

This being the case I thought I should ask the prince a question that I had already put to several clove farmers: 'Given the seriousness of the situation, do you think the people of Ternate should make an effort to cut back their carbon emissions?'

Considering his family's special relationship with the clove tree, I had imagined the prince would see the matter differently from the ordinary clove farmers I had spoken with. But the answer he gave me was similar to what I had heard from others on the island. It could be paraphrased as: 'Why should we cut back? That would be unjust to us. The West had their turn when we were weak and powerless and they were our rulers. It's our turn now.'

The prince's response came as no surprise to me because I had heard its like many times, not just in Indonesia, but also in India, China and many other places. For the farmers, as for the prince, the burden of history's injustices far outweighed the material realities and imminent threats of climate change. Having to tolerate a disrupted environment was, for them, a sacrifice that had to be endured for the sake of a wider national aspiration.

It is in much the same spirit that the inhabitants of cities like New Delhi and Lahore endure toxic levels of pollution, despite knowing that the air they breathe will shorten their lives by several years. The damage to their health and well-being is seen as a sacrifice that is necessary, on the one hand, to enjoy a certain standard of living and, on the other, to advance a wider collective aspiration to a better place in the international order. It is by this route that coping with environmental hazards comes to be blended with some of the notions of sacrifice and suffering that underlie nationalism. By the same token, attempts to impose limitations on the carbon emissions of poor countries are widely seen as a covert means of preserving the economic and geopolitical disparities of the last 200 years, since on a per capita basis the carbon emissions of the Global South are still a fraction of those of affluent countries.

These perceptions are mirrored in the West by the idea, now widely prevalent on the right, that the Global South is trying to deprive affluent nations of the hard-earned fruits of their success. In the US, the idea of imposing limits on America's carbon emissions is also perceived by many as an infringement of national sovereignty, which is guaranteed ultimately by the country's overwhelming military dominance.

In short, nationalism, military power and geopolitical disparities are essential to the dynamics that have repeatedly stymied efforts to reach a global agreement on rapid decarbonization. In that sense it could be said that conflict and national rivalries are fundamental drivers of climate change. Yet these issues are rarely discussed in conferences on global warming, which have come to be focused instead on technocratic and economistic 'solutions' of various kinds. It is no coincidence that the literature on climate change, which is overwhelmingly produced by Western universities and think tanks, is also mainly centred on technical and economic issues.

As a result, there is an immense gap between perceptions of climate change in the affluent countries of the Global North, which are almost all beneficiaries of centuries of colonialism, and those of the Global South, most of which were subjected to some form of colonial domination. In the North, global warming is largely framed by technology, economics and science; in the South, the same phenomenon is conceived of in terms of disparities of power and affluence that can all be traced back to the geopolitical inequities established in the era of colonialism.

In the South, issues like violence, race and geopolitical power are implicit in the perceptions of people like the clove farmers of Ternate. In the North, which is essentially secure in its position atop the global pyramid, these issues are rarely discussed, and climate change is generally treated as a problem of governance that can be resolved through processes of negotiation within multilateral institutions like the UN.

But there is a very significant contradiction here. Multilateral institutions are mandated to operate on the assumptions that all nations and peoples are equal, and that wealth and welfare should be justly distributed between nations. Geopolitics, on the other hand, is founded on a completely different set of notions. It is not intended to bring about equality and justice, but rather the opposite. It is explicitly about maintaining a structure of dominance—or, in other words, inequality.

The dissonance between these two spheres—that of multilateral global governance on the one hand and geopolitical power on the other—is so great as to be almost irreconcilable. While the structures of global governance produce seemingly endless streams of 'solutions' and treaties, the repeated breakdown of international negotiations points to a different, largely hidden, reality. This unacknowledged dynamic was once summed up by a Singaporean journalist with the following words: 'It is our will to power that will help us cope with one of the big driving forces of the future: climate change.'[1]

In other words, global leaders may speak a certain language during international negotiations, but when we examine what they are doing it would seem that their actions are indeed driven by a will to power. That perhaps is why affluent nations were able to find only 10 billion USD for the fund to help countries that are exceptionally vulnerable, but had no difficulty in increasing their defence spending by 1 trillion USD. This suggests that contrary to what global leaders may say publicly, many of them are actually preparing for a future of intensified conflict.

Given the intractable nature of the world's geopolitical disparities, what can be done to address the planetary crisis? How can the aspirations of the people in the Global South be met when it is clear that humanity would asphyxiate if everybody were to adopt Western lifestyles?

One element of this challenge that provides some encouragement is that the aspirations of the middle classes of the Global South are essentially mimetic. That is to say when an Indian or Indonesian says, 'Now it's our turn', what they are really saying is, 'I will not be wealthy or content until I have what the Other has.' It follows from this that if the supposedly wealthy Others were to change their ways and adopt substantially different lifestyles, then this could have a significant impact on aspirations across the world.

In this regard, the emphasis that Fridays for Future has placed on finding new ways to live is of vital importance. And the fact that their message has resonated so widely, even in the Global South, is a rare cause for encouragement.

(First published in *The Climate Book*, edited by Greta Thunberg, published by Penguin Random House, 2022)

# 2

# WITNESSES

Each of the six essays in this section grew out of the research I undertook for my four historical novels: *The Glass Palace* and the three volumes of the Ibis Trilogy: *Sea of Poppies, River of Smoke* and *Flood of Fire*. In all these books, subaltern characters like sailors ('lascars'), soldiers ('sepoys') and indentured workers ('girmitiyas') play important roles, and since such figures rarely leave any but the faintest marks on the historical record, writing about them required the unearthing of a great deal of obscure material.

The difficulty was particularly acute in relation to lascars who were pioneers in many respects, but who seem to have never wanted to leave behind any record of their personal experiences of seafaring. Only through diaries and memoirs written by others do we sometimes catch impromptu glimpses of these elusive seafarers. One such is the handwritten journal on which the essay 'Of Fanás and Forecastles' is partly based: it is the work of an English cadet called Robert Ramsay, who travelled to India in 1825 to join the colonial army. Ramsay's journal entries were written on board a ship that was in constant motion, pitching, tossing and heaving, yet he wrote with extraordinary ease and fluency, even though he was only nineteen at the time. Indeed, one of the pleasures of reading handwritten journals of the era before English spellings and punctuation were standardized, is that back then even ordinary young soldiers and sailors, merchants and traders seem to have been able to compose long, fluid sentences that flowed effortlessly over entire pages without a break.

The central character in the last book of the Ibis Trilogy, *Flood of Fire*, is Havildar Kesri Singh, who is part of the British Expeditionary Force of the First Opium War of 1840–42. In writing about Kesri Singh, I was constantly confronted with questions like: What did sepoys think of their British officers? What was it like for Bihari soldiers to be sent overseas to fight people who were not their own enemies?

These questions are very difficult to answer because nineteenth-century sepoys have not left behind any first-hand accounts of their overseas campaigns. This lack of first-hand documentation is particularly puzzling because (as I have written elsewhere): 'millions of Indian men served in British armies over several hundred years, going back to the seventeenth century. Many were upper caste, literate men, yet it was not till 1902 that a soldier by the name of Thakur Gadadhar Singh published a first-hand account of his wartime experiences'. To fill this gap in the documentary record, I began to look for accounts written by Indian military personnel during the First World War, and this was what introduced me (as recounted in the first piece in the section) to the work of Santanu Das, which in turn, led me to the two truly amazing books, both written in Bengali, on which three of the pieces in this section are based. The first of these books is Mokshada Devi's *Kalyan-Pradeep* ('Kalyan's Lamp'; 1928), an extended commentary on the letters of her grandson, Captain Kalyan Mukherji, who was a doctor in the Indian Medical Service. The second, *Abhi Le Baghdad* ('On to Baghdad'), is by Sisir Sarbadhikari who was a member of the Bengal Ambulance Corps, and is based on his wartime journal; the book itself was not published until 1958. Mukherji and Sarbadhikari both served in the Mesopotamian campaign of 1915–16: they were both taken captive when the British forces surrendered to the Turkish Army in 1916 after enduring a five-month siege in the town of Kut al-Amara—the greatest battlefield defeat suffered by the British empire in more than a century.

Mukherji and Sarbadhikari were both transferred to prisoner-of-war camps near Ras al-'Ain (now in Syria), which was in a region where many Armenians were then being massacred. The essay 'Shared Sorrows', based on Sarbadhikari's account of what he saw, was written for a conference on the Armenian genocide that was held in Yerevan in 2012. During my stay in that beautiful city I was moved to see that the role of Indian soldiers in protecting Armenians in a later phase of the war has been richly memorialized.

'Wordless Pasts', evolved out of my research on the event that forms the backdrop of the final section of *The Glass Palace*: the great Indian exodus out of Burma that followed upon the Japanese invasion of that country during the Second World War. Millions of Indians embarked upon this long, and lethally difficult march, yet the number of published accounts of it, written from Indian points of view, is vanishingly small. (It is a matter of no little pride for me that *The Glass Palace* struck a powerful chord with many survivors and their relatives, and that my blog [amitavghosh.com/blog] has since become a clearing house for materials on this subject.)

I wrote the essay that was based on this diary a couple of years after the publication of *The Glass Palace*, at about the time that I was exchanging letters with Dipesh Chakrabarty about his book *Provincializing Europe* (which is probably why echoes of this piece can be seen in my correspondence with him that has been reproduced in the 'Conversations' section). I had by then lost touch with Mrs Ahona Ghosh, so I was not able to publish the essay. Fortunately, my ever-diligent copy-editor at HarperCollins India, Shatarupa Ghoshal, was able to trace Mrs Ghosh and obtain the necessary permissions, so it has now become possible for the piece to appear in print at last. But the fact that I could not publish this essay earlier was in a way fortunate because it meant that I was able to revise and rewrite it for this collection: it is fitting, I think, for it to conclude this section, since all the essays in it are attempts to account, in one way or another, for the recurrent absences and silences that are so marked a feature of India's colonial history.

# SEVEN

# Santanu Das and the First World War

First World War writing is an old interest of mine, so when I came upon a book with the intriguing title *Touch and Intimacy in First World War Literature*, I picked it up at once.[1] I noticed that the writer had an Indian-sounding name—Santanu Das—but I had never heard of him before.

The book's first chapter is called 'Slimescapes' and it is about the ways in which First World War writers dealt with the tactile experience of trench warfare. It seized my interest immediately:

> In everyday trench life, the boundaries of the body can no longer be policed, as bodily fluids are perpetually on the brink of spillage. In *Blasting and Bombardiering*, the officer breaks wind at the sound of shelling; men vomit as they collect corpses in Graves's *Goodbye to All That* and Cloete's *A Victorian Son*. Winterbourne defecates in his trousers in *Death of a Hero*, as does the young boy in Remarque's *All Quiet on*

> *the Western Front*. Just as bodily fluids leak out, similarly mud and slime seep in: Céline speaks of 'eating Flanders mud, my whole mouth full of it, fuller than full'; in 'A Night of Horror', the narrator writes: 'The suffocating mud and slime / Were trickling down my throat'. Remarque, towards the end of his novel, observes: 'Our hands are earth, our bodies mud and our eyes puddles of rain.' Membranes have become permeable: the skin can no longer separate the inside and outside, the self and the world. (52)

I read the book at a stretch, finishing it in a couple of sittings (I don't think this has ever happened to me before with a book of literary criticism). But one thing puzzled me: If the writer was Indian, as his name suggested, why had he made no reference to the 1 million Indians who were on the Western Front during the First World War? Was this deliberate, and if so, why?

Upon googling Santanu Das, I learnt that he was on the faculty of Queen Mary University in London, and that *Touch and Intimacy* had been awarded Britain's prestigious Philip Leverhulme Prize, which carried a cash reward of 70,000 pounds sterling at the time!

I discovered also that Santanu had already addressed some of my queries: he had recently edited a book called *Race, Empire and First World War Writing*, for which he had written a long introduction as well as the essay 'Indians at Home, Mesopotamia and France, 1914–1918: Towards an Intimate History'.[2]

I had the impression that Santanu had studied in Kolkata at some point, so I sent a message to a friend, Sukanta Chaudhuri, who, together with his wife, Supriya Chaudhuri, has inspired a generation of literature students at Kolkata's Jadavpur University. Sure enough, it turned out that he had taught Santanu briefly. He introduced me to Santanu over email.

I don't often write fan letters, but I relished writing this one.

Dear Santanu (if I may),

I read *Touch and Intimacy* a few months ago and have wanted to tell you since then that it is the best work of literary criticism I've read in years. As I said to Sukanta, it is really very rare nowadays to come across critics who actually seem to like the bodies of work they're writing about—and since it is perhaps even more rare to come across a critic who actually writes comprehensible prose, it could be said that you are in danger of becoming the Snow Leopard of Literary Criticism! (I should add here that I am sure Sukanta and Supriya played an important part in steering you away from the prevalent fashions ... It's wonderful to see that some aspects of Kolkata's intellectual legacy have survived against all the odds.)

In any event your empathy for the First World War writers was very moving to me because I've liked that body of work since my college days (I feel I have an almost familial connection with Robert Graves et al because my wife wrote a biography of Laura Riding and spent a long time in Mallorca, talking with Beryl Graves). I was glad also to see that your book has been very well received—this recognition is richly deserved. Congratulations!

Santanu wrote back to say that a friend of his had given him *The Shadow Lines* when he was leaving for Cambridge and that he had subsequently written his undergraduate thesis on it. So our correspondence got off to a good start.

It so happened that I was due to travel to London soon afterwards. I arranged to meet Santanu, and we had a long talk over dinner about the project that he was then working on, and which has since been published as *India, Empire, and First World War Culture: Writings, Images, and Songs* (2018). This, in my view, is the single most important book to be published on the Indian subcontinent's involvement in the First World War.

*Race, Empire and First World War Writing* is an ambitious collection: it attempts to cover the whole spectrum of non-European involvement in the First World War, with articles on soldiers and auxiliaries from China, Vietnam, India, West and North Africa, Jamaica and elsewhere.

To provide an idea of the scale of this involvement, here are some numbers:

- 1,40,000 contract workers from China were recruited by the British and French governments between 1916 and 1918; they did most of the cleaning up of the battlefields of Flanders.[3]
- Between 1915 and 1919, 48,922 Vietnamese soldiers and 48,254 Vietnamese workers were recruited to serve in France. They were sent to battlefields, hospitals, construction sites, commercial businesses and agricultural regions.[4]
- The total number of Indians who served in the war, up to 31 December 1919, was 8,77,068 combatants and 5,63,369 non-combatants, making a total of 14,40,437. In addition, there were an estimated 2,39,561 men in the British Indian Army serving in Mesopotamia.[5]
- 1,40,000 West Africans were recruited into the French Army to serve as combatants on the Western Front.[6]

In other words, the major imperial powers, France and Britain, drew heavily on the resources of their colonies in fighting Germany, which was a latecomer to the colonial race. What did the Germans make of this? Christian Koller addresses this question in his article 'Representing Otherness: African, Indian and European soldiers' letter and memoirs'.[7] He writes:

German Propaganda met the introduction of colonial troops on the Western Front with a deeply racist campaign that represented the non-white colonial soldiers as beasts. They were described in terms that negated their quality as regular military forces: 'a motley crew of colour and religions', 'devils', 'dehumanised wilderness', 'dead vermin of the wilderness', 'Africans jumping around in a devilish ecstasy', 'auxiliary rabble of all colours', 'an exhibition of Africans', 'an anthropological show of uncivilised ... bands and hordes' or the catchphrase 'the black shame', which quickly rose to common usage in the early 1920s when French colonial troops were stationed in the Rhineland area. In summer 1915, the German Foreign Office put into circulation a memorandum titled *Employment, contrary to International Law, of Colored Troops upon the European Theatre of War by England and France*, in which many atrocities were attributed to colonial soldiers, including the poking out of eyes and the cutting off of ears, noses and heads of wounded and captured German soldiers. (128)

Another objection raised by German propaganda against the employment of colonial non-white troops on European battlefields was its alleged impact on the future of colonialism and the supremacy of the 'white race'. If African and Asian soldiers were trained in the handling of modern arms, if they saw the white nations fighting each other and were allowed to participate in these fights and experience the white soldiers' vulnerability, they would lose their respect for the white race once and forever. After the war, they would turn their weapons against their own master. German propaganda argued that the French and British policy of deploying colonial troops in Europe was a flagrant breach of white solidarity and should be condemned by every civilised nation. (128-29)

The view that the use of non-white troops on European soil amounted to a war crime seems to have been quite widely held in Germany during the war. As Santanu points out in his introduction, Max Weber, the sociologist, was among those who 'complained about "an army of niggers, Ghurkhas and all the barbarians of the world"'.

But as Koller shows, these views were not held by Germans alone.

> In spite of the significant differences between the French and British attitudes towards their respective colonial troops, certain common perceptions and prejudices were discernible, moving between racism and exoticism. Many of these find their most vicious and exaggerated form in German discourses. [But] such prejudices could also be found among the neutral voices from the front. (134)

The articles in this collection are, almost without exception, of absorbing interest. But I must admit that I am particularly beholden to Santanu Das's contribution, 'Indians at Home, Mesopotamia and France, 1914–1918: Towards an Intimate History', because it motivated me to seek out two books that I had heard about but never read, mainly because they are extremely difficult to find. They are *Kalyan-Pradeep: Captain Kalyan Kumar Mukhopadhyay, I.M.S.-er Jiboni* ('Kalyan-Pradeep: The Life of Captain Kalyan Kumar Mukherji, I.M.S.') by Mokkhoda Debi (1928) and *Abhi Le Baghdad* ('On to Baghdad') by Sisir Sarbadhikari (1957).

The works are extraordinary in the exact sense of the word: in my view, they both deserve places of honour in the canon of twentieth-century Indian writing. Yet they are almost completely unknown: they were self-published and have been out of print for decades (I was fortunate to find copies in the National Library in Kolkata).

Both books are about the Mesopotamian theatre of the war and were written in Bengali. This in itself is quite remarkable because at that time, Bengalis, like most other Indians, were not classified as a 'martial race' and were ineligible for recruitment in the British Indian Army. They could only join as doctors or medical auxiliaries. That indeed is how these two works came to be written.

Even though these are war narratives, they are in some respects strikingly different from their Western equivalents. They are, for instance, deeply embedded in family and community: war might be the main subject, but family—women relatives in particular—was essential to the making of both.

This is how Santanu describes *Kalyan-Pradeep* and *Abhi Le Baghdad*:

> Captain Mukherji, a member of the Indian Medical Service, was appointed a military doctor to Indian Expeditionary Force D. He was in Mesopotamia from his arrival at Basra on 9 April 1915 till his death from high fever in 1917 and was posthumously awarded the Military Cross ... After his death, his eighty-year-old grandmother wrote his biography, *Kalyan-Pradeep: The Life of Captain Kalyan Kumar Mukhopadhay, IMS* (1928), extracting his war letters in full. Sarbadhikari's memoir, on the other hand, has a tantalising textual history. It was based on his secret Mesopotamia diary, written in captivity, which was broken up into individual pages and hidden in his boots during the horrific march from Samarra via Mosul to the POW camp in Ras al-'Ain in July 1916. Later, the contents of the faded pages were copied into a new diary which was hidden underground and retrieved at Ras al-'Ain. Both men were Bengalis from Kolkata, yet due to differences in rank their experiences varied significantly. (78)

I believe these two books to be of inestimable value—as literature, as testimony and as historical documents. It is shocking, and deeply unjust, that they have vanished from public memory even in Bengal.

I devoured First World War writing in my teens and twenties, visiting the British Council Library in Kolkata to seek out those books—but the writers I read were all European. I had no idea then that Kolkata had produced its own First World War books, just as good, if not better, than those I had been reading.

It is not too late to give these books their due: if anything, it is urgently necessary—not least because it needs to be recognized that global engagements are not new to Indian writing.

# EIGHT
## *Abhi Le Baghdad*

Sisir Sarbadhikari's *Abhi Le Baghdad* (On to Baghdad) is, in my view, one of the most remarkable war memoirs of the twentieth century.

In no small part does the book owe this to the diary on which it is based. This diary (in various iterations) accompanied Sarbadhikari through his travels around Mesopotamia, Syria, Turkey and the Levant. It went on many gruelling marches with him, hidden in his boots. He kept it with him even in prison camp, where its discovery could have resulted in disaster for him. That it survived the war is nothing short of a miracle.

Sarbadhikari explains the history of his journal quite late in the book, in a brief paragraph.[1]

18 March 1917

After this I couldn't write in my journal for about a year. In the first place, opportunities were hard to find. Apart from that,

> I had to tear up many of my notes for fear that they would be found; I re-wrote some of them later; but I couldn't with some. You [the reader] mustn't make the mistake of thinking that the diary that I've referred to so far, and which I'll refer to again, was my original diary. (156) After the surrender at Kut, I ripped apart my diary, tore the pages into pieces, and stuffed them into my boots; using those scraps I filled out a new journal later—in Baghdad. This journal too was ruined when I crossed the Tigris on foot. But the writing wasn't all lost, because I had used a copying pencil. I dried the book and used it for my notes of the march from Samarra to Ras al-'Ain. At Ras al-'Ain I had to bury the diary for a while but it didn't suffer much damage. In the infirmary at Aleppo, I wrote it out again. (157)

These notes lend an extraordinary immediacy to *Abhi Le Baghdad*. Sarbadhikari's descriptions of battles, forced marches and prison camps are sometimes startlingly vivid. I know of nothing like it in Indian writing (although I have a feeling that a similar text may exist in Marathi, since many of the soldiers who fought in Mesopotamia were Marathas).

But it isn't just the immediacy of the text that makes the book so remarkable: it is something about Sarbadhikari himself. Not only is he a fine observer, but he is also to a quite astonishing degree free of rancour and prejudice. Despite the horrors that he witnesses and experiences, he never loses his ability to perceive the humanity of others, 'enemies' and captors included.

He evidently became quite fluent in Turkish, and this gave him unusual insights into the lives of ordinary Turkish soldiers: he understood that many of them were worse off than the prisoners they were guarding. There is sometimes an almost ethnographic detachment in his writing. There is also something very winning about his lack of grandiosity and pretension: never does he try to 'come the old soldier'—the whole book is pervaded by a kind of ingenuousness.

These qualities are unusual in any depiction of war, but they are particularly so perhaps in memoirs of the First World War. For this was a time when writers, sometimes even very gifted ones, had difficulty in recognizing the humanity of people outside their own class, let alone those of other races, religions and nations.

The quirky appeal of Sarbadhikari's sensibility is evident in his choice of title. Here is how he explains it:

> Major-General Charles Townshend, the Commanding Officer of the 6th Poona Division, said in his Order of the Day of 3 November 1915, 'We have successfully taken Sahil, Qurna, Kut al-Amara and other such places so our aim now is to move on to Baghdad.' We all assumed that Baghdad would be easily taken; that any other result might be possible never so much as entered our minds. In many units, British officers began to say that they would celebrate Christmas 1915 in Baghdad.
>
> But instead of taking Baghdad we were forced to retrace our steps and retreat. After Umm al-Taboul there was a rear-guard action and we had to go on marching, without once halting for a rest. Marching beside me was a Muslim sepoy of the 66th Punjabis: he had taken his boots off his badly blistered feet, and tied them together by their laces; with his rifle in hand he was limping along and saying to himself, 'Ya Allah, abhi le Baghdad,' meaning '"On to Baghdad," you said; now enjoy this.'

## 2. Joining Up

*Abhi Le Baghdad* has much in common with *Kalyan-Pradeep*. Sisir Sarbadhikari's war experiences in Mesopotamia and his time in captivity overlapped closely with Capt. Kalyan Mukherji's. They were in the same places, often at the same time, and they knew each other. They were both from Calcutta and belonged to families of lawyers and doctors; they were both well informed and widely read.

Capt. Mukherji was in his early thirties at the start of the war, married and with a child. He was also a doctor and a career officer of the Indian Medical Service (the medical wing of the British Indian Army). Sarbadhikari was in his early twenties, and he volunteered to serve as a private in a hastily formed auxiliary medical unit—the Bengal Ambulance Corps (BAC). Sarbadhikari mentions Capt. Mukherji a few times, but he himself never figures in Capt. Mukherji's letters to his family.

There is some degree of overlap even in the history of the two texts. Capt. Mukherji's letters became the basis of his grandmother's book, *Kalyan-Pradeep*, which was published eleven years after his death in a POW camp at Ras al-'Ain. Sarbadhikari's book was published forty years after the war, in 1958. Santanu Das, who has interviewed Sarbadhikari's daughter-in-law, Romola, tells me that she was instrumental in collating his notes and persuading him to write the book.

Both books were self-published: evidently publishers did not think that these works would be of interest to the reading public of Bengal. It is easy to imagine how dispiriting this must have been for the two families. It is a tribute to their persistence that the texts found their way into print and have survived.

However, these similarities are incidental, for in form, style and even content, the two books bear almost no resemblance to each other.

This is how Sisir Sarbadhikari's story starts.

> 1914
>
> I've just passed my B.A. and have nothing much to do. No, that isn't quite correct, I've actually entered my name in the

rolls of the Law College, and I am looking for a job. Meanwhile, the First World War has broken out. Of course, at that time nobody knew that this war would come to be known as the Great War, or that some twenty years later it would earn the designation 'First' following on another World War. When we first heard the news none of us were particularly interested. Who cared where Sarajevo was and which Archduke had been assassinated there? We barely took the trouble to look at the reports in the newspapers. We thought it was just a little bit of bother that would soon be sorted out.

But it wasn't. On 4 August, England declared war on Germany and Austria. Within a few days troops were dispatched from India to France. Now everybody was suddenly eager to know more about this war.

At this time Bengali leaders decided that this was a golden opportunity to establish a foothold in the armed services.[2] They held a meeting in Calcutta's Town Hall and it was resolved that they would write to the Viceroy requesting permission to send an Ambulance Corps, staffed with doctors and volunteers, to the front. Soon it was learnt that permission had been granted and that recruiting offices had been set up. One such office was set up in College Square: I went there, entered my name and signed the forms.[3]

Sarbadhikari was so keen to volunteer that he actually pulled strings to get into the BAC. Fortunately for him, an uncle of his, a prominent doctor, had played an important part in setting up the corps. Evidently a bit of nepotism was necessary even when one was volunteering to risk his life on foreign soil.

Sarbadhikari's eagerness to join was largely based, by his own account, on the 'Spirit of Adventure' (he uses the English phrase). This same spirit, he writes, would prompt him to volunteer for service again during the Second World War, when he was over fifty. So it was that he found himself under siege in not one but two world wars, the second time in Imphal in 1942, when the town was besieged by the Japanese.

### 3. From Calcutta to 'Aziziya

Sisir Sarbadhikari moved into the BAC barracks in Alipore on 1 April 1915. The volunteers' training was completed in three months, at the end of which the corps' total strength was 117: it was led by five British officers—a colonel and four lieutenants. As for the rest, there were seventy-two non-commissioned officers (NCOs) and privates, and forty-one camp followers (cooks, bhishtis, sweepers, etc.).

Sisir and the other volunteers left by train from Calcutta's Howrah Station on 26 June and reached Bombay on 28 June.

On 30 June, the volunteers watched as the 6th Poona Division embarked from Alexandra Docks.

> On the 30th heavily loaded ships left with Indian battalions. They were all Marathas. Some said they were going to Egypt, some said France. Their parents, wives and children came to see them off. Tears flowed! Slowly the ships began to move and the battalion bands struck up 'Auld Lang Syne'. (12)

The Ambulance Corps left a couple of days later, on the *Madras*, a hospital ship.

> At 9.30 a.m. on 2 July the ship pulled away from the dock. It had been just two days since the Marathas' families had come to see them off—with copious tears. No one came to see us off but we were still pained by the thought that we were leaving our country. The surprising thing was that when we

> left Calcutta none of us were as sad as we were now. Amongst those who came to see off the Marathas there was an old man who wept as he asked his son if he would ever return to the country. Would we return either? But thoughts like these did not weigh on us much at that time. (13)

The *Madras* reached Basra on 9 July, and a couple of days later, the BAC was sent upriver to Amara. They remained there for a month and a half before being dispatched northwards. On 10 October, they reached 'Aziziya after a series of forced marches but were still well behind the frontline.

It so happened that Capt. Kalyan Mukherji was marching with them part of the way, and on 10 October, he wrote a letter home:[4]

> Thirty-two lads from the Bengal Ambulance Corps marched with us with five stretchers.
>
> The poor fellows aren't accustomed to this kind of thing and their eyes and noses were flowing. In the first place they have to put up with the dhamkaoings of the Sahib officers; then they have to associate with lowly doolie-bearers; nor is the food to their liking—and on top of that they have to march 20 miles a day. They're in a bad way.
>
> Most of them say, 'If we had known that it would be like this then which damn fellow would have volunteered? We thought we'd see a few battles, pour water into the lips of the wounded, tie bandages and show everyone how brave Bengalis are (they're very enthusiastic about all of this)—but we haven't even heard the sound of artillery, let alone do any of that; all we do is work as coolies. They're going to kill us with these marches.'
>
> Ever since they said they'd send a Bengal Ambulance Corps into service in the field, I knew that these kids had no idea what

> they were getting into. A daily 20-mile march, and rationed water on top of that—they never even dreamt that it would be like this. But even then they're willing to put up with it, so long as the officers don't treat them as coolies.

Capt. Mukherji probably had good reason for his rather harsh judgement of the BAC volunteers. Like millions of young men in Britain, France, Germany and elsewhere who were signing up for the war, Sisir and his comrades clearly had no idea of what they were getting themselves into; with barely three months' training before being sent into the field, many of them may well have regretted joining up.

There is also a touch of the professional's scorn for the amateur, the career officer's disdain for the short-service soldier, in Capt. Mukherji's tone. But it was he who was behind the times. This was not a war of professional soldiers—the great majority of the men who were drawn into it were, in fact, volunteers like Sisir.

However, it seems that Capt. Mukherji soon changed his mind about the 'kids'—and they, for their part, soon heard plenty of artillery. The Battle of Ctesiphon began on 22 November 1915, six weeks after Capt. Mukherji wrote the letter above. On the retreat, he met up again with Sisir and the other BAC volunteers.

Writing about this encounter, Sisir notes: 'Capt. Puri was in command of our convoy. Capt. Mukherji was with him; he had been injured and his arm was still in a sling. He told [Havildar] Champati that the officers had been all praise for the BAC during the battle of Ctesiphon.' (45)

## 4. The Battle of Ctesiphon

Sisir Sarbadhikari and his fellow volunteers of the BAC arrived in Iraq on 9 July 1915. In the months that followed, General Townshend's

British Indian force pushed steadily north, towards Baghdad. The Turkish Army offered little resistance, and such hitches as there were came mainly from within.

> Yesterday (23rd October) a Pathan sepoy of the 20th Punjabis deserted after firing on a Sikh havildar. There were many Pathans in the 20th Punjabis: they had said quite clearly that they would not fire on Baghdad-sharif. So the 20th Punjabis have been sent back to Amara. (27)

By late November, General Townshend's 6th Division was closing in on Baghdad. But between them and the city lay the ancient township of Ctesiphon (also known as Salman Pak), where a large Turkish force was waiting for them in a well-entrenched position.

> On the morning of 21 November, the Ambulance Corps received orders telling them to be ready at all times because an attack was imminent. They were then told that the march would start at nine that night.
>
> 'Fall in' was at seven and once again we went over the rules of night marching. But this time one thing that was emphasized was that we were to be very careful in using our water. In the event of victory in the battle (and we took it for granted that victory was inevitable) we would have to march straight on to Baghdad and there would be no water for 20–30 miles.
>
> Why did we think that victory was inevitable? Our 6th Division had repeatedly defeated the Turkish forces and taken places like Qurna and Nasiriya; we could not imagine that this division would now face defeat.
>
> At 9 p.m. the 6th Division and the 30th Brigade began to advance for the attack on Ctesiphon. We moved noiselessly.

> Some 20,000 men marching and not a sound. Even the horses that were pulling the cannon and mules of the transport carts were quiet. Even they seemed to understand that we were in enemy territory. The earth was soft and dry along the route so our boots and the hooves of the animals made no noise. It was almost unnatural—so many men and animals on the move but not the slightest sound. (33)
>
> The march ended at 1 a.m. on 22 November. It was very cold that night: 'We curled ourselves up like dogs and waited for the day to dawn so we could warm ourselves in the sun.' (34)

When dawn came, Sisir decided to make some tea and lit a fire. But one of the other volunteers warned him about wasting water—there might be none through the rest of the day.

> I said: 'No water? Are you crazy? This "jackal fight" will be over in a trice and we will be in Baghdad at around three in the afternoon; there'll be no shortage of water then.' Perhaps when I said this the unseen goddess was laughing in secret: I certainly did reach Baghdad but not at three that day—rather, after some six months and in completely different circumstances.
>
> (The phrase 'jackal fight' was thought up by Jacob [another volunteer]. And I can't blame him. I've heard that in the British Parliament, Lord Curzon had compared the war in Mesopotamia to a 'river picnic'.)
>
> By this time the fighting had started in earnest: the boom of cannons could be heard continuously. Battalions were advancing one after another, right before us. In front of us were the 66th Punjabis; now they moved too. We understood that our turn was coming.

We began to advance slowly. Now there was no sound other than the boom of cannon fire and the report of rifles. We marched on with the whine of bullets passing over our heads and shells exploding behind us. We had to advance with great care. After every few moves we would have to fall into a 'lie down' position, while shells and bullets fell like hail all around us. Many were killed and wounded.

… The first wound that I bandaged was of a havildar in the 110 Maratha Light Infantry, by the name of Gul Mohammad. He had travelled with us on the P7 steamer from Basra.

As we advanced we gave the wounded 'first aid' and left them all together in dressing stations. There were many such small dressing stations …

No matter where we went, the arch of Ctesiphon was always visible ...

Capt. Murphy was commanding us now. He was a cool-headed man. At one point when the firing got very heavy, he ordered us to lie down. When we were prone we saw, about 300 yards ahead of us, the men of the 104th battalion retiring at the double. We retreated 100 yards and lay down again …

The hours slipped by but the 'jackal fight' showed no sign of coming to an end. All this while we were treating the wounded. Around us were innumerable dead bodies. Everyone started to say that a great number had been killed. Apart from our own brigade, wounded men from other brigades came to us too. Everyone was saying the same thing, that many had been killed and wounded. But we could see that for ourselves.

In the meantime my water bottle had run dry. My chest was splitting with thirst. Then I spotted a mule lying dead, with two containers of water (small tanks of galvanized tin) tied to it. I ran joyfully towards it, hoping to fill my water bottle. When I got there I saw that there wasn't a drop of water in the tanks. The bullet that had killed the mule had also punctured the tanks.

There was a dead sepoy nearby, and his bottle had a little water. I used it to wet my lips and throat.

Soon it was dark. The fighting was still going on but not at the same rate as before ... (35–37)

Later that night, the troops began to pull back.

Those whose legs weren't badly hurt went with us, leaning on our shoulders. We put two British officers whose legs had been badly fractured on stretchers; the slightest shaking would give them unbearable pain. One of them kept saying softly, 'Please don't give me more pain than you can help.' Around his neck was a gold chain with a cross; he was holding it in his fist ... (39)

We left behind those who were badly wounded. They couldn't stand, let alone walk. When they saw that we were leaving they began to weep, and who could blame them? They were very vulnerable in that condition. We tried to reassure them by saying that we would send transport for them soon ...

We didn't have far to go but we had to move very slowly because of the wounded. We were almost walking on tiptoe because of the two British officers with fractures. On top of that there were many dead bodies on the road so we had to move carefully. We tried not to step on them but it wasn't always possible. There was no space for one's feet. (40) ...

Ctesiphon, the next day and afterwards.

What I saw after I woke up on the morning of the 23rd defies my powers of description. On all sides the corpses of men and animals. In some places they seemed to be in each other's arms; in some places men had been pinned under animals and were lying there, groaning. In front of the trenches, along the lines of barbed wire, was where the greatest number of wounded lay. In some places men were hanging from the wires; some were dead (they were the lucky ones) and some were still alive. Here was a severed hand hanging from the wire; there a foot. One man was hanging on the wires with all his entrails tumbling out. In some trenches four or five men had died with their limbs thrown over each other—Turkish, Hindustani, British, Gurkha, all mixed up together. (42)

One man's limb in another man's stomach, another's in someone's eye, that's how they were lying. And in the midst of this some were still alive; bringing them out was impossibly difficult.

I saw a Sikh sitting with a smile on his face—his white teeth were shining in his black beard. I thought, why are you smiling at a time like this, have you lost your head? When I approached I saw that he had been dead a while. He must have grimaced in pain as he was dying. (43)

…

As the hours went by we became increasingly thirsty. During the night we'd suffered from the cold, now we were suffering from thirst. The wounded called for water with increasing desperation. The white soldiers said: 'A drop of water for Heaven's sake.' We had to turn our water bottles upside down to show them that we had no water. (44)

Then the fighting started again. It seemed as if the Turkish trenches that had been seized the day before were now being fought over again. At around 3 p.m. bullets were raining down on the V.P. [the designated 'vital point']. That was exactly where the wounded had been brought. Many of them were killed by bullets and many sustained new injuries. Those who weren't hit could see others being wounded around them and tried to get away—even though they were unable to move. They were seized by a kind of terror—and who can blame them?

The wounded were then loaded on carts and moved back. But the convoy did not have a large Red Cross flag, so it was mistaken for an ammunition column and was heavily shelled by the Turkish artillery.

Here too many of the injured were killed and many acquired new wounds. Many mules were killed; some panicked from the bullets and ran into the fields, dragging the wounded with them. Then darkness fell and the bombardment ceased so we were ordered to bivouac there.

By that time we were desperate for food and water. Twelve hours ago we had been given two chapatis and a bottle of water, after that nothing. Amulya [another BAC volunteer] and I set off to look for food and found a piece of bread in the haversack of a dead white soldier. We divided it between us and were eating it in the dark when we realized that the bread had a peculiar taste. Then we understood. The bread had soaked up the soldier's blood, hence the taste. (45)

## 5. The Siege of Kut al-Amara

After its defeat at the Battle of Ctesiphon in November 1915, the British Indian 6th Division retreated southwards, towards Kut al-Amara. During this time, the usual order of battle was reversed and the medical staff, like Sisir Sarbadhikari, found themselves in the thick of the action.

> A rearguard action is exceptionally difficult … On the one hand you have to engage the enemy and at the same time you have to keep moving back, and in such a way as to minimize the loss of men and weaponry … Ambulance staff are at great risk in a rearguard action. Normally, ambulance staff stay with or to the rear of combatant units. In a rearguard action the order is reversed. The wounded would be left behind while the regiment continued to retreat (59) and either the stretcher bearers or we ourselves would have to move them back. In other words, we were working between two fires. (60)

Many of the wounded were evacuated on paddle steamers: Sisir and the other volunteers of the Bengal Ambulance Corps were kept busy, carrying stretchers onto the vessels.

> A subedar of the 104th Rifles was very fat and as we were lifting him into the steamer, someone said—'Baap-re-baap, how heavy!'
>
> Even though he had spoken softly the Subedar sahib heard him and said, in a very sober voice—'What do you mean heavy? Just three maunds [about 240 lbs; 109 kg].' We all laughed. Despite his wounds, he hadn't lost his sense of humour. (47)

On 24 November, the BAC volunteers were loading stretchers onto a steamer, when the serang called out to them; he was a warrant officer from Chittagong and they had met him before. He said:

> 'From your faces it seems you haven't eaten in days; come aboard and eat some dal and rice.' We were charmed by his graciousness and couldn't say no. He couldn't give us much and it looked as if what he gave us was from his own portion, but that act of generosity was unforgettable. He was Muslim,

> we were Hindus, but we shared the same language: Bangla—that was why he wanted to help us.

The Turkish forces were in constant pursuit of the retreating 6th Division.

> A short distance away a huge Turkish encampment had arisen, with innumerable tents. It had come up overnight, like Aladdin's city. We didn't need binoculars to see them moving around. (57)

But in the midst of all this:

> Our regimental pet was a sheep. Sailen [a BAC volunteer] had bought it in Amara—it was very little then, and we took pity on it. This sheep stayed with us all along. At the battle of Ctesiphon it sat in a tent with Prabodh [a BAC volunteer] … (because it was with us at Ctesiphon we called it Tessie). She had one fault and that was that if one didn't pull her along with a rope she would simply stand still. When bullets began to rain down on us we decided that we would untie the rope and let Tessie run for her life. But she wouldn't run; she bleated and stared sadly at our faces. Then Prabodh said, 'Let's take her along, whatever is in her future will happen.'
>
> Tessie came all the way to Kut with us. During the siege of Kut, when there was nothing to eat but horsemeat, the local Arabs offered us one hundred rupees for Tessie—they would have sold the meat for thirty or forty rupees a seer. (We had bought Tessie for 1 rupee and 5 siccas). Needless to say we didn't accept the Arabs' offer. At the end, when the Turks were almost in Kut we gave her to the officer's mess. (57-58)
>
> …

> Marching beside me was a Muslim sepoy of the 66th Punjabis: he had taken his boots off his badly blistered feet, and tied them together by their laces; with his rifle in hand he was limping along and saying to himself, 'Ya Allah, abhi le Baghdad,' meaning '"On to Baghdad," you said; now enjoy this.' (61)[5]

On the night of 1 December:

> Our feet were in a terrible state. They'd get a little rest during halts, but then they would freeze in the cold. It was December. In that region, in the open, the temperature would drop below freezing after midnight. We would sit for a while, then lie down and then get up and do double mark time. Or else our blood would have stopped moving in our veins. (61)
>
> …
>
> At dawn we started marching again. On the 2nd, after marching through the day, General Townshend's hungry and exhausted troops entered Kut al-Amara.
>
> On the way many soldiers had been parted from their regiments and were marching alone. Not all of those who'd been separated made it to Kut; many probably lost their lives on the way to Arabs.
>
> Some had bandaged heads, some had their arms in slings, and many were limping.
>
> When the victorious 6th Division was advancing triumphantly, then too there had been several bandaged heads and numerous arms in slings; at that time too there were many who were limping—but those things didn't hurt as much then as they did now. These things weighed on our minds much more during the retreat. When an army is winning its morale is high.

> …
>
> Given the circumstances it was normal for our spirits to fall a little. But it was also true that our morale had not dropped to rock bottom. Like the sepoys, we had great faith in the British lion and we believed that victory would come in the end. We thought this was but a temporary setback, that the British would do everything possible to redeem their prestige.

The siege of Kut al-Amara began on 7 December, with some 10,000 British and Indian troops being surrounded by an Ottoman force that initially consisted of about 11,000 men (it was augmented later).

Along with the rest of the Bengal Ambulance Corps, Sisir was billeted inside a date orchard.

> This was a favourite target of the Turks; bullets whistled by without interruption. In this orchard some tents were put up to house the hospital … On the 6th, the orchard took so much fire that the hospital was moved to the bazaar. But before that some patients were killed by shells. One shell, instead of bursting above, hit a sepoy who was lying in bed in one of the tents; it took off half his face before burying itself. The man rose to his feet as he was dying and then fell to the ground. His eyes, nose and mouth were all gone, there were only holes in his face, spouting blood. The sight was so ghastly that it created terror amongst the others in the tent. (65-66)
>
> The Turks had a well-choreographed daily routine. Through the whole day they would bombard us; in the evening there would be rifle fire, an incessant whining of bullets. Not that there wasn't any machine-gunning rifle-volleys during the day. One morning I was sitting beside a young fellow called Anthony, of the I.G.H. [the Indian General Hospital], drinking

tea, when a bullet hit him in the forehead. He died right there and his body fell on me.

Another day a sepoy of the 7th Rajput's was sitting and chatting with us, when eight bullets hit him in the shoulder, just two or three inches apart. Those were the kinds of wounds a machine gun could inflict. (67)

...

January (1916) went by in hope and despair. It was very cold. We had lost most of our things at Ctesiphon, blankets included. In Kut we were given blankets—one to lie on and one for cover; they didn't keep the cold out. It was raining heavily and the roads and lanes were filled with mud and water. (73)

February 1916.

With the start of the month all kinds of rumours began to circulate. Some said that a relieving force would arrive in the second week of this month, some said on the 25th ... At one point it was said that the 6th Division would fight its way out of Kut and join up with the relieving force. But this plan had to be abandoned. There were some 40,000 Turkish soldiers in the trenches that surrounded us; not only were we outnumbered, but they were in trenches whereas we would be in the open. (75)

8th. News: the 13th British Division was coming to relieve us from Egypt. This raised everyone's hopes. There were two Indian divisions in the relieving force; now there would be a British division as well. Our deliverance was certain.

9th. Today our ration of firewood was suspended—and why just firewood, much else too—and instead of that we were issued a cigarette-tin of crude oil, for eighteen of us. (75)

22nd. From the morning onwards there was a great uproar. Everyone was told to be ready. The relieving force might arrive at any moment; we would have to meet up with them and bring them into Kut. Everybody was very hopeful. (78)

23rd. No sign of the relieving force. All our hopes dashed.

29th. We heard that the Russians have taken Kermanshah. A plane dropped our post.

*The Times of India* of 13 January says that an approver in the Lahore Conspiracy case has testified that many guns had been sent there from Germany.

February went by. Food was short, and on top of that, because of the shortage of clothing, we had to wear just one set of clothes. We couldn't change; nor could we bathe. Everybody was covered with lice. They would swarm all over us, under our clothes. The torment was indescribable. For lack of meat or fresh vegetables, scurvy broke out. (78)

A bombardment started on the morning of 1 March. Enemy airplanes dropped bombs several times. We had no planes in Kut, and even if we had I doubt they'd have been able to take off; with so many enemy soldiers close by, they'd have been shot down before they could get into the air. At about two in the afternoon, I had just come off duty from the hospital and was standing in front of my billet when a plane circled above and dropped a bomb. I was standing right below, and the plane had come very close. It slowed down a bit, and then let go of the bomb—we stood there as if hypnotized. I could hear the whistle of the bomb, and I could see it coming towards us, like an arrow: at first it was like a dot, then a football; and when it was right above me it was like a kolshi.[6] There were a couple of people in the billet; it seemed to me that all of us who were there would be finished in a moment. But that didn't happen;

> if it had then this account would not have been written, nor would you have to put up with reading it. The bomb fell but didn't go off. There was the sound of something heavy hitting the earth. Only then did I call out to those who were sitting inside the billet. (79-80)
>
> It was only a few days since we had returned to the date orchard. There was a Gurkha encampment near us. We were walking around when a plane appeared and dropped a bomb. A Gurkha was standing outside his tent, smoking, and the bomb fell near him. For a while there was only smoke and dust. When it cleared we saw only chunks of flesh and bone; the earth around there had turned into blood-soaked mud.
>
> I remember the scene to this day. (80)

## 6. Surrender at Kut al-Amara

After the first week of December 1915, some 10,000 British and Indian troops were pinned down in the town of Kut al-Amara in Iraq by an Ottoman force of some 11,000 men. The British made several attempts to relieve the town, but the attacks were all repelled.

At the start of the siege, General Townshend, the commander of the British Indian force, had estimated that the garrison at Kut had enough food to last one month. But these stocks had to sustain not only the troops but also the townspeople, of whom there were some 6,500. As the weeks went by, food ran critically short.

In the meantime, Sisir Sarbadhikari and his fellow volunteers of the BAC clung to the hope that a relieving force would soon break through.

> 4 March. It's rumoured that a relieving force will arrive on the 14th or 15th. Some think the Russians will save us. I don't have much faith in that, not many do. (80)
>
> We're hungry all day long.

It is rumoured that the Turkish general has sent a proposal to our general saying there's no point in wasting any more lives and we should come to an understanding. Our general didn't agree to it.

10th. Our rations are being cut daily since the relieving force retired. Arab houses are being searched to see if they've hidden away any food. Food has been found in many houses. They'd buried it in the earth. (82)

16th. Some Muslim sepoys have fled from Kut and run over to the Turks—in other words they've deserted.

In wartime, other than mutiny, there is no greater crime than desertion. If caught, the punishment is also extreme: death.

In Kut desertions happened from time to time because of hunger. First, there was the suffering of hunger; on top of that these sepoys were being made to fight those of their own faith; these were the reasons why Muslims deserted. Looking back, I have to say that desertions were few; it is surprising that there weren't more.

One day a young fellow of the 119th Regiment was caught trying to escape. Some Sikhs were on their way back from the trenches when they saw the chhokra walking past the trenches. This made the Sikh Subedar suspicious and he brought the fellow to the O.C. of the 119th. The chhokra was unable to provide a satisfactory account of his actions. There was a summary court-martial. Sentence: death! The firing party was picked from his own company—perhaps it included men from his own village? Or perhaps even a relative? He was blindfolded and his chest was laid bare by the medical officer of the 119th who turned him to face the firing party; the Adjutant looked on. After it was over, the medical officer, Capt. Ubhaya, examined him to make sure he was dead. (83)

March went by too. For food all we had was a little horsemeat and some flour mixed with dust. We'd eat the flour after mixing it with water. We'd cook the horsemeat on some embers of coal-dust mixed with crude oil, and eat it half-cooked. Even now many sepoys cannot bring themselves to eat horsemeat. Their condition is beyond description … (85)

At this awful time Ranada[7] did something that helped a lot of people. He went out into No-Man's Land where there was a constant storm of gunfire; heedless of the danger, he brought back grass, leaves, herbs and things like that. A lot of greenery had sprouted after the rains. We'd boil and eat these. When there was enough we'd give some to the I.G.H. ... This saved many of us from scurvy. Ranada didn't know fear. He was always smiling and cheerful.

Despite everything, the eighteen of us would drum up a noise and have fun. Every evening we would sing. Our billet became a small club … An artillery driver called Malaband used to come often. (86) He was a God-fearing man; but in the end he lost his mind and killed himself. Several others killed themselves in Kut. First, there was the hunger and all the other physical torments; on top of that no news from home. There's nothing strange about losing your mind in those circumstances.

Whoever came to our billet was charmed by the behaviour of our havildar, Champati. If Champati had not been our havildar we would not have earned quite as much of a good reputation as we did. He was a man of rare patience and humility. He was the right havildar for our Bengali temperament. We were not quite accustomed to military discipline, so instead of being harsh he would get us to work with either kind words and pats on the back, or gentle scoldings. (87)

In April, the British made some ineffectual attempts to supply the town by plane (this is said to have been the first air supply operation in history).[8]

> April 1916. Every day we hear the cannon of the relieving force; from the 5th to the 7th we could not only hear them but we could also see the flashes of the shells and the smoke. The relieving force had taken some trenches and attacked Saniyat. Everyone's hopes rose.
>
> Over the last few days the rations have been cut daily.
>
> We were certainly short of food ourselves but the people of Kut suffered much more. The rations they were given amounted to nothing. They now concluded that the English would not be able to relieve Kut, so many groups tried to leave.
>
> The Turks sent word that any Arabs who tried to leave Kut would be shot. The local Arabs were an additional burden on us so the Turks didn't want them to leave. But even after this was made clear to the Arabs, some would try to escape every night. Very few were able to flee, most were shot by the Turks. (88)
>
> …
>
> Rumours are flying that the relieving force will arrive tomorrow—if not then there's no hope. (89)
>
> We thought the relieving force had arrived. In the morning things became clearer. Climbing up on the roof we saw that a steamer was stuck in the river, some distance away.
>
> We learnt later that the steamer was called *Julnar* and it was on its way to Kut with forty-eight days' rations.
>
> Unbeknownst to us the Turks had cut off the river, so it could be said that they had closed the door to Kut. (90)
>
> After this we all concluded that there was no further scope of relief. After spending so many days in hope, none of us had imagined even in our dreams that this was how the curtain

would fall on the siege of Kut ... It was the thought of rescue that had seen us through the worst moments of suffering. Amongst our physical torments the most terrible was hunger; that was with us twenty-four hours of the day. The agony of it is something that nobody can understand without experiencing it. (91)

27th. From today there is a three-day armistice. We hear that Townshend is holding discussions with Khalil Pasha regarding our surrender. Some say that we will all be paroled and sent back to India; some say that only the medical units will be released.

28th. There's not a grain left of our rations.

29th. This is a day not to be forgotten. Orders saying that the Turks did not want to release us on parole or any other grounds were published; we would have to surrender unconditionally. We were directed to destroy all our weapons. There were some forty cannons in Kut—they were all spiked. Thousands of rifles were broken and burnt. Boxes of ammunition were thrown into the depths of the Tigris. In this way all our armaments and ammunition was destroyed. (We heard later that the Turks had retrieved some of the ammunition from the river.) (92)

No rations again today.

Townshend sent out his last communiqué. Along with that he published a copy of his letter to Khalil Pasha.

Parts of this letter are below:

*Kut-el Amarah*

*29th April 1916*

*The G.O.C. has sent the following letter to the Turkish Commander-in-Chief:*

*Your Excellency*

*Hunger forces me to lay down our arms and I am ready to surrender to you my brave soldiers who have done their duty as you have affirmed when you said, 'Your gallant troops will be our most sincere and precious guests.' Be generous then; they have done their duty; you have seen them in the Battle of Ctesiphon; you have seen them during the retirement; and you have seen them during the siege of Kut for the last five months. You have seen how they have done their duty and I am certain that the military history of this war will affirm this in a decisive manner.*

*I am ready to put Kut into your hands at once; but I pray you to expedite the arrival of food.*

*Sd. Charles Townshend, Maj. General*

This was how the curtain fell on the historic siege of Kut. (93)

The surrender at Kut was viewed at the time as the greatest defeat the British had ever suffered in Asia. According to the website www.firstworldwar.com: 'It was the greatest humiliation to have befallen the British Army in its history. For the Turks—and for Germany—it proved a significant morale booster, and undoubtedly weakened British influence in the Middle East.'

## 7. The Road to Captivity

General Charles Townshend, the commander of the British Indian force at Kut al-Amara, surrendered to the Ottoman commander, Khalil Pasha, on 29 April 1916. The force had been under siege since early December 1915, and their stocks of food were completely exhausted.

This is Sisir Sarbadhikari's description of what happened next.

29 April. Turkish troops entered Kut after 1 p.m. When we first entered Kut as a victorious force in September 1915 the Arabs had greeted us with ululations, dancing and applause;

all that was acted out again now. Those who wanted to take it further kissed the uniforms of the Turkish officers; but many earned blows and kicks for their efforts. The Turkish officers said, 'None of this is sincere, it's just an act.' They understood that very well; if the British had come instead of the Turks it would have been the same. (94)

It was hard to know when the Turkish troops had been issued their uniforms. Their clothes were in a ragged state; many didn't have boots. Roughly speaking their uniforms were like this—a coat of a khaki-ish colour, pants of the same colour, with puttees.

Most of them did not have shoes; those who did were wearing either German shoes, or our old boots. They had knapsacks on their backs, with greatcoats rolled up on top. On their heads they wore a kind of topi, made of cloth. A small water-bottle; on their belts two big cartridge pouches on either side; in their hands a Mauser of the German pattern. Some had a big bundle tied to the top of their knapsack—five or six of them would eat from those. Their faces had been burnt to a coppery sheen by the sun; it was clear at a glance that they were a hardy lot. No matter what their clothes, they were very good soldiers.

The officers' uniforms were quite good. Boots with leather gaiters. (94-95)

Among the Turkish soldiers there were some who snatched our things. One entered the hospital and pulled off Captain Kane's boots; another grabbed Phani Datta's watch from his arm. But those who committed these outrages were few. Considering the poverty of the Turkish soldiers, what is surprising is that there wasn't more looting. The looters were few. And when their officers were informed, they gave the soldiers hell and made them return the goods …

We heard a Turkish soldier shouting, 'Postal, postal,' near our billet and ran to give him our letters—we had heard that they would make arrangements to send our letters to India so we had kept them ready. He explained to us that he wanted our boots and was willing to pay. We didn't know then that 'postal' was the word for shoes. Anyway none of us sold our boots. Who would sell their boots then? For one thing there was no hope of getting more; and on top of that we heard that we would have to march 600–700 miles, and that too mainly through the desert, to get to our POW camps in Turkey.

1 May 1916. From today our regiments began to leave Kut one by one. For now to Camp Shamran, and from there to Baghdad. Where we will go from there nobody could say. Everybody would have to march. After five months of hunger, our physical state was such that it was difficult to march even a single mile—and now who knew how many miles we would have to walk …

2 May. The Turks took an interpreter from the Officers' Hospital, right next to us. The man did not want to go but they forced him. All day there was the sound of firing in the serai. We heard that those inhabitants of Kut who were considered traitors—that is those who had collaborated with the English—were being shot. Did the interpreter go that way too?

…

Today down by the riverbank we saw an awful sight. In Calcutta we'd seen tripods made of bamboo in front of coal shops to serve as hoists. Seven such triangles had been erected—a man had been hung from each one; the bodies were still strung up. (95–97)

…

> Among the seven were Kut's sheikh, his nephew, his son-in-law and a Jewish man, Sassoon. Their crime was helping the English.
>
> They had tried to escape but had got caught. Later we heard that they were whipped before they were hanged—so badly that the flesh of their backs was all torn up; Sassoon could not bear it and jumped off the roof of the serai.
>
> On the way back to the billet we saw a woman who was tearing out her hair and wandering about like a madwoman. Some said she was the sheikh's wife, some said the daughter.
>
> Their tragedy was a hundred times worse than ours. (98)

After this there were rumours once again that the Indian medical staff would be paroled and sent back to India.

> 8th. We ate what little we had and at about 1 p.m. we went to the riverbank. Our names were called out one by one and we were searched. What luck that they didn't make me take off my boots! Otherwise I don't know if this story would have been written. My diary was hidden in my boots.
>
> A Turkish officer got off the steamer *Julnar*. We thought that now they would let us get on the steamer. But that didn't happen. The officer had brought orders countermanding the instructions for sending us to India; we would be imprisoned in Turkey. What our state of mind was then, it's not in my power to describe. We all returned to our billet with our blankets and haversacks. (101)

On 12 December, the prisoners embarked on steamers, to be taken to Baghdad.

> The white or British soldiers are behaving very badly with the black or Indian sepoys; they're even beating them! They say that it is because of the Indians that they lost at Kut! It's unimaginably vile.
>
> The astonishing thing is that even when complaints are taken to the British officers, they do nothing. The whites are sitting in comfort in the lower deck, every one of them has space to sleep. We're on the upper deck—there's no roof over our heads, and we scarcely have enough space to sit.

On 13 December, the arch of Ctesiphon came into view.

> Remembered the battle of Ctesiphon six months earlier. Remembered many things one by one—the night march, how Sailen used to walk as though he was fast asleep … things like that.
>
> On the evening of the 17th, Baghdad. The innumerable minarets of Baghdad came into view from a long way off. The steamer dropped anchor and we disembarked. (102-03)

Sisir Sarbadhikari spent the rest of the war in prison camps in Turkey and the Levant. He survived the war and returned to India in January 1919.

Sarbadhikari's account of his captivity is, in many ways, even more compelling than his account of the campaign. Here my intention was only to provide a sense of the extraordinary vividness and drama of his narrative. These excerpts will, I hope, give readers some idea of why I believe this to be one of the finest of all First World War memoirs.

# NINE
# At 'Home and the World' in Iraq, 1915–17

Mokkhoda (Mokshada) Debi's *Kalyan-Pradeep* (published 1928)[1] is, in essence, her tribute, as a grandmother, to her daughter's son, Kalyan, who was a casualty of the Mesopotamian campaign of 1915-16.

Mokkhoda Debi was a minor literary figure in Bengal at the turn of the twentieth century. Like Rabindranath Tagore, she was born into the Brahmo Samaj, and like many Brahmo women, she was well-educated and widely read. She married a lawyer and spent many years in Bhagalpur in Bihar. Kalyan Mukherji was her daughter Binodini's son. Born in 1883, he lost his father at the age of eleven and was brought up in straitened circumstances. While still quite young, he seems to have conceived the ambition of becoming a doctor and joining the Indian Medical Service (I.M.S.). At the time, this was the British Indian Army's medical corps, which boasted many distinguished doctors, including Ronald Ross, who won the Nobel

Prize for Medicine in 1902. (Ross figures prominently in my *Calcutta Chromosome*.)

For an Indian, joining the I.M.S. was no easy matter. As with the Indian Civil Service, the examinations were held in England. Kalyan studied medicine in Calcutta and then managed to work his way to England as a ship's doctor. In England, he was taken in by a relative who had married an Englishman: they supported him and sent him to Liverpool for further studies in medicine. (Mokkhoda Debi's account of Kalyan's life in England is one of the most interesting parts of the book.)

Kalyan passed the medical service examination on his first try and returned to India. After serving for a while on the North-West Frontier, he married, had a daughter and moved back to Bengal. In March 1915, he was ordered to join the Expeditionary Force that was being assembled to invade Mesopotamia. He left Calcutta on 13 March 1915 with another Indian member of the I.M.S., a Dr Puri, who was a close friend of his. (Dr Puri figures in both *Kalyan-Pradeep* and *Abhi Le Baghdad*; he was evidently an admirable man, courageous, loyal and a fine doctor.) Kalyan died of a fever two years later in a Turkish POW camp in Ras al-'Ain. He was thirty-four. For his role in the campaign, he was awarded a Military Cross.

While in Mesopotamia, Kalyan wrote several letters to his family. The letters are reproduced in full in the book, but they account for only a small portion of the text (which is over 400 pages long). The rest of the book is devoted to family history, reflections on the Indian past and, most significantly, a detailed account of the disastrous British Indian campaign in Mesopotamia in 1915 and 1916.

Mokkhoda Debi was clearly a woman of great gifts. Although some of her ideas are undoubtedly odd and even objectionable, her account of the Mesopotamian campaign is painstakingly researched and carefully narrated. But what makes the book truly extraordinary is its curious juxtaposition of domestic life and war—'the home' and 'the world', in other words. Tagore's great novel of that name (*Ghare Baire*; 'The Home and the World') was published in 1916, and Mokkhoda may well have read it. Yet the manner in which she creates her own connection between her home and the world is completely different from that imagined by Tagore.

This is perhaps the most compelling thing about *Kalyan-Pradeep*—its extraordinarily intellectual and imaginative ambition. Mokkhoda Debi was clearly no rebel, socially speaking. Yet the book is itself an act of rebellion, for it is an assertion of her right to narrate the story of the world as a woman. She lays claim to this right through grief and bereavement, as a grandmother's privilege.

The voice of the book is profoundly maternal, at times nurturing and at times riven with pain. Yet the story is one of soldiering, imprisonment and war. It is as if the very act of describing masculine violence in a woman's voice were a way of restoring a primal balance.

**2.**

The tension between the voices of the grandmother and the military historian runs through the length of Mokkhoda Debi's *Kalyan-Pradeep*. It is reflected even in the form of the book: the sections are numbered in the manner of a military dispatch.[2]

> 8. On 7 October 1914, the Government of India appointed Brigadier-General Delamain the commander of the expeditionary force for the invasion of Iraq and sent him these instructions: 'When "A" Force departs for Europe from Bombay on 16 October, "D" Force must leave with them. Your orders are to part company with "A" Force while at sea and to sail on to the Persian Gulf. When you reach the British-controlled islands and territories of the Gulf you and your forces are to make inquiries about the Turkish forces and their

readiness. You must use your own judgement. Another force will soon be dispatched to reinforce you. You orders are to safeguard British rights and interests in the Persian Gulf; the Shaikh of Muhammara is our ally, you must support him. When the fighting starts, you must take every measure for the protection of Basra.' (227)

9. On 10 October, a special messenger carried these orders from the Military Department in Simla to General D in Bombay. On 16 October, twelve large troopships departed from Bombay as ordered, carrying A Force and B Force; D Force was secretly mixed in with them. The forces were escorted by British warships.

Three days out to sea another British warship was sighted. Now at General Delamain's command, the troops and equipment of D Force were separated from the others and moved to four ships. The next day it was announced that their destination was the Persian Gulf island of Bahrain. Upon their arrival two days later, it was learnt that a transport ship and a warship had been sent from Karachi carrying the rest of their equipment. (228)

And here is Mokkhoda Debi, the grandmother, describing Kalyan's departure:

7. In March (1915) it was more or less decided that Kalyan and Dr Puri would go to the port of Karachi with their regiments—he was to leave Calcutta by train as soon as the date of his ship's departure was wired to him. So he decided to await his orders in Calcutta.

8. One by one, Kalyan visited all his friends and relatives, taking his leave and seeking their blessings. At this time he stayed mainly with his mother and did his best to console her.

One day he said to her: 'Ma, aren't I your loving son? Look, if God brings me back safely from the theatre of war then the womenfolk of Bengal will regard you as the mother of a hero. Just think how proud you will be. Don't make yourself sick by crying and falling into despair. In your mind you must hold on to hope.'

9. Dr Puri came to Calcutta from Kohat on 10 March and after that he and Kalyan spent most of their time in Fort William. They would come home late in the afternoon.

A wire came ordering them to leave on 13 March. I went to see Kalyan the day before his departure, in the late afternoon. Binota [Kalyan's daughter] was then as lovely as an English doll. Her hair was curly and there was always a smile on her face. But when she saw me she became quite sombre. Kalyan tried to make her smile by playing with a handkerchief and some orange peel but this had no effect on Binota. Then Kalyan said: 'You see, Grandma, she's going to grow into a grim-faced woman. Was I like that when I was her age?' I understood then how much he loved his daughter.

10. I spent a long time with Kalyan that evening, with his daughter on my lap. Then I blessed him and went home. That was my last meeting with him. I didn't see him on the day when his yatra began, but I prayed constantly for his well-being. I did not think that I wouldn't see him again. (209–11)

**3.**

Kalyan Mukherji's letters from Mesopotamia are for the most part short, hurried and matter-of-fact. But some of them, as Santanu Das has remarked, are among 'the finest in the grand pantheon of First World War letters'.[3]

His first letter from Mesopotamia was written on 13 April 1915, soon after he reached Basra.

> Ma, we've arrived safely. We had a good time on the ship. Dr Puri and I were on the same ship. All the trained troops from Kohat have arrived. About 40,000 of them.
>
> Let that be: arré Ram! Can this be the Basra of Caliph Haroun al-Rashid? Chhi, chhi! There's not the faintest sign of the famous roses of Basra; instead there are shallow little creeks filled with knee- or waist-deep water from the Tigris. Every one of these khuds is home to hundreds of thousands of frogs. They come in all sizes, but most are big bullfrogs. What a fearsome roar they have! It's enough to deafen your ears. Men can't hear each other talk. (250)

The tone of the letters changes when Capt. Mukherji reaches the front line. On 26 July 1915, he writes from Nasiriya:

> Ma, you must have read in the papers that there's been a lot of fighting in Mesopotamia. The English[4] have secured a great victory. And there can be no doubt of it this time. It happened before my eyes, from beginning to end.
>
> On 16 July, I was about to go out for a ride in Basra but just then we received orders to pack up our things, load them on steamers and depart in a couple of hours.
>
> We left our patients in the hospital and set off as soon as we could ... Leaving on the 16th we arrived here on the 19th. ... On landing we knew at once that we'd reached the enemy lines. The sound of their cannon was loud and clear.
>
> ...
>
> We heard that our generals' tents were a mile and a half from the firing line; and the Turkish trenches and nullahs were

200–300 yards away. As for us, let alone tents, we weren't even allowed to have cots. One set of clothes, one blanket and a raincoat and five doolie-loads were all we were permitted.

Why should I give up a chance like this? I'm senior, I said, so I'll go. Leaving the junior doctor in charge, I set off at 5 a.m. Yes, and by that time two shells had hit our camp.

Around sunset, when we reached the pre-arranged spot, I let the others off and set up our dressing station. I heard that our trenches were 300 yards from there, and the enemy trenches were another 200–300 yards farther.

We were sheltered by a 4 foot wall; people warned us: when the bullets start to fly, it's best not to leave the shelter of the wall. There was not a breath of wind behind the wall; fiercely hot. It was swarming with mosquitoes, insects, frogs.

At 10 p.m. a storm of bullets began. Exactly like a hailstorm. Honestly. I'm not exaggerating. Sheltering behind a wall in a date garden. Boom boom! Hiss hiss! Bullets flew for half an hour.

Every night the enemy soldiers would waste some 60,000 rounds; but without wounding anyone. Why they would fire like that—wasting lakhs of bullets—only they know. We stopped paying attention.

As soon as the firing began everyone would go to their places behind the wall and then we would spend some time chatting. Our troops didn't fire in reply. Every night they would fire a few times, for ten or fifteen minutes and after that they probably fell asleep. In the four days that I was there no more than seven or eight were wounded.

Anyway, on the night of the 23rd we received orders telling us that the next day at dawn the fighting would start in earnest. We would attack. By 5 a.m. we had to be ready to treat the wounded, with bandages, medicines, iodine, milk, brandy etc. all prepared. At dawn our artillery barrage began.

'Boom-boom' some twenty or twenty-five cannons firing together. After twenty minutes or so our troops moved up and began to advance, firing over our heads. We were out of the line of fire all along. Once or twice some bullets flew over our heads but didn't hit any of us.

After two or three hours, the enemy was driven back by the storm of bullets. And after that of course there was the suffering of the wounded to deal with.

At about 3 p.m. a band of enemy prisoners and wounded arrived. From 6.30 a.m. till 1 p.m. I didn't have a chance to breathe. A river of blood, red—all around. I myself, soaked in blood, to the skin. Whom … whom should I treat first? … Why this bloodshed!! What can I say? In my life I won't forget that sight.

Yesterday evening we came to the town of Bijit.[5] On the way I saw the battlefield. What I saw—I couldn't ever describe it. Today the English have hoisted their flag here.

I left behind my bedding and all my baggage and clothing. We've advanced 7-8 miles. I'm still wearing the blood-soaked shirt from the day before yesterday. I've wired them to send on my things—can't wait for them to arrive.

I hope you're all well.

Your Kalyan (289–94)

**4.**

Within a few months of reaching Iraq, Capt. Kalyan Mukherji had arrived at a devastatingly clear summation of the war. On 20 October 1915, in 'Aziziya, he wrote a letter that is, in my view, one of the most remarkable of the twentieth century.

As for the war, what is there to discuss? Unless something surprising happens suddenly, I don't see why a war of this kind should not go on for twenty years. So long as Germany can keep itself supplied with provisions and weaponry I don't think this side[6] will be able to advance. Nor does it seem possible for Germany to advance any further into France.

England is the teacher. The love of country that England has always taught, that same love of country whose virtues are sung by all civilized nations—that is what all this bloodshed is for. Grabbing someone else's country—that's 'Patriotism'. Patriotism—that's what builds kingdoms and empires. To display the love of country, love of race, by seizing a piece of territory, at the cost of thousands and thousands of lives, this is what the English have taught.

Now the youth of our country have started to emulate these vile ways of loving one's nation. As a result, all kinds of horrifying things have started to happen; people are dead and bombs have been thrown at a blameless Viceroy. I spit in the face of patriotism.[7] As long as this narrow-mindedness is not wiped off the face of this earth there will be no end to bloodshed in the name of patriotism. Whether one man throws a bomb from a rooftop or fifty men hurl shells from a cannon—this bloodshed, this madness, all spring from the same cause.

In this one year of war a crore[8] of people (English, German, Russian, French, Indian, African together) have been killed or wounded. Another one crore families are heartbroken because of 'Selfish nationalism: a most inhuman sentiment'. In other words, this war is proof that this brutal and selfish love of country … this awful, malign sentiment is an obstacle for all humankind.

There's nothing much to report from here. I am well.

Your Kalyan (333–35)

It is profoundly humbling to read this letter, written almost a century ago, in the context of the many wars and conflicts that have riven the Indian subcontinent in the decades since Independence. Extreme circumstances often produce extraordinary perceptions. It is as if the battlegrounds of Iraq had granted Capt. Mukherji a Cassandra-like gift of prophecy.

Few indeed were the statesmen, intellectuals and politicians who had an equivalent depth of perception. One of those who did was Rabindranath Tagore. Like Capt. Mukherji, Tagore was both opposed to imperialism and wary of nationalism. In his 1916 novel *Ghare Baire*, the character Nikhilesh expresses views on nationalist terror that are similar to Capt. Mukherji's; and in his 1916-17 lectures on the subject, Tagore is similarly impassioned in his critique of nationalism.

> Does not the voice come to us, through the din of war, the shrieks of hatred, the wailings of despair, through the churning up of the unspeakable filth which has been accumulating for ages in the bottom of this nationalism—the voice which cries to our soul, that the tower of national selfishness, which goes by the name of patriotism, which has raised its banner of treason against heaven, must totter and fall with a crash, weighed down by its own bulk, its flag kissing the dust, its light extinguished?'[9]

Considered in the context of the early days of the Indian freedom struggle, Tagore's critiques of nationalism have often been regarded as anomalous. But Tagore was always closely attuned to the international situation, and he would certainly have tracked the progress of the war, in Europe and in Mesopotamia, with great care. What is more, he may even have known—at least at second hand—about the reports that Capt. Mukherji and others were sending home from the battlefield. This is not unlikely, for Capt. Mukherji, like Tagore, was from a family that belonged to the Brahmo Samaj, which is, after all, a small community. Nor was Capt. Mukherji the only Brahmo to serve in Mesopotamia at that time; there were several others.

Capt. Mukherji and Rabindranath Tagore followed two different routes to arrive at the same conclusion: neither of them wanted to see Europe's history of national conflict re-enacted on the Indian subcontinent. What that trajectory represented for Tagore was not freedom but a different kind of enslavement: 'Those of us in India who have come under the delusion that mere political freedom will make us free have accepted their lessons from the West as the gospel truth and lost their faith in humanity.'[10]

**5.**

The British campaign in Mesopotamia proceeded at a brisk pace through most of 1915. British and Indian troops swept northwards, brushing aside Turkish resistance and advancing confidently towards their ultimate objective: Baghdad. But the Turkish forces were waiting for them in a carefully prepared defensive position in the ancient town of Ctesiphon, 16 miles south of the city.[11]

The British commander General Townshend decided to attack early on the morning of 22 November.

The night before the battle, Capt. Kalyan Mukherji wrote a letter to his family:

> 21-11-15
>
> Ma
>
> Since I last wrote to you, we have advanced another 12-13 miles towards Baghdad. The battle will start tomorrow. I'm doing well. I don't know when you'll get this letter. We don't

know when the ships will take the next post to the south. I'm writing in the hope that the steamer will take our letters when it carries the wounded down. The post office is on the ship.

Let's hope the battle will last just a day and that we will reach our destination without difficulty.

Your Kalyan (347-48)

The British attack on Ctesiphon started the next morning. This is Mokkhoda Debi's account of the battle:

> 5. The Turkish soldiery was battle-hardened and brave, and their aims were, in a sense, completely clear. They had settled into the trenches of Ctesiphon and taken the opportunity to rest as they waited for the British attack. They were willing to risk everything for their country, their honour, and for the safety of Baghdad. Their leader, Nuruddin Pasha, was an extremely seasoned man, fully the equal of General Townshend in education, intelligence and strategic skill. (350–51)
>
> ...
>
> 9. At 6 a.m. [on the 22nd], the British launched their attack and it continued, like a great storm, for four hours. The Turkish troops matched their fire, bullet for bullet, and succeeded in blocking their advance. (353)
>
> ...
>
> 12. In this battle, Nuruddin Pasha showed that his grasp of strategy was superior to General Townshend's. He had held many troops in reserve, under the command of General Jevad Bey, to use as a 'trump' ... At two in the afternoon Jevad Bey's reserves began to cause great problems for the attackers. It ended with the British gathering their scattered, weary troops and retreating along the same route that they had used for their advance. (354–55)

…

4. It slowly dawned on Townshend now that he had been defeated in the battle of Ctesiphon; no hope of victory remained; there would be no 'victory-march' into Baghdad; the best he could hope for was to withdraw his troops safely to the south. (357–58)

On 25 November, Kalyan wrote another letter home:

Ma

What happened during the battle of the 22nd cannot be described. I will try to write about it later. On that day I was hit by a bullet in the elbow. I was lucky that it didn't hit me anywhere else. The wound was slight. There's a small hole where it entered. But it isn't out yet. It lodged itself just before exiting—that's where it hurts. I didn't have to go to hospital. If the pain doesn't stop then I'll have to get an 'X-ray'. I had a lucky escape. I hope you're all well.

Your Kalyan (364)

**6.**

After their defeat at Ctesiphon on 22 November 1915, General Townshend's troops (consisting principally of the 6th Poona Division) were driven back to the town of Kut al-Amara, where they had established a fortified base. Here, surrounded by the Turkish forces, they were besieged from early December to the end of April 1916.

Towards the end of that period, Kalyan wrote this letter:

Kut-el Amarah

26-4-16

Ma

It has been almost five months since I sat down to write to you. I've often thought of writing in these months but since nothing was known about when we would be able to send letters, I never got around to it. Since yesterday people here have come to accept that we will not be relieved. The troops have been on half-rations for the last month and even those have been steadily cut over the last fifteen days, but despite these measures there's only enough food to last three more days.

After three months with very little to eat, the troops are starving. The mortality rate in the hospital has soared. In the last fifteen days many have died for lack of food. Of what use is medicine now? There's nothing to eat. People are coming to the hospital because starvation has made them weak. With nothing to give them, how can we help? Apart from that, there are no medicines left either.

We, meaning the officers, have all lost a lot of weight. Even then, despite eating nothing through the day, none of us have fallen sick. I haven't suffered that much. Apart from our rations of four ounces of atta and a pound of horsemeat, I've occasionally bought a little food from the bazar. But I've still lost a lot of weight. I won't talk about our lack of food though, for my health is fine, and I've even lost a bit of my paunch.

...

The siege started on 5 December and it is now 26 April. But it's some consolation that things will be decided one way or another in the next three or four days and we will find ourselves either on this shore or that. We'll probably end up on the other shore. There's no way we could break out of the enemy's encirclement and rejoin our own side.

...

Don't worry at all. Remember: if I am imprisoned I won't be in the midst of the fighting. I don't know when or how this letter will reach you. I'm writing it anyway. I'll send it if the opportunity arises. If they don't imprison the patients who are in the worst condition—if they send them down to Amara—then this letter will go with them. (402)

Three days later, Kalyan wrote another letter, in English:

29-4-16
Ma

On account of hunger, our General was obliged to surrender today. The Turkish flag has been put up and the British flag taken down. Turkish troops entered the town this afternoon.

Now for goodness sake don't die of fright ... please cheer up. I shall let you know afterwards how often you might hear from me and how to send letters to me.

Yours,
Kalyan (403-04)

Soon after the surrender, Kalyan wrote home again.

1-5-16
Ma

I wrote you a letter on 26 April and a postcard on the 29th. Listen to what happened on the 29th. Our commander, General Townshend, laid his arms at the feet of Turkey's Halil Bey and surrendered. Before that, the British flag had been lowered and the Turkish flag had been raised on the fort. The two commanders shook hands. Halil Bey behaved with the greatest courtesy; he returned Townshend's arms and took him off somewhere with the greatest kindness. What can I tell you, Ma, of how well Halil Bey treated us? How much fresh food and water he had readied for us! And he let us have it all. After consuming all of that, it was as if our lives had been renewed.

Halil Bey's orders to us were: 'Enjoy yourselves for three days—eat as much as you want and write as many letters as you like. After three days you will have to move elsewhere—and then you will be allowed to write only one letter a week, of four lines.'

[In Kut] we had consumed our rations in a couple of months. Towards the end even our water had run dry. In the fort's courtyard we dug forty wells and found some water. It was bad, muddy water. In the end, all our mules were slaughtered and one pound of meat was distributed to us. Many died for lack of food.

...

My friend Puri and I are fine. We are quite fit as well. At times the water situation was difficult, but we used filters before drinking it. What we went through during the siege is beyond description. When we came here, after our defeat at Ctesiphon, our numbers were 10,000 or 11,000; now it is less than half that. It's horrifying! Even now we have hundreds of patients, many will not survive. So much water from the Tigris has entered the fort that everything has turned to mud.

...

You mustn't do yourself harm by worrying about me. I want to see you when I get home. I'm perfectly all right. I have to write four other long letters. I'll take your leave for now.

Yours,

Kalyan (405–07)

## 7.

After the defeat and surrender of General Townshend's Indo-British forces at Kut al-Amara, Capt. Kalyan Mukherji was sent to a prisoner-of-war camp in Ras al-'Ain. This town is now technically in Syria, but it lies right on the Turkish border.

In 1916, when the Indian POWs came to Ras al-'Ain, a great number of Armenians were incarcerated in concentration camps around the town. This was the most terrible phase of the Armenian genocide, and the Indian POWs would certainly have known what was happening in the camps around them. Capt. Mukherji's contemporary and fellow prisoner Sisir Sarbadhikari refers frequently to the mass slaughter of Armenians in his war memoir *Abhi Le Baghdad*: indeed his book suggests that the lives of Indian and Armenian prisoners sometimes became quite intricately intertwined. But there are no references to Armenians in the postcards Kalyan Mukherji sent home from Ras al-'Ain. His messages were very brief and were meant principally to allay his family's anxieties; in any case they would have been written with the camp's censors and guards in mind.

Here is Mokkhoda Debi's account of the final chapters of her grandson's life.

> 4. After reaching Ras al-'Ain, Kalyan sent his mother a few lines in English on a postcard on 15 June 1916. This is the Bangla translation of what he wrote: 'They give us very good, fresh food. We are eating lots of milk, almonds, rotis and fish. Our faces have regained their colour and our strength has returned. Puri and I are still together. I'll feel still better if I receive a letter from you. We are all well.'
>
> ...
>
> 6. From long before that month, Binodini's [Kalyan's mother] health had been declining because of her anxieties

about her son. Then something happened that made her condition even worse. In the month of June, she received news from Cooch Behar that Kalyan's daughter had died of an illness of the stomach at his in-laws' house. After this terrible news, Binodini never left her bed again: her health broke down completely and she lost all her strength.

7. Kalyan came to know about his daughter's death and his mother's illness from our letters and after that he wrote to his mother every month, trying to give her hope and strength. What those short, four-line letters said in sum was this: 'Ma, you must look after yourself, you must get better. I really want to see you—I will soon be home again. Don't go away before I come. So what if my first child died? You lost yours too. When I come home again, I will have many children, don't worry about that. I am desperate to hear from you, to receive your letters. If you are unable to write yourself, then let my wife take down the words from your lips. I'll be really happy if I hear from you … I am fine here but I worry a lot about you.'

9. On 29 October it was as if Binodini knew that her life would end that day. Her younger son Kamal's second child had been born twelve days earlier. From the morning onwards Binodini began to ask to see the newborn's face, so the child was brought to her from his uncle's house.

10. Many relatives went to see Binodini that day—she took leave of all of them. She even predicted the exact time when she would bid farewell to this world.

11. That day, it rained through the evening and into the night. Seeing how hard it was raining, Binodini prayed: 'Dear God, please don't drench those who will have to go to perform my last rites.' Her prayers seemed to find a loving reception. At ten the rain stopped, and shortly afterwards, at midnight,

Binodini eluded the sorrows of this world and made her escape.

It rained no more that night. The next day it was sunny until 5 p.m. and then it started to rain again. Needless to say, those who went to perform Binodini's last rites were not drenched. (410–13).

1. That October we received two postcards from Kalyan. Word of his mother's death was sent to him in November but, as we learnt later from his friend Dr Puri, the news did not get there till 3 March (1917).

2. We received no letters from Kalyan in December (1916). Towards the end of January 1917, two postcards arrived. They said: 'A terrible sickness has hit our camp.[12] Many have fallen very ill. Dr Puri fell ill too. It took me two months to save him. I didn't have time to write.'

3. After that we received a letter written by Kalyan in February 1917 and another in March. There was no indication in them that he had heard of his mother's death. He wrote only: 'Many are dying. If they don't move us from here no one may survive.' (415)

4. In April there was no news of Kalyan. Then on 21 May we read in the newspapers: 'Capt. Kalyan Mukherji died of a deadly illness on 18 March.'

5. Later, on 25 May, we received a letter from a grief-stricken Dr Puri. He wrote:

*Kalyan saved my life with his own hands. But I was unable to save him. I tried everything. It was my fate!!! I saw to it that his last rites were performed—as far as the conditions here would permit—to my satisfaction. And I will see to it that a marble plaque, with an inscription, is placed upon his memorial.*

*On 3 March Kalyan received a letter with news of his mother's death. After that he lost interest in everything. He ate much less and*

> *couldn't sleep at night. On 9 March he fell ill with a slight fever. Over three days his condition worsened. From 12 March he became delirious. But his enunciation was quite clear even in his delirium; he spoke in Bengali—words poured out of him. Even though the other doctors and I could not understand exactly what he was saying, we knew he was talking to his mother. His grief was so great that there was no mistaking it. After six days, on 18 March, his delirium ceased. And later that night it was all over.* (416-17)

The ending of the narrative, and the manner in which the final parts are shaped, suggests that Mokkhoda Debi believed that Capt. Mukherji's life had ended in a fashion that mirrored the death of his mother.

She writes of the death of her grandson and her daughter as if both had been brought about, ultimately, by the same cause: the grief of separation—'biraha'. It is as if, in writing the coda to their lives, she were invoking an ancient lament, sung over the centuries by women whose menfolk had left home to serve as sepoys.

# TEN
# Shared Sorrows: Indians and Armenians in the Prison Camps of Ras al-'Ain, 1916–18

*In Memory of Stephen Vertannes (1959–1978)*

**1.**

Armenians have been connected with India for a very long time. The foremost chronicler of the subcontinent's Armenian community, Mesrovb Jacob Seth, tells us that it was at the express request of Akbar, the great Mughal emperor, that Armenians settled in Agra in the sixteenth century. Akbar also took an Armenian wife by the name of Mariam Zamani Begum. By the time the English arrived at the Mughal court, the Armenians were already well established there: it was they who helped the East India Company acquire the Diwani of Bengal, which was a crucial step in the building of the British empire.[1]

For many years, Calcutta, the city of my birth, was home to the biggest and most vibrant Armenian community in India. Even in my own childhood, Armenians were an important presence in the city. As a boy, I heard stories about famous Armenian boxers; my father would reminisce about old hotels and boarding houses that had once been run by Armenians. I would often walk past the Armenian School, which happened to be housed in the birthplace of the English novelist William Makepeace Thackeray.[2]

These connections and memories may explain why Armenian characters have figured often in my books. In my novel *The Calcutta Chromosome*, one of the key characters is a Mrs Aratounian (a family of that name once ran a hotel in Calcutta); in my most recent book, *River of Smoke*, there is an Armenian watchmaker from Egypt by the name of Zadig Karabedian (he is the nephew of Orhan Karabedian, the icon painter whose work can still be seen in the Church of the Mu'allaqa in Cairo).

As a writer of fiction, I am accustomed to creating characters and inventing stories. But I also often deal with historical sources, and every now and again I come upon something that serves to remind me that reality often exceeds fiction in its improbability. Certainly, I could never have invented a story like the one I am going to recount here. The events date back to the latter years of the First World War, when groups of Indian soldiers and paramedics were imprisoned in the vicinity of Ras al-'Ain, in what is now Syria. Some of the worst massacres of the Armenian genocide occurred in the vicinity of this town, and through force of circumstances, the lives of the Indians and the Armenians often became closely intertwined.

The reason the story has survived is that one of the Indian prisoners happened to write about his war experiences forty years later. His name was Sisir Sarbadhikari, and his book *Abhi Le Baghdad* (or 'On to Baghdad') appeared in 1958:[3] it was self-published and was probably only ever read by a handful of people. But the fact that the text was committed to print is the key to its survival. It meant that a copy of the book had to be deposited in the National Library in Kolkata—this was the very copy that I sought out last year.[4]

Sisir Sarbadhikari was (as am I) a Bengali from Calcutta and he too belonged to a middle-class Hindu family. This adds greatly to the improbability of the story, for in the early years of the twentieth century, the chances that a young man from such a background would find his way into the front lines of a military campaign were close to nil. This is because Bengalis were not eligible for recruitment into the British Indian Army, which drew its soldiers (or sepoys) from certain specially designated 'races'.[5]

The army's recruitment policy excluded most Indians and was widely resented, partly because it was felt to be based upon demeaning racial stereotypes, and partly because it blocked access to one of the most important sources of employment in the colonial economy. The bar did not, however, apply to the army's administrative and medical wings, and many Bengalis found their way on to the military payroll through this route. When the First World War broke out, some prominent Bengalis decided that the army's medical services might be a means of furthering their claim to serve in the ranks of the regular military. To that end, they offered to raise a unit of voluntary ambulance workers in support of the war effort. They reckoned that such an offer would not be refused at a time of crisis, and they were right. They were quickly granted permission to form a unit that came to be known as the Bengal Ambulance Corps (BAC).

This was the unit that Sisir Sarbadhikari volunteered for in 1915. He was in his early twenties and had just earned his bachelor's degree. Such was his eagerness to join the BAC that he actually pulled strings to get in: he would later attribute his enthusiasm to the 'Spirit of Adventure', of which he evidently had more than his fair share. Nor was he the only eager volunteer: some were so enthusiastic that they falsified their ages in order to enlist. One of them, Bhola, was only sixteen when he joined up—he would become a close friend of Sisir's, and he too would end up in the camps of Ras al-'Ain.

The BAC was a small unit, with a total strength of 117, of which about a third consisted of 'camp followers'—that is to say, cooks, sweepers, water carriers and so on. It was led by five British officers and about a dozen Indian non-commissioned officers (NCOs). The remaining sixty or so members of the unit were privates, of whom Sisir was one.

Although lowly in rank, Sisir was from a family of well-educated middle-class professionals—a class that is often referred to in Bengal as 'bhadralok' or 'gentlefolk'. Sisir himself was well-read in English as well as Bengali: his book is embellished with lines of English and Bengali poetry, and he frequently refers to Xenophon and other figures from antiquity.

Many of the other volunteers seem to have been from circumstances similar to Sisir's. They were not the kind of men who would have joined the regular army as privates, even if that had been a possibility. If the Ambulance Corps appealed to them, it was probably because its medical associations lent it a touch of middle-class respectability.

The BAC volunteers were given three months' training before being sent off to Bombay to join the 6th Poona Division, which was on its way to Mesopotamia under the command of Major General Charles Townshend. They left Bombay on a hospital ship, the *Madras*, on 2 July 1915 and reached Basra a week later. From then on, they accompanied the 6th Poona Division as it advanced steadily northwards, towards Baghdad.

In the first few months of the campaign, the British Indian forces met with little resistance from the Ottoman Army. The going was so smooth that the campaign was described as a 'river picnic'. But just south of Baghdad, at the ancient town of Ctesiphon, General Townshend's army ran into a large and well-entrenched Ottoman force. The British advance was blocked, and the 6th Division was driven back to a small town called Kut al-Amara. There, with just one month's rations in store, the British Indian force endured a siege of five months—at appalling cost. Many soldiers died of hunger and disease before General Townshend surrendered to Khalil Pasha, the Ottoman commander, on 29 April 1916.[6] At the time this was thought to be the greatest defeat that the British had ever suffered in Asia.

On 12 May, Sisir Sarbadhikari and the other prisoners of war were sent to Baghdad on a steamer. Sisir remained there for a couple of months, and then, on 19 July, he and some other prisoners were dispatched to Samarra, about 60 miles away, by train. Then began a series of gruelling marches, in the burning heat of the Mesopotamian summer: the prisoners were driven brutally northwards through inhospitable country with very little food and water. British accounts of the march speak of floggings, starvation and terrible cruelties: 'troops (British or Indian) falling out of the line of March from sheer exhaustion were left to perish either of starvation or the probability of being murdered by the Arabs'.[7]

Cruelty and hardship figure in Sisir's narrative too, but his tone is stoic, almost dispassionate, and he often pauses to reflect on history and comment on the beauty of the countryside. Of the horrors of the march, the recollection that was to remain most sharply etched into his memory was of the shouts with which the guards would wake the prisoners in the small hours of the night. (121)

In twenty-five days, the prisoners marched from Samarra to Mosul, by way of Tikrit, Sargat and Hamam al-Alil. It was after leaving Mosul that they began to see signs of the devastation that had been visited upon the Armenians of this region.

## 2.

But before I come to that, I'd like to say a few words about Sisir Sarbadhikari's book. *Abhi Le Baghdad* was self-published, as I've said, and it seems to have vanished quickly into obscurity. I first learnt of its existence through the work of a military historian, Kaushik Roy, but it was an essay by a brilliant young literary critic, Santanu Das, that prompted me to seek it out.[8]

A detailed account of the making of *Abhi Le Baghdad* will be of immense value, not just in relation to the book itself but also in regard to the muteness from which it emerges. For the most remarkable thing about *Abhi Le Baghdad* is that it was written at all: it is almost a lone voice, piercing a profound and puzzling silence.

In the 150 years before the First World War, hundreds of thousands of Indian soldiers had fought for the British empire, at home and abroad; during the First World War alone, over 1.5 million Indians were deployed to different fronts. Yet, mighty though these legions may have been in the field of battle, outside it, they were as silent as an army of ghosts. Almost everything that is known about them is spoken in the voice and language of the soldiers' masters, the British. The number of accounts authored by Indian military personnel in this time is so small as to be counted on the fingers of one hand. As a full-length published memoir of the First World War by an Indian, *Abhi Le Baghdad* thus stands almost alone on its shelf.[9]

India's literary silence about the First World War is especially notable because this great conflict was an enormously fecund subject for soldiers of other nations. In England, France, Germany and elsewhere, it generated prodigious amounts of writing of many sorts. Yet even in this vast corpus, *Abhi Le Baghdad* commands a place of special notice because most of the writing about the war came from officers: Sisir's memoir is one of the few accounts to be written by a low-ranking private. (The greatest of all First World War memoirs, Erich Maria Remarque's *All Quiet on the Western Front*, was another.)

*Abhi Le Baghdad* is remarkable also because it is based on a very unusual source: a journal that Sarbadhikari kept through his time in the Middle East, including his years in captivity. His notes went on gruelling marches with him, hidden in his boots; at the Ras al-'Ain camp, where their discovery could have resulted in disaster for Sisir, they were buried underground. Yet despite the attendant dangers, Sisir seems to have continued to make regular entries in his journal whenever circumstances permitted. There was only one prolonged break, during the months between March 1917 and April 1918.

The journal travelled back to Calcutta with Sisir and was put aside for decades. In his brief account of the writing of *Abhi Le Baghdad*, Santanu Das suggests that the book might never have been written if not for the encouragement and support of Sisir's daughter-in-law, Romola Sarbadhikari.[10] It is not uncommon, of course, to come across war memoirs based on notes made 'in the field'—but few indeed were the journals that survived the sort of captivity that Sisir had to endure. Indeed, it was this journal's very existence, insistently miraculous, that seems to have prompted Sisir's daughter-in-law into midwifing the book into existence.

The dates and details also serve to make his account unusually persuasive. There is no showing off, no dwelling on personal injuries and hardship. For all these reasons, *Abhi Le Baghdad* is a book that is not just gripping to read but also very persuasive.

**3.**

To return now to Sisir's narrative. On 25 August, when he and his fellow prisoners reached Mosul, they still did not know where they were being taken. It was in Mosul that they received word of their destination: the Hindus (and Sikhs) were to be separated from the British and Muslim POWs; they would be sent to Ras al-'Ain, where they would work on a rail line. (124)[11]

Although Sisir does not make much of it, there is something distinctive about his use of the word 'Hindu' here. The word does not occur often in the text, and until this point in the narrative, it has never been used to imply that the various non-Muslim groups in the British Indian Army had felt themselves to be 'alike', and different from their fellow Muslim soldiers. His use of it in this sense here suggests to me that Sisir and his comrades were surprised and disturbed to learn that the Indian POWs, who had served together on the battlefield, were now to be split up along religious lines.[12]

Many of them would probably have concluded that Hindus and Sikhs, being neither Europeans nor co-religionists of the Turks, would be sent to the worst camps of all.[13] Their apprehensions would surely have deepened when they learnt that they were being sent to an area where thousands of Armenians had been confined to concentration camps. The sense of being singled out for a shared plight may have contributed to the bonds of sympathy that developed between these Indians and the Armenians they encountered.

From Mosul, the prisoners marched to Tell Kaaf.[14] Shortly after this, they entered a markedly different landscape:

> Here everything is beginning to change,[15] from the climate to the landscape and the appearance of the houses. It's much cooler than before and the nights are cold. The terrain is no longer flat or undulating, we are now marching through mountainous country; the houses don't have mud walls and roofs, they are made of stone. Before, there were no trees and no greenery, it was desolate, *barren*.[16] Here trees can be seen. Amongst the stone houses, those that are clean, well kept and nice looking belong to the Christians ('Nasrani') ... We are now on the frontiers of Kurdistan. The Kurds' villages are mostly perched on mountaintops, in inaccessible locations. How people reach them is beyond our reckoning. The Kurds aren't wanderers like the Bedouin ('Badu'), they do some farming. (124-25)

Sisir's first mention of Armenians comes a few days later, on 18 August. In the course of that day's march, the prisoners encountered two rosy-cheeked Armenian boys, eight to ten years old. Sisir notes that they had crucifixes on their chests. 'From what they said to us in broken Arabic,' he writes, 'we understood that the Turks had slaughtered their father and older brothers; where their mother was, they did not know.' (126)

On 23 August, the prisoners came to a small village.

> From a distance the small stone houses, cradled by the mountains, were as pretty as a picture. On approaching them we saw that they were empty of people. A dog emerged from an abandoned house ... At that time, we didn't know that the inhabitants of these villages were Armenians; the men had been slaughtered and the women and children had been driven away. (129)

Sisir's description of the village is accompanied by a few lines from Oliver Goldsmith's poem 'The Deserted Village':

> *Along thy glades, a solitary guest ...*
> *Amidst thy bowers, the tyrant's hand is seen,*
> *And desolation saddens all thy green.* (129)

Sisir recounts another story about this village: when he glanced into a well, a swarm of insects flew out. He explains that he had not intended to drink from the well; it was merely out of curiosity that he had looked inside. 'It was not at all advisable,' he writes, 'to drink from these wells; there were Armenian corpses rotting in many of them.' (129–30)

Over the next few days, as the prisoners marched north, they saw other empty, abandoned villages; a couple of them had been burnt down. After some forty days of marching, they reached a town called Nisibeen,[17] now on the border of Turkey and Syria. Sisir writes,

> In antiquity Nisibeen was a Roman town. Examples of their building styles can still be found. On the river the Roman Bridge is still standing and it is used by heavy army trucks ... Nisibeen is quite a big settlement; food is easily available there. The Khabur River (the Habur of the Bible) flows through the centre of the town so water is plentiful. It's different from the places we've seen so far; a fine place for bivouacking troops. The people are cultured and well dressed. None of the Armenian inhabitants are left. The local people who remain are all Muslims or Syrian Christians. (131-32)

Sisir would return to Nisibeen later, but his first stay there was quite brief. The prisoners soon continued their northward march, reaching Ras al-'Ain on 2 September. They had marched for forty-six days from Samarra to Ras al-'Ain, covering some 500 miles. (133)

This is how Sisir describes the camp at Ras al-'Ain:

> For shelter [we had] Bedouin tents; like those at the Baghdad rest camp. There were gales all the time, with swirling sand—it was like sticking needles in the body.[18] A hospital was nominally set up in a small room and serious patients were sent there. Medicines and supplies were few; but at least there was shelter from rain and wind ... Rations were irregular ... they'd come after two or three days. They didn't give us any firewood for cooking; we had to wander three or four miles gathering twigs and camel dung. There were no trees to get branches from. (138)

On 7 September, 100 prisoners started working on the rail lines. A few weeks later, the guards turned the officers' quarters upside down during a search. It was now that Sisir buried his diary, fearing that it would be found. He did not dig it up again until the trouble stopped. (140)

Over the next few weeks, the camp's medical facilities were expanded. New doctors arrived, among them some Armenians. The relations between the Indian medical staff and the Armenian doctors were not always easy. Sisir writes,

> One day, the hospital's Armenian doctor swore at Champati [an NCO] and had Sundar Singh thrown behind bars. The reason was that an Armenian prisoner from Russia complained about the hospital being staffed by Indians; he said they gave the Indian patients better food. Being an Armenian himself, the doctor created an incident without inquiring further. On informing Captain Puri, Sundar Singh was let off. There was always friction between us and the Russian prisoners. After this it got worse. (141)

In November, typhus broke out in the Indian camp. An epidemic of the disease had already ravaged many of the Armenian camps in the Ras al-'Ain area. It now began to take a serious toll on the Indian prisoners. Several members of the BAC came down with it, among them Sisir's friend Bhola, the sixteen-year-old who had exaggerated his age to get into the corps. Sisir himself escaped this outbreak. He was occupied in tending to the stricken when it was decided that he would take the most serious patients to Aleppo (Halbe).[19] Sisir was reluctant to go because he did not wish to be separated from his friends. He did not know it, of course, but the order that sent him away from Ras al-'Ain was a blessing in disguise. The coming winter would decimate the prisoners who remained in Ras al-'Ain. Many would die of disease, exhaustion or the cold. Had Sisir not been sent to Aleppo, he may well have been among the casualties. Later, he would write: 'That was our first winter in Turkey and we had no clothes to speak of; many didn't have boots ... [The prisoners] would be taken to work barefoot on the line, in the snow. They would get frostbite at first and then the flesh would fall off and the wounds would turn gangrenous.' (167-68)[20] E.A. Walker, a British officer, estimated that 75 per cent of the Indian prisoners died in that first year.[21]

On 19 November, Sisir left for Aleppo on a mail train with some fifty seriously ill patients. They travelled in awful conditions: locked in a windowless compartment, they had to relieve themselves in the corners. But these circumstances did not prevent Sisir from noting that the stations were pretty, with tiled roofs—'like stations in Europe'. (143)

They arrived in Aleppo a day later. The city created a strong impression on Sisir.

> Aleppo is not like the cities we have seen so far—Baghdad and Mosul. The houses are nice to look at; the roads aren't bad. We hear that it looks like towns in Europe. The people on the streets look cultured; their clothes are nice; European costume predominates. There are people of many communities—Turks, Syrian Christians, Rumis (that is Greeks) and Jews. (144)

On arrival, Sisir and his patients were sent to the general hospital (or Markaz Khastakhana), where some wards had been set aside for POWs. (144)

Sisir's account of his stay at the hospital is surprising in many respects. Even though thousands of Armenians were dying in the camps of Ras al-'Ain a short distance away, in this Aleppo hospital, Armenians were still an important presence. The commanding officer, Lieutenant Colonel Bagdasar Bey, was an Armenian, and most of the doctors were Christians. Sisir writes that some were Nasranis ('Nazarenes' or Syrian Christians), others were Rumis ('Byzantines' or Turkish Greeks).

Sisir was put into a ward that was run by an Armenian doctor called Saghir Effendi, about whom he wrote: 'a wonderful man, he takes good care of the prisoners'. But Saghir Effendi was not to remain in the hospital for long. In January 1917, he stopped coming. Sisir writes: 'We hear that he has been sent on to the firing line. We were saddened to learn of this. We will never forget his kindness.' (151)

Among the others who worked in the ward, there was an Armenian woman called Marum, who was especially kind. 'How well she looked after us!' Sisir remarks. (145) But this evidently did her no good in the eyes of the authorities, for she was soon transferred to another ward and then dismissed altogether. (151-52)

It is impossible not to wonder about the state of mind of the hospital's Armenian staff at a time when so many members of their community were being killed in nearby camps. Although the situation of the Indians was completely different, the plight of the Armenians would certainly have resonated with them: they knew well what it was to serve an empire in which they occupied a position of subservience.

Even in captivity, the Indian POWs were constantly reminded of their inferiority in the imperial hierarchy. Sisir touches on this theme often, especially in relation to the sums that were disbursed to the POWs according to the laws of war. On 12 February 1917, he records that an official had visited the hospital and distributed money to the prisoners: 'Five liras for the whites, four for the Russians and three liras for us. The money comes from British or Indian POW funds, but still the Russians get more than us. Not only are we a defeated race, we're black on top of that.' (153)[22]

The following year, in July, he returns to this theme:

> Some funds have arrived for us from the Red Cross Society—three liras for the British, and one and a half liras for us. We all refused it ... [But] after much persuasion ... we agreed to take the one and a half liras. What we said when we refused the money was that white soldiers are paid higher salaries in India (Bharatvarsha) because they are serving in a foreign country and therefore have extra expenses. ... But that argument doesn't work in this instance. Turkey is not our country, just as it is not theirs ... The differences and distinctions that have been created between whites and blacks in all things is deeply insulting to us. A Hindustani sepoy receives half the pay that a white soldier gets; his clothing and uniform is different too—the white's is better. But the white Tommy and the black sepoy both put aside their love of life to go to war, they both suffer equally—yet in the midst of shared hardship, everything possible is done to make things better for Tommy.[23] Even his rations are different—Tommy drinks his tea with sugar, we drink it with jaggery. And what tea it is! Sacks of it lie in front of the store; people walk over it with their boots. If there's a canteen then we aren't allowed into it; only whites can buy from them ... A lot can be written about this. (187-88)

**4.**

Towards the end of November 1916, Sisir too was struck down by typhus. For about a month, he was so sick that at times he did not know whether he was dead or alive. (148) But in December, he was once again the beneficiary of a stroke of good fortune: his friend Bhola was also sent to the general hospital in Aleppo. After that Sisir's health began to improve steadily.

In Sisir's description, the conditions at the general hospital in Aleppo appear as a startling contrast to the situation in the camp at

Ras al-'Ain, where Indian prisoners were suffering terrible hardships. In the hospital, on the other hand, the POWs were in some ways better off than the Turkish soldiers who were being treated there. Sisir often remarks on the difficulties that the Turkish soldiers had to deal with: 'They were in a bad way,' he comments, 'they didn't have money for cigarettes and would beg from us.' (160)

Elsewhere, he writes: 'Today there was a pitiful sight in our ward. The Turkish soldiers don't receive any pay; they are all poor; they don't even have money for cigarettes. Some of them ask us for money; but mainly they pick up butts from the street, take the tobacco out and use it to roll cigarettes. Four or five butts yield one cigarette.' (154)

Sisir evidently made great progress with the Turkish language during his stay at the hospital. 'We were quite friendly with the Turkish soldiers,' he writes. 'None of them were literate but they were friendly and warm. They used to say, you can't fight us now, so we are all brothers or kardeshes. The word "kardesh" was much in use.[24] If they saw someone they didn't know, they would call him kardesh. We did the same.' (157)

The Turkish soldiers at the hospital were themselves quite a diverse group. While most were from Anatolia, there were also some from Bulgaria and Albania. (158) Sisir notes that there 'was no lack of bad men amongst them ... Many a time we were insulted by them and we often had to suffer their blows.' He describes how he once went to the hospital's barber for a shave and was spat upon for no reason; he also mentions a corporal who would beat Indian patients without cause. (159)

But the Indians and Turks also discovered many commonalities:

> We would talk about our countries and about our own joys and sorrows. If we said that we have this or that in our country but you don't have it here, they would say, 'How can things improve in our country? All we do is fight, and that too with

> big and powerful countries. If you go into our country you'll see, even the fields are lying fallow. Who's to do the work? Everyone's away fighting; only the women are at home.' (158)
>
> One thing they always said was this: 'What are you going to gain from this war? Why are we cutting each other's throats? You live in Hindustan, we live in Turkey, neither of us had ever met, we have no quarrel with each other, but at the behest of a couple of men we've become enemies overnight.'

Sisir pauses to ask: 'Is this what's in the heart of every soldier, in every country, at all times?' (158)

Then he continues: 'There was a man from Edirna-le or Adrianopolis who used to say, "How will things improve? Sultan Abdul Hamid put a curse on our heads because of which we'll have to be at war for a hundred years. Why he put such a curse on us I cannot say, kardesh."' (159)

Sisir tells some touching stories about his kardeshes. For example:

> An old Turkish soldier came to our ward to collect cigarette butts. He was bent over with age, but he happened to look up and catch sight of a young Turk in one of the beds. He gave a shout and then we saw that they were hugging each other with tears rolling down their faces. After they had calmed down a bit, we learnt that they were father and son; for three years they had had no news of each other—and today this sudden meeting! ... In Turkey this kind of thing is not unusual—fathers don't hear from their sons; the sons don't know where their fathers are; householders go off to fight and don't know what's going on at home. They get news when they go back, or when others from their area return from leave. (155)

He follows this with a story that graphically illustrates the conditions of soldiering at that time:

> There was a Turkish soldier in our ward, about thirty years of age, who had been wounded in the fighting. With him was a pretty young girl of about five or six. Her name was Farida. She used to play with all of us. The soldier had no one at home to leave his daughter with, so he took her with him when he went to fight—he brought her to the hospital too. During the fighting he would leave her in some safe place in the care of one of his comrades ... [One day] I asked him: 'Kardesh, if you had been killed in the fighting what would have happened to your daughter?' He smiled and said, 'Allah bilior.' 'Only Allah knows.' I never saw this kardesh looking gloomy. And the girl? She was always cheerful, busy playing. (155-56)

Amongst Sisir's particular friends in the hospital, there was an Armenian called George. Sisir writes:

> His home was in Diyarbakır; his sons and daughters had all been killed; he had somehow managed to escape to Aleppo with his life. George was given the job of cleaning the toilets. There was a huge hall, with many toilets side by side. George lived in one corner of this hall—he ate and slept there. On cold evenings we used to sit with him and warm ourselves at his brazier, and then we would talk. (159)

Sisir's stay at the hospital came to an end around June 1917, when most of the Indians were discharged. But for a while, his luck held: amazing to relate, while other Indian POWs were dying of hunger and disease at Ras al-'Ain, through a providential turn in the wheel of fortune, Sisir and Bhola were sent to a rest-home (liaqat-khana) to recuperate. The rest-home was in the Jewish part of Aleppo, and they spent two months there. Only after they were discharged did they learn that the Hindu POWs were to be sent to Ras al-'Ain once again, while the Muslims would go to Islamiyah and the British to Belemedik. (165)

On returning to the vicinity of Ras al-'Ain, Sisir found many changes. The railway line had been extended in the months that he had been away, and the Indian camps had advanced with it. The construction of the lines was being overseen by Germans, and they had taken charge of many of the area's camps and hospitals. For a while, Sisir was in a camp that looked towards the town of Mardin,[25] which he describes as being 'in the interior of Armenia'. He writes: 'We heard that the city of Mardin was empty ... there were no people in it. The houses were abandoned and it was like a ghost town.' (168)

Sisir was then dispatched to another camp before finally ending up in a German-administered hospital in Nisibeen. It was here that he would become deeply enmeshed in the fate of Armenian refugees. 'When I reached Nisibeen,' he writes, 'there were no Indian, British or Russian prisoners there. I was the only prisoner of war. The rest were Armenian mohajers [refugees]; they were all women, only one had a little boy with her.' (170)

> I was given a small tent to live in and the big tents of the mohajer women were close by. There was no one to speak Hindi or English with, let alone Bengali; only with Meinhof [a German officer] would I exchange a few words in English. When there were chats and conversations with the mohajers, they were always in Turkish. One of the mohajers, old Mary, would patiently inquire after the smallest details of my home and family. She was sad to learn that I had lost my mother; she

> would say that this was why I had been able to go to war; if I'd had a mother she would not have let me go.' (170-71)

Sisir was assigned to the camp's hospital, but his duties were mainly administrative. 'Two Armenian mohajer boys, Yakob and Ilyas, worked for me in the office,' he writes.

> Yakob was some twenty years old; he was from a very ordinary background, and couldn't do anything that required reading and writing. Ilyas was from a well-off family: he was about fifteen and knew a little French; he didn't have much to do—his job was to write down telephone messages. (175)
>
> Ilyas's home was in Erzurum. He and his father, mother, older sister and brother lived there in peace until the war started. When the Turks began to kill the Armenians, Ilyas's father and brother were not spared. They were dragged out of their Erzurum house and forced to move, here today and there tomorrow. There were many others in their group—apart from all the Armenians of Erzurum, people in the towns and villages along the way were also herded together with them. They were brought to a place where they were told: Now the menfolk will be separated from the others; they will go to a different camp. (176)
>
> [The Armenians] knew already that the men would be killed, that there was no other camp; it was a lie—they were actually being taken to be slaughtered. There was much weeping and many tears, the women clung on to the men and would not let them go. But what could come of that? The men were dragged off by force; Ilyas's father and brother among them. The next day one male from that group managed to escape, bringing back the news that all the men had been killed. He

> himself had been badly wounded but was still alive. However, after a few hours, he succumbed to his wounds. (176)
>
> After that the women and children were driven along, only to be abandoned in cities along the way. They had to forage for themselves, keeping themselves alive as best they could. On the way, Ilyas was separated from his mother and sister; after much wandering he ended up in Nisibeen. When the Germans started building the railroad they assumed the responsibility for the Armenian mohajers and that made things a little better for them. (176)
>
> From what we hear, these terrible mass killings were not perpetrated by Turkish soldiers; they were done by Chechens and Kurds. Before we got to Ras al-'Ain many Armenians had been brought there and killed. Sachin [a BAC volunteer] was in Ras al-'Ain long before us; he told us that he had once witnessed the killings. A group of Armenians was made to stand up, their hands were tied, and their throats were slit one by one. Sachin said that those who did the killings were Kurds. There was a hill behind our camp in Ras al-'Ain, it was on the other side that these deeds were done; Sachin once stole off there in secret and witnessed them with his own eyes. (176-77)

The word that Sisir uses to describe these killings is worthy of note. Earlier, when writing about the killings of Armenians, he generally uses the word 'kâtâ': literally 'to cut' or slaughter. But here he uses the word 'hatyakanda', literally 'killing-deed', signifying mass killings.[26]

Sisir was not the only Indian in the camp for long: it soon began to fill up with British, Russian and Indian POWs, including many other members of the BAC, Bhola among them. (172)

As the months went by, the prisoners learnt that there had been a revolution in Russia, that Istanbul had been rocked by unrest and that British and Indian troops were making rapid advances in Palestine and Mesopotamia. By the middle of 1917, it was apparent that the tide of war was turning in the Middle East and the Turks were being beaten back.[27]

For the Armenian refugees, this created a new set of anxieties, for they were now seized by the fear that the Turks, faced with the prospect of losing the war, 'would slaughter those of them who were still alive—and this time even the women would not be spared.'

But it still came as a surprise to Sisir and his friends when they discovered that the Armenians were planning an escape: it was Ilyas who revealed this to them.

> Ilyas looked on Bhola and me like older brothers and we too loved him like a younger brother. In 1918, towards the end of August or the beginning of September, when the Turks were in a much-weakened state, Ilyas came to us one night. At the time Phoni, Bhola and I were living in one room ... Ilyas and Yakob were living a little distance away. What he whispered, after waking us, was this:
>
> For a few days [the Armenian mohajers] had been conferring in secret on matters such as how best they might escape to places that were now under Russian or British control. It seemed that they had not included Yakob in all this, perhaps because those who were planning to escape were all residents of Erzurum and its surrounding areas. Yakob's home was much further south.
>
> Now their destination had been decided on—where it was Ilyas did not yet know. They would flee that night; horses had been arranged. He had come to take his leave of us. Whatever warm clothing we had between us we gathered and gave to Ilyas—the poor fellow had hardly any clothes.
>
> He held me tight! None of us could say a word; nor was there any need for anything to be said.

> In the dead of night Ilyas left. We never saw him again.
>
> Did he manage to reach home? Did he find his mother and his sister? (177-78)

Here Sisir quotes a line from a poem by Tagore: *'Those who lose everything gain the whole world.'* (178)[28]

Ilyas and his fate weighed heavily on Sisir for a long time. Later in the book, he writes:

> I still think of [Ilyas]. A boy of fourteen or fifteen; a really good fellow. Did he manage to get back to Erzurum in the end? Or did he die on the way? What happened to his mother and sister? It's not that these questions arise only in relation to Ilyas, thousands of Armenian families are dealing with this. (189)[29]

In early October, the situation in the camps suddenly changed. Sisir was told that the hospital was to be shut down at once and all the patients were to be discharged. This had a dramatic impact on the mohajers. Sisir records:

> The Armenian women began to weep. For so long they had been sheltered by the Germans—it was like being in the lee of a mountain; the Turks couldn't do anything to them. Now they were afraid that as soon as the Germans left, they would be slaughtered; this time even the women wouldn't be spared.
>
> Every day Yakob would come to us, lamenting and crying; he would say that he was trapped while Ilyas had got away in time. (But did he get home? Poor Ilyas!) [But] we didn't worry so much about Yakob, he was a clever fellow, tricky one might even say. (190)

Within a few weeks, things came to a head. 'Everything's in an uproar!' writes Sisir.

> [Only] the Turkish soldiers seem to be indifferent; secretly they must be glad it's over. When the fighting's over they'll heave a sigh of relief. It's the Germans who are the most fearful; they're worried that they'll get stuck in Turkey and fall prisoner to the British. But the greatest terror is amongst the poor Armenians. Old Mary, Dudu, Haiganoush and Jarohi—all of them are crying out loud, asking: 'What will happen to us now?' Amongst them Dudu speaks some English. She has a boy of six or seven, and to please the Germans she had named him William. She's a clever woman, with an eye to the main chance. Now maybe she will change the name.
>
> Most of [the mohajers] are from Diyarbakır, Urfa, Siwas, Kaisariya, Maras, and Aindhab or Mardin. Later they had begun to come from Van and Bitlis. (191)

Soon after this, the Germans decamped. The POWs and Armenian refugees were left to subsist on the hospital's remaining stores of food. (191) The British were known to be advancing northwards but there was still no sign of them. This created great confusion.

'We run into our Armenian colleagues every day,' writes Sisir. 'They're in despair. But what can we do for them? If the British arrive soon, they'll be safe.' (193)

At the beginning of November 1918, Sisir writes:

> I'm overjoyed at the thought of going back home, but at the same time I am despondent at the thought of the [Armenian] mohajers and their fate. We've worked together for so many days; we've shared sorrow and joy. They have become like our

> own. I wonder, even if the Turks don't kill them, what will they find when they reach home? Who will they return to? Who knows if they even have any homes left? (194)

On 17 November, the POWs were informed suddenly that a train would come for them that night. Sisir and his companions went to the station well ahead of time because they were concerned about finding a covered wagon. Sisir explains that this was because Turkish trains ran on firewood—there being a shortage of coal in the country—and the engines couldn't work up much steam: 'At the slightest incline the engine would wheeze as if it had run out of breath, and flames would shoot out of the chimney, burning everything nearby.' (198) This was a hazard in an open wagon because cinders and flames would be blown backwards, and would often cause fires. Sisir recounts travelling in an open wagon once with one of the BAC's camp followers, a sweeper by the name of Jumman. A flaming cinder happened to fall on Jumman's turban and flames shot up from it. Between the two of them, they managed to put out the fire, but Jumman said afterwards, 'Lucky that I'm not a Sikh or my hair would have been burnt.'

Sisir and his four friends were lucky to get a covered wagon, and they settled down in it at about nine that night.

> After an hour or so, we heard Yakob's voice whispering to us from the outside. When we went to him he said that we had to make space for him somehow in our wagon. (198) 'Have you gone mad?' we asked. 'How can that be done? To take you into our wagon will be dangerous not just for you but for us too. If the Turks find out they'll give you such a beating that you may die of it; and who knows what will happen to us? There'll probably be a court-martial. We can't do anything like that.' (198-99)

> But Yakob was stubborn, he began to weep. He said the blame would be his alone; if the Turks caught him then there was nothing to be done; he would die anyway if he remained in Nisibeen; if he was going to die then he might as well make an attempt to escape. In the end we let him in. There were only four of us in that wagon—Phoni, Jagdish, Bhola and I. Had there been anyone else we wouldn't have dared.
>
> Although we let him in, we couldn't of course let him sit on a bench where anybody could see him; he had to be hidden. The only hiding place was under the bench. Herein lay the problem. Yakob may have been young, but he had a big belly; it was impossible to get him under the bench. In the end Bhola pressed his belly and somehow shoved him in. Yakob's pants' buttons popped open and his chest and stomach were grazed and bloody. He remained there that whole night and the next day and night as well. After that he got off at a station; he said he would be all right from there on. (199)

On 26 November, Sisir and his comrades reached Tripoli; and on 4 December, they boarded a ship that would take them to Port Said. But before they could embark, there ensued one of the strangest episodes in this story. At the centre of it was one of the BAC's 'camp followers', the sweeper called Jumman. It's best that Sisir tells the story himself:

> When we were marching [northwards] from Mosul, Jumman saw an Armenian child on the banks of a stream near Ras al-'Ain and picked him up. His mother must have died and his father must have been killed ... Jumman took on the responsibility of looking after the boy and named him Babulal. He used to call Jumman 'Baba' [father]. (175)[30]

This story would be hard to believe if it were not confirmed by other sources. E.A. Walker, an English officer, came upon a group of 'Indian sepoy prisoners in a holding camp at Ras-el-Ain' in 1916. He noted in his diary, which is now in the Imperial War Museum, that they 'had with them a "small Armenian boy of about ten or so" who was the sole survivor of thousands of Armenian women and children who had been massacred.'[31]

Sisir notes that Babulal soon began to speak Hindi and that once he was old enough, he began to work as a fifer for the BAC.[32] This was a job that by long tradition of the British Indian Army had been performed by orphaned Eurasian boys—so the tale is not as unlikely as it may sound. But at Tripoli a problem arose:

> Before embarking on the ship to Suez, Jumman was told that he would not be allowed to bring Babulal with him. An Armenian padre came to take Babulal away. But why would Babulal go to him? He made a huge fuss and cried up a storm of tears; and Jumman wept too, holding on to the boy. In the end Jumman was allowed to take Babulal home with him. (175)

Babulal, Jumman, Sisir and their surviving comrades reached India on 8 January 1919.

# ELEVEN

# Of Fanás and Forecastles: The Indian Ocean and Some Lost Languages of the Age of Sail

In the age of the sailing ship, indigenous sailors from the Indian Ocean area—Arabs, Chinese, East Africans, Filipinos, Malays and South Asians—made up the 'lascars'. This truly diverse group gave the world, in the eighteenth and nineteenth centuries, the Laskari language, the language of command on ships, drawn from English, Malay, Hindustani, Chinese, Malayalam and the entire Babel of languages spoken on board. The lives of the lascars should be of more interest today than ever before because they were the first Asians and Africans to participate freely and in substantial numbers in a globalized 'workspace'.

## 1

Bangladeshis, like Armenians and Gujaratis, often tell stories about the unexpected places where their countrymen are to be found. One location I have never heard mentioned, however, is a website maintained for the benefit of the Australian 'family history community': it was there that I came upon the ship's manifest of the *William Stewart*, a 596-ton vessel that arrived in Sydney on 8 November 1854, having made the journey from England to Australia with a crew of forty-four.[1] The ship was captained by one Mr Charles J. Riches and had only a single mate, a Mr Webb of London. Of the others on the list, only a handful (possibly seven or eight) were white sailors; the rest were lascars of various grades.

Who then were these lascars? The brief notations on the list reveal more than might be expected: although most of them were Muslims, there were some Christians and Hindus among them too. The oldest was a man of forty-eight, from Sylhet in what is now Bangladesh, and the youngest was a sixteen-year-old from Madras—but for the most part, these men were in their twenties and thirties, by no means young according to the standards of an age when English and American seamen commonly began their careers in their teens. The seniormost lascar was one Serang Mohammad, a thirty-two-year-old sailor from Bombay; next in seniority were the two tindals, one of whom was from Chittagong and the other from Bamnell, a place that has the distinction of being unknown to Google. For the rest, twelve of the lascars were from what might be called undivided Bengal—places such as Sylhet, Barisal, Noakhali, Calcutta and Howrah; six were from various ports along the east coast of India, including Madras; one of the seacunnies, Roderick by name, was probably a burgher from Colombo; two others were from Goa; two were Malay; two were probably Arab-African; and another two were, in the vocabulary of the time, 'Manila-men', meaning Filipino.

The crew of the *William Stewart* was by no means exceptional in its heterogeneity. The *Tynemouth*, a steamship of 1,228 tons that sailed from Hong Kong to Australia in 1858, had a crew of seventy, of whom thirty-six were white sailors, all English except for four

Germans. The others were lascars of various grades, of whom seven were from Bengal. As for the rest, they were from places too various to list severally: Daman, Cochin, Gorakhpur, Munger, Bencoolen (off Sumatra), Massawah (in East Africa) and so on. On lists like these, the term 'lascar' has so wide an application that we might well wonder where the word came from and what it means. The term appears to be an Anglo-Indian adaptation of the Persian/Urdu 'lashkar'/'lashkari', meaning 'soldier' or 'army'.[2] In passing between languages, the word appears to have taken on the connotation of 'mercenary' or 'hired hand' and was applied in this sense to a certain kind of sailor. The transition seems to have occurred first in Portuguese, in which the words 'laschar'/'lasquarim' have been in circulation since about 1600 CE: as with many other nautical terms, it was probably through a Lusitanian route that it entered English.[3] The nautical usage of the term is, however, distinctively European: in the Indian subcontinent, for example, the word is still generally used to mean 'army' or 'militia'.[4] The extended meaning of 'sailor' would appear to have been introduced to the subcontinent by Europeans; when thus used today, it has a touch of both the exotic and the archaic. In sum, the word 'lascar', as used on the manifest of the *William Stewart*, belongs to two kinds of jargon, the nautical and the colonial, and its meaning is specific to those contexts. What then is this meaning? When placed beside a crew list like that of the *William Stewart*, the *Oxford English Dictionary*'s terse definition ('East Indian sailor') would seem to be no less misleading than that of those well-known nineteenth-century lexicographers Albert Barrère and Charles Leland ('Malay sailor'). In actual use, the term was applied to all indigenous sailors of the Indian Ocean region—'native' would have been the operative category of the time—which is to say that it referred indifferently to Arabs, South Asians, Malays, East Africans, Filipinos and Chinese. That a single word should cast so large a net is puzzling only from a landward and contemporary perspective; for European sailors of an earlier era, the word 'lascar' would have been paired with, and opposed to, another similar term, 'kanaka', which referred to the native seamen of the Pacific.[5] With an ocean as a referent, it is scarcely surprising that both these terms cast their net very wide; scarcely surprising either that both suffered the same fate, drowning under the derogatory racial freightage that came to be loaded upon them.

That lascars were a richly cosmopolitan group is beyond question. Yet no matter whether they were from—South Asia, East Africa, the Arabian coast or the Malay Archipelago—these sailors were lumped together once they stepped on board. Words often create their own reality: it is easy to imagine that living in the cramped bowels of sailing ships, coping with conditions of extreme danger and difficulty, men from every edge of the Indian Ocean came to share in an experience that, although similar to that of sailors everywhere, was different in that it was salted with a particular kind of brine.

## Diversity in Ship Crew

It is common nowadays to hear 'diversity' being spoken of as though it were some thrilling new invention. But it is unlikely that there were ever any more diverse collections of people—albeit only men—than the crews of merchant ships in the age of sail.[6] No one was more keenly aware of this, or represented it to better effect, than Herman Melville, especially in the startling fortieth chapter of *Moby Dick*, where the *Pequod*'s crew begin to sing in a great outpouring of tongues and it becomes apparent that this small Nantucket whaling ship is a floating Babel, with sailors from Holland, France, Malta, Long Island, the Azores, Tahiti, Sicily, the Isle of Man and China. There is, of course, a token lascar, whose contribution to the merriment consists of: 'By Brahma! boys, it'll be douse sail soon. The sky-born, high-tide Ganges turned to wind! Thou showest thy black brow Seeva!'[7] Nor is this the only Asian on the *Pequod*: Captain Ahab's mysterious company of private harpooners consists, Melville tells us, of Parsees. The unlikeliness of this should cast no doubt either upon Melville's curiosity or his powers of observation—for he was one of the very few nineteenth-century writers who actually took the time to look at the world of the lascars with some attention. In his autobiographical novel, *Redburn*, based on his earliest experiences as a seaman, he writes of a vessel called the *Irrawaddy* that was docked in Liverpool when his own ship arrived there. The *Irrawaddy* was a 'country boat', which was the term commonly applied to ships built in Asia in the Western style. In Liverpool, the *Irrawaddy* and her lascar crew were something of a curiosity.

> Every Sunday, crowds of well-dressed people came down to the dock to see this singular ship … It was amusing … to watch the old women with umbrellas, who stood on the quay staring at the Lascars, even when they desired to be private. These inquisitive old ladies seemed to regard the sailors as a species of wild animal, whom they might gaze at with as much impunity, as at the leopards in the Zoological Gardens.[8]

Melville too was fascinated, and one Sunday, he went aboard the *Irrawaddy* to take a dekko. He found a group of lascars eating on the fo'c'sle deck:

> Among them were Malays, Mahrattas, Burmese, Siamese, and Cinghalese. They were seated around 'kids' full of rice, from which, according to their invariable custom, they helped themselves with one hand, the other being reserved for quite another purpose. They were chattering like magpies in Hindostanee, but I found that several of them could also speak very good English. They were a small-limbed wiry, tawny set; and I was informed, made excellent seamen.[9]

The chain of command on the *Irrawaddy* was no different from that of any other 'country boat' that made the crossing to England: such vessels might be built in India, they might be owned by Indian merchants, they might be manned entirely by lascars, but their officers were almost always white 'Free Mariners'.[10] The captain of the *Irrawaddy*, accordingly, was an Englishman, as were the three mates, master and bo'sun.

> These officers lived astern in the cabin where every Sunday they read the church of England's prayers, while the heathen at the other end of the ship were left to their false gods and idols. And thus, with Christianity on the quarter-deck, and paganism on the fo'c'sle, the *Irrawaddy* ploughed the sea.[11]

One night, Melville got into a conversation with a lascar who gave his name as 'Dallabdoolmans'. Melville found that he spoke English well and was quite communicative, 'like most smokers'. He wrote:

> It is a Godsend to fall in with a fellow like this. He knows things you never dreamed of; his experiences are like a man from the moon—wholly strange, a new revelation. If you want to learn romance ... take a stroll along the docks of a great commercial port. Ten to one, you will encounter Crusoe himself among the crowds of mariners from all parts of the globe.[12]

Melville wrote *Redburn* from memory when his first voyage was long in the past, but his visit to the *Irrawaddy* clearly made a powerful impression, for more than a decade later, he was able to recall Hindustani/Bengali words, such as 'sagoon', 'teak'. He probably got the lascar's name wrong, but the fact that he went to the trouble of recalling it is still of enormous significance—for in the annals of nineteenth-century nautical writing, the lascar, when he appears at all, is almost always a figure unnamed. Melville's account is almost unique in this regard, and his memory was perhaps not entirely to blame for the mangling of Dallabdoolmans' name. It is easy to imagine that a nosy young writer who inquired after the name of an Asian or African transient in today's Europe would be given a similarly misleading answer. Lascars like Dallabdoolmans were probably wary of making themselves conspicuous, and this may be one reason why the names recorded on nineteenth-century ships' manifests seem too sketchy to be real markers of personhood. For it is a fact that when a lascar stands out from the generality of his brethren in the historical record, it is almost always because he is the subject of some kind of legal or disciplinary action. Thus, for example, we have the case of Abdul Rhyme in 1649, a lascar who was convicted while at sea for having sex with a fellow member of his crew, a sixteen-year-old Londoner by the name of John Durrant. Several witnesses testified that the relationship was consensual, but in the eyes of the ship's captain, this served only to deepen the gravity of the offence, since it implied that the English boy had willingly entered into a liaison with a 'Hindoosthan peon'. The accused were both sentenced to forty lashes, and it was specified that their wounds were to be rubbed with salt.[13] Or there is the 1814 case in which a lascar was whipped to within an inch of his life in East London: the incident caught the attention of a magistrate and became something of a scandal. The lascar in question had been whipped by none other than his own serang, who, on being arraigned, offered the defence that he was merely applying the custom of his trade, with the consent of his employers, the East India Company.[14]

## Forerunners of Today's Migrants

Like many paperless migrants in the West today, lascars were probably suspicious of public scrutiny, so it behoves us to note that theirs is not the least of the many curtains of silence that we seek to pierce when we inquire into their lives. The truth is that their lives are of more interest today than ever before—for the very good reason that they were possibly the first Asians and Africans to participate freely, and in substantial numbers, in a globalized workspace. They were among the first to travel extensively; the first to participate in industrial processes of work; the first to create settlements in Europe; the first to adapt to clock-bound rhythms of work-time (the shipboard regime of four-hour work-shifts, or watches, was one of the most exacting disciplinary regimes ever invented); and the first to be familiar with emergent technologies (nautical engineering itself being one of the pioneering technologies of the industrial age). Not least, the lascars were among the first Asians to acquire a familiarity with colloquial (as opposed to book-learnt) European languages. They were thus in every sense the forerunners of today's migratory computer technicians, nurses, high-tech workers and so on. Indeed, they encountered many of the same problems that contemporary Asian and African workers face, with their Western counterparts doing everything possible to limit their access to the most profitable labour markets. The British Navigation Laws of 1814 and 1823, for example, imposed rigid restrictions on the employment of lascars and played no small part in crippling the Indian shipping industry, which had shown itself to be fully capable of competing with its British counterpart.[15]

Today, thanks to the work of pioneering scholars like Isaac Land, Rozina Visram and Michael Fisher, a great deal more is known about lascars than was the case even ten years ago.[16] We know, for instance, that lascars were a substantial presence in London even in the seventeenth century, and possibly even earlier; we know that they could, by law, be paid a fraction of a white sailor's wage and that to hire them was an easy way to expand profit margins. We know that in many Asian ports, well-organized chain gangs recruited sailors through such methods as kidnapping and debt bondage. We know that contractors would sometimes sell their kinsmen's children into virtual servitude, and that often, on reaching their destination, unscrupulous shipmasters would abandon these young men and boys on the streets of London and Glasgow.

Yet it remains true that much of what is known about lascars pertains to the shore; about their life at sea, we know very little. How, for example, in the Babel of tongues that was a lascar-manned sailing ship, did people communicate? Or, to put it differently, how could they afford not to?

## 2

The sailing ship is perhaps the most beautiful, most environmentally benign machine the world has ever known. But what really sets it apart from other machines is that its functioning is critically dependent on language: underlying the intricate web of its rigging is an unseen net of words, without which the articulation of the whole would not be possible. To work a sailing ship efficiently, dozens of men must respond simultaneously to a single command; failure to do so could mean the difference between tacking a vessel neatly and tipping her over on her beam ends. But to learn a series of commands is not enough: on a sailing ship, as in a language, verbs need nouns to create meaning. And in one of its aspects, a sailing ship is precisely a vast, floating lexicon, with thousands of named parts—not just every rope, but every gasket, leech and pin has its own name. This is why the technology of sail generated a shipload of lexicographers: from the sixteenth century onwards, most maritime nations in Europe needed dictionaries of sail, many of which were enormous compilations, hundreds of pages in length. It is one such that provides us with a refracted glimpse of the rigging of words that underlay the ropes of lascar-manned vessels.[17] This is Lieutenant Thomas Roebuck's *An English and Hindoostanee Naval Dictionary*, first published in Calcutta in

1811. Born in 1781, Roebuck was a skilled linguist, who had served a rigorous apprenticeship under the famous John Borthwick Gilchrist, author of the first major Hindi–English dictionary. From 1806 to 1809, Roebuck was in Edinburgh, assisting Gilchrist to prepare his lexicon. After that, while travelling to Calcutta on the Hon'ble Company Ship *Larkins*, Roebuck passed his time by compiling his *Naval Dictionary* with the help of the ship's serang, a man called Ulee from Kachh (Kutch). Roebuck found Ulee to be a 'most intelligent man', extremely 'willing and active', but on arriving in Calcutta, he took the precaution of cross-checking his entries with three other serangs, Shekh Duolut of 'Chutganw' (Chittagong in today's Bangladesh), Shekh Mohummud from 'Koolabu' (possibly Colaba, which was then an island adjacent to Bombay) and Yoosoof Surhung from 'G,hog,ha' (probably the coastal town of Ghogha in Bhavnagar district in Gujarat).

Roebuck did not long survive the publication of his dictionary, dying of a fever in Calcutta at the age of thirty-eight. But he did live to see the proof of his work's usefulness, for in 1813, two years after its first publication, his dictionary was reprinted by the East India Company's booksellers in London. In 1882, it was revised and reissued by a missionary called George Small, under the title *A Laskari Dictionary or Anglo-Indian Vocabulary of Nautical Terms and Phrases in English and Hindustani.*[18] Under that name, it continued to circulate well into the twentieth century.

## Word List to Dictionary

Thus, it took only seventy years for a word list of technical terms to evolve into a dictionary for a named language. The evolution of Laskari was undoubtedly speeded by the rapid expansion of shipping in the nineteenth century, but the dialect was already centuries old by the time Roebuck compiled his dictionary. The clearest proof of this lies in its contents, a large number of which are derived from Portuguese.

Indeed, Laskari was probably the conduit for the introduction of many of the most widely used Portuguese-derived words in India. Consider the word 'balti', for instance; derived from the Portuguese 'balde', it probably referred originally to a ship's buckets: today, no Indian household is without a complement of tin or plastic baltis, just as no English town is without its supply of 'balti chicken'. Similarly, the word 'kamra', derived from the Portuguese 'camara', which is today used to mean 'room' in many Indian languages, almost certainly came from the Laskari use of it to mean 'cabin'. The antiquity of Portuguese influence is evident also from the frequency with which Laskari resorts to it in naming the basic anatomy of the ship: the Laskari for cutwater, for example, is 'tâliyâmâr', from Portuguese 'talhamar', and the word 'trikat', meaning 'fore', as in 'fore-mast', comes from the Portuguese 'traquete'.

For the rest, much of the ship's taxonomy comes from Hindustani and other Indian languages: thus, a deck is a 'tootuk', a mast is a 'dol' and a sail is a 'serh' or 'pal'. Some of these terms have a rustic directness: the truck, or seal of the mast, becomes, for example, a 'laddu'. These terms in turn enter ever-more specific and complicated combinations with other linguistic influences to describe the many parts of the vessel. The Laskari term for fore-top sail, for instance, is constructed by joining 'trikat', 'gâvî' and 'serh', to form 'trikat-gâvî-serh' (or simply 'trikatgâvî'); similarly the fore-t'gallant sail is the 'trikat sabar'; the fore-royal, the 'trikat tabar'; the fore-topmast-staysail, the 'trikat-gavi-sawai'; and the fore-t'gallant-stu'nsail is the 'trikatsabar-dastur'. And so on.

English, however, was the principal resource that Laskari drew upon in describing a ship: thus, a hawser becomes a 'hansil' in Laskari; a jack block becomes a 'jugboolak'; a martingale becomes a 'mâtanghai'; and the cable known as the messenger becomes a 'masindar'. In this process of naming, languages often met and married with curious and picturesque results. On many sailing ships, at the intersections of some of the masts and yards, there were small ledges that provided sailors temporary refuge from the harassment and surveillance of their superiors: there they were wont to spend their leisure time, smoking, gossiping and telling tales. In English, these intersections were called 'cross-trees': Laskari took some of these syllables and turned them into 'kursi', a homonym for the commonly used Arabic-derived Hindustani word for 'chair'. No doubt that was exactly the purpose served by this happy intersection of spar and mast. The words for the complex set of lateral masts that project forward from a ship's bow—the jib, jib boom, etc.—also produced interesting intersections of language. The spar that sprouted from the head of the ship became a 'jîb', which means 'tongue' in some Indian languages; from a crossing of Arabic, English and Hindustani came the word for flying jib, 'fulâna jîb', which might be translated as the 'anyone tongue', and the outermost part of the jib boom, where many a lascar lost his life, was the 'shaitân jîb', or the 'Devil's tongue'.

As befits a language that was used by such a richly varied assortment of people, Laskari was profoundly eclectic in its influences. Consider the names for its ranks: 'serang', the most senior, is thought to be derived from Malay; the next, 'tindal', from Malayalam; the word for helmsman, 'sukkânî' (rendered in English as 'seacunny'), comes from the Arabic for rudder (sukkân); the word for steward, 'ishtor', was an obvious adaptation of the English; and 'kussab', a lower rank, may have come from Persian. However, no one seems to know the derivation of the word for sweeper—'topas/topaz'; and one of the most interesting of these words does not actually find a place in Roebuck's dictionary: it is the word 'arkati', meaning 'pilot', which is thought to be derived from the state of Arcot, near Madras, the nawab of which once had in his employ all the pilots in the Bay of Bengal.[19] The Laskari word for 'mate'—and officers generally—is 'malum', from the Arabic 'mu'allim', or 'knowledgeable'. But how were the first and second mates distinguished from each other: Were they 'burra' and 'chhota', or 'pehla' and 'doosra'? Roebuck provides us with no clue.

Directional words are possibly the most frequently used terms on a ship, and the most basic of these are 'for'ard' and 'aft'. The Laskari equivalents of these, according to Roebuck, were 'âgil' and 'pîchhil'. To anyone familiar with Hindi/Urdu, these would appear to be mishearings of the words 'âgey' and 'pîchhey'. But no: Roebuck assures us that this is how the words were pronounced by lascars, and he was certainly in a position to know. Two other directional terms, 'starboard' and 'larboard', became, in Laskari, 'jamnâ burdu' and 'dâwâ burdu', or simply 'jamnâ' and 'dâwâ'.

Anyone who has spent any time with sailors and boatmen in Asia will know that they do not conceive of their vessels as inanimate objects: from Roebuck's dictionary, it would seem lascars, similarly, figured their vessels as living things. The most striking example of this is the Laskari word for the kamra known as the fo'c'sle. The English word comes, as the spelling indicates, from 'forecastle' and dates back to an era when there was indeed a castellated fortification at the head of every ship. But in time, the word came to refer to the farthest forward of all the vessel's kamras, which consisted of a shallow, curved space between the bows. Being right above the taliyâmar, this was the dampest, most uncomfortable part of the ship, and so naturally it was where the lowliest seamen were lodged. To be a fo'c'sleman, in English, meant much the same as shipping out 'before the mast'—it was to be a scrub, a Jack, a Tar, a lascar. But the Laskari language, through an odd conceit, lends this crowded, cramped, foul-smelling kamra a small touch of poetry. The lascars' word for it was 'faná', or hood, as in the flared head of a cobra—and, of course, if a ship were to be thought of as a creature of the sea, then this would be exactly the part of its anatomy to which the location of the faná would correspond. Similarly, the word for the yard—the spar from which a sail hangs—is 'purwan'. Roebuck writes of this: 'Purwan,

I think is compounded of Pur, a wing, or feather, and Wan, a ship, which last word is much used by the lascars from Durat (properly Soorut), etc., so that Purwan, the yards of the ship, might also be translated (as) the wings upon which the ship flies.' If a ship was a living thing for lascars, was it always conceived of in the feminine, as was the case with European sailors? It is impossible to know, of course, but I suspect not. The word for 'dismasted', for example, is 'lundbund', which means literally 'phallus-tied' or 'dismembered', a locution that would make sense only if the mast were—at some register of speech—figured as a phallus. Roebuck's own gloss on this is very odd: he speculates that the term 'lundbund' comes from 'nunga-moonunga', meaning 'stark naked', which suggests that he was either overcome by an attack of pre-Victorian prurience or that he did not know what the word 'lund' meant. (This is not impossible, since it is a common Indian trick to persuade foreigners that 'lund' means, variously, a cloth bag, a bedspread, a miniature painting or whatever else it is that a hapless tourist might wish to buy in the bazaar). The word for 'command' in Laskari—which came to be used widely in English too—was 'hookum'. Some of these provide interesting insights into the nature of the relations between lascars and their malums. For example, Roebuck translates the hookum 'Heave and rally!' as 'Hubes, mera bap!' (lit: 'heave, my father') and goes on to add that 'sometimes a little abuse is necessary; as for instance "hubes sâlâ! buhan chod hubes!" (properly "buhin chod hubes") or "hubes huramzadu!"'[20]

## Grammar

So far as the grammar of Laskari is concerned, Roebuck insists that no matter how promiscuous its vocabulary, the language is fundamentally (as every Indian likes to say about their tongue) very 'chaste', insisting that 'there is little difference between the rules of the high or Court Hindoostanee, and the dialect spoken by the Lascars'.[21] In other words, the syntax of Roebuck's Laskari is, or so he claims, that of pure Urdu/Hindustani. This assertion is difficult to accept: If it were true, how could Laskari serve as disparate a group of people as the lascars seem to have been? Is it conceivable that unlettered Malays, Arabs and Africans were fluent in Urdu? Even among South Asian lascars, most were Bengalis, Tamils, Goans, Kachhis, etc., and most were uneducated: it defies credulity that they could speak 'courtly Hindustani'. What is more likely is that Roebuck's Laskari was used only in relation to matters pertaining to the running of the vessel: it was really just a language of command. For the rest, the lascars probably used, among themselves, a series of contact languages and pidgins made up of elements of Swahili, Malay and Hindustani. To communicate with officers and white passengers—and possibly often among themselves as well—they probably used variants of the Sino-Portuguese-English pidgin that came to be associated with the South China Coast. This marvellously expressive dialect once flourished in many corners of the Indian Ocean but, like Laskari, it did not outlast the age of sail.

**3**

What then was the texture of daily life aboard a ship with a large complement of lascars? The library of Western nautical fiction, vast as it is, has little to say on this subject, and the lascars themselves, inveterate storytellers though they are said to have been, were resoundingly silent about their experiences, at least on paper.[22] The passengers who travelled with them, however, were anything but: the length and tedium of long ocean voyages appear to have provided them with not just the time and leisure but also apparently the compulsion to describe in detail everything they saw and experienced. Although many of their diaries and journals survive, few have been published—no doubt because most of them are just as tedious as the voyages they write about. But there are some exceptions. One such is the *Journal of a Voyage from Gravesend to Calcutta by a Cadet in 1825* by Robert Ramsay, the manuscript of which lies in the collections of the National Maritime Museum at Greenwich in England.[23] Ramsay was a very young man when he travelled to Calcutta in 1825 on the *Lady Campbell*. His journal does not make for easy reading—his handwriting, terrible to start with, worsened considerably in bad weather—but he was an uncommonly good diarist.

Ramsay's diary tells us that the *Lady Campbell* had seventy-four lascars on board, and this company is presently revealed to consist of an assortment of Africans, South Asians, Malays and Chinese. Although Ramsay does not say so, it seems likely that these men had embarked on the *Lady Campbell* not as part of her crew but as paying passengers—this being necessary because of the legal restrictions on the employment of lascars. Yet it is clear from Ramsay's journal that, paying passengers or not, the lascars were still expected to work—and this might well have been the cause of bitter resentment on their part. In any event, there was trouble from the start. This is how Ramsay describes their embarkation on 3 January 1825 from Gravesend:

> The lascars came from two different vessels; and have therefore two Serangs; one company consists of 60, the other of about 12:—the Serang (or bo'sun) of the 60 having ordered one of his men to work, on the man's refusing, struck him. The man resented it, and a contest ensued; the 1st Mate gave the Serang a rope's end and desired him to beat the man which was done, the Serang beating him over the head & face; the man caught the Serang by the hair, which was coiled up on his head, and pulled him by it, the other Lascars looking on and talking very fast in their tongue;—Mr Murphy [the mate] called the

Serang, the Tindal (bo'sun's mate) and some more Lascars to the quarter-deck and asked the Tindal why he did not assist the Serang as was his duty;—the Tindal replied it was not his business, that the Serang was in the wrong; and that he was not a countryman of the Serangs; (the Tindal was a gloomy, sulky, strong, determined looking Malay); Mr Murphy told him if ever the Serang was insulted again and he (the Tindal) did not assist the Serang he should be flogged; and told the Serang to acquaint him (Mr Murphy) if he did not; the Serang replied the Tindal was as bad as the man; they were ordered forward when in a little the Serang & Tindal were at very high words; Mr Murphy came and ordered the Tindal on the Poop;—the latter refused; force was tried without effect; at last two sailors were ordered to take him; the blacks supported the Tindal and a scuffle ensued; but the sailors fists soon cleared the way and the Tindal was dragged to the Poop by the bo'sun, like a bundle of rags; the Armourer was sent for and the Tindal remained in irons on the Poop till dinner-time:—the Lascars were then all ordered below and threatened:—during the scuffle a black woman, Squinting Nancy, a passenger, having come to England as a Nurse, threw a large piece of iron in the direction of the Men! but falling short it hurt none:—what an Amazon!:—in the afternoon Mr Murphy sent for her and told her if she ever did that again she would be put in irons like the Tindal; she denied having thrown the iron and set up a pretty chattering:—another black woman joined today;—when it is cold the English sailors work to warm themselves, but the Lascars cannot work for the cold, in a warm climate this will be reversed; a Lascar who has been in England only eight days has lost the use of his feet from the cold.

There was more trouble the next day: 'A Lascar having struck the Serang was placed on the Poop; another Lascar with a bayonet in his hands placed sentinel over the culprit ...' On 5 January, yet another lascar was in trouble, being 'put on the Poop before Breakfast for stealing tobacco from one of his neighbours'. Once at sea, the relations between the lascars and the others degenerated still further, leading to some oddly farcical confrontations on matters ranging from the serving of grog to personal hygiene. At noon on 20 January,

> the Lascars were ordered to bring their beds on deck; on their refusing, Mr Murphy ordered three of the hammocks to be cut down for that purpose; this raised a great irritation among the Lascars, and the African (to whom I gave my old black waistcoat on Wednesday) even threatened Mr Murphy:—The African was ordered on the Poop but he refused to go, and when it was attempted to take him the Lascars came to his assistance;—after a considerable scuffle the African, an old surly Arab and two other ringleaders were put in irons, chiefly by the officers; the African and another were quite furious, vowing deadly revenge against the Second Captain:—I had never seen the blacks turn out in such numbers before; there was a dense crowd on the lee side, from the Poop to the forecastle; pre-eminent above the rest was the Lascar cook,—as black as ever demon was pictured—entirely naked, except a dirty rag about his waist;—and with a long charcoal stick in both hands;—several others had pieces of wood; nothing but the bayonets would set them forward, and a sepoy had a jag from one;—some of the Cadets who were below came up in a great hurry when the musquets and bayonets were called for; Mr Moore brought up his regimental sword, scabbard and all;—Mr Corfield a cutlass;—others bayonets and Mr Burroughs brought up and flourished his walking cane, which he said was quite sufficient for these fellows;—as for myself, I stood all the time on the Poop, peeling an orange;—the

butcher was rubbing the sick dogs all the time with the greatest sang-froid, merely saying when any of the Lascars came too near him 'Get out of the road you d-d rascal';—at sunset the prisoners were taken down and ironed below; a watch was put over them and the ladies, especially Mrs R was much afraid; the Butler was much offended at Mrs Clayhill's speaking to him about the offensive smell he had from the Garlic he eats, and was appeased with much difficulty …

The next day, 21 January:

Shortly after breakfast all hands were mustered on the quarter-deck, the Europeans on one side and the Lascars on the other; the prisoners were brought up and everything being arranged the captain began by stating his firm opinion that this disturbance among the Lascars was chiefly owing to dissatisfaction among the European sailors; that first the Bo'sun's and then the other Messes began to refuse their grog, for what reason they know best, and yesterday when the Lascars resisted the officers of the ship, with sticks in their hands, not above three sailors came to the officers' assistance, but stood looking on, on the forecastle;—that there was not a more easily managed people in the world than Lascars, and that even if he had given the seacunnies grog (a thing never done before), if that was any object;—that in future he should no more trouble himself whether the Lascars assisted in navigating the vessel or no;—during this harangue the Captain was repeatedly interrupted by a sailor with a broken nose called Nells, who said he was the first that refused grog & he then addressed the Serang on refusing to bring up his bedding, and his allowing his men to resist the officers taking a man aft who had even threatened the 1st Mate; that he would now make an example of these four men and if ever a Lascar lifted, or threatened to lift, a stick to any officer he should be shot whatever should be the consequence, and that he (the Serang) should not leave the vessel till his conduct was inquired into by justice; the Capn then repeated to the African the expressions he had used to Mr M and descanted on the heinousness of his crime as intelligibly as possible; then turning to the Lascars he shewed them the sticks they had used, and threatened summary punishment to whoever should shew the least disaffection in future; the African was then tied up and his shoulder bared, rather against his will, and the gunner stood all ready with the Cat in his hands; in the mean time both Serangs begged for the criminals release, and the Capn at last yielded, or seemed to yield to their solicitations, on condition that if any Lascar behaved in such a manner again, both Serangs and Tindals should be flogged as well as the culprit;—when the African was to all appearances just about to be flogged, half of the Lascars went away to the forecastle rather than see his punishment;—the almost naked cook made a prominent figure again amongst the motley group; his looks were as scowling as ever and altogher he was a perfect representation of the D_l without wings;—the other Lascars seemed quite submissive when all were assembled & the Capn was just about to speak a pistol was heard to go off in Mr M's cabin; a servant had been loading it when it accidentally went off close to Mr Strathfield; the ball hit the roof and retorted back on Mrs S; on the report of the pistol the greatest anxiety was depicted on the face of the Lascars; plenty of arms had been taken out of the arms chest in case of necessity, but none were brought on deck; when the prisoners were released the Lascars went about their duties with the greatest alacrity ... When the men were called out to set the fore stun'sail yesterday afternoon, the Lascars refused to come

> up; Mr Murphy went down and told them if they did not work we should never arrive at Calcutta; 'Ah,' says they, 'when we get to Calcutta, we will take you to the Police.'

Despite the mutual contempt and hostility, tensions on the *Lady Campbell* remained within the bounds of what might have been described in the English of the day as a banyan-fight (a 'tongue-tempest' that 'never rises to blows or bloodshed').[24] The vessel made steady progress, and even when the weather turned foul, as it did on 17 April, the passengers were not denied the comforts of the table.

> Last night rolling exceeded all we had met with off the Bay of Biscay; in our Cabins everything broke adrift and floated about in the water which came plentifully down the hatchways. The thumping of our cots against the trunks or sides of the cabins prevented our having much sleep. Mr C's bottles of lime-juice, lavendar water & c were found lying on the floors without their necks. The close smell below was excessive and all forenoon the foul air could be seen rising through the hatches as if it was steam from a boiler. The Cutter was nearly lost in the night from one of the davids [davits] or large pieces of wood which support it giving way.—The day was as bad as the night.—endeavouring to keep in a sitting posture afforded excellent exercise. The milkman fell and emptied the contents of his pitcher over himself,—a sudden lurch placed Mrs H on her posterior close to the Lee Scuttle while coming to dinner, and last tho not least, while endeavouring to arrange my cabin I was pitched on one of my trunks and was glad to get off with a cut under one of my eyes. The scenes at the cuddy table baffle my powers of description:—'eat and drink while you can', is the only way to get on; to have one hand at liberty for a whole minute was a rare occurrence. Legs of mutton, pork,

> hams, potatoes etc had no idea of remaining on their dishes:—the table-cloth was died with soup, butter, mustard, wine, beer & c. and the clothes of many shared the same fate:—the chairs were very fond of skating, making their owners measure their length upon the floor; Mr C split Dr H's door with his head … It is extraordinary how the cook managed to dress the dinner in such stormy weather; there is the same variety of dishes, tarts etc as at other times; a little delay being the only difference. The present cook is a China-man who got into the ship among the Lascars; he soon became an assitant in the galley and was found to be a most expert hand, so much so as to excite the envy of his superior …

On occasion, the passengers amused themselves with games and other diversions. Ramsay remarks of one such: '… after dinner there was a game of Leap-Frog, the Lascars seemed highly amused with it …' Later Ramsay describes a theatrical evening, performed, or so the passengers believed, in the privacy of an awning on the quarterdeck. Amongst the various skits that were staged there was one of a 'drunken Blackey'. During the performance of this piece, Ramsay happened to look up: he found that many lascars were watching the skit from up above, their faces framed by rents in the awning.

And so they went their ways, lascars and live cargo, each watching the other's enactments through tiny cracks in their wooden world.

(First published in *Economic and Political Weekly*, vol. 43, no. 25. An earlier version of this article was the keynote lecture for 'Eyes Across the Water: Navigating the Indian Ocean', a conference sponsored by the South Africa/India Research Thrust at the University of the Witwatersrand, Johannesburg, South Africa, in August 2007.)

# TWELVE

# Wordless Pasts: The Indian Exodus from Burma and the Writing of *The Glass Palace*

As a novelist, history is, for me, one of the limiting conditions of the imagination. What I mean by this is that history is of interest to me in that it creates unique predicaments for human beings—characters, in other words—but it cannot carry a novel on its own; only characters can: in this, a historical novel is no different from any other kind of fiction. Yet it is also true that characters cannot be realized outside the circumstances they live in, and since it is history that creates those circumstances, it is an essential aspect of the realization of character.

Let me cite an example: In 1941, in Malaya, Indian soldiers of the British colonial army found themselves in a predicament—fighting a war for freedom on behalf of an empire that held their country in subjection. Their condition was not without analogy: the

Greeks in the Ottoman Army, the Serbs in the Austro-Hungarian Army and many others have had to deal with a similar dilemma. Yet the conditions of the Indian soldiers in Malaya were different in ways that came to be realized only within the actual moment that framed their actions. This moment was constituted not just by their ties and loyalties but also by such specificities as the terrain they found themselves in, the food they were served and, indeed, even the weather. To my mind, as a novelist, my duty to history lies in a commitment to reproducing those elements of the past that create the environment of a character's predicament. But to know everything about a predicament is still to know nothing at all about how any human being may respond. It is in this sense that I find history to be a limiting condition of the imagination. Yet it is a condition that demands a certain scrupulousness, not merely for ethical reasons but also because of the simple fact that the predicaments of history, when carefully retrieved, are usually of far greater interest than any that a novelist could imagine unassisted.

But there arises here a question that I, as an Indian, have frequently been forced to confront. How does a novelist write of the past when the predicament of his characters is shaped precisely by a willed wordlessness, an intentional silence, a refusal, or inability, to acknowledge the legitimacy of an overarching narrative? This is a question that is forced upon us by the history of colonial India—indeed, by all colonial histories, replete as they are with examples of events that occur as symptoms of unknown motives and unspoken intentions. In northern India in 1857, what precisely was the thinking behind the passing of chapattis from village to village? Who set the movement in motion and why? What was the meaning of this strange connubium? It is no accident that we still do not know the answers to these questions. We are not meant to know; those who circulated the chapattis did not want us to know, and they succeeded in their intention. Perhaps they intuitively realized that knowledge is inseparable from conquest and, therefore, to challenge their conquerors was also to refuse to translate their intentions into the language of instrumental means and ends. For a novelist, this circumstance creates a specific challenge: How do you recreate in words the predicament of an intentional silence?

In posing this question rhetorically, I run the risk of suggesting that I have an answer. I do not. Nor, as a novelist, am I ultimately required to provide one; as I see it, I am required only to present the story as best as I can, leaving it to readers to draw their own conclusions.

The following is one such story. Its background consists of an event that was described by the British historian Hugh Tinker as 'A Forgotten Long March'. In 1941, when the Second World War spread to Asia, Rangoon was predominantly an 'Indian' city, in that the majority of its population consisted of people of subcontinental origin or descent. According to the 1931 census, there were slightly more than 1 million Indians in Burma at the time; of these, some 60 per cent (617,521) were born in India. The social consequences of Indian migration into Burma are too complex to go into here. Suffice it to say that through the 1920s and '30s, there were powerful currents of hostility towards the Indian presence in Burma: in 1930, bloody anti-Indian riots broke out in Rangoon and many thousands were killed. As a result, there was an increasing nervousness within the Indian population in Burma.

Japan entered the Second World War on 7 December with simultaneous attacks on Pearl Harbour and northern Malaya. On 23 December came the first Japanese air attacks on Rangoon, which created absolute panic in the city. It is important to remember that very few civilians had expected the war to spread to Asia. The survivors I spoke to were almost unanimous on this. The attitude is hard to account for, because in military circles, Indian as well as British, it was well-known that the Japanese were preparing for war. Similarly, British municipal authorities had made preparations for air raids: trenches had been dug and an Air Raid Precautions authority, modelled on similar bodies in London, was set up in Rangoon and other cities. Yet, psychologically, the civilian population of the British territories in Asia appears to have been completely unprepared for the catastrophe that lay ahead. I have in my possession several accounts of how people stood on the streets of Rangoon, staring as the first Japanese planes swooped down on their bombing runs. It was as though they could not believe that the war would come to them; in their own eyes, they were simply not important enough to become a battleground for history. Their role was to serve as an audience.

In thinking and writing about this period, I have frequently asked myself why this was so. I don't know if there will ever be a satisfactory answer to this—certainly, if there is, I don't claim to know it—but it seems to me that this attitude is illustrative of a particular aspect of the psychology of colonial rule: one in which the political disempowerment of a population creates a distancing from immediate events, even where they constitute a clear and present danger. Possibly, for Indians as well as many Southeast Asians, a century of Pax Britannica had removed all memory of war and civil uncertainty. I do not mean to say that there were no conflicts in this period, for there certainly were. Yet British imperial success was due in no small measure to the fact that the spheres of the civil and military were kept strictly segregated. Soldiers came from certain castes and groups, and over time, through careful administrative policies, they were segregated from society at large. They lived in cantonments, and when they were seen in public, it was always from a great distance—a distance underscored by the racial and other mythologies with which the business of soldiering was surrounded. When Indian soldiers were sent to war, the rest of the nation rarely saw any of the consequences: there were no body bags, literally or metaphorically, and such consequences as there were were felt only within those villages and districts from which the soldiers had been recruited. Even though Indian soldiers fought in every important conflict of the late nineteenth and early twentieth centuries—the Boxer Rebellion, the Boer War, the First World War, a succession of Mesopotamian campaigns, etc.—their compatriots were never anything other than distant spectators in relation to these conflicts. They had no say whatsoever in matters of recruitment or deployment: in other words, they had absolutely no control over how their countrymen were used. What can we make of this? On the one hand, it was surely a good thing that civilians were spared the spectacle of violence, and it is certainly true that this was a luxury the empire amply afforded its Indian subjects. Yet it is also true that if a society is ignorant of the consequences of conflict, then it runs the risk of forgetting that conflicts do have consequences. Those who forget this are inevitably forced to relearn it in very painful and perhaps tragic ways. Often, looking back on the recent history of the Indian subcontinent—particularly the nuclear situation—it seems to me that this is one of the most implacable of the many ghosts that have haunted the region over these last fifty years.

On 25 December 1941, there was a second Japanese air raid on Rangoon. The air raids, coming in quick succession, created chaos in the city. Once it became evident that the war had indeed arrived upon the city's threshold, there was a rapid breakdown of law and order. Indians, already wary after the riots of the past decade, began to panic. Suddenly thousands of Indians began to move northwards. But without them, the city simply could not function: Indians made up almost the entire working class of Rangoon. The dockworkers were the first to abandon their jobs. This meant that essential supplies could not be unloaded from the ships in the docks. Many of the vessels became sitting targets for Japanese bombers. Indian workers were also responsible for clearing the city's nightsoil; in their absence, there was an immediate breakdown of the city's rudimentary sewage system.

The British did everything they could to discourage the Indian migration. They sealed off some of the exit roads from the city and they sent prominent Indians to cajole the migrants to return, promising them safety in government-organized camps. It was at this point that administrative action made race and class into the determinants of survival. For example, the British issued orders that no adult Indian would be allowed to leave Rangoon by ship as a deck passenger. This effectively trapped the working class in Rangoon, for only the wealthiest Indians could afford to travel other than on deck. Soon even these routes were cut off: the major steamship company British India Steam Navigation Co. confined its allocations mainly to 'Europeans' (the standard euphemism for white people).

In January, it became clear that the Japanese were advancing rapidly and that the British forces would not be able to hold them off. In his memoir, *The Changing of Kings*,[1] Leslie Glass, a British civil servant posted in Rangoon at the time, writes:

> Every Japanese air raid increased the steady stream northwards of the city population, and more and more institutions ground to a standstill. One afternoon, I joined in a bizarre and melancholy foray to shoot all dangerous animals in the zoo, as all their keepers had decamped. Tigers, panthers and poisonous snakes were killed and the deer released in the park, except for one which we shot for fresh meat. When we had gutted the poor beast, we threw its entrails into the lake and great fish thrashed and swirled in the course of their unusual meal. (138)

The British then began preparations for evacuating their government: the civilians were left largely to fend for themselves. Indians began to stream out of Rangoon and central Burma, and soon vast crowds clogged the principal roads. The British government tried valiantly to discourage people from leaving, but the marchers would not be dissuaded. The difference in perception between the British and the Indians on this issue is itself illustrative of the psychology of colonial dependency. The British appear to have been at a loss to understand why the Indians believed themselves to be threatened by the Japanese invasion. As colonial masters, they were perhaps aware that the Japanese would, if anything, go out of their way to court and placate the Indian population, if only to create a springboard for future advances. Yet British wartime propaganda was largely based upon appeals of loyalty to the empire, presumably predicated upon the idea that Indians identified themselves with Britain's interests. Two questions suggest themselves here: Were these appeals for loyalty made, as it were, in bad faith? Or was the internalization of colonialism so advanced among the Indians that they were incapable of perceiving the operation of a racial logic of fealty—one that was evidently acknowledged but unvoiced by British officialdom?

For their part, many Indians saw themselves not as a group separate from the British but also as colonists, extensions of their master's house. Some evidently believed that they would be a hostage population in the hands of the Japanese; others thought the Burmese would turn upon them once the protective hand of the British was removed. As it happened, well over half the Indian population chose to remain in Burma. They were not singled out after the British withdrawal—and were spared the suffering of the exodus. Not the least aspect of the tragedy of this terrible event is that it was largely unnecessary: it was an instance in which a dependent population's sense of identification with its master overrode the colonizers' insistence on separating themselves from their subjects.

In the initial stages, the exodus moved in two directions. The easterly route, over the Arakan Hills into Chittagong, which was used by an estimated 200,000 Indians,[2] was relatively short, though also very dangerous.

The other route lay farther to the north, essentially following the courses of the Irrawaddy and Chindwin rivers, and was several hundred miles long (depending on the starting point). The final crossover into India was through uncharted terrain, over the mountains that separate Manipur from Burma.

Though British planes and boats did stay in operation in northern and central Burma through the first quarter of 1942, they were used mainly for the evacuation of 'European' personnel. There are innumerable stories of how these fleeing officials sometimes used their transportation privileges to carry away pianos and dinner sets, while their subordinates had to make their way on foot, abandoning everything. I also possess many stories, some very touching, of the subterfuges that Indians resorted to in order to avail themselves of 'European' facilities.

In his article 'A Forgotten Long March',[3] Hugh Tinker states that in the early phases of the air evacuation, 'Europeans and Eurasians were in the overwhelming majority'. Then, 'after protest by Indian leaders, the proportions were reviewed'. On 9 May, the air route was shut down altogether—now only the mountain route remained.

Tinker remarks:

> Because the thousands on the march included every section of the Indian community in Burma, one might have supposed that some among them—teachers, writers, social workers perhaps—would have recorded their memories of the experience. Perhaps some did: but it has not been possible to trace any such personal account. For most, it was an experience they wanted to forget: and who anyway was interested in reading their experiences? They were not heroes: either to other Indians or to the Burmese or the British.

Tinker is both right and wrong. He is right in that the great majority of the published accounts of this march were written by Europeans; Indian sources are indeed very hard to come by and I think we need to ask ourselves why this is so. One clear reason is that Indians were largely complicit in viewing themselves as the objects rather than the subject of history. (This itself raises many very important questions:

for example, what are the circumstances in which people assert the right to narration?)

But Tinker is also wrong in asserting that Indian accounts do not exist. Some were written in Indian languages—and evidently Tinker did not have access to them. Equally, many others were preserved in oral narratives. These have, of course, largely perished now because few survivors remain. (This is why it is a matter of great urgency that those who know of any survivors should hasten to write down their accounts.) Some may have been written but not published. We might ask why the writers did not publish their accounts—and here again I think the answer is simply that Indians did not see themselves as 'making history'.

Some other answers to Tinker's question are suggested by the one Indian account that I have managed to find. It was written by a Bengali doctor, Dr Shanti Brata Ghosh, many years after the event—in 1978, to be exact—and was given to me by his daughter, Mrs Ahona Ghosh of Kolkata (no relation).

The narrative is written in English, and the account commences in March 1942.

> I was with the IBP & Co. [Indo-Burma Petroleum] then posted to Indaw, a little oil colony in the wilderness of the Upper Chindwin District of North Burma. The Japanese had already occupied South & Central Burma and were fast advancing towards the North ... In the meantime, I had to consider about safety and departure of my family (wife & 2 kids, 4 & 3 yrs) to avoid a last hour scramble in disorder ... Being under conscription ... I couldn't accompany my family but obtained [leave] permission for 24 hours to arrange and see them off from Mawlaik (IBP HQ approx. 30 miles downriver & across from our own river station at Pantha). Indaw is a further 35 miles to the interior with intervening hills, numerous streams

and dense forests. The transport is normally by pony, elephant or foot, but at this time the first two were not available—having been sold out. Starting early in the morning on foot, with the family and a couple of coolies to carry our 2 suitcases we reached Pantha by evening fall. Here we were informed that neither steam launches nor country boats were available, all having been commandeered by the Govt. as also the services of coolies in general to help evacuation of refugees. Nevertheless, not all villagers had given up their river crafts and in great secrecy a dinghy (canoe) was found and hired out at purchase cost.

We rested at Pantha overnight and started early in the morning on our precarious river-trip minus the 2 coolies. They would rather go their own way than be caught and held by the Govt. for helping in the refugee camps. In March the river flowed smooth and I kept steering as close to the banks as possible though how much it would keep in case of an overturn I did not like to think. However, paddling with the tide and using utmost caution, we reached Mawlaik in approaching dusk (how different from the sophisticated rowing practice we had at the university). The scene at the riverbanks at Mawlaik was bewildering and [it] still gives me the shudder to think of it. The sea of refugees in their thousands appeared to be crawling around like … insects in pain—men, women and children of all ages, some from near, others from far & very far, all collected at the bottleneck in a heterogenous conglomeration with but one object and thought—escape into [the] safety of the soils of India. There was a single steam-launch tied up at its mooring a little away from the jetty. The sight made me feel insignificantly small and nervous but it was a case of 'now or never' as I had to arrange the family's passages on the steamer, find accommodation for the night and get away in the morning to report back for duty. Between us we managed to land on the muddy bank and then on to higher grounds where we were immediately swallowed up by the crowd and became one with them. Inside a vast crowd it is not unusual to lose one's sense of direction and it was after a long and arduous chase that I located the Camp commandant's office. Here, I introduced myself, explained my business and requested for help. The Colonel was much concerned with my plight but regretfully said it would have been so much easier a fortnight ago when a planeload of refugees left by air for the last time. Now he had only a single steamboat, preparing to make its own last trip at dawn, and unfortunately already jam-packed. The Japs, he said, were already up north in a bid to cut the retreat of the British troops and further attempts at evacuation would be extremely hazardous … I insisted that he make some arrangement on this boat for my family, or else it would not be possible in my present mental state to continue to work for the Company—notwithstanding conscription [NB in effect he threatened to desert]. The Colonel thought for a moment, brought out 3 tabs (bamboo shavings cut to size for tickets and coloured for classification), handed them to me and asked me to report at pre-dawn. I was to know the following morning that these were 1st class tickets meant for European families only. After a hurried thanksgiving and goodbye, I made my way to my waiting [family] and precious possessions, clutching at the tabs as though I held the solution to all my problems …

[The next day] Dawn was still a few minutes away when we started for the appointed place. Just as boarding the boat was about to begin Col. Summerville appeared shortly with his staff and the tab holders were asked to embark. It is to be noted that though thousands of the less fortunate would be denied passage in the boat, there was no stampede, no jumping the line but a quiet procession of the tab holders in a most disciplined manner. Were they preoccupied with their own immediate relief, or were they pondering over the fate of the vast majority that were about to be abandoned?

Soon it was our turn to board the boat, and the commandant was good enough to conduct us to the 1st class accommodation where a few European families were already ensconced—possibly overnight. We were introduced and welcomed as co-passengers more likely from a sense of co-sharers of a common misfortune than pure love of an allegedly inferior race …

[The boat was heading upriver and the commandant allowed it to make a stop at Pantha, so that Dr Ghosh could go back to his post. So he stayed with his family for a few more hours.]

We tried to keep up a bold front amongst ourselves lest any sign of weakness or breakdown be transmitted to the dear children and disturb their composure. They had so far behaved admirably though completely flabbergasted by the unusual happenings … Rarely they would look at us with questioning eyes, little knowing that we were to be separated in about a couple of hours which made it more difficult to meet their gaze—leave alone telling them. So we tried to keep our minds off the immediate issue and talked of casual and irrelevant things.

Pantha finally came into view and I felt the most difficult moment had arrived and I was only too eager to get away rather than stand and suffer the suspense. The plank was lowered and after a hurried embrace and kisses I left them with the words: 'Do not be afraid: you are not alone in this, look after the kids and yourself. I shall soon follow you and catch you up in your trek.' Climbing up the steep bank I looked back to wave them

> a final Good Bye but the boat had turned [and] crossed over to midstream.

This was only the beginning of the family's journey—the boat was taking Mrs Ghosh and her children as far as Tamu, the roadhead from which the trek itself would begin. Ahead lay dense malarial jungles and mountains several thousand feet high. Mrs Ghosh would have to confront these obstacles alone with her two children. To make things worse, Mr Ghosh discovered that his wife had been held up at Tamu. Frantic with worry, he finally persuaded his British superior officer to send a telegram to the camp commandant.

> The reply came promptly, saying, 'Mrs Ghosh and 2 children doing well; leaving Tamu immediately.' Later on I would know what had caused their delay at Tamu from my wife.
>
> There were two routes from Tamu—the shorter, cleaner and better managed one was exclusively for the Europeans, and the other, much lengthier, unclean and relatively wearisome for climbing, and overcrowded, for the Asiatics. My wife had differences with the authorities over her preferences for the European route ... She refused to budge unless permitted passage by the shorter route. This privilege was denied her until the telegram by the WM [works manager] had reached and then it was all sweet and prompt. The 3 days delay was certainly worthwhile as the alternative presented hazards of unrelieved crowding, lack of hygienic measures, epidemics, abandonment and not infrequently death from lack of proper medical attention and care.

Dr Ghosh stayed at his post until his company decided to evacuate Indaw because of the Japanese advance. The British were following a 'scorched earth' policy in retreat to deny the Japanese any resources: they were destroying roads, bridges, oilfields, blocking rivers, blowing up food storage facilities, etc. Dr Ghosh's group was told to blow up their oilfield and destroy all equipment, including a water-pumping facility. Naturally there was huge resistance to this from local villagers, and Dr Ghosh found himself having to act as the intermediary. These are his comments on what followed:

> The arguments, points and counter-points went on long, back and forth until the locals finally lost patience and threatened us with extermination even before we could leave Indaw—not to speak of the rebels en route who would be only too glad to deal the final stroke to end the last vestige of [the] white regime from their country. Racial superiority and prestige of the ruling powers are fine, but life is sweeter still. The management submitted to their demands in a gesture of goodwill.

Soon after this, Dr Ghosh left Indaw and started on the homeward journey to India. He mentions that the one valuable possession he took was his radio set. Their group consisted mainly of British company employees. Dr Ghosh and his subordinate, Prakash, were the only Indians, and they were given the job of recruiting coolies, which they did. Dr Ghosh writes:

> Being the only Indian amongst the group [of officers], I often found myself alone and it was possible on that account that I was not meant to share all the discussions that were held … amongst the white group. There was one exception however—the engineer, who was born of British parents, but unfortunately in India—a stigma which was those days looked

down upon by British-born subjects. A sort of rapport had long been established between him and me …

He continues:

It was dark in the jungles under the half moon as we reached Sittaung, an old abandoned oilfield and the starting point of our long march ahead. The camp commdt and other officers, some uniformed, were there to meet us. The WM was the first to get out and immediately entered into what appeared to be an important discussion while we stood a few feet apart. What passed between them couldn't be known, but as the new group left, the WM turned to me and very blithely said (and it still rankles within me), 'Look here, Doc, that's the Indian camp over there (indicating with his big hand) and I think you and your men will be happier there with them. Just find out a "basha" for yourself. We are moving over the bungalow, meet us in the morning around 7 o' clock. Good night.'—curt and dry just like that. With these parting kicks, he turned about and proceeded towards the bungalow with his brother officers, leaving me in a complete daze. The Indian camp as could be made out in the light of the moon was a vast area of jostling crowd[s], men and women engaged in loud talks or arguments, children howling. There was a stench of urine and excreta and pungent smoke rising in the air from hundreds of improvised ovens where each family had cooked its own food. If there was a common kitchen, I did not feel like exploring. We had depended solely on the company's supply of tinned foods. In contrast the bungalow at a little distance away was fully lit and dazzling despite the 'Black out' routine. The treatment meted out to us was shabby, humiliating and offensive, unbecoming of a responsible officer … Prakash and I felt small before our men who no doubt also got the message. We found a basha nearby but after its usage by refugees before us the atmosphere was stifling. We sat out on the river bank but we still had to eat. When at Pantha, someone had joked about carrying my radio set, saying there were hundreds of cars, fridges, radio sets etc. lying abandoned on the wayside because the climb was so arduous that all that a person could carry was his own weight and sometimes even that would be too much … In a depressed mood I parted with my radio—just threw it into the river and followed up with stones to render it unserviceable to anybody. After that there was nothing to do but to wonder where was the food to come from. We had to muster strength for tomorrow's climb, so I asked Prakash if he would be willing to try our luck at the bungalow. He went but soon returned empty-handed and sobbing. He had met the WM in the dining hall, seated at the table with scores of other officers, all Europeans and having their fill of food and drinks. He thought the WM might have been tipsy. He had mentioned my name and stated the purpose of his intrusion. The WM … told him in the hearing of others that the Indians had no taste for tinned foods but there was that big river where fresh fish wouldn't be a difficult catch. Prakash withdrew amidst laughter from other chairs and felt better for the fresh air outside the banquet hall. My head started throbbing with the rank insult and I started along the bank to meet the WM, quite oblivious of consequences. But half way, I discerned in the moonlight somebody coming my way with a big load in his arms. He turned out to be my friend, the India-born engineer … he had brought over … enough food and drinks (beer) for the lot of us and more … It would be difficult to analyze his motives for going out of his way thus to show his

> concern. Was it just plain fellow-feeling in our distress? Was it his antipathy and disdain for those who had refused to look upon him as their equal? Or was it just a case of humanism vs colonialism?
>
> However, we decided we must have our own back, and soon a plan of action was evolved to which all concerned were in agreement. We told our boys that starting from tomorrow, we stop having anything to do with them—[with] the emphasis on luggage lifting. They were to be left to manage their own luggages …
>
> On meeting the [European] group the next morning, we were greeted with 'Hello Doc, good morning, did you have a comfortable night?' 'Good morning, everybody. Yes, we had a very comfortable night with our friends in the Indian camp, thanks to you, but if you are thinking of starting late, we are on our way to join our Indian friends on the march and wish you good luck.' 'But your coolies, where are they? Should have been here by now.' 'I have not the faintest idea, they scattered last night.' Prakash & I left them as they stood in shocked silence and wended our way towards our first big climb. As we gained height, we took a bird's eye-view of the situation below. It was a sweet satisfaction to watch the group as some of them [were] down on their knees, [while] others [were] stooping to their open suitcases, trying to sort out the essential items they would now be carrying themselves. We did not meet them again through the remaining trip.

This account is a striking contrast to British accounts of the same events. To put the matter simply, 'European' accounts of the Long March focus broadly on the challenges posed by the terrain, the incredible physical hardships, the hunger, the disease, the mud and rain, the struggle to stay alive in conditions of unimaginable adversity. They are, in short, narratives of survival. In Dr Ghosh's account, these elements take second place: his narrative is centred on his family and on the question of race. It is curious to think that when he sat down to write about his experiences, some thirty-six years after the event, his most vivid memories were not necessarily those that related to the struggle for survival or hunger or hardship, or even the war itself: what he remembered most clearly were his conflicts with his white colleagues.

I would like to return now to the question I posed earlier: Why are there so few Indian accounts of this great exodus? One possible reason—as suggested by Dr Ghosh's account—is that it is very difficult to write about a wartime circumstance in which your loyalties are not sharply defined: that is to say, when it is not clear that you belong to either of the parties that are at war.

Another difficulty for the Indian participants of the march was that their memories were as much of racial divisions as they were of survival. And this itself may have been the principal reason for their reluctance to tell these stories—because the explicit acknowledgement of race as a governing principle did not come easily to literate and middle-class Indians, most of whom were upper-caste and accustomed to thinking of themselves as belonging to a ruling elite. They were thus in the irreconcilably conflicted position of wanting to claim privileges that they knew would be denied to their less fortunate compatriots. To then find that they themselves had been excluded from the inner circles of the colonial power structure, by reason of not being 'European' (read 'white'), would have come as an epistemic shock that upended their sense of their place in the world. Many who lived through such events would never sufficiently recover their sense of their own historical agency to the point of being able to narrate their experiences. Only a few, like Dr Ghosh, would regain that confidence in one's own sovereignty that makes it possible to think of oneself as a historical protagonist: and when this happened, stories would come pouring out of them like water surging over a crumbling dam. This is what makes Dr Ghosh's diary so poignant: it represents a personal assertion of the freedom that his nation's hard-won independence had bestowed upon him.

(I am deeply grateful to Mrs Ahona Ghosh and Ms Suhana Dipona Basu for sharing Dr Ghosh's diary with me. Thanks are due also to Dr Madhumita Mazumdar for putting me in touch with Mrs Ahona Ghosh.)

# 3

# TRAVEL AND DISCOVERY

Travel has always been an essential part of my work. As I describe in another essay in this collection, 'The Making of *In an Antique Land*', my journey as a writer began in a small village in the Nile delta, in Egypt's Beheira province. It is no coincidence, therefore, that several of the essays in this collection deal with that experience, including the first piece in this section, 'Confessions of a Xenophile'.

From the early 1990s onwards, my interests turned eastwards, in the direction of Cambodia, Burma, China and Indonesia. The writing of the Ibis Trilogy took me to China several times, mainly for research, but my journey to Yunnan, in 2011, with my seventeen-year-old son, was an exception in that it was undertaken purely for pleasure. On rereading the essay that came out of that trip, 'The Mountains Are High and the Emperor Is Far Away', I am still surprised that it was not until I had reached my fifties that it occurred to me—an inveterate traveller—to get on the short flight that connects Kolkata to Kunming. There are few places in the world that are as beautiful and as interesting (and have such exceptionally delicious food) as Yunnan. No one who has ever set eyes on the Tiger Leaping Gorge is likely to forget it; yet very few foreigners venture there, Indians least of all.

Indonesia is another country that I have always found to be of absorbing interest, and so when the Ministry of Education and Culture in Jakarta reached out to me with an offer to organize a tour in any part of the country that I wanted to visit, I accepted without hesitation (I will forever be grateful to John McGlynn, the preeminent translator and publisher of Indonesian literature, for forwarding the invitation).

I had long wanted to see the part of the archipelago that was once known as the Spice Islands or Moluccas (Kepulauan Maluku) because of the pivotal role it had played in the history of the European colonization of Asia. But these islands have never been easy to get to and were also off-limits to foreigners for several years for political reasons.

Fortunately, the ministry not only made it possible for me to travel to Maluku but also sent a large team with me to translate and act as guides (I would like to include here a few special words of thanks for the leader of the team, I Gusti Gede Irawan). The visit was revelatory beyond anything I could have imagined, and it eventually provided the anchoring narrative of my 2021 book *The Nutmeg's Curse*.

# THIRTEEN
## Confessions of a Xenophile

Next to my own country, India, there is no place in the world that has been more important to my development as a writer than Egypt. It is now nearly twenty-eight years since I first landed in Cairo on 19 April 1980: I was then twenty-four years old, and I had come to explore what was to me a new—but not entirely unknown—world. The immediate pretext for my journey was research: a short while earlier, I had won a scholarship that took me from Delhi University to Oxford to study social anthropology. My dream was of writing fiction, but like many an aspiring novelist, I felt I lacked the necessary richness of experience. The writers I admired—V.S. Naipaul, James Baldwin and others—had gone out into the world and watched it go by: I wanted no less for myself. The scholarship was a godsend because it allowed me to choose where I wanted to go, and in my case that was Egypt. Through the good offices of Dr Aly Issa, an eminent anthropologist from Alexandria, I was soon installed in a small village in the Governorate of Beheira, near the town of Damanhour: in my book *In an Antique Land*, I give this village the name 'Lataifa'. My home there consisted of a recently vacated chicken coop on the roof of a mud hut; at the time there was no electricity in the village, although there was, as I recall, a supply of piped water.

Lataifa and I were undeniably a shock to each other. There was the question of language to begin with: I spoke very little Arabic, and what I knew was of a laboriously classical variety. Thus, even simple operations such as asking for water could cause great outbursts of laughter. In the process, however, my hosts and I discovered one medium of communication where we were on equal terms: this was the language of *aflaam al-Hindeyya*—that is to say, Hindi film songs. When all other efforts at communication broke down, we would burst into song—this was no small accomplishment on my part as I am a terrible singer. But many of the younger people in the village sang very well and knew innumerable Hindi songs. Indian filmi music thus became a shared language and opened many barriers and earned me many invitations to meals. The Hindi films that were best known in Lataifa were of the '50s and '60s vintage—films that featured such stars as Raj Kapoor, Nargis, Padmini, Manoj Kumar and Babita. The 'good-hearted vamp' and 'cabaret dancer' Helen was another popular figure. Everyone in the village had a few favourite scenes, and I would often be asked detailed questions about these episodes. This was a great trial to me, as I was by no means an expert on the films of that era. Often children would be called out to perform, which they would do with the greatest gusto. There were even minor specializations, some boys being regarded as particularly good performers of Raj Kapoor numbers, while others were experts in reciting dialogues and soliloquies. The performances were almost always by boys, as I remember, and it was quite the sight to see young jallabeyya-clad fellaheen attempting to imitate the dance numbers of scantily dressed actresses like Helen. Even more astonishing were the recitations, for it would happen sometimes that children would reel off large chunks of Hindi dialogue without knowing a word of the language. Hindi films also provided me with a certain name recognition, for although the megastar Amitabh Bachchan was not as well-known in the Middle East then as he is now, there were plenty of people who knew of him. It was thus not as difficult as it might have been to introduce myself.

Yet while I had reason to be grateful to Hindi films in some respects, there were others in which they made my life exceedingly difficult. One of these was the matter of cows. I must admit that until I went to live in Lataifa, I had no idea that cows played such an important part in Indian films: from the recurrence of this animal in everyday conversation, one might well have imagined that Bollywood is a veterinary enterprise, and that cows, rather than Raj Kapoor and his ilk, were the true stars of Hindi films. Every day, several times daily, I would have to deal with barrages of questions on the matter of cows: Did I worship cows? (*Inta bita'abud bi bagara*? Literally, 'Are you a devotee of the cow?') At what time of day did I conduct my devotions? Could they please witness my prostrations? Was there not a risk of being splattered with dung? Had I ever considered transferring my allegiance to the camel? And so on. Although these interrogations were often wearisome, there was also something touching about the attitudes of my friends. When we were out walking in the fields, they would slow their pace if we passed a cow: it took me a while to understand that they were allowing me time to perform my secret oblations. In the ploughing season, it often happened that we would go past a field where a team of oxen was being driven on with a stick or a whip: on many such occasions, my friends would run ahead to berate the poor ploughman, telling him to stop beating his animals for fear of hurting the sentiments of 'Doktor Amitaab'. In vain would I try to persuade them that cows were frequently beaten in India: they wouldn't believe me, for had they not seen otherwise in Hindi films?

The other principal association that rural Egypt had with India was the matter of water pumps, which were, of course, very important in rural communities. In those days, Egypt imported so many water pumps from India that in some areas these machines were known as 'makana Hindi'—or simply as 'Kirloskar', the name of a major pump-manufacturing company. Purchasing a water pump was a great event, and the machine would be brought back on a pick-up truck with much fanfare, with strings of old shoes strung around the spout to ward off the evil eye. Long before the machine made its entry into the village, a posse of children would be sent to summon me: as an Indian, I was expected to be an expert on these machines, and the proud new owners would wait anxiously for me to pronounce on the virtues and failings of their new acquisition.

It so happens that I am one of those people who is hard put to tell a spanner from a hammer or a sprocket from a gasket. At first, I protested vigorously, disclaiming all knowledge of machinery. But once again no one believed me; they thought I was withholding vital information or playing some kind of deep and devious game. Often people would look crestfallen, imagining, no doubt, that I had detected a fatal flaw in their machine and was refusing to divulge the details. This would not do, of course, and in order to set everyone's fears at rest, I became, willy-nilly, an oracle of water pumps. I developed a little routine wherein I would subject the machine to a minute inspection, occasionally tapping it with my knuckles or poking it with my fingers. Unsurprisingly, no machine failed my inspection: at the end of it I would invariably pronounce the water pump to be a 'makana mumtaaza'—a most excellent Kirloskar, a truly distinguished member of its species.

Yet even as I was disclaiming my relationship to those water pumps, I could not but recognize that there was a certain commonality between myself and those machines. In a way, my presence in that village could be attributed to the same historical circumstances that introduced Indian pumps and Hindi films to rural Egypt. Broadly speaking, those circumstances could be described as the spirit of decolonization that held sway over much of the world in the decades after the Second World War; this was the political ethos that found its institutional representation in the Non-Aligned Movement. We are at a very different moment in history now, when the word 'non-aligned' seems somehow empty and discredited; today the movement is often dismissed not just as a political failure but also as a minor footnote to the great power rivalries of the Cold War. It is true, of course, that the movement had many shortcomings and met with many failures. Yet it is also worth remembering that the Non-Aligned Movement as such was merely the institutional aspect of something that was much broader, wider and more important: this, as I said before, was the post-war ethos of decolonization, which was a political impulse that had deep historical roots and powerful cultural resonances. In the field of culture, among other things, it represented an attempt to restore and recommence the exchanges and conversations that had been interrupted by the long centuries of European imperial dominance. It was in this sense the necessary and vital counterpart of the nationalist idiom of anti-colonial resistance. In the West, Third World nationalism is often presented as an ideology of xenophobia and parochialism. But the truth is that many of these movements of resistance tried very hard, within their limited means, to create a universalism of their own. Those of us who grew up in that period will recall how we were animated by an emotion that is rarely named: xenophilia,[1] the love of the other, the affinity for strangers—a feeling that lives deep in the human heart but whose very existence is rarely acknowledged. People of my generation will remember the pride we once took in the transnational friendships of such figures as Nehru, Nasser, Nkrumah, Sukarno, Chou En-lai and others. Nor were such friendships anything new. I have referred above to the cross-cultural conversations that were interrupted by imperialism. These interruptions were precisely that—temporary breakages; the conversations never really ceased. Even in the nineteenth century, the high noon of empire, people from

Africa, Asia and elsewhere sought each other out, wrote letters to each other and stayed in each other's homes while travelling. Lately, a great number of memoirs and autobiographies have been published that attest to the depth and strength of these ties. It was no accident, therefore, that Mahatma Gandhi chose to stop in Egypt in order to see Sa'ad Zaghloul before proceeding to the Round Table Conference in London. This was integral to the ethos of the time. Similarly, it is no accident that capitals like New Delhi, Abuja and Tunis have many roads that are named after leaders from other continents. Sometimes these names are unpronounceable to local tongues and cause annoyance or laughter; occasionally they are dismissed as empty gestures. But the fact that such gestures are not without value becomes apparent when we reflect that we might search in vain for roads that are named in this fashion in such supposedly global cities as London, New York and Berlin. These gestures, in other words, may be imbued with both pomposity and pathos, but they are not empty: they represent a yearning to reclaim an interrupted cosmopolitanism.

If I am to think of what drew me to Egypt in 1980, it was, at bottom, the very impulse that I have been describing here—a kind of xenophilia, a desire to embrace the globe in my own fashion, a wish to eavesdrop on an ancient civilizational conversation. Admittedly, this impulse could have taken me to many other places, but the opportunity presented itself at a time when I was just becoming aware of the ties that had once linked Yemen and China, Indonesia and East Africa—and, most significantly for me, India and the Middle East. As one of the centres of the world, Egypt has always had a special attraction for travellers, and it seemed fitting that this was where I would come. Thus it happened that in 1980 I found myself living in a small village in the Governorate of Beheira.

I have said earlier that the Non-Aligned Movement was merely the institutional aspect of a much broader and older cultural and political tendency. But it needs to be acknowledged here that neither I nor any of the other elements of India that were present in rural Beheira—the pumps and the Hindi film songs—would have been able to find a place there if not for the existence of the Non-Aligned Movement. In its absence, the people of Lataifa would not have known of any foreign films other than those produced by Hollywood; their water pumps would have been of European or Japanese make; and as for myself, I would either have failed to get a visa or not have been permitted to reside in the countryside. It was only because of the good relations that prevailed between India and Egypt that I was able to do what I did. It is important, I believe, to acknowledge this, for no matter how sincere an individual's desire for cultural communication might be, it is impossible for such exchanges to occur in the absence of an institutional framework.

In other words, it was decolonization and its aftermath that made it possible for me to live for a time in Egypt. I say this in a spirit of the deepest gratitude, for this period was critical to my development as a writer: for me it was the equivalent of writing school. While living in Beheira, I maintained a detailed journal, in which I made extensive notes about my conversations with people and the things I saw around me. Not only did this teach me to observe what I was seeing, but it also taught me how to translate raw experience on to the page. It was the best kind of training a novelist could have and it has stood me in good stead over the years. Much of my writing has been influenced by this time in my life.

For any writer, reading is as essential as writing, and in this regard too my time in Egypt was absolutely vital to my literary formation. Although I have always been a voracious reader, I have never in all my life read as much as I did in Lataifa—partly because there was not much else to do: like most rural communities, Lataifa was a quiet place where nothing much happened. It was there that I read Gabriel Garcia Marquez's *One Hundred Years of Solitude*, and I would not perhaps have felt its influence as intensely as I did if I had been living elsewhere. *One Hundred Years of Solitude* alerted me to the possibility that the movement of time may often be felt most powerfully in places that appear to be far removed from the main currents of history: Lataifa was one such place, an Egyptian Macondo.

It was in Lataifa also that I discovered contemporary Arabic fiction. I had, of course, heard the names of such writers as Taha Hussein and Tawfiq al-Hakim, but their work had a special resonance because I was living in a place that was so much like those they described. A writer who was to prove particularly significant to me was Tayeb Salih: his novel *Mowsam al-Hijra ila ash-Shimaal* ('Season of Migration to the North') would have a strong bearing on my own work. Dislocation and migration, the crossing of boundaries and borders are central to this novel, and these were themes that resonated very significantly with me: my first novel, *The Circle of Reason*, is about a group of migrant workers that travels from India to the Gulf, and it reflects some of the same concerns that Tayeb Salih addresses in his seminal book.

And then there was the towering figure of Naguib Mahfouz. To me, as to many others the world over, the situations and characters that Mahfouz wrote about were instantly recognizable, intimately familiar. One reason for this is that Mahfouz's entry into the world of his characters is often through the interior passageways of the family. Of course, the family is one of those territories that the novel, as a form, has most successfully claimed for itself everywhere: all around the world there are novelists who, like Mahfouz, build their books on families and their histories, on the endless cycle of birth, marriage and death. But in Mahfouz's hands, this invitation into the family has an extra dimension of excitement. This is because in Egypt, as in India, the family is often a secret, curtained world, protected from the gaze of outsiders by walls and courtyards, by veils and laws of silence. To be taken past those doors into the forbidden space of failed marriages and secret desires, the areas that lie most heavily curtained under the genteel ethic of family propriety, is to prepare oneself for the pleasurable tingle of the illicit. And once past that curtain, we discover, with an almost guilty delight, a quiet murmur of furtive gropings, dissatisfaction and despair that confirms everything one has ever suspected about one's neighbours—no matter whether they be in Calcutta or Cairo. In Mahfouz's hands, the intricacies of family relationships become a kind of second language with which he demonstrates the dangers that lurk on the margins of a world that strives for an unattainable respectability in circumstances of poverty and deprivation. The predicaments he presents are the stuff of life in the crowded, teeming cities of India as well as Egypt: this is a world of disappointments, aspiration and hypocrisy, where people look for meaning and authenticity while being marooned between great wealth and unimaginable poverty.

Over the years, although I have forgotten much of my Arabic, my work and my understanding of the world have been greatly enriched by many other Arab writers: Nawal El Saadawi, Abdelrahman Munif, Gamal al-Ghitani, Elias Khoury and Ghassan Kanafani, whose *Men in the Sun* I consider to be one of the finest works of post-war fiction. It is possible that I would have discovered these writers even if I had not lived in Lataifa, but I doubt that my readings of their work would have had the same resonance had I not lived in Egypt.

The world today is very different from that of 1980, when I came to Egypt. The conversations and exchanges that recommenced in the post-war period are now in danger of being broken off again. Today, especially in the Anglo-American world, capitalism and empire are once again being packaged together in a bundle that is scarcely distinguishable from the old 'civilizing mission'. Indeed, one of the outcomes of the horrifying attacks of 9/11 was that it led to an extraordinary rehabilitation of imperialism, not merely as a political and military force but also as an ideology—one that has resulted in the unfolding catastrophe in Iraq.

It is strange to think that the fall of the Berlin Wall is still widely read as a vindication of 'capitalism'. The truth is that the world's experience over these last fifteen years could more accurately be read as proof that untrammelled capitalism leads inevitably to imperial wars and the expansion of empires. If that were not the case, then surely the almost uncontested reign of a single system would prove to be an epoch, if not of universal peace, then certainly one in which there would be a broad agreement on the means of ensuring peace? Yet what we see is exactly the opposite. We find ourselves in a period of extraordinary instability and fear, faced with the prospect of an endless proliferation of thinly veiled colonial wars. In fact, there is less agreement on the means of ensuring peace today than there was at the time of the founding of the United Nations.

Empires always profess, and sometimes even believe in, noble ideals: the problem lies with their methods, which are invariably such as to subvert their stated aims and ends. This is because the processes of conquest, occupation and domination create realities that become alibis for the permanent deferral of the professed ideals. Thus did some Jacobins argue for the necessity of slavery in France's colonies; thus did the author of *On Liberty* preside over hundreds of millions of conquered Indians; thus does torture come to be reconciled to the promise of liberty. None of this is new. Let us recall that the slave trade in the eighteenth century—arguably the foundational commerce of speculative capitalism—was long justified on the grounds that it bestowed freedom on Africans by removing them from the tyrannies of their native continent; let us recall that the export of opium to China, enforced by Western arms, was justified in the name of 'Free Trade'.

The packaging of 'capital+empire' is still beribboned with these processes of double-think. Those who set out to remake the world in their own image will not be satisfied with an imperfect portrait; for them the flaws in the depiction will be an invitation to rip up the old copy and start again. And since no simulation will ever be as good as the original, the process will repeat itself again and again. Capitalism+empire, in other words, is a programme for permanent war—the prospect once beloved of Trotskyists and now embraced afresh by neo-conservatives. Yet this is not the whole picture, for the West is not a monolith: even within the Anglo-American world, there are powerful forces of resistance to the neo-imperialist model of politics. And as for Europe, it has charted an entirely different course in which negotiation and compromise have been given much greater value than confrontation and force.

Empires are not the sole threat to the continuation of our conversations: over the last fifteen years, in many parts of Asia and Africa, we have seen a dramatic rise in violent and destructive kinds of fundamentalism, some religious and some linguistic. These movements are profoundly hostile to any notion of dialogue between cultures, faiths and civilizations. They are movements of intolerance and bigotry and they mirror the ideology of imperialism in that they seek to remake the world—or at least their corners of it—in their own images. What is more, they are deeply and viscerally hostile to all forms of the arts: just as Mahfouz was attacked by Muslim fundamentalists in Egypt, so too in India have Hindu fundamentalists attacked museums and libraries, exhibitions and artists. If these fundamentalists—no matter of what stripe—are allowed to have their way, it is not merely conversation that will cease; art itself will no longer be tolerated.

Against this background, it is tempting to look back on the days of non-alignment with some nostalgia: indeed, there was much that was valuable in that period. Yet it would be idle to pretend that solutions can be found by looking backwards in time. That was a certain historical moment and it has passed. If I have reflected on it here, it is not my intent to suggest that we should try to turn back the clock—as religious fundamentalists seek to do—nor is it to fall back on an ideology of permanent victimhood, such as that which the French rightly castigate as 'tiers-mondisme'. I have pointed to that period rather to evoke the desires and hopes that animated it, in particular to its strain of xenophilia, to its yearning for a certain kind of universalism—not a universalism merely of principles and philosophy but one of face-to-face connections, of everyday experience. Except that this time we must correct the mistake that lay at the heart of that older anti-colonial impulse—which is that we must not only include the West within this spectrum of desire but also acknowledge that both the West and we ourselves have been irreversibly changed by our encounters with each other. We must recognize that in the West, as in Asia, Africa and elsewhere, there are great numbers of people who, by force of circumstance, have become xenophiles in the deepest sense, acknowledging—as Tayeb Salih did so memorably in *Mowsam al-Hijra ila ash-Shimaal*—that in matters of language, culture and civilization, their heritage, like ours, is fragmented, fissured and incomplete. Only when our work begins to embody the conflicts, the pain, the laughter and the longing that come from this incompleteness will it be a true mirror of the world we live in.

(Delivered as a lecture at the Arab Writers' League Conference in Cairo, 2008. A version of this essay was also published by *Outlook* in 2008.)

# FOURTEEN
# The Mountains Are High and the Emperor Is Far Away

The last place you would expect to meet Brian Linden is Xizhou, a village of some 3,000 souls in a far corner of southwestern China, in the province of Yunnan. A forty-something native of Chicago, Brian is tall, blue-eyed and looks as though he belongs on TV—perhaps in a soap opera, for he also has the likeable distractedness of someone who is accustomed to being waylaid by changing storylines.

Xizhou sits beside a branch of the old Burma road: Burma is a day's journey away, and the Indian border is not much farther than the nearest big city, Kunming. This is, in other words, the kind of place where it used to be said in the old days: 'The mountains are high and the Emperor is far away.'

The landscape in this part of Yunnan is as crumpled and fractured as the bonnet of a car after a head-on collision. Tectonic plates grinding into each other with titanic force have created jagged mountains and deep valleys, some of which are worlds unto themselves, inhabited by distinct ethnic groups. The area around Xizhou is populated by one of the most remarkable of these, the Bai, a community that has been successful in many fields, including business.

That Xizhou is no ordinary village is evident even before one enters it. The setting is dramatic: the village sits in the middle of a vast, prodigiously fertile valley, at a height of over 2,000 metres above sea level (around 7,000 feet). Towering above it to the north are the majestic ridges of the Azure (Cangshan) mountains, which rise to heights of over 4,121 metres (13,520 feet). The dense banks of cloud that come rolling over the peaks are mirrored in the waters of Lake Erhai, which sprawls over 42 kilometres of the valley's floor. It does not seem at all far-fetched when the local people tell tales about their valley being so beautiful as to arouse the jealousy of the gods.

But the road that leads to Xizhou is no heavenly highway: it is clogged with traffic and fringed with grimy workshops and dismal eateries. Suddenly, out of this shabby industrial detritus, there appears like a mirage a garden arranged around a serpentine pond. Islands planted with clumps of ornamental bamboo lead to an exquisite many-roofed pavilion, surrounded by peonies and flame-shaped cypresses. I was to discover later that this was once a library, built in the 1940s by four of the village's richest families: the Yan, the Dong, the Yang and the Ying.

These were dynasties of no ordinary wealth: in their heyday, they presided over mercantile empires that extended throughout China and Southeast Asia: some even had offices in London and New York. These families also placed great store by education. Some of their members distinguished themselves in the imperial civil service examinations; some became well-known scholars and academicians. In the 1930s, when the Japanese invasion forced many institutions to withdraw from central China, Xizhou was home for eight years to a college that was affiliated to Yale University in the US. The Buddhist temple complex in which the college was housed is now looked after by a solitary old lady: the grounds are overgrown but the altars are still tended and incense is regularly offered.

How did this small village, situated in what was once a remote place, accumulate so much material and cultural wealth? Yunnan itself had much to do with this. The province is immensely rich in mineral resources, and its valleys are well-watered and exceptionally fertile. Yunnan produces some of the world's most valuable teas, and its botanical endowments are legendary (to cite just one example: Britain has two varieties of oak; Yunnan has 146). The old fortified city of Dali, 18 kilometres south of Xizhou, has been described as 'one of the most famous cities in botanical history'. For a century and a half, the region has been a magnet for plant-hunters who have discovered here some of the world's most beautiful garden plants. In the right seasons, the slopes around Xizhou are ablaze with flowers: rhododendrons, azaleas, camellias, irises, lilies, gentians, incarvilleas, primroses and rare orchids, including the fabled Golden Gate pleione.

Yunnan also sits astride some of the world's oldest and busiest trade routes: some major branches of the ancient horse-, silk-, and tea-trading routes ran past it, connecting Burma and Thailand with central China and lands farther west. In Xizhou, evidence of this mercantile past lies close to the surface: farmers regularly chance upon inscriptions, pottery, figurines and stelae that are a thousand years old or more.

But the period in which Xizhou really came into its own was much more recent: it was the time of China's precipitous decline, in the late nineteenth and early twentieth centuries. One of the instruments of China's undoing in this period was, of course, opium, most of which was grown in India and smuggled into China with the active connivance of the British East India Company. The drug was prohibited by the Imperial court in Beijing as early as 1729 CE, but the resources from the trade were so important to the financing of the Raj that the British went to war in 1841 CE to prevent the enforcement of the ban. This war, and the other conflicts and upheavals that followed, led to the collapse of the last dynasty and ultimately to revolution.

In the early years of the drug trade, Indian opium came to China mostly through Canton (Guangzhou) and other ports. But in the mid-nineteenth century, a new overland route opened up through Bengal, Assam and Burma into Yunnan. Soon the farmers of Yunnan began to grow their own opium, and by the late nineteenth century, Yunnan had become, along with Bihar and Malwa, one of the world's most important opium-growing regions.

What part did opium play in Xizhou's prosperity? Nobody ever mentions it. People speak instead of mines, textile factories and so on. But in Xizhou's dusty antique shops, along with artefacts from other eras, there are many ornately carved opium pipes. No one looks askance upon these anymore: China has been so successful in its battle against opium that these pipes are now no more threatening than the tiny shoes that were once worn by women with bound feet.

That period of great wealth has also left another happier legacy: an extraordinary architectural endowment consisting of no less than 111 multi-courtyard buildings constructed in the Bai style, with beautifully carved doorways, windows, screens and gates.

It was this part of Xizhou's heritage that brought Brian Linden to the village in 2006. His parents ran an antique store in Chicago, and he had grown up restoring old furniture and other objects. An exceptionally able student, he won scholarships to major universities and for a while even worked on a PhD in Chinese history at Stanford. But that didn't quite suit him, so he knocked around the world doing many different things, including a stint with the CBS bureau in China. One day, while out jogging in Beijing, he was spotted by a Chinese director who recruited him to star in a film called *He Came from Across the Pacific*: to this day Brian is sometimes recognized by people who saw him in it. Brian has a celebrity's ease with fame, which is just as well, since he has already become—as the secretary of the local branch of the Communist Party said to me—'the icon of Xizhou'.

One morning, we strolled down to the village market. Women dressed in the colourful attire of the Bai were selling wild mushrooms collected from nearby fields and forests. I had never seen so many varieties of mushroom in one place: long-stemmed and short-stemmed, knobbly and smooth, some as small as a fingernail and some that had the heft of a joint of meat. Fortunately, there was a little two-table eatery nearby so we went over and asked for a sampling of the market's wares. In a minute, a 'ba-ba' was fetched fresh from one of the food stalls in the market: a thick paratha-like flatbread, it was stuffed with minced chives and pork. Then came Chinese bitter melons cooked with freshly laid eggs and chunks of Yunnan's storied ham; this was followed by a frittata-like omelette made with wildflowers—these blossoms are called 'peacock flowers' in Chinese (Jîn què-gên; *Caragana sinica*), but they are tiny and subtly flavoured. Next was a plate of crisp puffs: they were made from the local goat cheese, cut into ribbons and fried. At some point, a preparation of glistening short ribs of pork, resting on a bed of red chillies, appeared, and a bowl of delicious fresh greens, tart with garlic and green chillies. The greens were a kind of water spinach that is known as the 'empty-heart vegetable' because of its hollow stems (apparently this plant often serves as a metaphor in songs of unrequited love). As for mushrooms, I forget how many dishes and bowls there were of them: some came stewed in a light broth; some had barely felt the touch of heat; some were flash-fried with slices of green chilli and garlic.

The gods could be forgiven for envying this feast.

At the end of the meal, the proprietor served his own home-made orchid wine, which contributed much by way of conviviality. At the table next to ours was a cheerful family from Sichuan. After a round or two of toasting, one of the Sichuan party produced a newspaper cutting: this, he said, was what had inspired him to bring his family to Xizhou—a report about an American who had set up an inn and arts centre in an old house with a view to making it a destination for artists, writers and musicians from across the world. The picture that accompanied the article was of Brian's wife, Jeanee, who is Chinese-American, and his son Shane.

Our new friend pointed to the picture and laughed. 'Once upon a time,' he said, 'we used to carry pictures of Chairman Mao. Now we carry pictures like these.'

Brian's dream—the Linden Centre—is housed in the last traditional mansion to be constructed in Xizhou. The story goes that the owner designed every detail himself but was only ever able to spend one night under its roof in 1947. After the revolution, he was allotted a couple of rooms elsewhere in the village and came to be known as 'Paper Box Yang' because he spent the rest of his life peddling boxes.

When Brian first saw it, the three-courtyard mansion was in a state of near-collapse. Recognizing its possibilities, he appealed to the authorities to let him use it for his centre. Amazingly enough they agreed, even though there were powerful real-estate interests trying to block his bid.

'They realized,' says Brian, 'that what I wanted to do wasn't just about money. This is the part of China that people don't see. China isn't all about mass-produced shoes and plastic toys. There's a vision here too.'

The local authorities certainly do have an ambitious vision for Xizhou: they would like to restore all the old mansions and turn the village into a major tourist destination. But some of the villagers have other visions. One day, Brian took me to visit a 500-year-old house: in the Ming era it was a rambling four-courtyard mansion; now it is occupied by several families who were allotted rooms there after the Revolution. They will not budge. Xizhou's old Confucian temple is being used as a chicken coop and is on the verge of ruin;

the authorities would like to restore it, but the family to whom it was allotted after the Revolution won't hear of it. One morning, we went to visit the village chronicler. He has compiled a detailed inventory of all the artefacts and antiquities that were destroyed in Xizhou during the Cultural Revolution: the account was published and then suddenly withdrawn, probably at the behest of the authorities. But the work of remembrance goes on undeterred in a tiny study that looks like an anchorite's retreat.

This is, to me, one of the most appealing aspects of Xizhou: here history is not yet an inert object of consumption; it will not tamely submit itself to plans and projects. The village's past is rich and deep and has the resources to push back.

I asked Brian about the difficulties that he himself had had to face: Were licences difficult to get? Did palms have to be greased?

Brian's answer startled me. 'No,' he said. 'I would say this part of it was easier than in the States. I used to run a gallery in Wisconsin and it took years to get licences there. The building codes and other regulations made it impossible for the small guy to succeed. It's like politics in the US—you have to be rich to get ahead. It was different here; I found China so open, so willing to help. I could sit down with the fire brigade and discuss things directly. I don't want to sound naïve—I know that it may be because I'm a foreigner. But there is a tremendous collective pride: people don't want China to lose face.'

For Brian, the Linden Centre is both a dream and an enormous risk: he has sunk all the money he could raise into it. 'We are just ordinary people in the States,' he said of himself and his wife. 'We don't have anything to fall back on if this fails. That's scary to me as a father and a husband.'

For the moment, the problems that Brian has to face are those of success rather than failure. The centre has had a great deal of coverage in the Chinese media and is flooded with visitors. Sometimes Brian and his staff are hard put to cope. The Linden Centre was not conceived as a conventional hotel and it does not offer multi-starred comforts. Hot water is available only for a few hours each day; mosquitoes are a problem; the kitchen provides excellent food but it shuts down at eight; there are no TVs in the rooms and since Xizhou, like any other farming village, turns in soon after sunset, guests must look inwards for entertainment.

But none of this detracts from the centre's appeal. Many of the guests are Chinese: prominent artists, affluent young couples and highly placed officials and executives. Some have the courtly manner and meditative bearing of classical scholars; they divide their time between practising Tai Chi and quietly contemplating the surrounding rice fields. They appear to be deeply grateful to Brian for providing an antidote to the frantic pace of China's cities.

But it isn't only to those seeking seclusion that Xizhou appeals. My seventeen-year-old son, Nayan, was travelling with me and he loved the Linden Centre. Where else in the world can a teenager go for walks in the clouds and bicycle down to a lake where fishermen use cormorants to catch fish? Where else can he eat spicy pork ribs and tiny whole fresh-water crabs, and, with his saved-up pocket money, buy figurines that date back to the time of Genghis Khan?

Western Yunnan is traversed by four of Asia's mightiest rivers: the Salween, the Irrawaddy, the Mekong and the Yangtze. In places, the last three run almost parallel to each other, like troughs in a sheet of corrugated iron, except that their gorges are thousands of metres deep.

The road that runs past Xizhou leads to the steep valley carved by the Yangtze: at times it descends right to the bank of the river, which is in its infancy here but is already a broad torrent, flowing at the pace of a rushing mountain stream. Presently the road comes to one of nature's miracles: the magnificent Tiger Leaping Gorge. Here the Yangtze, racing to keep pace with the fast-rising mountains, has sliced an almost vertical channel through the upwelling rock. At

3,900 metres (12,795 feet), the gorge is more than twice as deep as the Grand Canyon, and yet in places, the gap between its sides is so narrow that it does not seem impossible that a tiger could span it in a couple of bounds. It is astounding to think that the stream pouring through this narrow defile has sustained one out of every ten human beings ever to walk this Earth.

From here it is only a couple of hours by car to the edge of the plateau that becomes Tibet farther west. Roughly 3,300 metres (10,800 feet) above sea level, the region is slung like a hammock between the Himalayas and the Hengduan mountains to the north: it is a region of winding streams, rolling hills and flower-strewn alpine meadows. Although it falls within the borders of Yunnan, the area has the status of a Tibetan autonomous region. One of the pioneers of the tourist industry in this area is a woman from a Kolkata family: Uttara Sarkar. Diminutive in stature, with a wide face and an even wider smile, Uttara is in her mid-fifties. Like Brian, Uttara has lived in many places and her voice is inflected with Indian, African, Chinese and British intonations (she carries a UK passport).

Uttara grew up in Uganda, where her father had a sugar cane plantation. The family left before Idi Amin seized power, and Uttara finished her education at North Point in Darjeeling. While she was studying there, her class was invited to visit Nepal by a fellow student who happened to be a scion of the royal family—this was none other than the future, and now deposed, king Gyanendra. The visit led to a long-lasting involvement with Nepal, and Uttara went on to join a leading eco-tourism company. She spent many years in Nepal and was briefly married to a British-Nepali. But eco-tourism was her real love, and she prides herself on having been one of the industry's pioneers in such difficult, high-altitude locations as Lahaul-Spiti, Ladakh, Zanskar and Mustang. She also worked to establish the overland tourist routes to Tibet, and it was while travelling there that she became interested in the eastern part of the Tibetan culture area, known as the Kham region. A fortuitous romance with a man who had roots there brought her in 1989 to the region's centre, a county town that was then known as Gyalthang (Zhongdian in Chinese).

The old town is a tangle of narrow lanes paved with stones that still bear the marks of the mule trains that once passed this way. Uttara stayed with her boyfriend's relatives in the old town. Electricity was available for only two hours each day and she had to go to the water spouts in the town square to wash. She fell in love with the place and returned several times, even after her relationship with her boyfriend had ended. Her friendships with local people deepened, and in 1995, a Tibetan businessman from Gyalthang invited her to join him in setting up a hotel.

She ran the hotel for seven years and then, after selling her interest, started a couple of new ventures of her own: a travel business and a café, which is a combination of restaurant, bar and coffee shop, housed in an imaginatively restored building that was once the residence of a tea-trading family.

Her account of her experience is not unlike Brian's. 'The county government was amazingly helpful,' she told me. 'Otherwise it would have been impossible for me to develop the project. They really made me feel welcome and were supportive in every way. It's easier to do business here than in any other place I've worked in. If there's an idea you want to develop, and you succeed in putting it across, then the authorities are very pragmatic about making it happen.'

According to Uttara, it was this pragmatism, and not some absurd flight of romantic fancy, that led to the renaming—or rather rebranding—of Gyalthang: it is now officially known, believe it or not, as 'Shangri-la' (Xianggelila in Chinese).

The Tibetan legend of an earthly paradise called Shangri-la was given worldwide currency by the British writer James Hilton in his 1933 novel *Lost Horizon*. Interestingly, Hilton never set foot in Tibet or China; he wrote the book in a London suburb and died near Hollywood. This did not deter several counties in Sichuan and Yunnan from claiming that they matched the book's setting. They petitioned Beijing for permission to appropriate the name, and Beijing responded by appointing a commission of historians, anthropologists, geologists and other experts to look into the matter. After two years of deliberation, Gyalthang was declared the victor. It is now, by administrative fiat, the earthly embodiment of a place invented by a writer who never left the Western hemisphere.

Shangri-la is, in other words, a completely postmodern creation: not quite a product and not quite a place.

The rebranding of Gyalthang might seem absurd to anyone who beholds the hideous concrete blocks and half-excavated building sites of the new town—but then had Hilton's fictional utopia ever existed, this is probably the fate that would have befallen it. For the moment, the name does not seem to have attracted an inflow of tourists comparable to that of Yunnan's other major tourist destinations. The area's most important religious site, the Ganden Sumtseling Monastery, built centuries ago on the model of Lhasa's Potala, suffered extensive damage during the Cultural Revolution. It is still being restored. Visitors are comparatively few and seem to consist mostly of Tibetan pilgrims. The old town is also being slowly rebuilt: no doubt it will soon be beset by surging crowds, but for the moment, it is still uncrowded and quaint, the atmosphere dimly reminiscent of Kathmandu in the 1980s. Whiffs of marijuana waft by on the fresh mountain breeze.

Atop the valley's sacred hills there are many secluded, serene temples where the world seems very far away. One afternoon, Uttara, who is a practising Buddhist, took us to visit the Ringha Monastery, some 15 kilometres from the town. The road wound through forests of shimmering birch and soughing conifers. We came to a meadow that was carpeted with wildflowers. Uttara led me through it, pointing out clumps of anemone, pedicularis, salvia, delphinium and a native species of edelweiss. Here and there, standing alone, was a brave aster or a tenacious gentian. She came to a euphorbia that was turning colour and cried out in delight: this was a shade of red that she was seeing for the first time.

She seemed so content and happy that I felt bound to ask: 'So is this your Shangri-la?'

She thought about this for a bit. 'There are many challenges here, of course,' she said, 'but most of them are in your mind—and if a place can help you see that, then what else is it but Shangri-la?'

(First published in *Condé Nast Traveller*, 8 November 2011)

# FIFTEEN
# The Spice Islands

## 1.

At my writing desk, as in my kitchen, I find it impossible to escape the lure of spices. Their flavours enliven many of my passions: history, cookery, botany and, of course, storytelling.

Some years ago, my interest in spices spilled over into my garden, and I started to grow my own turmeric, galangal, ginger, black pepper and cinnamon. The experience has taught me a great deal: I have learnt, for instance, that there is a huge difference between home-grown and store-bought spices—the latter are but a pale shadow of the former. The hand-picked, sun-dried pepper from my garden in Goa has a citrusy freshness and complexity that I've never encountered in commercial varieties.

Growing my own spices has also made me wonder why some of them are used in dried forms and some are not. Consider ginger, for example: many Western recipes call for dried, powdered ginger, an ingredient that some Indian cooks would consider an abomination. Yet many who scorn dried ginger have no qualms about using dried turmeric and chilli, even when they are available fresh. In Southeast Asia, by contrast, freshly plucked chillies and 'raw' turmeric root are usually preferred and account, in no small measure, for the vividness that is characteristic of the cuisine of the region. In flavour, as in colour, fresh turmeric has a brightness and subtlety that dried versions cannot match.

Nor are spices the same everywhere; as with chillies, there are many varieties of turmeric and ginger. Indian turmeric, which is bred to be dried, differs from Indonesian varieties, which are grown to be used fresh. There can be no doubt, in any event, that provenance makes a significant difference to the taste of many spices: these great builders of flavour are themselves flavoured by elements of the microenvironments in which they are grown.

Yet spices rarely fall within the ambit of the localism that is now so enthusiastically celebrated in the culinary world. Famous European chefs, renowned for their use of the freshest local ingredients, continue to unashamedly publish recipes that ask for a generic 'pinch of curry'; restaurants that name the very village in which their meat has been pastured remain silent about the origins of the spices with which it is flavoured. The reason for this, perhaps, is that historically many spices were by definition non-local—they always came from faraway places. After all, even in India, cloves, nutmeg and mace, familiarly known as laung, jaiphal and javitri, were exotic imports until just a couple of hundred years ago.

But need it be thus? Often, while reading weighty tomes on the spice trade, the historian in me has been interrupted by my culinary self, which slips in questions such as: If the tastes of fresh, raw turmeric and ginger are so different from the dried versions, then what about freshly picked cloves and mace? Could they perhaps also be used 'raw'? Surely, in places that have long familiarity with these spices, local cooks have experimented with them when they are fresh from the harvest?

My curiosity on this score was keen enough that I did not hesitate when an opportunity arose to visit Indonesia, at the invitation of the country's Ministry of Culture. When asked which part of the country I wanted to travel to, I knew exactly where I wanted to go—the fabled Spice Islands, once known as the Moluccas.

**2.**

The Spice Islands are the original home of two spice-producing trees. One is *Myristica fragrans*, which produces nutmeg and mace: the former is the seed and the latter is its lacy outer covering. The second tree is the one that bears the clove, *Syzygium aromaticum*. Historically, these trees were each endemic to two small clusters of islands, about 500 kilometres apart. The clove had its home in the northern part of the archipelago, in what is now the Indonesian province of Maluku Utara (North Maluku), while the nutmeg tree was indigenous to the Banda Islands in the south, now a part of Maluku province.

In size, the islands of the Moluccas are very small: on maps they look like berries, suspended just beyond the hornbill-head of Papua New Guinea. The largest in the chain, Halmahera, is less than half the size of Bhutan. But by a strange quirk of fortune, the original spice-growing islands are tiny even in relation to Halmahera; they are visible only on maps of very large scale. It is as though destiny had embarked on a controlled experiment, depositing two priceless treasures with pinpoint precision in order to observe the outcome.

Politically, it was the clove that gained ascendancy. The islands that came to dominate the archipelago in pre-colonial times were the historic centres of global clove production: Ternate and Tidore (pronounced Ter-NA-tay and Ti-DOR-ay). The half-rhyme of the islands' names is a verbal echo of the mirrored drama of their topography: both islands are dominated by beautifully shaped conical volcanoes that rise to a height of over 1,700 metres (5,000 feet). From the air, flying over the narrow channel that separates Ternate from Tidore, the two islands present a breathtaking sight with their twin volcanoes soaring above the turquoise blue water, their towering craters encircled by haloes of cloud. The dense greenery of the volcanoes' slopes is broken only by dark streaks of solidified lava and the rust-red roofs of the picturesque little settlements that cling to their skirts.

The islands' idyllic appearance is not the least of the reasons why it is difficult to think of the Moluccas as pivotal to world history. Ternate and Tidore seem, at first glance, to be barely touched by the grimy workings of time. Then there is the matter of their remoteness. In an age of shrunken distances, Ternate and Tidore are still difficult to get to. They are separated from Indonesia's capital by two time zones and some 3,500 kilometres. To reach them by sea from Jakarta takes weeks. Flights are few and most of them require a change of planes in northern or southern Sulawesi, either in Manado or Makassar. The Banda Islands are even harder to travel to and generally require a six-hour journey by ferry. If ever there were a periphery, far removed from the great global centres of history, where would it be if not here?

But the Spice Islands confound questions such as these. The biggest settlement in the archipelago, Ambon City (formerly known as Amboyna), is a busy modern port, with many ships anchored in its harbour. In the city centre, high-rise buildings vie with church steeples and minarets; at rush hour, traffic slows to a crawl. In Ambon, the hum of modern life is loud enough to create an impression of a bustling, globalized blandness. But this is, in fact, strangely at odds with the realities of Ambon's encounter with globalism. Here, in 1622, ten Englishmen and two of their associates ran afoul of the Dutch East India Company and were tortured and executed by Dutch officials. This incident, which came to be known as the Amboyna Massacre, was by no means the worst colonial atrocity in the Dutch East Indies, but it sent shock waves across the globe and was memorialized in a 1673 play by the poet John Dryden. The massacre did not, however, immediately dislodge the English from the Spice Islands: for the next few decades they clung tenaciously to their toeholds in the Banda Islands.

The Anglo–Dutch conflicts of the seventeenth century were among the earliest global wars, and the part that Ambon played in them was reprised during the Second World War, when the island became a fiercely contested battleground for Japanese and Allied forces. The Japanese succeeded in seizing the island after an intense bombing campaign in which much of Ambon City was destroyed. Of the thousands of Allied soldiers who were taken prisoner, some 300 were summarily butchered. Once more the site of atrocities committed by foreigners, Ambon was witness to one of the largest war-crime trials of the post-war period.

Nor did Indonesia's independence put an end to Ambon's travails. In the 1940s and '50s, the region was rocked by rebellions and army actions. Then, in 1999, the Moluccas were convulsed by a years-long wave of communal violence that pitted Muslims against Christians. Ambon, with its large Christian population, was particularly badly hit. The violence eventually subsided, and over the last decade the Moluccas have been through an extensive process of reconstruction and rebuilding. Today Ambon's churches bear fresh coats of paint and the city has no lack of bars and clubs featuring local singers and musicians. If tensions remain, they are hidden from the eyes of the casual visitor. To all outward appearances, the city could well serve as a showpiece for Indonesia's rapidly expanding consumer economy.

## 3.

Ternate, the largest town in the northern Moluccas, is much smaller than Ambon, yet here too the hum of an accelerating economy can be quite clearly heard. The town's streets are lined with neat, brightly painted houses and well-stocked shops and markets. A grand new waterfront mosque with soaring minarets crowns its main thoroughfare, which also winds past busy wholesale bazaars, several large modern malls and at least one immense 'hypermarket'. The town has a fine, comfortable new hotel with fast internet connectivity; ATMs are ubiquitous, as are signs marking evacuation routes in case of a tsunami or eruption.

The abundant signs of a vigilant local administration, the excellent roads and infrastructure, and the absence of any visible signs of poverty form a stark contrast to out-of-the-way areas elsewhere in the world. Anyone familiar with India or Egypt, for instance, might wonder how Indonesia is able to deliver goods and services in such profusion, across thousands of kilometres of ocean, when those countries struggle to provide much less over land.

But this presumes, wrongly, that transportation is easier over land than sea: it is because of the ocean that these seemingly remote islands have always been so closely tied to the currents of history. Cloves have, for instance, been found at an Aramaean–Assyrian archaeological site in Tell Ashara, Syria: they arrived there around 1,721 BCE. They had probably crossed the sea in short steps, going first from Ternate or Tidore to what is now Makassar and then on to the Middle East via Java, Sumatra or India (the cloves that are mentioned in the Vedas would also have come from these islands).

It was the sea too that permitted the Melanesians, the greatest seafarers and navigators of antiquity, to settle on these islands as they sailed across the oceans, from Madagascar to Easter Island. Perhaps it was they who first carried the cloves of Ternate and Tidore to the Asian mainland, where they became an essential element not just of many cuisines but also of innumerable indigenous medical systems. Such was the demand for them in the ancient world that a cycle of trade and travel came into being, linking the Spice Islands to east Africa, the Arabian Peninsula, Persia, India and, perhaps most importantly, China, which remained for millennia the single most important market for cloves.

Along with people, goods and coinage, the trade in cloves brought beliefs and ideas of many sorts. Hinduism and Buddhism are sure to have figured among them at some time, but in this part of Indonesia, neither religion has left spectacular traces of the sort that are to be found on islands like Java and Sumatra. Nor is there much evidence of Chinese cultural influence, except, curiously, in the islanders' dominant religion, Islam. Along with traders from Gujarat and the Arabian peninsula, China's Hui Muslims are thought to have played an important part in the Islamization of the islands. In any event, by the early sixteenth century, when Europeans first came to Ternate and Tidore, the islands were being ruled by Muslim sultans whose authority extended from Papua in the east to Ambon and the Banda Islands in the south.

Both Ternate and Tidore were sustained by the clove trade, and their sultans competed actively with each other to attract traders from different countries. This was the practice of many other rulers of ports and city-states in the Indian Ocean, including, for example, the aptly named Samudri Rajas (or Zamorins) of Calicut. These rulers could not afford to offend one group of traders over another; their prosperity depended on the number of merchants they could attract to their ports, and to that end they would cut taxes, offer goods at lower prices and provide land and protection for foreigners and their places of worship. Ruler competed against ruler and merchant against merchant; often there was not much to distinguish the one from the other.

These practices were very different from those of Europe and the Mediterranean, where maritime powers commonly sought to monopolize the trade in certain goods. One of the most lucrative of these monopolies was that of the spice trade, which had for several centuries belonged to the Venetian Republic. But this was essentially a transhipment trade that depended on alliances with the Islamic realms of the eastern Mediterranean, most notably Egypt. By the time Asian spices reached Venice, they had already changed hands many times in the course of their long journey across the Indian Ocean and Arabian Sea. This gave other European maritime powers very good reasons to find an alternative route to the Indian Ocean—by doing so, they could at one stroke destroy Venice's monopoly, weaken the Muslim states of the Middle East and also eliminate the chain of middlemen who profited from the handling of spices on their journey to Europe.

So it happened that spices became the grail that launched the great voyages of the Age of Discovery: they were the prize that caused Christopher Columbus, Vasco da Gama and Ferdinand Magellan to hoist their sails. What they all hoped to do was control the mechanisms of the spice trade and create monopolies. On reaching the Malabar coast, Vasco da Gama lost no time in trying to impose terms that would exclude other buyers, particularly Arabs and Muslims, from the pepper trade. But pepper was too widely cultivated for a monopoly to be feasible. The tiny, almost defenceless islands where clove, nutmeg and mace were found offered much greater scope for monopoly building—or so it must have seemed to the Portuguese, who soon set off in search of the 'spiceries' of the East Indies. In 1512, just ten years after seizing Goa, they arrived in Ternate, where they immediately tried to take exclusive control of the trade in cloves. But their European rivals were hot on their heels: first the Spanish, followed by the Dutch and the English, who fought each other as pitilessly as they did the inhabitants of the Moluccas.

Ultimately it was the Dutch who triumphed, and the Moluccas became the foundation of their empire in Asia, with its first capital at Amboyna. It was in the Moluccas too that the British acquired their first Asian possessions, two tiny nutmeg-growing islands in the Banda archipelago called Ai and Run. They would cling doggedly to Run Island for decades and be richly rewarded for their tenacity. The Dutch were so eager to evict them from their toehold in the East Indies that in 1667, they signed a treaty in which the English gave up their claim on Run in return for the confirmation of their right to territories on the other side of the planet. Included among these was another island—Manhattan.

**4.**

The clove tree was very picky in choosing its home. Ignoring the larger islands in the Moluccas, it zeroed in on the small chain of volcanic islands that stretches southwards from Ternate. Here, as nowhere else, a number of different factors fell into alignment in such a way as to create the perfect environment for this gift of the Earth.

But what the Earth gives it can also take away. This became shockingly clear to me at the first clove garden I visited in Ternate. Overlooked by Mt Gamalama, the garden was in a wonderfully scenic location. A few of the trees were in bloom, their leaves dotted with clusters of yellowish-pink buds, but most of the others were dead or dying, their branches leafless and their trunks ashen.

This was happening all over the island, I was told, and the farmers I spoke to were unanimous about the cause: the climate had changed in recent years, they said; there was less rain and it fell more erratically. This in turn had led to the spread of blights and disease. The prolonged drought has also been accompanied by another unprecedented phenomenon: in March this year, a wildfire had raged for three days on the slopes of Mt Gamalama. A forest fire of this intensity was new to the islanders' experience.

In other words, the delicate balance of the islands' environment has changed; no longer is their alignment well suited for the clove. This is but one of the many ways in which the Spice Islands seem to be emblematic of a much larger predicament—for human civilization too was able to flourish only when a great number of physical systems fell into place several millennia ago with the dawn of a period of relative climatic stability.

The journey of the clove is itself illustrative of the pace at which civilization accelerated once the conditions were right. The earliest forms of writing appeared around 3,200 BCE, and within a millennium and a half, cloves had already become articles of luxury consumption more than 10,000 kilometres from the islands where they grew. From then on, the demand for them mounted steadily, not so much because of the purpose they served but because of what they had come to represent. Cloves were a product that people needed in order to keep up with others, or to prove a point to their neighbours. They were the progenitor of the luxury good—the Fabergé egg or the Gucci handbag—except that they played that role for thousands of years.

'[The clove] is the precious Commodity,' wrote a seventeenth-century Spanish historian, 'which gives Power and Wealth to ... Kings and causes their wars. 'Tis the fruit of Discord ... for it there has been, and still is, more fighting than for the Mines of Gold.'[1]

What this passage describes, however, is just a moment in the life cycle of this commodity. Eventually seedlings of cloves and nutmeg were smuggled out of the Moluccas and transplanted elsewhere. As spices became more easily available, they lost their mystique. In Europe, where foods had once been very heavily spiced, tastes changed, and the per capita consumption of spices began a long, steady decline. By the late eighteenth century, the Dutch East India Company was mired in corruption and effectively bankrupt.

This cycle too is representative of something much greater than itself—it is a cautionary tale about processes of phenomenal growth that burn themselves out, depleting the very resources that fuel them. Today, like the cinders of a dead fire, evidence of the astonishing energies that were once generated by the clove and the nutmeg is littered across the Moluccas: the most revealing of it is the fortifications that stretch across the islands. Few are the places on Earth that possess so dense and varied a collection of gun emplacements, citadels and strongholds.

The earliest of the Spice Island forts was erected by the Portuguese in Ternate, in the sixteenth century, but some of the most imposing, like those of Tidore, were of Spanish origin. The Dutch forts came a little later, starting in the seventeenth century, and some of them are still in use today as military bases.

Most of the Maluku forts are now ruins, carefully tended by the authorities. They are well worth visiting, not only for their picturesque locations, but also because their very existence bears witness to the influence that spices have exerted on history and on the planet.

But the energies generated by the Spice Islands were not only of a military nature: priests, dreamers and poets were also drawn into their orbit. St. Francis Xavier came to Ternate by way of Goa in 1547. One of his converts was a former queen called Nukila, who had once led a rebellion against the Portuguese. She was to become a figure of legend, not only in the Moluccas (where she is known as Rainha Buki Raja) but also in Europe: the Jacobean dramatist John Fletcher was inspired by an earlier Spanish novel about her to write his 1647 play *The Island Princess*. Another visitor who came to Ternate by way of Goa was Luís de Camões, author of the Portuguese national epic *The Lusiads*: one of its verses is thought to be a description of Ternate. Even Cervantes, author of *Don Quixote*, was not immune to the influence of the Spice Islands: he invented a Moluccan character for one of his 'exemplary novels' of 1613.

But the flame of literary interest that the Moluccas had ignited in Europe withered with the fortunes of its prime commodities. In the nineteenth century, the Moluccas were instead written into the history of science by Alfred Russel Wallace, Charles Darwin's fellow formulator of the theory of natural selection. Indeed Wallace's hallowed position in the annals of science rests upon an essay and a letter (the famous 'Letter from Ternate') that were sent from the Moluccas to London in 1858.

Wallace was the author also of one of the great travelogues of the nineteenth century, *The Malay Archipelago*. He spent three years in Ternate, and in his chapter on the island, he writes: 'About the centre of [the town] is the palace of the Sultan, now a large untidy, half-ruinous building of stone ... The sultans of Ternate and Tidore were once celebrated through the East for their power and magnificence.'

The dynasty that holds the sultanate of Ternate is one of the world's oldest, and its scions still command a great deal of authority on the island. The last sultan died recently and the succession is yet to be settled, but one of the main contenders, Hidayat Mudaffar Sjah, a son of the late ruler, still lives in the palace. I spent an hour with him there, and was glad to find that the palace is no longer the half-ruin of Wallace's description: it is elegant, airy and unpretentious, with a wide courtyard that faces Mt Gamalama.

Mr Sjah told me that his family had ruled Ternate for some 800 years and that the islanders believed that the dynasty had a special relationship with the spirit of the place, particularly Mt Gamalama. He too feels that connection very powerfully, even though he grew up mainly in Jakarta.

It was strangely moving to be seated in the shadow of the great volcano, talking to someone who was directly descended from the ruler who had welcomed Europeans into his realm in the hope of adding a new set of customers for its cloves. Little did that long-ago sultan know that he was helping to set in motion a cycle of consumption that would ravage the lives of his descendants and subjects, ultimately depleting the value of the very commodity on which the island's fortunes were founded. Nor could he have known that those ever-spiralling cycles of consumption would ultimately change the planet's climate in such a way as to endanger the clove in its ancestral homeland.

I mentioned this to Mr Sjah and he answered with a smile: the clove, he said, had been both a blessing and a curse for the island.

His words reminded me of other stories about ambiguous offerings—the apple of Eden, for example, and Pandora's box—that were given to human beings as a test of their wisdom and prudence. If Mt Gamalama were a capricious god, it could have chosen no better test than the clove.

**5.**

The islands of the nutmeg are a world apart from those of the clove. The first hints of this appear as the ferry from Ambon approaches Gunung Api, the principal volcano of the Banda Islands. Although Api is more active than Ternate's Gamalama, it is neither as tall nor as imposing. If a volcano could be said to create a sense of sheltering intimacy, then this would certainly be true of Api.

The volcano's size signals a distinct change of scale: the Bandas are small and intimate; they have the look of a mid-ocean atoll, distant from everywhere, a universe of its own. Here the hum of Indonesia's acceleration is scarcely audible.

In the lee of Gunung Api lies a channel of startlingly clear water. The island of Banda Neira is on the far side, as is the eponymous town, the largest settlement in the chain. When the ferry noses into the channel, a string of low, brightly coloured houses appears, lining the waterfront. On one side of the main jetty is a rambling yellow-and-mauve building with a long arched veranda: this is Hotel

Maulana, Banda Neira's oldest; it sits right by the water, across the channel from Gunung Api.

As the ferry comes in to dock, a crowd converges on the jetty; a band begins to play and the town seems to wake suddenly from a long siesta. Shopkeepers race to open their shutters, a market appears, selling fruit and innumerable varieties of dried fish. The hubbub speaks of another time, recalling sailors' accounts of canoes rushing out at the sight of a distant sail, of water-borne markets clustering around arriving ships, their hulls laden with fruit, poultry and other treats.

The town's main street is a short walk from the jetty. It is lined on both sides with colonial-era mansions that once belonged to Dutch nutmeg planters and dealers. In the 1930s, some of these were turned to another use: by then the Banda Islands had become a kind of oceanic Siberia, where troublesome radicals were banished by the Dutch colonial government. The most prominent of Banda's exiles were Sutan Sjahrir and Mohammad Hatta, both leading intellectuals and major figures in Indonesia's anti-colonial struggle. The mansions that once housed them have now been turned into museums.

Hatta and Sjahrir's sojourn in Banda Neira had a transformative effect on the island. They set up an informal school that was attended by local children, among them the sons and daughters of a wealthy local family of Arab origin. On his release, Sjahrir took some of these children to Jakarta, and one of the boys, Mohammad Des Alwi, became a colourful globe-trotting adventurer who fell in and out of favour with Indonesia's leaders. From the 1980s onwards, Des Alwi began to spend more time on the Bandas and developed a vision for the island's future. It was he who founded the Maulana Hotel; he also set up a foundation that is working to preserve the heritage of the Bandas.

I was told all this by Des Alwi's daughter, Tanya Alwi, who is herself a remarkable character. Schooled in Hong Kong, Malaysia,

Switzerland and the US, she has travelled widely and met many famous people, including President Obama. Now she divides her time between Jakarta and Banda Neira, and helps run the family hotel and her late father's foundation.

It was Tanya Alwi who led me around the centre of the old town, an improbable little square that looks as though it belongs in one of the spookier tales of the Brothers Grimm. On one side of the square is a seventeenth-century Dutch church, paved with centuries-old gravestones; the building was badly damaged in the riots of 1999 but has since been completely restored. On the far side is a sprawling Dutch East India Company warehouse, presided over by a curious little statue of King William III of the Netherlands. Next to the warehouse are the former residences of the islands' most senior colonial officials—empty, echoing buildings with an air of ineffable melancholy. A window pane in one of the houses has a suicide note etched upon it in French. The wreckage of a burnt-out Catholic church lies nearby: it was set on fire during the riots of 1999 and is yet to be rebuilt.

Overlooking the town square are the massive seventeenth-century ramparts of Fort Belgica, one of the largest and best-preserved of the Spice Island forts. On the other side, down by the waterfront, is an equally formidable hulk, Fort Nassau. The little town is enclosed like a nutmeg between these two stone-fisted citadels.

A few of the town's old mansions have been converted into small hotels and coffee houses for tourists. But the visitors who now come to the Banda archipelago are mostly drawn there not by its history but rather by its rich marine life and magnificent coral reefs. The latter are notable not only for their variety but also because they have mostly been able to weather the recent blight of bleaching that has devastated corals worldwide in the wake of a global rise in sea temperatures.

At a diving centre on Banda Neira's waterfront, I met Mareike Huhn, a marine biologist with a doctorate from the University of Kiel in Germany. Dr Huhn has been monitoring the Banda reefs for signs of bleaching, and was alarmed to see signs of it earlier this year. But the outbreak lasted only a few weeks and no more than 20 per cent of Banda's reefs were affected. Dr Huhn believes that the Banda corals owe their resilience to two factors. The first, they have a very high degree of biodiversity. 'A healthy reef with high biodiversity is more robust against bleaching,' she said. 'Site per site, of all the reefs that have been investigated, this one has the highest biodiversity.' Second, the Bandas are surrounded by very deep oceans, and cold water sometimes wells up from the abyssal depths, lowering temperatures at the surface—that is what seems to have happened this year.

But climate change has affected the Banda archipelago in other ways: it too has seen droughts and unprecedented wildfires. 'If higher temperatures persist,' said Dr Huhn, 'then Banda's reefs will also suffer.'

**6.**

Today the Banda Islands are so tranquil, sleepy and otherworldly that it is hard to imagine the extent of the violence that has been visited upon them. In the seventeenth century, they were the main theatre of imperial rivalry in the East Indies, with the Dutch trying to enforce monopolies on the islanders and the English doing their best to thwart them. The islanders, for their part, were obstinate in their resistance and made every effort to preserve their ancient trading relations with merchants from China, India and elsewhere. They frequently disregarded the treaties that were thrust on them, and in 1609, they ambushed a Dutch military contingent and killed its commander and some twenty-seven others.[2]

The incident persuaded a merchant by the name of Jan Pieterszoon Coen that a monopoly of the islands' spices could only be secured by doing away with the Bandanese and replacing them with Dutch burghers and freed slaves. In 1621, after having risen to the rank of governor-general, Coen brought an army of a couple of thousand soldiers and some 100 Japanese mercenaries to the islands. As had often happened before, talks with the elders quickly broke down and Coen soon found an alibi for an attack. What followed was a systematic orgy of slaughter, in which 14,000 of the islands' estimated 15,000 original inhabitants, including women and children, were killed or taken into slavery. Forty-four of the islands' elders were brought to Fort Nassau, where they were beheaded and quartered. '[They] died silently,' a Dutch witness later wrote, 'without uttering any sound except that one of them, speaking in the Dutch tongue, said "Sirs, have you then no mercy" but indeed nothing availed.'[3]

Coen's genocidal plan achieved its aim: the Bandas, and the monopolies in nutmeg and mace, remained secure in Dutch hands for the next century and a half.

At the time of the Banda genocide, the Golden Age of Dutch art had just dawned. This amazing efflorescence would create the images of Holland that have endured in global memory: of tranquil, rustic landscapes; serenely lit, tiled interiors; and God-fearing burghers and their bonneted ladies. A visitor who looks at these masterpieces today in Amsterdam's magnificent Rijksmuseum will be hard put to imagine that much of the wealth that underwrote this great outpouring of art came from an archipelago on the far side of the planet, nor will they see any hint of the violence that made it possible.

On Banda Neira the great killing of 1621 is memorialized by a few plaques, affixed to a small well: this is where the bodies of the forty-four Bandanese elders are said to have been thrown after their execution.

But the massacre is also remembered in other ways. The islands teem with legends about 'hantus' (ghosts) and, strangely enough, many of these tales of hantus are not about the victims but rather about tormented Dutch souls. One of the most striking of these stories was told to me by a man who swore that he had once seen tears pouring down from the stone eyes of the bust that stands in the compound of the old nutmeg godown.

Attributing remorse to this long-ago monarch is perhaps one way of making peace with history.

**7.**

And what of the question that had launched this journey: Are 'fresh' cloves and mace used in the cuisine of the Spice Islands?

A clove is actually a bud, picked unopened and dried. When the bud first appears, it is of a pale yellow hue, with four sepals enclosing an equal number of unopened petals; these lie inside, curled into a tight little ball. As it ripens, the bud changes colour, turning a delicate pinkish-red; plucked and dried at this point, the young bloom turns dark and its texture becomes hard and woody.

A freshly picked clove bud tastes milder and more interesting than a dried one. But so far as I could determine, the fresh bud is not used in cookery on the Moluccas. And this makes sense: to the people who grow them, cloves are, after all, merely merchandise.

In the case of the nutmeg, the story is a little more complicated. The fruit, which has a sharp, astringent taste, is used to make syrups and sweets. Fresh mace, peeled off the nut, is often made into tonics or chewed, like gum; the islanders swear that it is a good remedy for sleeplessness. The taste of raw, freshly peeled mace is like an explosion in the mouth: the scent is literally intoxicating—it induces a mild euphoria (both nutmeg and mace are known to have psychotropic properties). But once again, I could find no evidence of fresh mace being used in cookery. Indeed the commonest spice on the Spice Islands is no different from that of the rest of the world: it is the ubiquitous and all-conquering chilli.

But I remain convinced that newly harvested cloves and mace can be combined with green peppercorns and shavings of cinnamon bark to make a delicately fragrant, 'fresh' equivalent of tired old spice mixes like ras el hanout and garam masala. I do not doubt that such a concoction will one day transform the kitchens of the world and bring untold riches to its inventor.

(First published in *Outlook*, 30 January 2017)

# 4

# NARRATIVES

The title piece for this collection, 'Wild Fictions', was written in 2005 and 2006 while I was working on the first novel of the Ibis Trilogy, *Sea of Poppies*, and it was based on two texts that I stumbled upon almost by accident. One was a story called 'The Indian Hut' by Jacques-Henri Bernardin de Saint-Pierre (1737–1814), a major literary figure of the eighteenth century who wrote one of the earliest bestsellers, *Paul et Virginie*, a romantic tale set in Mauritius. The second was an article published in 1859 by the naturalist Edward Blyth, who was then the curator of natural history at the Asiatic Society in Calcutta. The article is dry and technical but there is a story in it, buried in the footnotes, and when I pieced it together I was struck by what it had to say about the ways in which European naturalists of that era envisioned India.

Much has changed since 'Wild Fictions' was written. While tiger populations have recovered in some parts of the country, the Forest Rights Act continues to be enmeshed in a protracted political struggle. However, the basic issue that the essay deals with, that is the conflict between exclusivist and participatory approaches to forest conservation, remains pressing and urgent. Today, at a time when environmental regulations are being loosened across India and forests are being opened up to corporate mining interests, it is of greater importance than ever before that the role indigenous people have played in preserving nature and wildlife be accorded proper recognition.

# SIXTEEN
# The Well-Travelled Banyan

No garment lies closer to the heart of the Indian male than the banyan. Yet, despite its hundreds of millions of adherents, the ubiquitous undervestment of the subcontinent gets little attention and even less respect: designers scorn it; dudes despise it; and its mere outline, were it to be discerned, would bring ruin upon an aspiring male model.

I confess that I, like most of my countrymen, am deeply attached to the humble banyan: like many of my fellow devotees, I have never been able to rid myself of the illusion, fostered in earliest childhood, that my banyan provides a necessary layer of insulation without which my shirt will not be dry and my chest will be defenceless against all the germs, viruses and malign humours that seek to invade it. But reason alone cannot explain the addict's attachment to this garment. For a true devotee, the banyan is much more than a mere article of clothing: at the deepest level, it is a marker of identity, a link with the past. This is why it annoys me when marketers attempt to rebrand the banyan as a 'sleeveless undershirt', 'singlet' or 'vest'. To call it anything other than a 'banyan' is to demean and disparage a garment that has every right to be proud of its distinctive name and lineage.

The destiny of a word can sometimes hinge on a tiny shift of emphasis. Notice how the word banyan, when referring to a humble article of clothing, is pronounced with the stress on the last syllable—banyán. Move the emphasis to the first syllable—bányan (like the tree)—and we have a word that is infused with spiritualism and freighted with overtones of ecological benevolence: a word so eminently fashionable, in fact, that hundreds of thousands of products, from soaps to spas and restaurants, have incorporated it into their brand names. Indeed it may well be one of the most popular brand names in existence: a brief googling produces over 4 million entries.

The words 'bányan' and 'banyán' may appear to be as unlike in their fortunes as a prince and a pauper, but they are actually twins and share the same parentage: both are derived from the name of a well-known Indian merchant community, 'bania'. The transition from 'bania' to 'banyan' began some 900 years ago, the process being set in motion by Arab and Persian travellers and scholars, some of whom used the word 'baniyân' as a generic term for Hindu merchants (the final consonant 'n' was probably added to indicate a collective noun). When Europeans arrived in the Indian Ocean, they adopted the Perso-Arabic usage, and 'banyan' became a general term for things associated with India. The banyan tree, *Ficus benghalensis*, is thus merely the 'Indian tree'. In matters of costume, similarly, the word 'banyan' probably referred to an item of clothing that was distinctive of India. This may have been an ancestor of a vest like those that Mahatma Gandhi used to wear, but it is hard to know for sure because nothing could be more unlike the Mahatma's simple 'angarkho' than the earliest surviving examples of the garment that went by the name 'banyan'. Several of these, dating from the late eighteenth and early nineteenth centuries, are on display at the Victoria and Albert

Museum in London: they are sumptuous, heavily embroidered ankle-length robes that look like ornate dressing gowns. They were typically worn by 'nabobs', or Britons who had made their fortunes in India.

But these were not the only banyans in use at that time: there was yet another garment that had an Indian association—one that is just as unexpected as the nabob's robe. In this other incarnation, the banyan was 'a sailor's coloured tunic', to quote Admiral W.H. Smyth, an eminent eighteenth-century authority on naval and nautical usage. In other words, at this stage of its evolution, the banyan was a prototype of the modern T-shirt. What is more, it was often accompanied by an accessory that was also of Indian descent: the 'bandhna', a head scarf that came to be absorbed into Western costume as the 'bandanna'.

How did a sailor's tunic come to be domesticated as our beloved Indian banyan? I believe the transition was effected by lascars—the Asian mariners who formed a large part of the sea-going workforce in the age of sail. These sailors may have been underpaid, but they were the earliest avatars of the global, well-travelled Indian. It is easy to imagine that their clothing possessed a glamorous appeal in the eyes of their countrymen and was thus adopted with a fervour not unlike that which would be lavished a century later on another article of workmen's wear: denim jeans. Thus did the 'banyan' (in the original sense of 'Indian') come full circle, having been reshaped and refashioned by a journey across the oceans.

In my novel *Sea of Poppies*, there is a character who has a theory about the banyan: he argues that the status of this garment has risen and fallen with the fortunes of the Indian subcontinent. When India was a land fabled for its riches, the word banyan was associated with extravagantly sumptuous robes; as the subcontinent's fortunes declined, the banyan dwindled into the humblest item of everyday wear. The implication of this, of course, is that as India's economy grows, the fortunes of the banyan will rise again, perhaps to a point where it will become, once more, a finely crafted garment. Designers, take note: there is no article of Indian clothing that has a richer, more varied and more cosmopolitan past than the banyan; a vaunted place in history awaits the couturier who can claim authorship of the next stage of its evolution.

(First published in *Dress: An Anthology Celebrating Clothes and Style* by *Vogue* India, published by HarperCollins Publishers, 2017)

# SEVENTEEN

## 11 September 2001

In 1999, soon after moving to the Fort Greene section of Brooklyn, my wife and I were befriended by Frank and Nicole De Martini, a couple whose lives were closely twinned with the towers of the World Trade Center. Both Frank and Nicole are architects. As construction manager of the World Trade Center, Frank's offices were on the eighty-eighth floor of Tower 1. Nicole is an employee of the engineering firm that built the World Trade Center, Leslie E. Robertson Associates. Hired as a 'surveillance engineer', she was a member of a team that conducted year-round structural integrity inspections of the twin towers. Her offices were on the thirty-fifth floor of Tower 2.

Frank is forty-nine, sturdily built, with wavy salt-and-pepper hair and deeply etched laugh lines around his eyes. His manner is expansively avuncular and nothing pleases him more than when the conversation turns to a subject on which he can offer his expert advice. For Frank, the twin towers were both a livelihood and a passion: he would speak of them with the absorbed fascination with which poets sometimes speak of Dante's canzones. Nicole is forty-two, blonde and blue-eyed, with a gaze that is at once brisk and friendly. She was born in Basel, Switzerland, and met Frank while studying design in New York. They have two children, Sabrina, ten, and Dominic, eight, who are unusually well-matched with mine, in age, gender and temperament: it was through our children that we first met.

Frank and Nicole's relationship with the World Trade Center was initiated by the basement bomb explosion of 1993. Shortly afterwards, Frank was hired to do bomb damage assessment. An assignment that he had thought would last only a few months turned quickly into a consuming passion. 'He fell in love with the buildings,' Nicole told me. 'For him, they represented an incredible human feat; he was awed by their scale and magnitude, by the innovative design features and by the efficiency of the use of materials. One of his most repeated sayings about the towers is that they were built to take the impact of a light airplane.'

On the morning of Tuesday, 11 September 2001, Frank and Nicole dropped their children off at their school in Brooklyn Heights, and then drove on to the World Trade Center. Traffic was light and they arrived unexpectedly early, so Nicole decided to go up to Frank's office for a quick cup of coffee. It was about a quarter past eight when they reached Frank's office. A half hour later, Nicole pushed back her chair and stood up to go. She was on her way out the door, when the walls and the floor suddenly heaved under the shock of a massive impact. Frank's office commanded a panoramic southwards view, looking towards the Statue of Liberty and the harbour. Now, through the thick plates of glass, she saw a wave of flame bursting out overhead, like a torrent spewing from the floodgates of a dam. The blast was clearly centred on the floor directly above: she assumed that it was a bomb. Neither she nor Frank was unduly alarmed: few people knew the building's strength and resilience better than they. They assumed that the worst was over and the structure had absorbed the impact: it was now a question of coping with the damage. Sure enough, within seconds of the initial tumult, a sense of calm descended on their floor. Frank herded Nicole and a group of some two dozen other people into a room that was relatively free of smoke. Then he went off to scout the escape routes and stairways. Minutes later, he returned to announce that he had found a stairway that was intact: they could reach it fairly easily by climbing over a pile of rubble.

The bank of rubble that barred the entrance to the fire escape was about knee-high. Just as she was about to clamber over, Nicole saw that Frank was hanging back. She stopped beside him and begged him to come with her, imploring him to think of the family. He shook his head and told her to go on without him. There were people on their floor who'd been hurt by the blast, he said; he would follow her down as soon as he had helped the injured on their way. She could tell that she would have no success in swaying her husband; his belief in the building was absolute; he was not persuaded that the structure was seriously harmed—nor for that matter was she, but now she could only think of her children. She joined the people in the stairway, while Frank stayed behind to direct the line.

Frank must have gone back to the Port Authority offices shortly afterwards, for he made a call from his desk at about nine o'clock. He called his sister, Nina, on West 93rd Street in Manhattan and said: 'Nicole and I are fine. Don't worry.'

Nicole remembers the descent as quiet and orderly. The evacuees went down in single file, leaving room for the firemen who were running in the opposite direction. All along the way, people helped each other, offering water and support to those who needed them. On every floor, there were people to direct the evacuees and there was never any sense of panic. On the lower floors of the building, there was even electricity. The descent took about half an hour, and on reaching the plaza, Nicole began to walk in the direction of the

Brooklyn Bridge. She was within a few hundred feet of the bridge when the first tower collapsed. 'It was like the onset of a nuclear winter,' she recalls. 'Suddenly everything went absolutely quiet and you were in the middle of a fog that was as blindingly bright as a snowstorm on a sunny day.'

It was early evening by the time Nicole reached her home in Fort Greene. She had received calls from several people who had seen Frank on their way down the fire escape, but he had not been heard from directly. Their children stayed with us that night, while Nicole sat up with Frank's sister, Nina, waiting by the telephone. It was decided that the children would not be told anything until there was more news.

Next morning, Nicole decided that her children had to be told that there was no word of their father. Both she and Nina were calm and perfectly collected when they arrived at our door; although they had not slept all night, neither their faces nor their bearing betrayed the slightest sign of what they had lived through. Nicole's voice was grave but unwavering as she spoke to her children about what had happened the day before. I was awed by her courage: it seemed to me that this example of everyday heroism was itself a small victory—if such could be imagined—over the unspeakable horror the city had witnessed the day before.

The children listened with wide-eyed interest, but soon afterwards they went back to their interrupted games. A little later, my son came to me and whispered: 'Guess what Dominic's doing?'

'What?' I said, steeling myself.

'He's learning to wiggle his ears.'

This was, I realized, how my children—or any children, for that matter—would have responded: turning their attention elsewhere during the age that would pass before the news began to gain purchase in their minds.

At about noon, we took the children to Fort Greene Park. It was a bright, sunny day and they were soon absorbed in riding their bicycles and scooters. Meanwhile, my wife, Deborah, and I sat on a shaded bench and spoke with Nicole. 'An hour passed between the blast and the fall of the building,' she said. 'Frank could easily have got out in that time. The only thing I can think of is that he stayed back to help with the evacuation. Nobody knew the building like he did and he must have thought he had to do it.'

Nicole paused. 'I think it was only because Frank saw me leave that he decided that he could stay,' she said. 'He knew that I would be safe and the kids would be looked after. That was why he felt he could go back to help the others. He loved the towers and had complete faith in them. Whatever happens, I know that what he did was his own choice.'

(First published as 'Talk of the Town: Sept 11' in *The New Yorker*, 24 September 2001)

# EIGHTEEN
# Wild Fictions

If stories play a vital role—as I believe they do—in our understanding of the world, then a question of pressing importance is: What are the tales that animate the struggle over nature that is now being waged all around the planet? Here is one such: it is called 'The Indian Hut' and is said to have been a favourite of Mahatma Gandhi.[1] This is how it begins: 'Some thirty years ago, a group of English scholars formed a society in London with the purpose of advancing the sciences and furthering the happiness of mankind by seeking knowledge in different parts of the world.'[2] There were twenty such scholars, and in order to better direct their inquiries, the Royal Society gave each of them a book containing 3,500 urgent and important queries. The most erudite of these savants knew Hindi as well as Hebrew and Arabic, and he set off in the direction of India, 'the cradle of all the arts and all the sciences'.[3] After three years of travel, he came finally to Benares, 'the Athens of India',[4] where he spoke with many a learned Brahmin and amassed an immense collection of manuscripts.

He was about to head back with this rich cargo of knowledge, when it occurred to him that despite having spoken with Jewish rabbis, Protestant ministers, French Academicians, Turkish mullahs, Parsee elders, Hindu pandits and so on, he had failed to clarify even one of the 3,500 questions he had set out with. On the contrary, he had succeeded only in multiplying the doubts that surrounded each of them. It came to his notice then that the most knowledgeable of the pandits of India was to be found not in Benares but in the temple of Jagannath in Orissa. The eager scholar set off at once for Calcutta, where the directors of the East India Company provided a palanquin and bearers to escort him to the great temple. Travelling southwards, the scholar decided that he would not trouble the learned pandit with trivial matters and would limit his inquiries to three questions of the most pressing significance. By the time he was shown into the temple's inner sanctum, he had settled upon the three queries that seemed to him to outweigh all others in importance: By what means was truth to be known? Where was the truth to be sought? Was it necessary always to reveal the truth to mankind?

The pandit had ready answers for all three questions. All truth was in the Vedas, he said, and could only be sought by means of the Brahmins, who alone possessed the secret of the language of truth. As for revealing the truth to mankind, why, said the pandit, prudence called for it to be hidden from most, while duty dictated that it always be made known to Brahmins.

These answers so dismayed the Englishman that he cried out in outrage: 'So the truth must always be made known to the Brahmins, who won't communicate it to anyone! The truth then is that the Brahmins are unjust ...'

There followed a great uproar, at the end of which the scholar was evicted from the temple and found himself heading back to Calcutta in an even greater state of dejection than before. On the way, while passing through a forest, he and his party were overtaken by a cyclone blowing in from the sea. They pressed ahead with the wind and rain raging around them until at last they caught sight of a small hut that was protected from the elements by hills, rocks and trees. The relieved scholar was of a mind to head towards the dwelling, but he could not persuade his entourage to accompany him. The hut belonged to Parayas, they said, members of one of the lowest castes of India, and they would not set foot in it.

'Then go where you want,' retorted the scholar. 'To me all the castes of India are the same.' So saying, he went inside and was warmly welcomed by the occupants, a man of gentle countenance and his wife. As the thunder raged outside, the scholar spoke at length with his host and soon discovered him to be a man of far greater intelligence and good sense than any of the savants and pandits he had met on his travels. How had this simple man acquired such wisdom? At last, unable to contain himself, he inquired of his host where his temple lay.

'Everywhere,' responded the Paraya. 'Nature is my temple.'[5] 'And from what book,' the scholar persisted, 'have you learnt your principles?' 'None but nature,' answered the Paraya. 'I don't know of any other.' 'Ah! That is indeed a great book,' said the Englishman, 'but who taught you to read it?'

'Misfortune,' answered the Paraya. 'Being from a caste that has an infamous reputation in this country, I was not able to be an Indian. Thus I made myself a man; rejected by society, I took refuge in nature.'

And as for the issue of whether the truth should at all be revealed to a world that so often rewarded honesty with persecution, the answer was: 'The truth should be told only to those with a simple heart.'

This, in short, is the narrative of 'The Indian Hut', a story published in 1791 by a Frenchman who had never set foot in India. The writer was Jacques-Henri Bernardin de Saint-Pierre (1737–1814), a novelist, naturalist and philosopher who was both a friend and disciple of Jean-Jacques Rousseau.[6]

Over the course of a varied and interesting life, Saint-Pierre accumulated many disappointments until the publication of his massive multi-volume work, *Studies of Nature*, which achieved an immediate and resounding success. Charles Augustin Sainte-Beuve would say of him later that he had done for tropical nature what Rousseau had done for the Alps. Saint-Pierre's unabashedly romantic and immensely popular novel *Paul et Virginie* was to earn the admiration of Alexander von Humboldt as well as Napoleon Bonaparte, who is said to have read it over and again in Saint Helena. No doubt the novel's themes of rejection, retreat and withdrawal held as much resonance for Napoleon as the novel's setting: the island of Mauritius, where Saint-Pierre had resided in 1768. Saint-Pierre's stay there produced what may well be his most lasting work, the Dutch-published travelogue *Voyage à l'Isle de France*.[7] While living on the island, Saint-Pierre joined the circle that surrounded Pierre Poivre, a French naturalist and administrator who had travelled extensively in Asia.[8] As is well known, the unique ecosystem of Mauritius had been seriously depleted by the first Dutch settlers.[9] By the early eighteenth century, the dodo had already been exterminated and the forests denuded. Recognizing the fragility of the island's natural environment, Pierre Poivre enacted a series of environmental measures based on his knowledge of the traditional forestry practices of China, India, Indonesia and the Dutch settlement on the Cape. Although short-lived, these measures have been adjudged to be some of the earliest state interventions motivated by ecological concerns.[10] Thus it could be said of Bernardin de Saint-Pierre that he assisted at the birth of ecological and environmental activism as we know it today: it is in this sense too that he shared in the authorship of a vision of nature whose influence was felt far beyond his time. Along with his much-admired mentor, Rousseau, Saint-Pierre was both a creator and a disseminator of the romantic vision that would so powerfully influence perceptions of nature not just in Europe but around the world: in time, kings, presidents and citizens would equally fall under its sway. That Romanticism played an important part in the creation of the first national parks in the US has been well documented; no less well documented is the fact that American parks like Yosemite served as models for the colonial administrators who created the earliest parks in Africa and Asia. Saint-Pierre's 'Indian Hut' is, therefore, no ordinary story: it has played a part in shaping and forming real ecosystems, including those of the country in which it is nominally set.

To offset Saint-Pierre's imagined encounter, here is a story about a real English scholar and one of his brushes with nature in India.[11] The date of the event is July 1852, a mere six decades after the publication of 'The Indian Hut', and its setting is Calcutta. The city's river, the Hooghly, is subject to the pressures of the tides, and in the past, it often happened that a high tide in the Bay of Bengal would cause it to flood the surrounding countryside. Thus it happened that on a hot July day in 1852, the Hooghly flowed over its embankments, swamping the low-lying wetlands that surrounded the city. When the waters receded, it came to be seen that a school of gigantic creatures had been deposited in a shallow wetland pond. Word of this discovery spread rapidly and in a few hours reached the ears of an Englishman by the name of Edward Blyth, who was then the curator of natural history at the Asiatic Society in Calcutta. Blyth was a naturalist of distinction and is credited with having anticipated some aspects of the theory of evolution.[12] He corresponded regularly with Darwin, who once described him as 'a clever, odd, wild fellow who will never do what he could do, from not sticking to one subject'.[13] Now, hearing of the gigantic sea-creatures deposited by the tide, Blyth set off immediately for the wetland. He arrived to find some twenty whales, their heads rounded and their bodies black with white undersides, floundering in the pond. The adult males were over fourteen feet in length, and the water was too low to keep them fully submerged; their short, sharply raked dorsal fins were exposed to the sun. The animals were in great distress and their moans could be clearly heard.

A large crowd had gathered but somewhat to Blyth's surprise they had not killed the whales. He had imagined that the animals would be set upon by the villagers for their meat and oil. He learnt instead that many of the villagers had laboured through the night to rescue the creatures, towing them through a channel into the river. Many had been saved, and those that remained were the last of a school of several dozen.[14] Blyth chose four of the best specimens, two males and two females, and had them secured to the bank with poles and stout ropes: his intention was to return the next day with the implements necessary for a proper dissection. Before departing, he did everything in his power to make sure the tethered whales would not be freed by the local populace.

But a shock awaited him the next morning: on returning to the site, he found that his chosen animals had been cut loose during the night. Now only a few inferior creatures remained in the pond. Not to be thwarted of these, Blyth got to work at once and quickly reduced the whales to 'perfect skeletons'. On examining the bones, he decided that he had discovered a yet-unknown creature and named it *Globicephalus indicus*. But a few years later, this identification was disproved; it turned out that Blyth had spent two days and much effort to no avail.

The text of Blyth's article makes no mention of the human interactions that resulted in the retrieval of the skeletons. The references from which I have reconstructed the event are consigned to a footnote, but, scant as these are, they leave no doubt that the villagers went to some lengths to free the whales. What was it then that prompted these people to exert themselves on behalf of the animals at the cost of incurring the wrath of an English sahib? The one thing we can be sure of is that their concerns were not the same as those that might have inspired a Saint-Pierre or a whale watcher of today. Possibly the lake in question was a public fishing ground owned by a family or the whole village. Perhaps the villagers were dismayed at the thought of their common property being colonized by a school of whales; perhaps they imagined that their carefully tended stocks of fish would be rapidly depleted by the gigantic creatures. These reasons would surely have been enough to lend some urgency to their efforts. Yet, compelling as these pragmatic reasons might be, I find it hard to believe that they were not allied also to a certain sense of awe, wonder and even compassion at the sight of the distress of these majestic creatures. Is it possible that there was no talk among the villagers of divine visitations, no stories told of signs from the heavens? I cannot conceive that there was not. Such emotions might appear to have little in common with an ecological awareness, but if indeed there is in cultures at large as well as in works of literature such a thing as an environmental unconscious, then surely it would consist in an overlapping of the pragmatic and the poetic—a broad acknowledgement of mutual dependence in which rights, mutual obligations and a sense of wonder are seamlessly merged.

As in Saint-Pierre's story, Blyth's encounter too was probably with Dalits, or with members of other disadvantaged caste groups. In both instances, the people are unnamed, but there the similarities end: Saint-Pierre's imaginary scholar converses with an individual, whereas Blyth finds himself dealing with a collectivity; where Saint-Pierre's Indian is a meditative recluse, worshipping in the temple of nature, the people that Blyth meets are of an eminently workmanlike frame of mind—far from sitting back to ponder the wonder that nature has delivered at their doorstep, they set immediately to work. What is more, the real English scholar, unlike Saint-Pierre's imaginary hero, has no interest at all in the natives and their ideas of nature: to him they are just a nuisance, an impediment in the production of perfect—if misidentified—skeletons. As for the animals, Blyth seems to have had neither the talent nor the inclination for forging any kind of relationship with them. In this, he would have been no different from other eminent naturalists of his period. His famous contemporary Alfred Russel Wallace once acquired a siamang in Sumatra, and found that the ape would spend hours playing with his Malay helpers while ignoring him. 'It took a dislike to me ...' Wallace tells us in his disarming way, 'which I tried to get over by feeding it constantly myself. One day, however, it bit me so sharply while giving it food, that I lost patience and gave it rather a severe beating, which I regretted afterwards, as from that time it disliked me more than ever.'[15]

While there are differences between Blyth's and Saint-Pierre's narratives, there are also many parallels and intersections. Where Saint-Pierre imagines nature as a sacred space and a temple, for Blyth it is a 'field' in all the varied senses of the term: in other words, it is an area that lies beyond the hearth and is uninhabited by design so that it may be subjected to cultivation—in this instance as an object of study. Where the visions coincide is that in both nature is uncontaminated by people: it is a domain defined by the exclusion of human beings. Thus did nature come to be imagined as an Eden too perfect for the fallen progeny of Adam and Eve.

Let us return for a moment to Blyth. What if, on discovering his school of stranded whales, he had indeed paused to ask the villagers for an account of their actions, as Saint-Pierre's scholar might have done?[16] The answer, I suspect, would not have been recorded—by either Blyth or Saint-Pierre—for it would probably have taken a very different form from the pithy aphorisms that Saint-Pierre accorded to his reclusive sage. The villagers, most likely, would have responded by telling a story—a fabulous tale that both Saint-Pierre and Blyth would have dismissed as a characteristically extravagant native fantasy, having nothing whatever to do with nature.

Here is a story of the kind they might have heard. It comes from the Sundarbans, the mangrove forests that in Blyth's day, as in Saint-Pierre's, extended to the very threshold of the city. Of the 4 million people who live in the Indian part of the Sundarbans today, the majority are Dalit and many are Muslim. Everywhere in this region, a figure known as Bon Bibi—'the Lady of the Forest'—is held in veneration and, as with many deities in India, is worshipped by the recitation of a verse narrative. But the first of the many surprises of the legend of Bon Bibi is that it begins neither in the Himalayas nor on the banks of the Ganges but in the Arabian city of Medina, one of the holiest places in Islam.

In this city, the legend goes, there lived a pious Muslim, a childless Sufi faqir called Ibrahim. Through the intercession of the Archangel Gabriel, Ibrahim came finally to be blessed with twin children, Bon Bibi and her brother, Shah Jongoli. On coming of age, the twins were told by the Archangel Gabriel that they had been chosen for a divine mission: they were to travel from Arabia to 'athhero bhatir desh'—the country of eighteen tides—in order to make it fit for human habitation. Thus charged, Bon Bibi and Shah Jongoli journeyed to the mangrove forest dressed in the simple robes of Sufi mendicants.

The jungles of 'the country of eighteen tides' were then the realm of Dokkhin Rai, a powerful demon king, who held sway over every being—animal, ghoul, ghost and malevolent spirit—that lived in the forest. Towards mankind he harboured a hatred that was coupled with insatiable desires; he had a limitless craving for the taste of human flesh, and when overcome by desire, he would take the form of a tiger in order to hunt human beings.

Powerful as he was, Dokkhin Rai proved to be no match for Bon Bibi and her brother, who quickly defeated the demonic hordes. Merciful in victory, Bon Bibi spared the demon's life but forbade him ever again to indulge his taste for human flesh. Following her triumph, Bon Bibi surveyed the Sundarbans and declared a certain number of them to be open for human settlement. The rest she allotted to Dokkhin Rai, ordaining that these remain wilderness to be ruled over by the demon king. Thus was order brought to the land of eighteen tides: by the creation of a balance between the wilderness ruled by the tiger demon and the areas of human settlement, which were Bon Bibi's own domain.

But this equitable dispensation was soon disturbed by human greed. On the edges of the tide country there lived a man called Dhona, who had put together a fleet of seven ships in the hope of making a fortune in the mangrove forest. Just before setting sail, Dhona discovered that his crew was a man short, and finding no one else at hand, he inveigled a boy into joining them. This lad was known as Dukhey—'sorrowful'—a name that was nothing if not apt, for he had long been cursed with misfortune: he had lost his father as a child and now lived in great poverty with his old and ailing mother. In parting from her only son, the old woman gave him a word of advice: were he ever to find himself in trouble, he should remember to take the name of Bon Bibi; she was sure to come to his aid.

The expedition set off and wound its way down the rivers of the tide country until at last it came to a promising island by the name of Kedokhali. But when Dhona and his men went into the forest, strange things began to happen: they were given tantalizing glimpses of plump hives hanging from branches of mangrove, but every time they approached, the hives would disappear only to reappear again at a distance. That this was the work of Dokkhin Rai was revealed that night when the demon showed himself to Dhona in a dream and proposed a pact in which they would each provide for the satisfaction of the other's desires. The sight of the boy Dukhey had reawakened the demon's longing for human flesh: if Dhona would but surrender the boy, he could have wealth beyond imagining; the forest would yield as much as could be carried on his boats and more.

Seized by greed, Dhona agreed to the bargain and the demon was quick to keep his word. At his orders, the bees themselves loaded Dhona's boats with a great cargo of wax and honey. When the vessels were full and could carry no more, Dhona summoned Dukhey and told him to go ashore to fetch some firewood. Suspecting a ruse, Dukhey pleaded with his captain but to no avail, for Dhona had chosen his course. Alone and disconsolate, the boy went into the forest to collect an armful of firewood. On his return, he found his misgivings confirmed: the ships were gone. It was in that moment of abandonment, as he stood alone on the riverbank, that he caught a glimpse of an enormous body covered with shimmering stripes of black and gold. The animal was none other than Dokkhin Rai in the guise of a tiger. The creature shook the earth with a roar and charged at its prey. At the sight of that immense body and those vast jowls flapping in the wind like sails, mortal terror seized Dukhey's soul. Just before he fell to the ground unconscious, he recalled his mother's parting words, and called out: 'O mother of mercy, Bon Bibi, save me, come to my side.'

Bon Bibi was far away, but she crossed the waters the instant she heard the cry. Taking the boy's unconscious body into her lap, she dealt a terrible chastisement to the demon, sending him fleeing back into the forest. Then, transporting Dukhey to her home, she nursed him back to health. When it was time for him to return, she sent him back to his mother on a gigantic crocodile that was loaded with a treasure trove of wax and honey. Thus was greed punished and balance restored between the wilderness and the domain of human beings.

This story, almost unknown outside the Sundarbans, saturates the lived experience of those who inhabit the mangrove forest. Travelling theatre companies go from village to village, staging Ramlila-like re-enactments of the legend; the verse narrative is recited every time the worship of Bon Bibi is celebrated. Although these rituals are Hindu in form, they begin always with the Muslim invocation 'Bismillah'. In a region where several hundred people are annually killed by predators, no local person will ever venture into the forest without invoking the protection of Bon Bibi. But Bon Bibi's indulgence is not easily had; it must be earned by the observance of certain rules that derive from the parables contained in the legend. Take, for instance, the belief that the wild parts of the forest are the domain of Dokkhin Rai: the corollary of this is the idea that to leave signs of human penetration is to invite retribution from the demon. So powerful is this prohibition that villagers will not urinate, defecate or spit while collecting honey or firewood. And let there be no doubt that the fear of the demon's wrath is far more effective than any secular anti-littering laws, for in the order of preventive sanctions, a municipal fine can scarcely be compared to the prospect of death by agency of storms and floods, tigers and crocodiles.

But this is merely an incidental injunction: the most important of the beliefs that relate to Bon Bibi have to do with the regulation of human need. Indeed the Bon Bibi legend is at bottom a parable about the destructiveness of greed: its fundamental teaching is that in the relationship between the forest and the sown there can be no balance except by placing limits on human desires. For Bon Bibi's devotees, the parables translate into the belief that the forest must never be entered except in circumstances of demonstrable need. In other words, to go into the forest while there is still food in the larder is to invite one's own death. The force of this prohibition is such that it extends backwards and forwards in time, so that of a man who has been killed it will often be said, 'There was a pot of rice still to be cooked in his house: he had no reason to go when he did.' Conversely, a man who goes a-foresting in the full knowledge of having left food behind at home will be haunted by the guilty awareness of his transgression so that his steps will be slowed and his senses dulled, and in the event of an attack he will be all the more vulnerable.

As with the stories of Bernardin de Saint-Pierre, the legend of Bon Bibi uses the power of fiction to create and define a relationship between human beings and the natural world. Nowhere does a term equivalent to 'nature' figure in the tale of Bon Bibi, yet nowhere is its consciousness absent; although ecological concerns are never named, the story is profoundly informed by the awareness that the literary critic Lawrence Buell termed 'the environmental unconscious'—a phrase that is all the more useful, in my view, because it does not invoke the cultural and linguistic freightage of the word 'nature'.[17]

Although the Bon Bibi legend is singular in its details, it is not unique in its vision of the relationship between human beings and the natural world: similar conceptions of balance, reverence and the limitation of greed are to be found in many other places.[18] The question of what impact these belief systems have upon the environment is not easily resolved: while it is by no means the case that indigenous peoples are always good custodians of the environment, neither is it true that their practices are always destructive. Today it is widely accepted that many such groups have indeed played an important part in the preservation and maintenance of forests and ecosystems. In the nineteenth century, however, the generally accepted view among academically trained European foresters was that the presence of people was always a threat and never an asset to forests: it was thought that where woodlands survived, it was despite, rather than because of, the people who lived in and around them. These ideas, propagated by the highly regarded German school of scientific forestry, exerted their influence on the Indian subcontinent through the forest departments of the British Raj, which were manned at the highest levels by Germans. These officials were trained to believe that it was everywhere their duty to rescue woodlands from 'backward' local populations, a grouping that did not exclude the peasantry of

Europe.[19] But the colonial context gave the foresters' efforts an extra edge of missionary zeal and the administrative structures of the Raj endowed them with powers far in excess of those they wielded at home. Many of these officials believed themselves to be surrounded by 'environmentally profligate natives' and thought it their duty to thwart the 'predatory hordes'; their efforts were silently abetted by India's nationalist elite, which was mainly urban and had little interest in the plight of forest dwellers.

The modern-day institutional successor to the colonial forest department controls a vast slice of Indian territory: the tracts that are classified as 'Reserve Forest' add up to more than a fifth of the country's land surface, an area larger than that of the two biggest states—Rajasthan and Madhya Pradesh—put together. National parks and wildlife sanctuaries are a small—but by no means insignificant—part of this domain: they form about 4.5 per cent of India's land surface, an area greater than Punjab, Haryana and Himachal Pradesh combined.

Although the forest department has now been subsumed under the Ministry of Environment, Forest and Climate Change, it continues to wield a near-imperial jurisdiction over its vast dominions: this is indeed a veritable inland empire, whose authority weighs upon a hundred million people—on none more heavily than those who live in the vicinity of national parks and wildlife sanctuaries. As it happens, many of these people are, in fact, environmental refugees, who have been evicted in the process of creating the parks—for the truth is that in their pristine state, these wildernesses were not uninhabited. In many parks—Ranthambore being a good example—traces of a centuries-old human presence can still be seen in the form of recently depopulated villages. It is the inhabitants of these settlements who have paid the price for the doctrine of nature's exclusivity.

When urban tourists visit national parks or sanctuaries, they have little conception that their experience of the wilderness is akin to that of spectators at a play: rarely, if ever, are they given a glimpse of the stage machinery that provides them with their experience—that is to say the administrative apparatus of eviction, restriction and so on that make these wildernesses conform to the tourist's notion of the 'pristine'. They are in this sense partners in the production of a wild fiction: it is their willing suspension of disbelief that makes the exclusivity of forests possible.

In effect, over many decades, there has been a kind of 'ethnic cleansing' of India's forests: indigenous groups have been evicted or marginalized and hotel chains and urban tourists have moved in. In other words, the costs of protecting nature have been thrust upon some of the poorest people in the country, while the rewards have been reaped by certain segments of the urban middle class. Is it reasonable to expect that the disinherited groups will not seek ways of resisting, whether it be through arms or poaching or the active destruction of the forests? This indeed is one of the reasons why the Naxalite insurgency—which the nation's most senior leaders have acknowledged to be the single most serious threat to the country—has found such fertile ground in India's heartlands.

The forest department is no different from any other arm of government in that some of its officers are idealistic and competent while others are corrupt and inefficient. But it so happens that the forest department holds sway in areas where there is little oversight, which means, unfortunately, that there is often greater scope for the abuse of bureaucratic power. Such indeed is the atmosphere of repression and secrecy in some of our parks that even influential outsiders risk retaliation if they bear witness to what they see. Not long ago, an eminent tiger biologist whose research suggested that officials were inflating their tiger population statistics had his equipment seized and was taken to court on an unrelated charge.[20] In another instance, the forest department is said to have filed thirteen suits of criminal trespass against conservationists who collected data on an environmentally harmful mining project in the Kudremukh National Park in Karnataka. This is what relatively privileged outsiders face in dealing with the rulers of India's forests: as for the realities that confront the people who live under this regime, they are perhaps best depicted in such harrowing works as Gopinath Mohanty's *Paraja* and the novels of Mahasweta Devi.

In short, the people who live in India's forests have had to contend since colonial times with a pattern of governance that tends to criminalize their beliefs and practices.[21] Ironically, the era of decolonization, with its growing awareness of environmental issues, has made their situation even more precarious by providing an overarching ideology to sanction their dispossession.[22] As Ramachandra Guha, in his avatar as a pioneering environmental historian, has pointed out, the consequences of this exclusivist approach have been harmful not just for the 'ecosystem people' but also for the very environment it sought to protect.

As an illustration, here is another real-life story set in one of the most picturesque corners of the subcontinent: the Hunza Valley of northern Pakistan, a high-elevation oasis overlooked by the majestic Karakoram mountains. The population of the valley consisted of a diverse mosaic of peoples, most of whom made their living partly by farming and partly by grazing their sheep and yaks on alpine summer pastures.[23] To this remote fastness there came in 1974 Dr George B. Schaller, an eminent zoologist. After a brief visit, Dr Schaller decided that 'northeastern Hunza would make a perfect national park', since it was 'scenically spectacular' and contained some rare wildlife, most notably the Marco Polo sheep. The fact that local people used some of the upland meadows for grazing was, Dr Schaller acknowledged, a problem, since 'by definition a national park should be free of such disturbances'.

The proposal took the fancy of Zulfikar Ali Bhutto, the then Prime Minister of Pakistan, who declared that 'it must become a world- famous park ... This is an iron directive.' Thus in 1975 was born the Khunjerab National Park. Since it was listed as a 'category two' national park, which involves the banning of all human activity, the machinery was set in motion for the exclusion of all human activity from this area. At one stroke, the way of life of the people of the valley was criminalized, despite evidence that there was no basis for the assumption of competition between wildlife and domestic animals. But the people who lived in the valley knew they could not survive without their grazing rights, and they decided they had no option but to resist: a local man is quoted as having said, 'First they can kill us, then they can come and make a national park.' There were lawsuits, followed by demonstrations and organized incursions into the forbidden areas. In the climate of protest and public anger, poaching and illegal hunting flourished, often with the collusion of government officials. The net result was that the park perpetrated exactly the effect it was intended to prevent: the extermination of the Marco Polo sheep, the numbers of which dropped from an estimated 300 in 1975 to 100 in 1980. A 1986 sighting suggests that the numbers may have dwindled to twenty-eight sheep at that time. If there is any upside to this story, it is that the government was eventually able to work out a more stable and equitable situation by negotiating with the villagers and giving them a stake in the park. Currently there is a dual management system in force in the park, and this arrangement has been judged by an expert to be 'the best possible way of safeguarding local resources'.

Today in India, the conflict between differing views of nature has been brought to crisis by two interconnected developments. One of these is a public awakening to the disastrous failure of India's flagship conservation effort, Project Tiger.[24] Although the scale of Project Tiger is far greater than that of the Khunjerab National Park, the two initiatives have had eerily similar careers. They were launched at almost exactly the same time, with support from the highest political quarters and massive funding from international agencies. However, after the expenditure of enormous sums of money and the displacement of a great number of people, it has suddenly been discovered that the population of tigers in the project's showcase reserves has diminished catastrophically: indeed the species may have been wiped out in some of the best-known forest areas. The one place where tigers have held their own is in the Sundarbans, where, despite an inordinate number of animal-related fatalities, people still display a general willingness to co-exist with the species—for which more is due in all probability to the Bon Bibi legend than to any governmental project.[25]

The second major development in the present conflict is a recent legislative initiative: the Forest Rights Act, which seeks to restore some of the rights that forest dwellers have lost in the 150 years since the first British edicts concerning India's woodlands.[26] The rights in question are pitifully modest: the Act would confer ownership of land (up to a maximum of 2.5 hectares per family) that is already occupied. The land at issue adds up to just 2 per cent of all forest land, of which none is currently under tree cover.[27] Moreover, the Act would forbid hunting while also imposing responsibility for protection, conservation and regeneration on those who receive rights. In other words, the Act represents a minimal effort towards the restoration of the forest dwellers' stake in the well-being of the place where they live. The measure is also belated recognition that the denial of these rights has led to exponential growth in poaching and illegal timber felling while creating conditions for a spreading Maoist insurgency.

Modest though these proposals are, the Act has been stalled by a coalition that includes the forest bureaucracy, some members of Parliament and a few well-intentioned conservationists whose experience and idealism are beyond question. Between them, this group has turned the Forest Rights Bill into an issue where the state must choose between 'tigers and tribals'.[28] Inasmuch as they have confronted the failure of Project Tiger, they blame it not on the plan's conception but on its implementation: inadequate personnel, the lack of high-tech equipment, even the allegedly advanced age of the forest guards. However, their proposals for the rectification of the situation are of a para-military nature. Never mind that this minatory approach to conservation has largely been abandoned even by the Western wildlife groups that once championed it; never mind that the rationality of a single-species approach to preservation is increasingly under question the world over.[29] Indeed issues of rationality and effectiveness have been largely abandoned, and instead there is an increasing invocation of the 'sacredness' of forests in the Indian tradition. Needless to add, such a view is anything but traditional: in the Bon Bibi legend, sacredness is not invested in the forest itself but in the deity who maintains a balance between the forest and the sown. The actual derivation of the sacredness that exclusivists attach to forests comes rather from the ideas of such Romantics as Bernardin de Saint-Pierre—none of whom had ever had to make a living from the woods. There could be no more effective demonstration of the extraordinary power that fiction has in shaping our ideas of nature: it is as if Saint-Pierre's imaginary Indian recluse were raised from the dead to haunt the real India of today.

Let us be frank in acknowledging the dirty little secret that underlies the exclusivist approach to conservation: it assumes the existence of populations that are too poor and too disempowered to adequately articulate their own interests. But while political disempowerment may have been more the rule than the exception in the Asia and Africa of the late twentieth century, it would be a mistake to imagine that this will continue forever. Soon refugees displaced by forest reserves will learn to organize: many will join those who have already taken up arms; others will form vote blocs and elect representatives who will carry their grievances to Parliament. In the long run, the greater threat to the environment may well come from the latter, for they will probably make it their mission to overturn the legislation that created the reserves. If this happens, and the path is cleared for millions of refugees to return to their ancestral villages, we may be sure that they will not look upon the forest as their forebears did; two generations of displacement will have made them angry and embittered. Quite conceivably they will return to the forest not in order to make it their home but to despoil it. This is why the exclusivist approach to conservation must be rethought: because it may well have the unintended consequence of creating an environmental catastrophe. Before that happens, we have to find some middle way, one in which the people of the forest are regarded not as enemies but as partners. And this in turn will require an acknowledgement that the idea of an 'untouched' forest is none other than a wild fiction.

Saint-Pierre, Rousseau and the Romantics of the nineteenth century have a justly honoured place in the history of environmentalism. To them goes the credit for creating an awareness of the fragility of the natural order in an age of machines. But to confront those very issues in the context of Asia and Africa today requires not just a rethinking of policy, but indeed reimaginings of nature: I use the plural advisedly, for it seems to me imperative that these imaginings be as varied as the natural world itself—and we are fortunate here in possessing a great wealth of stories to point us in other directions. But to recognize this is not by any means to call for a re-enchantment of nature in a manner similar to that of the Bon Bibi legend, not just because it would be futile but also because that view has very serious limitations and failings of its own. There are many places in the world where people stigmatize greed, acknowledge the necessity of limiting human need and believe in the principle of a balance between human beings and their natural surroundings. Although these ideas may have a wide appeal, their implications are always worked out in relation to the environment specific to the region in question. These systems are, therefore, necessarily local, and while they may be able to create a balance between the elements particular to their context, they are profoundly vulnerable (like ecosystems themselves) to disruption from the outside. Thus in the Sundarbans, with the introduction of commercial fisheries, great value has come to be placed on the microscopic spawn of prawns. As a result, fishermen have begun to trawl the waters with nets of very fine mesh. This means that the waters are being sieved in ways that are likely to have devastating effects on all aquatic life. That the Bon Bibi legend is silent on this matter is a sign of its limitations in the contemporary context.[30]

But there is another, possibly deeper, limitation to the legend's mystical conception of balance: it is a contract drawn up and signed by a single party, and it provides for no mechanism through which to understand the needs of the other protagonists; in this scheme of things, the forest has no means of articulating its interests.

It is this gap that is filled by the natural sciences, in particular the descriptive disciplines that are spoken of as 'natural history'—zoology, botany, geology and so on. These sciences direct a gaze of concentrated, interpretive scrutiny towards the curtain of signs that is called 'data'. Natural history is in this sense the indispensable science of interpretation that allows the environment to speak back to us. Although 'natural history' is by no means the only knowledge system to apply interpretive methods to the natural world, it is certainly the only one that is capable of universal application. Yet science cannot be the final arbiter in the matter of our relationship with nature for the very good reason that its procedures and methods cannot acknowledge or address questions of meaning, intention and lived history. The seriousness of this limitation does not become obvious until we consider the field of public policy. Since the conditions of scientific inquiry are such as to require a radical separation between the inquirer and the field of study, it is surely no coincidence that experts' responses to conservation challenges so often consist of attempts to recreate these conditions on the ground—primarily through the expulsion of people. It is as though they were seeking to mimic the setting of a laboratory within inhabited landscapes, an endeavour that can only be futile and, in the end, self-defeating.

In sum, the limitation of the sciences in relation to the natural world is that they cannot address its most important determinant, which is human action and subjectivity. These last are properly and necessarily the domain of politics. But the limitation of political action is that it cannot generate the imaginative resources that are necessary to a rethinking of the human relationship with nature. And yet the truth is that new policies will be impossible without such a rethinking.

The relationship between people and their surroundings constitutes as vast a spectrum of experience as the human mind is capable of conceiving—it ranges from a fisherman's knowledge of a river's rapids to Saint Francis of Assisi's meditations, from a child's wonder at the sight of a butterfly to public outrage at an oil spill. The very vastness of this spectrum points us to the reason why the human relationship with nature is so profoundly formed by fictional imaginings of it, whether they be the stories of a writer like Bernardin de Saint-Pierre, legends such as that of Bon Bibi or novels like Herman Melville's incomparable *Moby Dick*. It is my belief that only fiction can provide a canvas broad enough to address this relationship in all its dimensions; only in fiction can a reconciliation be effected between Bon Bibi and Saint-Pierre's recluse, between the quest of a scientist determined to prevent the disappearance of a species and the needs of a fisherman who must hunt in order to live. It follows then that if nature is to be reimagined in such a way as to restore the human presence within it, and not as predator but partner, then this too must first be told as a story. In India, we are fortunate in that our literary traditions, powerfully influenced though they are by the West, have never wholly succumbed to the romantic imagining of nature as a 'pristine', uninhabited temple. Such writers as Shivarama Karanth, Gopinath Mohanty and Mahasweta Devi have always been profoundly aware of the predicament of those who live in India's forests. That a meaningful debate on this issue is possible at all in today's India is due in no small part to their fictional explorations of this territory.[31]

(A version of this essay was first published by *Outlook* in 2008.)

# 5

# CONVERSATIONS

The pieces in this section are all parts of ongoing conversations with a wide range of scholars and friends. Some of these exchanges go back a long way, like the correspondence I initiated with Dipesh Chakrabarty after reading his book *Provincializing Europe*. I did not know then that our interests would converge again, on the subject of climate change.

The pieces on Shashi Tharoor's *An Era of Darkness* and Priya Satia's *Time's Monster* were written as reviews, but they are also parts of ongoing dialogues. In Shashi Tharoor's case, our conversations go back almost fifty years to our college years.

My engagement with Priya Satia's work is of a much more recent date, but it has given me new ways of understanding the role that ideas like 'progress' have played in the gestation of this time of monsters.

# NINETEEN

## *Provincializing Europe*: A Correspondence

On 14 December 2000, after reading *Provincializing Europe*, I sent an email to Dipesh Chakrabarty. I had never met or corresponded with Dipesh before this, and I was not aware that he was in Australia at the time. Despite other more pressing concerns, Dipesh was quick to respond, and over the next few days, we sent each other a series of emails centred on *Provincializing Europe*. Re-reading the correspondence later, we agreed that some of the themes and issues we had touched on might be of interest to others.

**Amitav to Dipesh, 1: 14 December 2000**

Dear Dipesh,

Although we have never met, I feel I have known you a long time because of the many friends and acquaintances we have in common. Recently I also met Uday Singh Mehta. I'd read his *Liberalism and Empire: A Study in Nineteenth-Century British Liberal Thought* (University of Chicago, 1999) this summer in Calcutta, and it had made a great impression on me. I felt that it was the most important theoretical work I'd read in many years. It so happened that I was doing a reading at Amherst last month—and who should be in the audience but U.S. Mehta! We had a long talk afterwards and he spoke very highly of you and *Provincializing Europe*.

I acquired a copy of *Provincializing Europe* soon afterwards. Reading it was an experience of such rare pleasure and excitement that I wanted to write to you while it was still fresh in my mind. First, I want to congratulate you on your extraordinary achievement. History is never more compelling than when it gives us insights into oneself and the ways in which one's own experience is constituted. I don't think I've ever read anything that does this more consistently than *Provincializing Europe*. It is truly a wonderful book, brimming with ideas and insights. To take just a few examples: I was deeply impressed by your discussion of the ways in which literature is imbricated in the emergence of modernity in India—particularly in your discussion of the place of Tagore's work in the culture of twentieth-century Bengal. I felt that it helped me understand an aspect of myself and my past that I had often wondered about but never quite comprehended—and I'd say the same about your discussion of the way in which India produced a wholly idiosyncratic version of the private/public aspect of modernity. The chapter on 'adda' was a particular delight—its insights were at once illuminating and hilarious (I am reminded particularly of the wonderful anecdote about the thwarting of Mahalanobis's attempt to functionalize 'addas').[1]

But *Provincializing Europe* is so rich in ideas and insights that it has also raised many questions in my mind, both large and small. I hope you will not mind if I take the liberty of addressing some of these to you.

First, the small questions: I was intrigued by your comment on Tagore's belief in the Goethean 'idea of world literature' (198). I wonder if you could give me a reference on this?

I was much struck also by your reconfiguration of the role of the family in Indian fiction. I agree substantially with your observation that this should not be read as a 'compensatory move'.[2] But as a writer myself, I'd like to take this a step further. Two of my novels (*The Shadow Lines* and my most recent, *The Glass Palace*) are centred on families. I know that for myself this is a way of *displacing* the 'nation'—I am sure that this is the case also with many Indian writers other than myself. In other words, I'd like to suggest that writing about families is one way of *not* writing about the nation (or other restrictively imagined collectivities). I think there is a long tradition of this, going back at least to Proust—and it's something that Jameson and Anderson (and even Bhabha) never seem to take into account.

I want to move on now to a broader set of issues. These are comments, really—and I very much hope that you will not take them amiss. They spring from certain perplexities that came to haunt me while I was writing *The Glass Palace* (which is, among other things, a historical novel). Please believe me when I say that I mean no disrespect in addressing these comments to you.

There seemed to me to be certain very important areas of silence in *Provincializing Europe*, and by the time I got to the end of the book, I felt that these silences had achieved, as it were, a piercing volume. To take one example: one of the most exciting aspects of *Provincializing Europe*, to my mind, is the way in which you attempt to restore meaning to subaltern resistance, even where those patterns of resistance make no sense from the point of view of modern citizenship, progress, etc. To this end I was particularly struck by the arguments on pp. 103 and 104 (Santal rebellion, etc.).[3] Yet, illuminating as these discussions were, I was struck also by the absolute silence on the one moment that brings all these issues to crisis—that is 1857. This absence seems all the more striking because this is surely the one case in which all the patterns you point to can be observed at their clearest. I find 1857 multiply interesting because the reasoning of the insurgents was *not* entirely opaque to 'reason' as it was in so many other anti-colonial insurgencies. It is also universally acknowledged to be the single most important anti-colonial uprising in modern history; by the same token, it was also possibly the most important event in all of modern Indian history. What is more, real subalterns (in the military sense) played a very important part in this uprising. Why then is there such a resounding silence on this subject in *Provincializing Europe* (as in so much else that has been written by the subalterns)?

Secondly, I do not understand (and this is a question I've also addressed to Uday Mehta) how it is possible to discuss J.S. Mill (or Bentham or any other nineteenth-century British liberal) without accounting for the place that the idea of race occupies in their discourse. That the idea of race was largely unacknowledged within these discourses does, of course, contribute to the difficulty of giving it its proper place within the edifice. But surely, to omit it altogether is merely to ignore the ground on which liberal thought is built. Take, for example, the idea of tutelage in liberal imperialism. This idea is after all founded implicitly on a theory of race: the 'not yet'[4] of which you speak is, in fact, a 'not yet forever' (which is merely a locution for 'never') and packed into the forever/never is the silenced term that makes this line of reasoning possible—'race'. In this sense, one of our tasks surely must be to restore, always and without flinching, the silenced term in the equation—the '+R' as I have come to think of it. Thus, in British India 'the rule of law' is actually 'the rule of law +R', and since legal procedures differed significantly when applied to Indians and British, this does, in fact, yield a much more accurate picture of the functioning of the legal system of British India than the unqualified term. Without placing the '+R' in its proper place, we cannot apprehend the real nature of the institution that was introduced under imperialism as 'the rule of law'. Built into this institution were the grounds for its own future subversion, for it was founded on an implicit understanding that the rulers were, if not quite above the law, then certainly subject to a different species of law than that which was applied to the ruled. I need hardly point out that the post-Independence successors to the colonial ruling classes have been quick to adapt this implicit exception to their own purposes: yet in acknowledging this, we must also acknowledge that these possibilities were built into the system at the very start.

To speak of the edifice of liberal ideas in the nineteenth century without confronting the issue of race seems to me much like discussing *The Tempest* (or Gray's 'Elegy' or *Jane Eyre*) without addressing the question of imperialism. Uday quotes a powerful passage from James Fitzjames Stephen: '[The British empire] represents a belligerent civilization, and no anomaly can be more striking or so dangerous as its administration by men, who being at the head of a Government founded on conquest, implying at every point the superiority of the conquering race … shrink from the open, uncompromising assertion of it …' Race, as Stephen recognizes, was the foundational social fact of the post-1857 empire—an idea embedded more in practices than in discourse—and it grew ever stronger from the mid-nineteenth century onwards. I was struck by this when I was researching the British response to the Japanese invasion of Malaya and Burma. In Malaya, while evacuating their government from the north, they stuck absolutely resolutely to the principles of race: trains were forbidden to transport 'non-Europeans' (this in a war that had its origins in Europe!). Similarly, in northern Burma in 1942, in a moment of total crisis, with hundreds of thousands of civilians heading for the mountains, the British still found time to set up 'white' and 'black' evacuation routes. Race was much more than just a tool of empire: it was (in the Kantian sense) one of the foundational categories of thought that made other perceptions possible.

In the last chapter of *Provincializing Europe*, you quote A.K. Ramanujan on how his father reconciled two apparently irreconcilable ideas.[5] To my mind, the questions that are implied there are more appropriately addressed to Mill, who saw no conflict between his hobby of theorizing about liberty and his day job as the overseer of the Indian empire. It was really he and others of his ilk who managed to believe two completely divergent things at the same time.

One final set of comments: even though *Provincializing Europe* deals largely (in one way or another) with resistance, you very rarely speak of the coercive apparatus of empire. In the chapter on 'adda', pp. 191–93, you give an example of 'Bangshalochanbabu' shutting down a discussion after Chatterjee says, 'He is a spy of the police, it is better to be careful ...' You cite this as a rare example of the subject of the 'adda' being shaped by censorial intervention. But in the broadest possible sense, could it not be said that all addas and indeed all (native) discourse in imperial India were shaped to a greater or lesser degree by the ever-present fear of intervention? Certainly, in reading B.C. Pal or Tilak or Lajpat Rai, it is evident that they were always conscious of the hand of the state and the possible consequences for themselves and their families. Is it then possible even to embark on a project of recovering 'Indian' visions of modernity under imperialism? For the traces of such thought that were actually committed to paper were, I suspect, always those that were the least compromising from a legal point of view. The visions that were articulated 'seditiously' would almost by definition be excluded from the project. It is worth noting that in most instances of insurrection, Indians (and Burmese) were very careful to shroud their projects in silence (e.g., Mutiny, Ghadar Party, Saya San rebellion, etc.).

To take this one step further: in reading contemporary Indian historians, I am often struck by the divergence in accounts of the 'persuasive' and 'coercive' dimensions of imperial rule. Military histories write of 'a garrison state' (Omissi); social and intellectual histories give us a different kind of picture altogether. But since it is the latter category that occasions most historical writing about India today, is it possible that we run the danger of getting a wildly distorted picture of imperial rule?

I realize that these questions and comments come from so far outside your broad paradigm that they may well seem meaningless. Please believe me when I say that I do not intend to offend by sending you these remarks—*Provincializing Europe* is a truly remarkable achievement and I feel enormously enriched by your insights. I am hoping that this will start a conversation (albeit digital), and if you have time, I would love to hear back.

With many thanks and good wishes.

Yours,

Amitav

## Dipesh to Amitav, 1: 14 December 2000

Dear Amitav,

Thank you for doing me the honour of reading my book with so much interest and for writing to me in such a spirit of generosity. I have long admired your work and discussed and taught it in my classes. I also have always sensed a connection with you—both through your writings and through the friends we have in common. Your praise and criticism mean a lot to me.

Unfortunately, I cannot print out messages from the computer I am currently using in Australia. (It belongs to my son and he is in hospital at the moment.) But I could read the attachment without downloading it, so I can respond from memory to some of your questions. I will see if I can get your message printed somewhere so I can respond to you more fully. But here are some preliminary responses.

Regarding Tagore and the idea of 'world literature' ('visvasahitya'). The topic is under-researched. As you know, the philosophically inflated use of the word 'world'—as in 'world outlook,' 'world spirit,' etc.—is a contribution of German romanticism. I had a hunch that Rabindranath's use of the word 'visva' in the name Visvabharati or in the expression 'visvasahitya' was an interesting case of translation. I have been fascinated by the way 'the world' came to figure in Bengali cosmopolitan and internationalist thought in the late nineteenth and early twentieth centuries. So the reference to Goethe and German thought was a quick way of signalling an area of interest needing more research.

On 1857: I take your point entirely. It would be very, very interesting for us collectively to revisit that moment of resistance. Many of my arguments regarding 'subaltern pasts' probably could have been better worked out using that instance / archive rather than that of the Santal rebellion. My choice of the Santal 'hool' was overdetermined by the fact that this was the rebellion discussed in Ranajit da's essay that my chapter attempted to critique. This still does not address your larger criticism about the silence regarding the coercive side of colonialism, but that will need a longer discussion that I hope to have with you in the course of our conversations.

Regarding race and liberalism. You are right. I kind of allude to it in the Introduction in referring to Fanon and others and then drop it. Thanks for making me aware of this problem. Why do I do it? I don't disagree factually about the place of race in imperial thought but have a question for you about the 'not yet'. Don't you think that historically one ought to make a distinction between imperialist attitudes in the settler-colonial countries where the white races genuinely wished death and destruction on the natives and in 'colonies' like India where the idea of 'self-rule' was promulgated right from the beginning (i.e., 1858)? I think there was more ambiguity in the cases of countries where imperialists acknowledged the existence of a prior 'civilization'. In other words, the 'not yet' functioned differently, it seems to me, in the two cases. Now the idea of civilization was itself a racist idea but it did produce significant differences in the way in which the Europeans treated the so-called 'primitives' and the allegedly more 'civilized' peoples. In other words, I do think that one has to acknowledge the ambivalence introduced into nineteenth-century European thought by the tension between the universalist aspects of 'science' and the particularistic emphases on 'race'. Some of our own 'primitivism', it seems to me, suffers necessarily from the same ambivalence.

Will write more again when I have had time to read your comments more carefully. But really wanted to thank you for taking the trouble to write to me. Your letter was one of the most welcome gifts I could have received on my birthday.

I will be back in Chicago towards the end of this month. Let's meet up sometime in person and do let me know when and if you visit Chicago.

With best wishes,

Dipesh

**Amitav to Dipesh, 2: 15 December 2000**

Dear Dipesh,

Thank you so much for taking the time to respond to my letter—especially since it appears to have arrived on your screen at a moment when you had many more important things on your mind.

Many thanks for your interesting comments on Tagore's usage of 'visva'. I think you are right in your intuitions and it would be interesting to see more research on this subject.

The point you make about race in imperial thought is well taken. It is true that Europeans generally did not embark on a genocidal project in India, as they did in the 'settler colonies'—but surely this had more to do with the sheer size and intractability of India rather than with notions of civilizational hierarchy? Could it be said that the Portuguese in their early years behaved substantially differently in the Konkan than they did in, say, Brazil? I'm not sure. Also, perhaps it's worth remembering that the savagery of sixteenth-century European encounters with 'other people' in the Americas, Africa and Asia was not calibrated, as it were, on a case-by-case basis. The violence was generated by their own recent history, by their encounters with people whom they generally acknowledged to be their civilizational equals—the North African Arab kingdoms in the case of the Portuguese and Spanish. Similarly, in the seventeenth century, the English in North America applied techniques (scalping, scorched earth) that they had already perfected in Ireland.

On the question of the promulgation of self-rule in 1858: this seems to me to be very clearly a political response to 1857. (One can't help wondering, why promise something for the future when so many people have died to make it clear that they want it now?) Equally, what is envisaged there is precisely a kind of perpetual deferment, as later articulated by Mill et al. In this discourse, race is the unstated term through which the gradualism of liberalism reconciles itself to the permanence of empire. Race is the category that accommodates the notion of incorrigibility, hence assuming the failure of all correctional efforts (and thus of tutelage).

To return to the question of the relationship between the ideas of 'race' and 'civilization': it would appear that in every important instance, procedurally, the latter was always subordinated to the former. It seems to me that the British did have a 'civilizational' hierarchy in India, but this had more to do with skin colour and 'race' than with elements of culture as such. This is much more clearly observed in the 'coercive' practices of empire than in the 'persuasive'. Thus, for example, the British insistence in the post-1857 period on making Punjab and the north-west the core areas for army recruitment. In army officers' memoirs, writings, etc. (on both sides), this is often presented as a clear case of, as it were, a racial alliance. Indeed, this was how it was sold (one sees this very starkly in the pamphlets the British distributed to the sepoys in Malaya at the time of the Japanese invasion). The Tamils, on the other hand—once one of the mainstays of the British Indian Army—came to be excluded because of racial theories. This despite the fact that Tamils had—by all the conventional markers—one of the most highly developed 'civilizations' in South Asia (not to speak of martial traditions). Instead, Tamils and many other east coast peoples came to be identified as ideal material for 'labour' and were thus shipped out to clear new colonial territories. Here we see the operation of an ideological logic that is in no way different from that which was employed in Africa and the New World: the civilizational calculus was clearly subordinated to the racial.

An aside: a quote from *Manual of Rubber Planting* compiled by A.T. Edgar and published in Kuala Lumpur in (mind this!) 1958. This is from a section entitled 'Some notes on labour and on the races of workers …':

> The three main races of South Indian estate workers are Tamils, Telugus and Malayalees. Each race has its particular characteristics, which have been described as follows:
>
> 'A Tamil will work well under constant supervision but is not as hard a worker as a Telugu or Malayalee. He is not generally ambitious … he prefers toddy to beer … A Telugu is generally a hard worker, industrious and thrifty … he is more clannish than a Tamil … is puzzled by trade unions, is not very receptive to argument or propaganda … A Malayalee is capable of hard work, and his work standards are high … He does not talk much, and is peaceful by nature, but is very sensitive and quickly upset emotionally …' (585-86)

If these ugly forms of racial stereotyping persisted in 'official' discourse into the '50s, imagine how much more powerful they were in the colonial epoch.

An anecdote: my father served in the British Indian Army and fought in Burma and North Africa. As a child, I remember hearing only idyllic stories of my father's life in the British Indian Army. Then one day, towards the end of his life (he died in 1998), he told me an altogether different story: at the siege of Imphal, he had turned away from the main battle to confront a South African officer who had called him a 'dirty n....r'. Suddenly these stories came pouring out of him: I was presented with a vision of army life that was completely different from that which I had grown up with.

I often ask myself: Why did my father (and in some sense all our fathers) avoid telling us these stories? There is a clue in your book: 'Bengali men experienced numerous instances of racial prejudice and humiliation ...' These stories must have been very hard to tell—especially because they were so much at odds with their vision of themselves as high-caste, 'bhadra' patriarchs. No doubt it was even harder to accommodate the idea that these were not merely 'numerous instances': they represented the system itself. For if they were to accept that, then all the versions of modernity they'd built up would crumble. Or perhaps they didn't tell us because they thought that we didn't need to know, that this was something they would keep from their children—recognizing perhaps the necessity of what Ashis Nandy calls 'the need to forget'.

Is it possible that we see this silence reproduced in our historiography for reasons that are not dissimilar? It strikes me that the historians who have written about race and imperialism in India are overwhelmingly European. The ideology of race is an ugly subject: Is it possible that we Indians flinch from it partly in self-preservation and partly because it so hopelessly contaminates that aspect of liberal western thought in which our own hopes of social betterment (as you are so careful to point out) are often founded? But then don't we have to ask also: At what point does our aversion to this subject become either complicity or denial?

Enough for now: I am sorry to bother you with so much again when you have many other pressing things on your mind.

With many thanks and good wishes,
Amitav

## Dipesh to Amitav, 2: 16 December 2000

Dear Amitav,

Your letter raises such interesting questions that I cannot help writing down a few words immediately. Yes, my son is seriously ill, and it is true that the fact of his being ill preys on my mind all the time; but conversations such as the one I am having with you also help to take my mind off it and connect me to some of the pleasures I have learnt to receive from life. So I can only thank you for your willingness and initiative in starting this dialogue.

The whole question of 'race' is indeed a silent question in India. Not just our experience of 'racism' at the hands of the Europeans. I have often thought about how we refuse to see the 'racisms' we, as Indians, practise towards one another. For instance, accounts of 'communalist' behaviour are often difficult to distinguish from what in the context of a Western country we will easily decry as 'racist behaviour'.

Yet why do we use the term racism as if it were something that only the whites did to the non-whites? This takes the question beyond the parameters of your discussion, but perhaps they are not unconnected phenomena. But let me return to your comments before I come back to mine. I do not deny the truth of what you say regarding cruelties perpetrated by the Spanish and Portuguese in their colonies, but wouldn't you think that the Enlightenment made a difference here? The calibrated scale of 'civilization' was after all an Enlightenment phenomenon. Where the Enlightenment seems special is in its universalization of different versions of the idea of equality, which allowed the colonized to charge the colonizer with self-contradiction (a lot of nationalism was that, wasn't it?). How else would I understand Fanon saying back to the European that he, the European, had made a travesty of his own principles of human equality? Or Gandhi saying that 'Western civilization' would be a good idea! Or think of Tagore's essay 'Sabhyatar Sankat'. Even the stuff I know about European settlement in Australia and their policies, with genocidal impulses built into them, all speak of deep dilemmas at the very heart of European thought, dilemmas introduced by seventeenth- and eighteenth-century ideas about being human, about property, ownership, international law and so on. (If you have not looked at Henry Reynolds' work on this subject, you may find it useful.)

The difference between our positions seems to boil down to this: How seriously do we take the ambiguity that lies at the heart of liberalism, the ambiguity caused by the tension between the universal applicability that it claims for itself and the unacknowledged racism that runs through it? I do not want to foreclose this discussion by producing an answer at this point (in part because I benefit from your interrogation of what you read as a silence in our work). But the question interests me.

There is a larger question that the story of your father's experience in the army raises for me. I have also heard somewhat similar stories from an uncle who served in the First World War as a junior doctor. Besides, as you will know, we grew up on stories of Vivekananda or Sir Ashutosh or even Vidyasagar combating racism in public places. Yet, as you say, race is not a major presence in Indian narratives. Why? Why is the coercive side of colonialism not admitted in the Indian narratives?

You ask a powerful question. In a different form, it has interested me for some time now. First, there is a question of understanding the various sites that allowed for racist practices. And there were variations internal to these sites, depending on their proximity to the ruling race. The army, the civil service—these were very specific kinds of imperial institutions, and I do not know if one can generalize the experiences particular to an imperialist army to the whole of the nation. Secondly, as you know, the cultural location of the institutions varied between groups and societies within British India. Punjab was much more intimately tied with the army, for instance, than Bengal. But I have a different question to put to you about the coercive forces of colonialism. I don't know if what I am about to say would be a correct interpretation of your rendering of your father's story, but you seem to see it as an instance of 'race'—and the overwhelming presence of the censoring/coercive side of colonial domination—circulating as a silence in our lives as untold, or belatedly told, family stories, somewhat in the nature of 'family secrets' that some psychoanalysts write about. It is an interesting approach, and may indeed be very productive in helping you to generate a new narrative about ourselves. For myself, I have wondered about whether or not the coercive side of British colonialism had a uniform reach throughout society. I have, for instance, often questioned (in my head) Ashis da's idea of 'the intimate enemy'. I think colonialism was 'the intimate enemy' for some, but I have seldom sensed it in someone like Rabindranath. I would not be surprised if there was something specifically postcolonial in the anguish that Ashis da expresses so powerfully in his book. Overall, the question of how we live fragments of joyful existence within structures of domination interests me a great deal. Having seen the Australian Aboriginals and read about their histories, lives and conditions, I do feel that Europeans dominated these unfortunate peoples in ways they never dominated us. There were spaces in our lives—so-called classical music would be a case in point—where we could use European institutional forms, syllabi, etc. (Bhatkhande would be a case in point) to our advantage without feeling deeply colonized. Aboriginal societies were just pulverized and sometimes wiped out. I do not think we—again, I mean the middle classes—suffered anything like that.

But this is not to block or mitigate the force of your question that opens up for me a new way of looking at race. And the whole business of looking at the Mutiny for a new understanding of colonialism is full of promise.

My very best wishes,

Dipesh

**Amitav to Dipesh, 3: 17 December 2000**

Dear Dipesh,

I am glad to know that this 'conversation' is serving the purpose of giving you something else to think about (I was concerned that it might be an annoyance at a time like this). For my part, I am glad to continue, for *Provincializing Europe* and your subsequent reflections have provoked me to think through many issues that have long been on my mind. Your last letter again was full of interesting ideas and suggestions and I'd like to give you my views on some of these matters.

You point to the ambiguity that lies at the heart of the Enlightenment. I accept this. But this being the case, should we not also acknowledge that this same dualism runs through many, if not most, philosophical traditions? Why should we so reflexively assume that the reformist spirit in nineteenth-century India derived its strength primarily from Enlightenment sources? We know that long before Bentinck, the Mughals as well as many major and minor Hindu rulers did everything in their power to discourage sati (I am referring here to Catherine Weinberger-Thomas's research in *Ashes of Immortality*). We know, similarly, that anti-hierarchical thought in India goes back through the bhakti period to the Buddha and Mahavira. Why should we so completely disavow the liberatory potential of these traditions?

(E.g.: Why should we assume that Dr Ambedkar was making a deathbed compromise rather than stating a deeply felt belief?) Why should we assume also that the egalitarian impulse in nineteenth-century India derived its power primarily from the Enlightenment (when indeed all the exegetical material goes against this)?

To take this further: In making these assumptions, are we not also accepting certain fundamental (but unstated) beliefs about colonialism? Are we not implicitly conceding the argument that imperialism was, in at least one of its aspects, an enterprise of social reform? This is worth asking because many Indians have been down this road before us, and I for one have come to be very interested in the ways in which they charted this path. Take Tilak, for example: His early essays give the impression that he accepted (perhaps even against his own will) the idea that there was an important reformist impulse in colonialism. But in a later essay (written in about 1906, I think, soon after a visit to Burma), Tilak went on to produce a very interesting deconstruction of this assumption. The argument goes something like this (so far as I remember):

> Yes, of course it is true that there are many evils in contemporary Indian society, that Hinduism has become a caricature of itself and is desperately in need of reform. These are all facts: but those who offer these facts as a justification for the imperialist presence in India are proceeding on a mistaken assumption. They are assuming that the British are here to reform us. They are wrong because our imperfection is not their reason for being here. They would be here anyway, even if our society did not have any of its present evils. If tomorrow we were to become a perfect society, they would still be here. If you doubt this, look at Burma: the Burmese had no caste system—they have always been egalitarian; the Burmese were not ignorant—they had complete literacy long before the British came; in Burma there was no sati and no mistreatment

> of women—women had a better position there than even in the West. Burma was not in need of reform, but this did not prevent the British from occupying and despoiling them. In many ways, they treated the Burmese even worse than they did us. Nor did their egalitarian social institutions help the Burmese in resisting the imperialist onslaught.

(Should you ever read *The Glass Palace*, you will see that there is an echo of this argument there—or perhaps I am simply rephrasing my own rephrasing.)

I was startled when I first read this essay. I was struck by the simplicity of the argument, which is not founded on a priori assumptions about imperialism but rather on one man's life experience. I had the sense that it had taken Tilak a long time to work through his assumptions (to 'pierce the veil', as it were). It made me realize that I too had been complicit at some unthought level with the idea (pace Tilak) that reform was inseparable from empire—and, on examination, one can see at once that this is simply not true. In fact, the British did everything they could to reinforce the hierarchical aspects of Indian society—indeed they introduced hierarchies of their own. That is why I think we should not reflexively assume that the egalitarian and liberatory impulses of nineteenth-century Indian society came solely or even primarily from Enlightenment roots. That there was an admixture of influences is undeniable: indeed it is to be celebrated. But inasmuch as Indians appropriated certain aspects of Enlightenment thought, it was *against* the will and the weight of the empire, and it would have happened (as in Thailand and Japan) whether there was an empire or not.

In sum: it is true that there is a profound ambiguity in Enlightenment thought. But it is also true that this very ambiguity was often used, sometimes quite deliberately, to dupe the colonial subject. We can see that this is so even today, when blatant expansionism is often cloaked in the language of reform and political 'progress' in the subcontinent and elsewhere. Given our history, it seems to me that it behoves us to approach these claims with great caution and scepticism.

To revisit the subject of race: I am intrigued by your comment about how we refuse to see the 'racisms' that Indians practise towards one another. Racism, as I understand it, is not just an exclusivist or supremacist ideology. It is an ideology that is founded on certain ideas that relate to science, nature, biology and evolution—a specifically post-Enlightenment ideology, in other words. I have often heard Western academics compare 'communalism' and 'casteism' to 'racism'. But are these legitimate comparisons? Let's take communalism first. Hindu and Muslim communalists hold many vile, false and hideous beliefs about each other. But does either group believe, for example, that the other has a lesser cranial capacity or a genetically diminished intelligence? I put it to you that they do not: that this question would appear meaningless, even absurd, if you were to put it to them. This is not in any way to diminish the horror of what communalists do indeed believe—but all horrifying beliefs are not the same, and conceptually at least we must be careful to make distinctions between them. Generally speaking, Indian communalists recognize that their conflicts are located in the social domain: I do not think they put a biological or scientific construction on them.

Similarly, racism and caste: you will perhaps remember that Louis Dumont distinguished between them in an appendix to *Homo Hierarchicus*. I was reminded of that recently while listening to a New York radio interview with Martin Macwan, the Dalit activist. The interviewer, who was African American, tried to press Macwan on the relationship between skin colour and caste. Macwan seemed to be a little puzzled at first and then remarked that there was no easy correlation in India (pahari Dalits, for example, being lighter-skinned than, say, plains Brahmins and so on).

I was struck by Macwan's initial puzzlement because his response reminded me of some of my own perplexities on the subject of race. During my student days in Delhi, I (like many others) read

James Baldwin, Langston Hughes, Fanon and C.L.R. James. I was by no means ignorant of the terms 'race' and 'racism', yet, in some profound way, I don't think I understood these terms at all. I thought of racism as a kind of cultural survival, a civilizational sediment on the model of superstition and 'aposanskriti'. Underlying this was the assumption that racism would disappear under the gaze of Enlightenment-influenced education. What I did not understand was that Enlightenment ideas were actually at the heart of racism: that this ideology incorporates certain elements of scientific thinking and it is precisely this that gives it its resilience. It has taken me a long time to understand that racism is comparable to casteism and communalism only in that it has the same murderous effects: its internal logic is quite different.

I don't think I was alone in mistaking the nature of racism. I believe it is because we South Asians fundamentally misrecognize racism that we are not able to give it its proper place within the history of colonialism. Colonial racism was an administrative and ideological practice that was applied to the Indian subcontinent: Indians inhabited the spaces it created without understanding or giving credence to the internal logic of its architecture (this is perhaps the other side of the 'dominance without hegemony' coin). I have become convinced that it is this problem—fundamentally epistemological—that underlies the 'silence' on the race issue in the historiography of colonial India. This silence is not the product of ill intention or bad faith or psychological avoidance (or, as you put it, the 'compensatory move'): at bottom, it is founded in an epistemological perplexity, a misrecognition. Nowhere is this more apparent than in the practices of the British Indian Army, where the idea of the 'martial race' was interpreted by Indian sepoys as referring to 'jati' or 'sampradaya', while British recruiters had a completely different view of the matter. (Someday I will recount to you the many strange stories I came across while interviewing old faujis.)

This is not the whole story, of course. There were many emergent discourses in India that incorporated the true Enlightenment idea of race—for example, the stuff about Hindus and Aryans and so on. Similarly, the relationship between the people of the Northeast and the Indian state does, to my mind, display many of the characteristics of institutional racism. Most significantly perhaps, the Indian perception of (and behaviour towards) the 'Sahib' incorporates many aspects of real racism—including elements of self-hatred, etc., which are familiar to us from the historical experience of North America and the Caribbean. The story is a very complicated one and I wish one of our theoretical heavyweights would work through it in detail. But I do believe I am right in claiming that the Enlightenment is the enabling condition of true racism in the modern (or colonial) sense, and that our ability to perceive and recognize it is also enabled and limited by the degree to which we are (or are not) true Enlightenment subjects. (Of course, this does not in any sense mitigate the true horrors of either communalism or caste.)

You make the important point that the Indian experience under colonialism was very different from that of the indigenous peoples of Australia and North America. You are absolutely right. To my mind, the Indian experience spans a spectrum of analogies. At one end, it is perhaps best compared to the experience of Ashkenazi Jews in eighteenth- and nineteenth-century Europe; at the other extreme, it is really not far different from that of the indigenous peoples of Australia and North America. For literate middle-class people (such as ourselves), the Jewish–German comparison is full of illuminating lessons: the debates about assimilation, for example; also the dawning awareness of the issue of self-hatred in groups that try to assimilate (in Felix Mendelssohn's parents, we see a prefiguring of Aurobindo Ghose's father, pace Ashis Nandy's brilliant essay). Similarly, many middle-class Indian debates about tradition/reform, etc., are clearly prefigured by German–Jewish debates on the relationship between reformist theology and Hasidism. As an Indian who writes in English, I frequently find myself reflecting on what it must have meant for, say, Benjamin or Celan to write in German, a language that was often inflected with a hatred for the traditions that they had been born into.

At the other end of the spectrum were the hundreds of thousands of Indians who lived through the population transfers that were set in motion by colonialism. I wonder if you have ever looked at the (very scant) material on the transportation of Indians to Southeast Asia. What these people endured is truly horrifying: the truth is that India was to the late nineteenth century what Africa was to the eighteenth—a huge pool of expendable labour.

An anecdote: you will have heard of the 'death railway' built by the Japanese to link Thailand to Burma. From *The Bridge on the River Kwai*, we get the impression that this railway was built mainly by 'European' POWs. In fact the labour force was about 80 per cent Asian—and a large part of it consisted of Indian plantation labourers from Malaya. Stranger still: many of the Indians actually 'volunteered' to work on this railway (other employment opportunities having ended with the war). One such Indian 'death railway' survivor, a Tamil, was still alive until a few years ago. A reporter heard about him and went to do an interview. In tones of horror, he asked the old man about the hellish conditions on the railway—the hunger, the disease, the torture, the unbelievable death toll. For a while, the old man answered in monosyllables, and then his patience ran out. 'You are right,' he said quietly, 'the conditions there were truly terrible for the Europeans, who had never lived through these things before. But you know, for us Indians, the life there was not much different from what we lived through here in the plantations.' It is only because these aspects of our history have been erased that we are unable to see that what happened in India was not always so different from what happened in Australia and the Americas.

The two ends of the spectrum are admittedly very far apart. Yet even in the middle-class Indian experience, there were constant irruptions of elements from the other end of the colonial spectrum. In Ramakrishna's theology, for example, I see many parallels with the radical turning away from the world that marks so many nineteenth-century Native American cultural practices (the Ghost Dance ritual comes to mind). I believe that the fundamental impetus of this theology came from the despair of recognizing an absolute impotence in the real world (I am reminded of the 'politics of despair' that you once advocated and have now renounced).

You make the very good point that in Indian (particularly Bengali) cultural discourse, there was very little anguish about the colonial situation. Again, you are right. But to my mind, the real question is: How else is it possible to assimilate subordination except by refusing to represent it to oneself?

You will undoubtedly have noticed that one of the key terms in Victorian discourse on India (especially in the latter half of the nineteenth century) is 'servility'. This is a term that intrigues me. You know, and I know, that there is nothing particularly servile in the Indians whom we encounter in our everyday dealings. On the contrary, it could well be said that Indians (of all classes) are often very contentious and self-assertive. Similarly, it is hard to imagine that an insurrection on the scale of 1857 could have been undertaken by a people, or peoples, who had become 'servile'. Nor do we ever encounter this representation in early Arab (or European) accounts of India. Yet the term recurs over and over again in British travelogues about India, even in the most sympathetic accounts written by people who were genuinely distressed to encounter this form of behaviour. This being the case, we have to assume that these reports were not without some kernel of truth. How do we account for this? I think once again 1857 is the key: in the aftermath of this event, the great mass of Indians did indeed acknowledge that they were a 'defeated people' (Bengalis had probably made this acknowledgement much earlier). I suspect that it was only in the aftermath of 1857 that most north and central Indians acknowledged that the British regime was not in India on their sufferance, as they had once assumed, that there was really, truly nothing they could do about it and that resistance, as they had once thought of it, was futile—the only grounds left for resistance were within the conqueror's terms. I believe that this recognition underlay all their subsequent attempts to appropriate modernity: I think we also have to accept that in their personal everyday behaviour this did indeed often translate into something that could be read as 'servility'.

It does not seem surprising to me that the subsequent accommodation of imperialism (in Bengal, for example) was based upon cultural forms that tried to make the domestication of colonial modernity as painless as possible. This was not just good sense: it was the only possible way. What else could they have done? But the key point so far as I am concerned is that these accommodations were always fragile and always precarious. Take the army again. Nobody bought the Indian accommodation of colonial rule more thoroughly than the people who served in the army. Not only was this accommodation not painful for them—they could not have imagined any other construction of reality. These men were not intellectuals—they had no investment in rethinking the cultural accommodations of empire. Yet one of the unwritten stories of the British Indian Army is that sepoys kept on mutinying, over and over again. And stranger still, once an Indian sepoy had seen, as it were, the other side of mutiny, he became the most passionate, the most incorrigible opponent of empire (as, for example, with the followers of the Ghadar Party). You may also have read accounts of the 1915 Singapore Mutiny: you will remember that the sepoy leaders went to their deaths hurling defiance to the last.

The best example of this was in 1941 in Malaya. In Jitra, in the aftermath of their defeat at the hands of the Japanese, the

Indian officers suddenly found themselves faced with the absolute disintegration of their worldview. At that moment, many of them underwent a kind of psychological crisis: they looked at themselves and saw something they could neither understand nor give meaning to. The cultural accommodations of colonialism, which they had so unhesitatingly accepted, evaporated in an instant. They suddenly realized that the construction that they had put on their world had no connection with their reality: it was as though history had pushed them through the veil and they had been blinded by what they had seen. This is why the early phase of the INA is so very interesting (you should read the accounts left behind by Shah Nawaz Khan and Prem Sahgal).

Although it is true, as you say, that we do not see this anguish reflected in Tagore, I think it is actually ever-present, straining against the smooth surface of his prose. For example, the constant refrain (which you refer to) of 'It's all a lie': this is stated most resoundingly in 'Kshudhito Pashan', and to my mind, this story is very explicitly a fable for switched identities (the frequent changes of clothing, etc.). Despite appearances, I think Tagore was always struggling to repress the very vision that blinded the followers of the INA in Malaya—and this struggle surfaces in his work in the constant refrain of 'it's all a lie'. This was precisely what the Indian soldiers said to themselves in Malaya: 'it's all a lie', the difference being that they had had to discover the fragility of their accommodations on the battlefield.

I have gone on at great length and must stop here. As you can see, this conversation has absorbed most of my attention over the last many days. It's proved to be an immense pleasure: it is very rare, in my experience, to come across an academic who has either the time or the inclination to listen to another point of view. I hope I am not trespassing on your patience.

With my best wishes,

Amitav

## Dipesh to Amitav, 3: 20 December 2000

Dear Amitav,

I cannot thank you enough for these conversations. They help to remind me of enjoyable things in life when I am, I must admit, a little weighed down by my son's illness and my own sense of helplessness in the face of it. I truly like the intelligence, passion, sensitivity and erudition that animate what you write. I learn from these exchanges even when we do not agree. What more could one ask of an intellectual sparring partner?

Besides, sometimes I feel our disagreements are often only partial or apparent, while sometimes they do perhaps run deeper. Let me deal with the first kind first. On the Enlightenment and its ambiguities, we are fundamentally in agreement, it seems. I agree with you that we need to understand the existing terms to which many of the Enlightenment ideas were assimilated. One of my complaints was that we, as scholars, often do not have the equipment or training with which to do that. We have nobody with the skills, for instance, of a John Pocock or Quentin Skinner. For all my respect for his work, and while I find his translations from Indian texts often beautiful (can't comment on their accuracy), I find A.K. Ramanujan's attempt to make our Virasaivas look like predecessors of modern democratic thought unsatisfactory. I do not dispute that there are a great many things to be mined in the bhakti traditions or in other texts that critique hierarchy. But what I bemoan is the fact that while the older commentarial traditions—in all their richness—seem lost to us, we have not been able to connect with them or revive them except in the most perfunctory of manners. I once heard my dear, respected and now-very-unfortunately-departed friend D.R. Nagaraj attempt to produce a critical commentary on the Mimamsa Sutras of Jaimini from the point of view of a modern pro-Dalit scholar. The scholarly apparatus in what he was trying to do was weak and inadequate to the task. So I agree with you about the need to explore our traditions, but I do hold that a lot of what we—scholars who write in English—say about these traditions is a bundle of unexamined assumptions and assertions based on a knowledge of these traditions that, textually speaking, is scanty. It amounts to what in Bangla we call 'porer mukhe jhal khaowa'.

But there is a sense in which, based on my admittedly shallow reading of our own traditions, I would argue that the Enlightenment—in combination with capitalism—was something special. It was special in the way in which it helped to make 'equality' into a universal category of secular life and ran it through every aspect of human activity, building it into all general measures of exchange. To me, it has always seemed interesting, for instance, that even some of the most aggressively egalitarian of subaltern or religious sects in India do not do away with the idea of the 'guru'. Later Sikhism is a major instance of this, but you probably also know of the Balahari and other sampradayas that Sudhir Chakraborty wrote about a few years ago. In any case, there are many such instances. I contrast that point with what Marx said about the logic of commodity production: that the principle of equality that underlies generalized exchange can be performed—and thus be made visible—only in a society in which the idea of human equality has attained the fixity of a popular prejudice (I am paraphrasing).

In other words, from where I stand, to acknowledge our debt to the ideas of the Enlightenment is not to thank colonialism for bringing them to us (your examples of Japan and Thailand are very pertinent here), and the Tilak quote is very interesting (and I do look forward very much to reading *The Glass Palace*). His argument would go for many of the tribal and indigenous peoples as well. Their societies often conformed better to the ideals the British set up as criteria for judging the quality of civilization. So there were absolutely no intellectual grounds for colonizing them. (I must say, however, that at least in the case of Australian Aboriginals, I personally do not always find their social customs—as described in ethnographies—attractive, though this is no argument for the 'civilizing mission'.)

To continue and move on to the question of race.

Here again, I agree with you that if one were to connect race with modernity, one would have to go to the more 'scientific' versions of it. I take your point here. And I accept the empirical facts about Indians having partaken of this kind of racism through the eugenics movement in the 1930s, the theories of Aryanism, etc. I also accept that one should distinguish between modern racism and simple prejudice (or even more virulent but older forms of ethnic hatred). But couldn't we expand the idea of 'science' to include modern knowledge forms such as sociology, anthropology, demography, etc., that governments and institutions use every day? Take the case of the idea of 'the dying race' and the way that was used—not only in the Indian censuses in the early part of the twentieth century but also in 'communalist' writings about Hindus and Muslims. And these in turn informed popular ideas about whether or not the Muslims bred faster than the Hindus. A sort of popular demographics came into play. In other words, the very practices of governing in modern bureaucratic ways entail the use of modern knowledge forms that also, thanks to the media, develop a life in popular culture, so that the distinction between simple prejudice and prejudice backed up by the pretensions of knowledge becomes harder to sustain. In that sense, I was arguing that there are homologies between racism and communalism. If you define racism very tightly, you run the risk of defining it away as does Dinesh D'Souza, from what I understand him to be saying in the American context: scientific racism is gone, so there is no racism left!

Our deepest—and for that reason, the most productive—differences are perhaps over this whole other question you raise about 'forgetting' subordination. If we were conducting this discussion in Bangla, then I would have put the question to you in this form:

*Rabindranath ki samrajyabaad bhule thakte parar nidorshon, na amader bishesh ouponibishik obosthay-o atmostho thakar nidershon?* I think the latter. But let me put the question as a problem of knowing and we can work on it together (for I am not sure what my answer will be). Suppose we come across someone who looks to us subordinated and oppressed but who does not give us any signs of being in that state, at least signs that we would recognize. How do we know then if this person has actually developed ways of forgetting that state or not representing that state to himself or herself? How do we know that ours is a truer representation of the 'deeper' facts of their life? Why could not we allow for the possibility that they have developed ways of living—life forms—in which our very questions are of lesser relevance?

I struggle with this possibility, and this is what bothered you the most in reading *Provincializing Europe*. I find your questions challenging, for they come out of another way of looking, from other struggles that are yours. But they are also shared struggles. My responses do not do justice to the many interesting cases and ideas you raise and mention, but I am very grateful for the conversation. It is always instructive to differ from someone one respects. It reminds of the possibilities for diverse interpretation that are innate to living. There are two other points I want to raise quickly. In your first ever letter, you made a very interesting and intriguing point about how writing about the family was one way of not writing about the nation. If possible, I would like to hear more about it. I found the thought arresting but could not develop it on my own.

Amitav, I want to thank you again for this exchange of thoughts. I have found it quite exhilarating to meet you in this way in cyberspace. I have now seen your mind at work and I truly respect it. Thank you for becoming my friend.

With my very best wishes,

Dipesh

## Amitav to Dipesh, 4: 21 December 2000

Dear Dipesh,

Thank you very much again for your thoughtful responses to my last letter. This correspondence has been a true pleasure: it has made me recall the intellectual excitement and urgency of my college days. But it has been better still in that there has been none of the combativeness and rancour that marred those exchanges. One of the subtler pleasures of growing older is that one comes to understand the true meaning of the Arabic saying '*ad-dunia wasa'a*'—'the world is wide'. To be able to understand and appreciate ideas that are different from one's own is a gift in itself: to look for agreement is really futile, since—let us face it—much of the time, it's quite a struggle even to agree with oneself.

Since I initiated this correspondence, I feel in fairness you should have the last word. So I'll try to be brief. First, to take the question of the novel and the family. Novels almost always implicitly assume a collective subject: this is what usually provides the background, milieu, setting, dialect, etc. Sometimes this collective subject is the nation itself (one sees this most clearly in the work of the magical realists). Sometimes it is a culture or a class (very common among Brits and Europeans) or (as in modern American writing) 'a generation'. All of these are clearly subsets of the nation—since the boundaries of the culture, class or generation are usually assumed to coincide with the boundaries of whatever country the writer happens to be from. In India, collectivities such as nation, class, generation, culture, etc., do not have the same imaginary concreteness that they do elsewhere (even today, I think). This is one of the reasons why Indian (and African) writers so often look to a different kind of collectivity: the family. In my case, the family narrative has been one way of stepping away from the limitations of 'nation', etc.; I think this is true also of many others. I could go on at length about this but will postpone that discussion till the day we meet.

Also, a few rejoinders:

- While it is true that we do not possess good commentaries on some anti-hierarchical movements in South Asia, this is certainly not true of Buddhism, Jainism or Sikhism, each of which could fill a library (or several) on its own. Moreover, even where it concerns the other more obscure traditions, I feel that we sometimes prevent ourselves from keeping a genuinely open mind simply for fear of being labelled 'nativist', 'indigenist', 'Orientalist' and so on. Useful as these terms are, we must not allow them to become tools for a new kind of intellectual re-colonization.
- If we acknowledge that the egalitarianism of anti-hierarchical movements in South Asia was incomplete, then we must surely also acknowledge the incompleteness of Enlightenment egalitarianism, which is inseparable, on the one hand, from 'Leviathan' and, on the other, from the disguised denial of the affirmed principle through such exclusionary mechanisms as race.
- The question of which of these traditions have had the most influence on contemporary Indian egalitarianism is surely moot for the very reason that you point out—that this egalitarianism continues to be imagined in ways that are quite different from the Enlightenment model (e.g., Lenin-puja in Calcutta; guru-ism in politics, etc.). Yet we surely cannot deny the force and vitality of contemporary Indian egalitarianism. If anything, this is evidence that contemporary Indian egalitarianism derives its almost-millenarian force from sources that are not necessarily the same as those in France or Russia, for instance.
- Your point on race and the mechanisms of the Indian state is well taken: the story is, of course, a very complex one.

- On Rabindranath: if you are taking the position that it is unacceptable to examine a text for meanings that go beyond the author's expressed intentions, then you are effectively throwing out 99 per cent of postmodern (as well as Marxist) literary criticism. While this would definitely make you popular with me, I suspect it would not go down quite so well with some of your 'post-colonial' friends and colleagues.
- As for Rabindranath, we can have no real doubt that race and colonialism were among his central preoccupations. These were explicitly the subjects of the novel that is acknowledged to be his prose masterwork: *Gora*. The title itself signals the preoccupation with race. Perhaps it is we who fail to read it as it was intended. And it is worth remembering that one of the notable features of *Gora* is that Tagore was ultimately unable to find the kind of resolution to these issues that he sought elsewhere. Also, generally speaking, so far as the Bengali vision of colonialism is concerned, we can surely only think of it as lacking in anguish if we omit (for starters) Bankim and Sarat Chandra.
- You make the very important point: *Suppose we come across someone who looks to us subordinated and oppressed but who does not give us any signs of being in that state, at least signs that we would recognize. How do we know then if this person has actually developed ways of forgetting that state or not representing that state to himself or herself? How do we know that ours is a truer representation of the 'deeper' facts of their life? Why could not we allow for the possibility that they have developed ways of living—life forms—in which our very questions are of lesser relevance?* This raises many vital issues, the most important of which is: How is it possible to recognize coercion when its traces are invisible, as they most often are? If you went to Burma today, you would see that people often appear light-hearted. People smile and laugh much more openly than they do in India, and you would be hard put to find anyone

who would talk about political or economic difficulties. But if you were to take all this at face value, you would be deeply mistaken about the circumstances of the Burmese people. It is one of the odder facts of history that oppression and coercion do not necessarily rob people of their capacity for joy and laughter: quite the contrary. There is (as you noted in one of your letters) a great deal of joy and laughter in the poorest bastis in India (just as there probably was on antebellum plantations in the Deep South and in the Caribbean). The broader question is: Is it possible to detect coercion in cultural matters at all? Where do we look? Battles and insurgencies are, after all, relatively rare: in its effects on everyday life and culture, coercion leaves few, if any, detectable traces—but this does not imply its absence.

Finally, please do not imagine that these (and the other issues I've raised) are intended as criticisms of *Provincializing Europe*. I believe very strongly that books should be read on their own terms. One of the lessons I've learnt as a writer is that it is hellishly difficult to say anything at all: to me what a book says is much more important than what it does *not* say. *Provincializing Europe* is a rich and insightful work, a singular achievement. It is without a doubt, one of the most important books I've read these last many years. The questions I've raised were not addressed to the book as such, but rather to you—and I raised them partly to share some of my own perplexities and partly to point to areas that I hope you will explore one day, for it would be fascinating to follow the writer of *Provincializing Europe* into those realms. It is in this spirit that I would like to add an observation and a final plea: the unintended effect of concentrating solely on the 'persuasive' and discursive aspects of the Raj is that it sometimes makes colonialism itself invisible, as though all that had happened was a consensual exchange of ideas between equals. Do you really believe that this was what happened—that this was the truth of the subcontinent's long subjection?

The beginning of this friendship has been one of the true rewards of venturing into cyberspace—I hope, however, that we will one day get to carry on the conversation in a less immaterial medium.

With many good wishes,

Amitav

### Dipesh to Amitav, 4: 22 December 2000

Dear Amitav,

It is you who deserve my grateful and warmest thanks for these exchanges. I was always—from your very first book—an admirer of your writing. But, of course, a person's work is often not a good guide to his or her personality. It has been a real pleasure to get to know you—your intellectual generosity and straightforwardness, your capacity to disagree without disrespect—through these letters. One day, I hope we will meet in flesh and blood and renew the bond. (Incidentally, I have just acquired a copy of *The Glass Palace* and will now read it with the added pleasure of the knowledge that the author is now somebody I think of as a friend.)

It is, again, kind of you to let me have the 'final word', but whatever I say cannot, of course, be final in any intellectual sense. The world is indeed big, and the trick, I now think, is not only to accept difference but enjoy it. India is also too big to be reduced to any unitary experience. Colonialism was no one thing. But our difference can be productive. You and I may not agree on everything. But I know that even when I disagree, the pressure of your thoughts will keep acting on me. And one day, I may see some of the things you see, share your passion or be better able to see through your eyes. Something similar may happen to you. Even if I never get to that point, the knowledge that someone I respect disagrees will lace what I think and how I think it. There is a fragment of a sentence from Heidegger that continues to intrigue me: 'to hear that which I do not already understand ...'

Often in listening to someone, I try to work out what this injunction may actually mean in practice. I am not absolutely clear, but it kind of works as an ethical horizon for me.

Before I respond to some of the points you make, let me thank you for your clarification re the novel and the nation. I will continue to think about your interesting point.

My first response is by way of clarification. Of course, there are long commentaries available on Buddhist, Jain and other systems of thought. My point was/is that our—I mean social scientists who write about democracy, citizenship, equality, etc. in modern South Asia (that includes myself)—access to these commentaries is often through English and often without any awareness of the problems of translation (both literal and intellectual). This is why I mentioned people like Skinner, who actually can enter the heart of the sources they use, so great is their mastery of Latin or Greek or other languages they need. Skinner's capacity, for instance, to talk about the literary characteristics of Hobbes's texts (their rhetoric, for instance) is something unparalleled in our scholarship. I don't disagree with you in the emphasis you put on our traditions and PE, at least in my head, was a plea to make these traditions into critical resources for, and guides to, living. (You perhaps know that I have often been called a 'nativist'!) But the task is immense and not to be done solely through English. When writing the chapter on Tagore, I became aware that—with the exception of Sudhin Dutta and Mohitlal Majumdar—very few of the poets criticizing him actually had any access to the rasashastras from which Tagore quoted in self-justification. Rabindranath's own knowledge of these texts was not authoritative (or so I learn from Subodh Sen Gupta's criticisms) but he had read Vishwanath's *Sahitya Darpan* at least and perhaps more. But even this was a big gap that separated him from the poets of the thirties. (And, interestingly, Rabindranath himself did not have the interest that his father had in Persian poetry and philosophy.) I blamed colonialism for this intellectual loss and was trying to argue: 'Let's once again make intellectual that which has become merely practical now.' As you can imagine, I don't have great expectations on this score but my sentiment remains.

And secondly, on anguish, colonialism and 'the intimate enemy' syndrome. I do not always factually disagree with you on *Gora*, etc. But perhaps I had not expressed myself clearly. Any self-respecting author in British India felt humiliated by colonial rule and the racist practices on which it was based. Bankim, Rabindranath and Sarat Chandra all felt profoundly insulted by it and were all angry about it (Bankim in some sense was consumed by this anger). That anger is absolutely legitimate and I consider myself an heir to it. But I distinguish it from 'the intimate enemy' position. By the latter, I mean a complex of feelings in which you feel that something that moulds your interiority also corrodes you from within, something Ashis da calls 'loss of self'. This is what I meant by anguish. You may tell me that I am using it in a special sense, but I needed to clarify my understanding in order to clarify our differences (if they still exist). I see some of this anguish in early Michael indeed. But not even in Bankim. Otherwise, he would not have been able to write what he wrote in defence of 'imitating' and learning from the English. (Sarat Chandra, I have to think about more, having always read him for other things.) And I don't think Rabindranath ever had anguish about his deep love for English romanticism or poetry in general. I see both him and Gandhi as two people who took the European idea of 'civilization' seriously and then asked themselves what it might mean to become civil(ized) Indians if civilizing were a matter of self-education and not something doled out by the imperialists. What you say about *Gora* is right. But I submit to you that Rabindranath lives on in middle-class Bengali lives much more—as he himself once predicted—through his songs. Ranajit da once described *Gitabitan* as Rabindranath's *Grundrisse*. If these songs were the expression of some of his deepest sentiments and thoughts, then while there is nationalism and nationalist anger in many of them, there is no anguish of the 'intimate enemy' kind.

My last point relates to oppression and its apparent absence in consciousness. Obviously, what we can infer about whether or not someone is deliberately or half-deliberately attempting to forget oppression depends on how we read the evidence. In many situations, it could be legitimate to infer such forgetting. My one question was: How do we distinguish between 'forgetting/silence' and life practices in which the imperative to forget may not be as salient as it is in the observer's framework? I do not ask this rhetorically, for I do not have an answer to the question, but it continues to bother me.

And secondly, I have often wondered if the feeling of oppression became more important or intense precisely when, because of historical factors, it was possible to (a) imagine the existing order as one, and (b) imagine secular and worldly alternatives to such an order. In other words, totalitarian rule would now hurt more viciously because people can imagine democracies. Colonialism hurt more when one could imagine alternatives—Mughal rule for the sepoys, self-rule for the nationalists. It is possible, similarly, that Bengali women who received education in the nineteenth century felt more oppressed (in the way they did) than their eighteenth-century counterparts. Some of my arguments were against the tendency to read this sentiment anachronistically into a period to which it may not belong (while there may have been other feelings of oppression in the past).

Enough said, Amitav. You will know what I mean and accept or reject as you find suitable. Now it is time to wrap up these exchanges. Let me end by heartily agreeing with you on one major point. Most of our deepest disagreements, as you said, are with our own selves. There is a constant need to test one's ideas, to doubt them, to prevent them from becoming a crust on the surface of one's mind. You have been a wonderful partner in this exercise. I am very glad and grateful that I met you in this way.

I will read you now with the special privilege of having got to know you a little.

My very best wishes for you and your family for the holidays.

Dipesh

**Amitav to Dipesh, 5: 23 December 2000**

Dear Dipesh,

Thank you again for your deeply reflective and thoughtful reply. Of course, the only reason why I even took the time to write to you is because I knew that we both started from similar positions and hold the same things dear and worth defending. I can think of no more than a handful of people with whom the effort would be even halfway worthwhile. The questions that we've been addressing are, as you said, part of a common struggle—and I am proud to be able to share that struggle with you.

This has been a wonderful and immensely rewarding correspondence. I hope we will be able to continue it one day as a real conversation. I sincerely hope that your stay in Australia goes well and my very best wishes to you and yours for the New Year.

Amitav

(Amitav Ghosh and Dipesh Chakrabarty, 'A Correspondence on *Provincializing Europe*', in *Radical History Review* no. 83, pp. 146–72.  www.dukeupress.edu)

# TWENTY
## Imperial Denial

### 1.

To anyone who knows the work of Fa-ti Fan, Prasannan Parthasarathi, Kenneth Pomeranz and Julia Adeney Thomas, it will be amply evident that *The Great Derangement* owes an enormous debt to their scholarship and their thinking, especially in regard to imperialism, global scientific exchanges and the trajectories of modernity in Asia and the West. That they in turn, and Rob Linrothe, have attended so carefully to this book is a true privilege for me: I am grateful to the *Journal of Asian Studies* for making it possible.

In reading the contributions to this round table, I was forcibly struck by the recurrence of certain words: 'imagining', 'imagination' and 'seeing'. These terms are, of course, central also to *The Great Derangement*, where, as Julia Adeney Thomas points out, I have tried to explore the ways in which 'our modes of representation have derailed humanity, blinding us to our real condition'.

My main concern in the first part of *The Great Derangement* was with the techniques and suppositions of the contemporary literary novel. But modes of storytelling in literature and the humanities have so much in common that there can be no question that Kenneth Pomeranz is right when he observes that the constraints that shape the writing of history 'may not be completely unlike those of realist fiction'.

This suggestion becomes even more interesting if we consider it in conjunction with the question Dipesh Chakrabarty implicitly poses in his seminal book *The Climate of History in a Planetary Age*:[1] Is the Anthropocene a critique of the motifs that have guided the writing of human history over the last 250 years? These motifs—equality, social justice and progress—all of which Chakrabarty subsumes under the 'blanket category' of freedom, are, of course, ultimately derived from the emancipatory ideals of the Enlightenment. As such, their influence extends far beyond the academic discipline of history: they are the guiding motifs of all the humanities and indeed of liberal-humanistic thought in general.

It follows, therefore, that in trying to identify the constraints that guide humanistic thinking, we must give due attention to these motifs. In light of this, Pomeranz's suggestion can be recast as the following question: Is it possible that in relation to climate change, the emancipatory motifs of humanistic thought function as blinders that restrict our range of vision?

The contributions to this forum hint at several ways in which this might be the case. Prasannan Parthasarathi, for instance, writes that our times 'may be seen as an age of imperial denial ... In popular—and even to some extent scholarly—circles it is difficult to persuade many that the present inequalities of the world are legacies of empire.'

The possibility that post-Enlightenment history may actually have exacerbated global inequalities and injustice is almost impossible to reconcile with an emancipatory vision of the past. This is certainly one of the reasons why 'imperial denial' is so pervasive within the academy and elsewhere.

But 'imperial denial' is not only a disowning of the past: it is also, and perhaps more significantly, a disavowal of the realities of the present day. After all, the 'present inequalities of the world' are not just bequests of history (as the term 'legacies' implies); they are also outcomes produced by the contemporary world order. Consider the disparity in the coercive abilities of the US and, say, the Philippines: the gap between them has not lessened since the end of the colonial era. Far from it. If anything, the difference is greater today than at any time in the past. In this sense, as Parthasarathi points out, empire is not only alive and well but is also an integral element of the history and political dynamics of climate change.

A hundred years ago, imperial power celebrated itself with parades, reviews and durbars, perhaps because it was then still open to contestation and, therefore, needed to make itself visible. Today empire manifests itself as an everyday reality, something that undergirds the scaffolding of the world to such a degree that it is no longer distinguishable as power at all. It has come to be conceptualized instead as 'cultural disparity' or 'international income distribution' and so on. These rubrics are so effective in masking the connection between the international power structure and what Parthasarathi calls 'the apparatus of violence that enforces our vast global inequalities' that the asymmetrical nature of those relations has become the unseen elephant in the room.

While writing *The Great Derangement*, it became clear to me that the unacknowledged realities of contemporary power are themselves central not just to the politics of climate change but also to the discourse on the subject. The reason why emissions, consumption, income inequality and other quantifiable metrics have come to dominate the discussion is precisely because disparities of power are both unquantifiable and difficult to acknowledge. This phenomenon is not so much 'denial', I think, as a blockage of some other kind, rooted quite possibly in the emancipatory motifs of humanist thought: those assumptions make it very difficult for liberal, well-intentioned people to accept and address the correlation between greenhouse gas emissions and power.

Let me illustrate what I mean. One of the most admirable aspects of the discourse on climate change is the patent altruism and good intention of the scientists who have brought this crisis to the world's attention. James Hansen, Michael Mann, Kevin Anderson and many others have argued forcefully for global justice in carbon consumption, repeatedly acknowledging the relationship between income and greenhouse gas emissions, and conceding (or even insisting) that the world's poor have a right to increase their emissions in order to improve their standards of living. Some of them have also made significant personal sacrifices, giving up air travel and going to great lengths to reduce their carbon consumption.

All of this is laudable, yet there is something that goes unacknowledged here: carbon consumption is not just (or even primarily) about wealth and standards of living. Thus the questions that altruistically minded people need to consider do not relate only to living standards and creature comforts: they must also address whether they would be willing to sacrifice influence and power. Were this to be factored in, even the most well-intentioned people may be inclined to rethink their positions.

Few Western university professors would object, for example, to betterments in the economic conditions of the average Indian or Chinese person, nor would they greatly mind sacrificing a few conveniences in order to achieve that outcome. But how would they feel about putting themselves in a position where Chinese or Indian institutions of learning exert upon them the same influence that American universities exercise upon the world? To look for an answer, we need only think of the controversy over the setting up of Confucius Institutes in American universities. The reality is that it is almost impossible to conceive of a situation in which Western universities or intellectuals would consent to rearranging their priorities in accordance with the needs and wishes of, say, China, Russia, Indonesia and India.

That the struggle for mitigatory action is ultimately a battle to determine who wields power over whom is perfectly well understood by those who oppose or obstruct it, silently, explicitly or by subterfuge. Yet this context rarely figures in the discourse on climate change, which continues to be ruled by emancipatory motifs. As a result, the struggle for mitigatory action has increasingly come to be conceptualized as a battle of ideas, or of conscience, even on the left.

Consider an argument advanced by Naomi Klein and George Monbiot, among others: that the Abolitionist and Civil Rights movements were moral struggles that could serve as models for the climate campaign. I have the greatest respect and admiration for Klein and Monbiot, but it is clear to me that this analogy, unfortunately, does not hold. There are many reasons for this: The first is that many other political and historical factors were also critical to the success of both Abolitionism and the Civil Rights movement. In the case of the former, the context consisted (among many other things) of the political pressures generated by slave rebellions and the Haitian Revolution; moreover it was at just that time that another vast source of labour—indentured workers—became available because of Britain's rapidly expanding empire in India. Similarly, the political and ideological struggles of the Cold War were essential to the success of the Civil Rights movement. In neither case can it be said that the movement's success was brought about primarily through emancipatory idealism.

Secondly, while it is certainly true that the Abolitionist and Civil Rights movements improved the lives of a great number of people, it is true also that the prevalent structures of global power were not fundamentally changed by either of these movements. This, however, is precisely the effect that a more equitable global emissions regime would have. Nor has this facet of the issue eluded climate change negotiators: indeed the Western approach to climate change negotiations has consistently been oriented towards the creation of an emissions regime that would change the global distribution of power as little as possible. This objective, which is both unacknowledged and probably impossible to attain, remains in my view the most important obstacle to effective mitigatory action.

Given the paucity of resources that are available to activists, it is not hard to understand why Klein and Monbiot would choose to present the struggle for mitigatory action within an idealistic frame. Yet it is also important, tactically and otherwise, not to lapse into idealist readings of history: otherwise we run the danger of placing our faith in a kind of secular spiritualism.

Parthasarathi points quite rightly to the ways in which global structures of inequality amplify climate change and suggests that mitigatory efforts would be enhanced by reducing inequalities. There is an implicit assumption here, one that underlies much of the literature on climate justice: that people everywhere want fairness, equality and justice for all. But the unfortunate truth is that where it concerns relations between classes, castes, nations and races, this has never been the case, least of all in the post-Enlightenment era.

Were we to stop reading emancipatory motifs into the Anthropocene, we would be faced with questions of a different order. What if it is precisely the prospect of a reduction in global inequities—especially where it concerns coercive force—that motivates the world's powerful to drag their feet on climate change mitigation? What if the only way to prompt them to act more decisively were to persuade them that mitigatory action would *not* change the inequities of the present order, that the status quo would be preserved unaltered? What if drastic action on climate change can be achieved only at the cost of *abandoning* the emancipatory ideals that have come to undergird our thinking?

The ethical and political dilemmas that this possibility conjures up are almost impossible to resolve. What, for instance, should be the properly ethical course for a country like India? Knowing that its population will suffer disproportionately, should it, for the sake of preserving life, proceed to make radical cuts in emissions, accepting that this will ensure the continuation of current inequalities, nationally and internationally? Or should it make all possible haste to improve living standards, at the cost of accelerated emissions, so that some may be better able to cope with what lies ahead? This is, after all, the strategy that has largely been adopted by the world's wealthy nations.

These dilemmas are almost never explicitly stated. Yet, arguably, they have a more immediate bearing on climate change negotiations than do many metrics that have been elaborated upon at great length, like climate budgets and so on.

**2.**

Julia Adeney Thomas's contribution suggests another way in which our imaginings of time and history influence our perception of the Anthropocene. Thomas argues that our blindness 'to our real condition' and our failure to act are the result of the 'distance between our abstract tools of understanding and the exuberant messiness of reality'. This in turn is echoed by Linrothe in his comparison of his own way of looking at the mountains of Zangskar with that of a hereditary headman and monk who has lived there for all his seventy-plus years. 'In person or in photography,' writes Linrothe, 'I don't *see* the difference that twenty-five of the deadliest years of the Anthropocene have made.'

Here then is the question that haunts our age of cosmopolitan omniscience: Everything in the phenomenal world has already been mapped, measured and weighed. Yet we know that something eludes us, that we cannot listen to glaciers in the same way that the Tlingit peoples of the Yukon and Alaska do,[2] that we cannot read waves and currents as Polynesian navigators once did. Is it possible then that our inability is rooted in the ways in which we use such words as 'mountain', 'glacier' and 'current'—all of which invoke a cosmopolitan universalism, a commensurability and comparability of phenomena wherever they may exist? Have these very words become 'abstract tools of understanding' that obscure other possibilities? After all, the monk from Zangskar would not claim to 'see' the mountains of the Andes in the same way that he 'sees' those that he and his forebears have lived with over generations. Nor would the Polynesian navigator claim to be able to read the currents of, say, the North Atlantic.

Indeed it is quite possible that the monk 'sees' certain features of his landscape precisely because to him they are not 'mountains', mere instances of a much larger class of things; they are specific, individualized presences with their own names, personalities and moods. In short, to 'see' in this way may also entail a blindness to other like phenomena.

But that is not the kind of seeing that Linrothe is seeking. For him, 'seeing' is much more than an act of perception: he is searching, in this instance, for a 'recognition of our collective imperilment'.

'Seeing' in this sense is a metaphor for looking ahead, for 'vision'. It too imagines the passage of time as linear and directional; discernible within it are the same emancipatory motifs that have guided history and the liberal arts—of history as a forward movement shaped by human agency.

But what if history is something else altogether—demanding metaphors of an entirely different kind? What if, as Carl Schmitt proposed, history is a labyrinth through which humanity blindly reels, knowing neither its shape nor entrance or exit?[3]

Certainly there can be little doubt as to which vision of history is better fitted to the predicaments of the Anthropocene.

**3.**

Kenneth Pomeranz and Fa-ti Fan have both mentioned the last section of *The Great Derangement*, which suggests that religious groupings may represent a sign of hope. Pomeranz describes this gesture as 'forced'—and he is probably right. A critical look at the world's major religions suggests that the Catholic Church under Pope Francis is very much the exception—almost miraculously so—in its responsiveness to climate change. Other major religions have come increasingly to be dominated by forms of belief that closely resemble those that arose in the Age of Acceleration (like certain kinds of Protestantism). They now consist largely of differently packaged admixtures of growth fetishism[4] and identity politics. This is true of 'Hindutva' in Narendra Modi's India and of the officially approved version of Islam in Recep Tayyip Erdoğan's Turkey.

If growth fetishism is at all contested in Asia, it is only by a few Buddhist groups and figures, most notably the Dalai Lama. Certainly no one who travels in the continent at this time can be blind to the signs of ever-quickening acceleration: vast forests of concrete rising everywhere; perpetually expanding networks of highways, packed with fast-growing numbers of vehicles; rapidly proliferating airlines offering ever-cheaper flights. The momentum generated by this acceleration is such that it would take decades to reverse course even if Asian governments were willing and able to make significant changes. But a change of direction is nowhere a discernible priority: this is a vast machine fuelled, on the one hand, by fusions of neo-liberalism and religion and, on the other, by the enormously powerful industrial lobbies across Asia and indeed the world that now hold governments captive.

In light of these realities it is undeniable that the last section of *The Great Derangement* is 'forced'. The only excuse I can offer is that I felt it necessary to look, as does nearly everyone who writes about climate change, for some rays of hope. Very few of us can claim to possess the clarity of vision that allowed Martin Heidegger to say, as he did half a century ago: 'Only a god can save us.'[5]

(Julia Adeney Thomas, Prasannan Parthasarathi, Rob Linrothe, Fa-ti Fan, Kenneth Pomeranz and Amitav Ghosh, 'JAS Round Table on Amitav Ghosh, *The Great Derangement: Climate Change and the Unthinkable*', in *The Journal of Asian Studies* vol. 75, no. 4, pp. 929–955.  www.dukeupress.edu.)

# TWENTY-ONE
## Storytelling and the Spectrum of the Past

**1.**

Never had I imagined while writing the Ibis Trilogy that these books would one day be the subject of a special forum in the *American Historical Review*. For a teller of stories, it is indeed a truly unforeseen privilege to participate in an exchange of this kind with four scholars as distinguished as Clare Anderson, Gaurav Desai, Mark Frost and Pedro Machado.

Of course, Anderson, Desai, Frost and Machado are also, willy-nilly, storytellers themselves. This is unavoidable because history and storytelling are so closely joined together that it is impossible to pick apart their roots: they are like two trees grafted upon each other as seedlings. It is not only in the linked etymologies of the words that the grafting is evident but also in the storyteller's dependence on the past, so inescapable as to be apparent in the rhetorical form that fiction most commonly employs: the past tense. History too once regarded itself as a literary art, and this forum is perhaps a sign that after a brief parting of the ways, history and storytelling are once again moving towards a convergence.

As for my own work, it will be clear from the acknowledgements in the trilogy that I owe an enormous debt to many historians whose work has, for the most part, helped me to understand the background and settings of the books. In some instances, however, the debt extends well beyond that. Take, for example, the episode from *Sea of Poppies* that Clare Anderson refers to in her contribution to this forum: 'the powerful scene when disgraced rajah Neel Rattan Halder first enters Alipore jail and is stripped naked, inspected, and tattooed on the forehead with the mark of *godna*'.

This scene was, in fact, inspired by the work of none other than Anderson herself, specifically her study of the treatment of convicts in nineteenth-century India: *Legible Bodies: Race, Criminality and Colonialism in South Asia*.[1] The book made a powerful impression on me for many reasons, not the least of which was its imaginative use of an official photographic archive. Anderson brought the plight of the convicts so powerfully to life that even as I was reading her book, I knew I wanted to explore these situations further. What was it like to be tried, jailed and sentenced to transportation in colonial India? I felt compelled to imagine those experiences from the points of view of the people who had lived through them.[2]

This endeavour could be regarded as deluded and self-indulgent, especially since a novelist's knowledge of the past is bound to be, in many respects, far less complete, far less rigorous, than that of the trained historian. But it also bears saying that approaching historical moments through the eyes of fictional characters does sometimes yield certain insights.

Take the parts of the trilogy that are set in the foreign enclave of Canton (Guangzhou), for instance. We are fortunate to possess detailed historical accounts of many aspects of late eighteenth- and early nineteenth-century Canton: much has been written about the city's trade relations, politics, art and material life, and botany and gardening; even the dialect in which business was conducted there (pidgin) has received careful attention.[3] But Canton's foreign enclave was a tiny place, a quarter of a mile in length and half that in width. Everyone knew everyone else, at least by sight; traders danced with each other at social occasions, and they were all great gossips.[4] The same merchants who made fortunes in trade also patronized the arts and collected botanical and zoological specimens. Like any community of people living in close quarters, they were divided by many petty rivalries and jealousies.

It is easy to lose sight of these peculiar circumstances while reading historical monographs on eighteenth- and nineteenth-century Canton. This is because the protocols of historical research impose certain constraints. In the same way that a novel is shaped by its protagonists, a historical monograph is shaped by its subject and the questions it asks. The trade historian sees a busy port; the historian of science sees a city with innumerable nurseries; the art historian sees a collection of studios. This limitation is also a strength, in that it focuses the range of the research and thereby gives the historian the right to assert claims to truth, or at least verifiability.

A work of fiction cannot make truth claims no matter how detailed and exhaustive the research. Yet, in rendering a setting through the eyes of individuals, a novel can take on the task of recreating the multifaceted nature of a character's experience. This project would not be possible, of course, if historians had not laid the foundations for it. But some things can elude even the highly disciplined and rigorous gaze of the historian.

Consider, for example, the episode that precipitated the First Opium War: Commissioner Lin Zexu's confrontation with Canton's foreign merchants from February to May 1839. This period is so densely documented that it is possible to work out from day to day, and sometimes from hour to hour, who was meeting with whom and what was being said in which of the enclave's thirteen factories.[5] As I sifted through this material, the picture that began to emerge was rather different from the one portrayed in historical studies of the origins of the First Opium War: the events seemed to be powered to a great degree by interpersonal relationships and conflicts. The patterns of factional rivalry, deception, manipulation and overwrought emotion that were hidden within the sources made the ultimate outcome seem much less inevitable than I had thought. Here was a world-historical event in the making—yet its course seemed to have been determined by a dynamic that will be familiar to anyone who has ever sat on a committee!

It was in this way too that I became aware of another aspect of the Opium Wars: the corruption that permeated the British campaign, extending from the procurement of below-grade provisions to the hiring of substandard transport vessels.[6] Corruption within Chinese officialdom is a recurrent theme in the literature on the Opium Wars; that something similar was happening on the other side is almost never mentioned.[7]

Archives are shaped by the eye of the beholder; the same materials will yield different impressions to a historian and a novelist, depending on what they are looking for. The point, however, is that they are both looking for *something*. This is why Pedro Machado is right, in my view, to describe historical fiction as 'a mode of enquiry'.

## 2.

Packed into the word 'history' are many very different ways of relating to the past. Only a small part of this vast spectrum is occupied by academic history of the kind that emerged in European universities in the nineteenth century. A much larger section is taken up by various modes of storytelling, ranging from epics and sagas to contemporary historical fiction.

Professional historians might insist, not unreasonably, that their discipline has a privileged position in relation to the past, not least because their procedures and scholarly apparatus protect them against the ideological pressures—like nationalism—to which the rest of the spectrum is vulnerable. But the truth is that academic history has also often been deeply enmeshed with nationalism, imperialism, communism and other ideologies; equally it has often critiqued and debunked the fallacies of popular history, myth and so on. As I see it, these engagements, sometimes complicitous, sometimes adversarial, continue to be close enough to establish that academic history belongs in the wider spectrum of discourses about the past (although its place within it is undeniably a special and privileged one).

In my view, what distinguishes contemporary historical fiction from both academic history and other forms of historical storytelling is the way in which it envisions the past. Take, for example, the response that Anderson's *Legible Bodies* evoked from me. As I noted above, my reading of the book made me want to explore the past in a distinctive way: I wanted to see it through the eyes of someone who had lived through certain experiences. In other words, I wanted to *inhabit* that moment; I wanted to know what it was like to be there at that time.

That we can never actually know what it was like to inhabit the past hardly needs to be said. Yet this kind of curiosity cannot be wished away either; it is as urgent, as primeval, as the desire for knowledge itself.

To live in a place is to be able to see it, to experience it through one's senses, to eat its foods, breathe its smells, rest one's eyes on its sights. The capaciousness of the novel as a form makes it well suited to this endeavour. In a study of trade, there is no place for banquets and gardens. The novelist faces no such restrictions. Within the pages of a novel, trade, banquets and gardens are all elements of the world its protagonists live in. It is precisely the effort to recreate this roundedness of experience that makes historical fiction a distinctive 'mode of enquiry'.

In order to relive the past, novelists are often forced to approach sources in a distinctive way; information about matters that might seem transitory to a historian may be of vital importance to a writer of fiction. The settings of the Ibis Trilogy are unfamiliar to most of us, their material background even more so. This is particularly true of the foreign enclave in Canton, which was visually and otherwise an admixture of an extraordinary range of influences, styles and tastes. Even experienced travellers were astonished by its uniqueness, its unfamiliarity.[8]

In order to make this place habitable, I had to make an effort to inhabit it myself, and this I did by trying to picture Canton's thirteen factories room by room, building by building. Fortunately this was not as difficult a task as might be thought, for the Chinese and European artists who worked in Canton have left behind remarkably detailed pictorial records of the city, particularly of the foreign enclave.[9] The visual sources are supplemented in turn by a wide range of textual materials authored by contemporary residents and visitors.[10] Moreover, a number of scholars, such as Carl L. Crossman, Valery Garrett, Patrick Conner, Jacques M. Downs and Paul A. Van Dyke, have also written about the enclave in great detail.[11] In short, the documentation of the foreign enclave is rich enough to provide a vivid picture of the setting.

But to envision the events that unfolded within this setting is another matter altogether. The queries that arise while imagining a scene are not always answered by historical accounts. Much may have been written about a well-known episode, yet in trying to visualize it, a novelist may be forced to comb afresh through contemporary letters, records and pictures. This is because some of the issues that need to be addressed in order to create a scene are of the following order: What was so-and-so wearing when such-and-such happened? What was the time of day? What was the weather like?

These questions are generally not of interest to historians who address long-term social, economic and political trends. There are, however, other branches of history in which such matters are essential. One such is military history: the overlap here is quite striking, especially when it comes to detailed accounts of battles. For the military historian, as for the novelist, weather, terrain, clothing, equipment and states of mind are all essential elements of a narrative. Nor is this the only commonality: it extends also to the treatment of time. Military historians must also contend with critical moments and decisive events: like novelists, micro-historians and others who are concerned with the unfolding of specific events, they work with the jagged edges of the temporal continuum. Historians interested in long-term trends, by contrast, depend on the aggregated time of the social sciences, in which the peaks and valleys of the temporal continuum are either flattened or ignored.

There is another significant respect in which the novelist's relation to the past is radically different from that of most historians. The historian's work could not begin without an idea of a recoverable past. Historians necessarily have a sense of responsibility to this past, and this contributes in no small measure to the importance of what they do.

But I as a novelist see this past through the eyes of my characters; my responsibility is to them; my task is to try to recreate their experience as faithfully as possible. This means that I can ignore certain kinds of material. I do not, for example, have to attend closely to secular trends in, say, cotton prices over a hundred-year period. I do, however, have to pay close attention to sudden fluctuations in value, and I have to try to figure out how a character would have responded to them. In this sense, the historian's past has a sweep that the novelist's doesn't.

The difference is between observing the flow of a river from the shore and from within the waters: the direction of the current is the same in both cases, but a swimmer, or a fish, has at every moment a million different choices and options.

As with any perspective, this has many limitations. One of them became evident to me in the process of writing this response. Mark Frost makes a number of points about the trilogy: he suggests that I was not fully abreast of revisionist writings on opium use and the Opium Wars, that I am not sufficiently attuned to colonialist perspectives and that Conrad and Kipling were better able to grasp 'the psychology and the psychosis of the Western imperial project'.

It seems to me that these opinions are perfectly reasonable in that they are consistent with a particular point of view, one that has certainly not lacked for proponents. In order to dispute them, I would have to write a story featuring characters with opposing views. One of those characters would probably want to point out that in considering the rights and wrongs of the nineteenth-century opium trade, the actual effects of drug use are a secondary matter; the prime issue is whether the British—and other European colonial powers—aggressively promoted the trade while *themselves fully believing* that it was capable of causing great harm.[12]

Perhaps I will get around to writing such a story some day, but for now I would like only to note that many of those who wrote most perceptively about the Western imperial project have sadly fallen into neglect—for example, Eduard Douwes Dekker (Multatuli), Leonard Woolf, J.R. Ackerley, Louis Couperus, Maurice Collis, Victor Segalen and Han Suyin.[13] This may be one of those canons where what is obscured is more revealing than what remains.

**3.**

Anderson makes an interesting point when she notes that it may be easier for novelists than historians to 'address questions of emotion and affect'. Of the two, oddly enough, it is the latter, in my view, that poses the greater challenge for the novelist: raw emotions do, after all, have a certain universality, while forms of feeling and affect shift over time in ways that are hard to translate. Consider, for instance, the prominence of words like 'impertinence', 'insolence' and 'impudence' in the nineteenth century. These expressions have almost vanished from modern English; the passions they once evoked are incomprehensible to most contemporary readers. A character who risks his life in order to avenge a perceived impertinence is now more likely to be seen as crazy or foolish than heroic or honourable.

Trying to recover this aspect of the historical moment was among the most testing challenges of writing the Ibis Trilogy. What does a wealthy, upper-caste man like Neel Rattan Halder experience when he has to clean another man's excrement? What is the nature of the fear that the sea (the 'kala pani' or 'black water') inspires in a woman like Deeti?

Questions such as these—and others that relate more generally to affect, emotion and intimacy—have also attracted the interest of many historians. In seeking answers to my queries, I was fortunate in being able to draw on a wide range of historical research, some of it of exceptional quality and insight.[14] Yet the effort was humbling as well, in that it forced me to recognize that some strands of affect and emotion are probably beyond our comprehension.

Take, for instance, the question of the nineteenth-century sepoy's subjective feelings about combat. Historians like Dirk Kolff, William Pinch and Nile Green have shown that pre-modern soldiering in India was deeply permeated by religious and mystical beliefs: although affect and emotion are not their primary concerns, their research leaves little doubt that the sepoy's experience of combat was also shaped by his beliefs.[15] But to try to understand what this might have meant for a soldier on the battlefield is to confront, in the starkest way, the unrecoverability of many elements of the past.[16]

This is why in crediting me with tackling the 'materiality of the sea', Desai may have granted me more than is warranted (I am glad to accept the compliment, of course). The truth is that it is almost impossible to fully comprehend, far less communicate to today's readers, what it was like to be at sea in the age of sail.[17] It isn't just the constant danger, the confinement, the extreme discomfort, the sexual tensions and brutality that are hard to represent; what is really difficult to convey is that danger and violence may not have been experienced as they are now. The violence that one encounters in accounts from that time is sometimes so casual and yet so excessive that the contemporary reader may have no rubric for it other than a clinical one like 'sadism'. Yet those acts were produced not by individual pathologies but rather by institutional arrangements that not only enabled but even enjoined certain kinds of behaviour.[18]

Another, more intimate, aspect of affective experience has been rendered almost alien to the modern reader by a process that Herbert Marcuse characterized as 'desublimation':

> [The] pre-technical world was permeated with misery, toil, and filth, and these in turn were the background of all pleasure and joy. Still there was a 'landscape,' a medium of libidinal experience which no longer exists ... a whole dimension of human activity and passivity has been de-eroticized. The environment from which the individual could obtain pleasure ... has been rigidly reduced ... The technological reality *limits the scope of sublimation.*[19]

It is perhaps because I did not grow up in a technological and desublimated world that Marcuse's observations carry a great deal of weight with me. In any event, I did try to convey through the texture of the language of the Ibis Trilogy a sense of a differently configured landscape of experience. This is why Desai's comment on the 'hypersexualization' of Zachary Reid in *Flood of Fire* is of particular interest to me: it is perhaps inevitable that Zachary should appear so when seen from a perspective in which sexuality has been intensified (or 'hyper'-ized) at the expense of a more diffuse kind of eroticism. But, conversely, it is also true that it is the very desublimation of our technological era that has made it possible even to attempt to portray this lost landscape. The interesting question then is whether such a feat of translation is possible or even permissible. The writer who came closest to succeeding at it was perhaps Marguerite Yourcenar.

What Zachary and Mrs Burnham certainly have in common is the gift of unbounded sublimation—and this expresses itself in Mrs Burnham's case (as it often did before our clinicized times) in euphemism. The attentive reader will notice that neither Mrs Burnham nor Zachary ever uses a sexually or anatomically explicit word or phrase: their relationship is sustained, even in its most physical moments, by sublimation. Nor is sublimation merely fantasy: it is, as Marcuse notes, 'a cognitive power which defeats suppression while bowing to it'.[20] For Mrs Burnham, this power becomes a curse; for Zachary, it may well be his salvation.

The Ibis Trilogy happens to be set in a period in which the world—especially the Western world—was beginning to experience what is probably the single greatest shift in affect that has ever occurred: the birth of the bourgeois sensibility.[21] This too is an aspect of Zachary's relationship with Mrs Burnham in *Flood of Fire*. Their circumstances—one an 'India-born' memsahib and the other an American freedman—could not be more different, yet they have this in common that they both find themselves on the cusp of this transformation. Although their journeys end very differently, they are both propelled by the most powerful of the anxieties that underlay the shift in sensibility occurring at that time: anxieties that relate to the body—for example, 'hysteria', 'onanism' and so on. Much has been written about the religious and literary dimensions of the transition to bourgeoisdom; this other aspect of it remains to a surprising degree silent and invisible, even though traces of it are ubiquitous in nineteenth-century materials.

No one who has read Thomas Laqueur's *Solitary Sex: A Cultural History of Masturbation*,[22] and Jean Stengers and Anne van Neck's *Masturbation: The History of a Great Terror* can doubt that the anxieties associated with 'onanism' amounted to a kind of terror.[23] These historians are careful not to suggest any simple or direct link between these anxieties and the birth of capitalism or the bourgeois sensibility ('Onanism and the Spirit of Capitalism' is a book yet to be written ...). What their work does show, however, is that this particular terror manifested itself just as the great bourgeois transformation was getting under way in the first half of the eighteenth century. They show also that the fear that surrounded onanism was a largely secular phenomenon and that it came to exert a powerful influence on a wide range of practices: medical, dietary, penal and much else. This anxiety was, in other words, inseparable from the birth of modernity itself. It was one of the mechanisms that brought into being the genteel yet highly sexualized world of the bourgeois.

**4.**

The contributions to this forum are so rich that it is impossible to respond to every point of interest. But I would like to comment briefly on an issue that Desai raises when he touches upon the possibility of future conversations between historians of India and China.

These conversations already exist, of course, and their echoes can be heard throughout the Ibis Trilogy. Tansen Sen's work, for example, has uncovered many new layers of complexity in Sino-Indian relations between the seventh and fifteenth centuries.[24] Madhavi Thampi has written about the circulation of goods, objects and people between India and China in the nineteenth and twentieth centuries.[25] Prasenjit

Duara's work on environmental issues in Asia shows that these conversations can offer new perspectives on the most pressing issues of our times.[26]

Matthew Mosca's account of the xenology of the Qing dynasty, *From Frontier Policy to Foreign Policy: The Question of India and the Transformation of Geopolitics in Qing China*, is another hugely important recent work on Sino-Indian relations.[27] Fortunately for me, the book was published while I was working on *Flood of Fire*: not only did it vastly broaden and deepen my sense of the relationship between China and the Indian subcontinent in the late eighteenth and early nineteenth centuries, but it also suggested all kinds of new possibilities.

The recent work of Anand Yang has opened yet another window into a vista that was of vital interest to me: the lived experience of Indian sepoys who fought in various campaigns in China. Yang's articles on this subject are based on an extraordinary memoir written in Hindi by Thakur Gadadhar Singh, an Indian subaltern who was in China in 1900-01, participating in the suppression of the Boxer Rebellion. Yang's detailed and sensitive reading of the memoir shows that Gadadhar Singh was deeply aware of the commonalities that bound India and China, and had a great deal of sympathy with China's faltering attempts to deal with the West.[28]

In pioneering the study of Sino-Indian connections, Duara, Mosca, Sen, Thampi and Yang have shown that this is a subcontinent in itself, and that its exploration has scarcely begun.

**5.**

One of the greatest rewards of writing the Ibis Trilogy was that it revealed to me the astonishing, almost unbelievable, breadth and variety of the work that contemporary historians are engaged in. From micro-histories to studies of gender and cuisine, this is indeed an embarrassment of riches, notable most of all for its openness to other disciplines and pursuits.

Things were very different when I made my first forays into historical research for my book *In an Antique Land*.[29] I remember showing a part of the manuscript to a brilliant young historian of my acquaintance: he came back to me with the considered opinion that the pages I had given him were worthless as history and that I would be well advised to throw them in the trash.

Did I ever think that I would live to see the day when a historian would describe that book as 'a seminal, and perhaps even foundational, text' (Machado) or 'ahead of the historical curve' (Frost)? The answer, unambiguously, is no.

That this has come about, and that the Ibis Trilogy can be the subject of a forum in the *American Historical Review*, has a significance that extends far beyond these three novels: it signals the arrival of a new era in thinking about and imagining the past.[30]

(First published in *The American Historical Review* vol. 121, no. 5 [2016]: 1552–65)

# TWENTY-TWO

## Shashi Tharoor's *An Era of Darkness*

In May 2015, the Oxford Union held a debate on the proposition 'Britain Owes Reparations to Her Former Colonies'. One of the invited speakers was Dr Shashi Tharoor, novelist, essayist, politician and social media star with a following of over 8.4 million on X (formerly Twitter).

Tharoor spoke in favour of the proposition, and his speech, when posted on YouTube, quickly went viral, garnering millions of views on some sites. In India, the highest in the land took notice: the rancour between the ruling BJP and the Congress (of which Tharoor is a prominent member) was temporarily set aside and Prime Minister Narendra Modi showered him with praise for having said 'the right things in the right place'.

Tharoor confesses that he 'was pleasantly surprised but also a bit perplexed' by the response.

> For one thing, though I had spoken well enough for my side to win the debate by a two-thirds majority of the audience, I knew I had made better speeches that had not acquired a tenth of the fan following this one had. For another, I honestly did not think I had said anything terribly new. My analysis of the iniquities of British colonialism was based on what I had read and studied since my childhood, and I thought the arguments I was making were so basic that they constituted what Americans would call 'Indian Nationalism 101'—the fundamental, foundational arguments that justified the Indian struggle for freedom. Similar things had been said by the likes of Romesh Chunder Dutt and Dadabhai Naoroji in the late nineteenth century, and by Jawaharlal Nehru and a host of others in the twentieth.
>
> Yet the fact that my speech struck such a chord in so many listeners suggested that what I considered basic was unfamiliar for many, perhaps most, educated Indians. They reacted as if I had opened their eyes, instead of merely reiterating what they had already known.

By Tharoor's own account, the response led to a kind of awakening: he realized that there is widespread amnesia about the colonial record, especially among young, educated Indians. It was this recognition that prompted him to expand his speech into his impassioned, eloquently argued book *An Era of Darkness: The British Empire in India*.

Tharoor and I were near-contemporaries at Delhi University and we both studied history as undergraduates. I, like him, have often been astonished by the extraordinary rehabilitation that the reputation of the British empire has enjoyed over the last few decades. This is partly the result of a many-fronted revisionist project, one of the aims of which is to establish, as Sanjay Subrahmanyam has argued, 'that the

British in the nineteenth century were practically indistinguishable from Indians in white-face, and that what has unjustly been termed "colonialism" is in fact really all about "dialogue"'.

This, at least, is a front on which there can be genuine and productive engagement because it actually requires detailed readings of the historical record. The revisionist project is far more dangerous on another of its fronts, where it is spearheaded by theorists with wider ambitions, like Niall Ferguson, who argue that the British empire's great virtue was that it was an 'essential engine of modernity'. The phrase is revelatory. What it tells us is that the defence of the British empire's history has come to rest not on the actual record of what happened in Britain's colonies but rather on a teleology that reaches towards an imagined future: it is in relation to a conjectural end point—'modernity'—that the empire is claimed to have been 'essential'.

Even if we ignore the fact that many very 'modern' institutions—like commodity futures' markets—existed in Asia long before the West, even if we set aside the possibility that colonialism may actually have retarded the modernization of the Indian economy, the question remains: Does modernity actually have an endpoint? Will there ever come a moment when we will be able to say, 'We are all equally modern now so empire is no longer essential'? Clearly not, or surely two hundred years of empire would have brought us there already. Hence, it follows that empire is still, and will forever continue to be, 'essential' so long as the always-unrealizable goal of 'modernity' remains unrealized.

This, in essence, is what imperial revisionism is about: although it purports to be about history, its true nature and purpose is of an altogether different order. This is evident, first of all, in the fact that the project's exculpatory energies are directed solely towards the British version of empire to the exclusion of all others (the Roman being the possible exception). The Portuguese, Spanish, Austro-Hungarian, French, German, Russian, Ottoman and Chinese do not figure in this narrative at all, or if they do, it is usually as objects of denigration whose benightedness makes the virtues of their British counterpart shine all the more brightly.

Equally revelatory is the chronology of the revisionist project, which came to the forefront soon after the end of the Cold War. This too suggests that the debate over the British empire is not about what actually happened in colonies like India in the nineteenth and early twentieth centuries; it is about the world we live in today and the political dynamics of the post-Cold War international order. This is because the global distribution of power that was created by the British empire is still very much with us in its post-war avatar as a broader American-led system of alliances in which Britain and her former settler colonies ('the Anglosphere') are the most important partners and actors. The argument about British imperialism is, therefore, actually one about whether the Raj should serve as a template for today and tomorrow (a connection that is made explicit in such books as Niall Ferguson's *Empire*).

The power and significance of these neo-colonial ideas should not be underestimated. Among their staunchest advocates are the neo-conservatives and liberal interventionists who have been the driving force behind many recent Western interventions. No less a figure than George H.W. Bush was also a votary. (A very senior Indian diplomat, a man well-placed to know, once told me that the former President's readings about colonial India had served as inspiration for the American war against Iraq in 2003. Perhaps he should have read a little more about Pakistan, which is, in many ways, the true successor of the 'garrison state' that was the Raj.) Nor are Indians immune to the appeal of neo-colonialism. On the contrary, many within the country's political elite are so keen to join the ruling ranks of the Anglosphere that they are all too willing to draw a veil over inconvenient historical truths.

Inasmuch as neo-colonialist ideas have been contested at all, it is by academics and theorists whose voices are scarcely audible within the public arena. This is precisely why *An Era of Darkness* is so welcome: as a hugely gifted writer and polemicist, Tharoor is eminently well-equipped to engage the new ideologues of empire on their own terms; indeed he has few equals in his mastery of their particular forms of rhetoric. He has the added advantage of being a scholar in his own right (he has a PhD from the Fletcher School of Law and Diplomacy at Tufts University). The skills he acquired then are deployed to great effect in *An Era of Darkness*: he presents a vast body of evidence with wit and flair, enlivening his narrative with anecdotes drawn from his experience as a senior functionary in the United Nations and as a politician. Rare indeed is it to come across an essay on history that is so readable and so persuasive.

Of the many important aspects of British imperial history that the book touches on, there is one of particular note: the Raj's extreme ideological rigidity in matters of economic doctrine. Its approach to famines was governed by an almost insensate belief in free-market principles. As Tharoor points out:

> The British tended to base their refusal to intervene in famines ... on a combination of three sets of considerations: free trade principles (do not interfere with market forces), Malthusian doctrine (growth in population beyond the ability of the land to sustain it would inevitably lead to deaths, thereby restoring the 'correct' level of population) and financial prudence (don't spend money we haven't budgeted for).

The consequence was that

> As India became increasingly crucial to British prosperity, millions of Indians died completely unnecessary deaths in famines. As a result of what one can only call the British Colonial Holocaust, thanks to economic policies ruthlessly enforced by Britain, between 30 and 35 million Indians needlessly died of starvation during the Raj. Millions of tons of wheat were exported to Britain even as famine raged. When relief camps were set up, the inhabitants were barely fed and nearly all died. It is striking that the last large-scale famine to take place in India was under British rule; none has taken place since.

Tharoor adds, aptly:

> While comparisons of human deaths are always invidious, the 35 million who died of famine and epidemics during the Raj does remind one of the 25 million who died in Stalin's collectivization drive and political purges, the 45 million who died during Mao's cultural revolution, and the 55 million who died worldwide during World War II. The death toll from the colonial holocausts is right up there with some of the greatest recent examples of man's inhumanity to man.

The sheer shock value of the last paragraph is itself a testament to the success of the last many decades of imperial whitewashing. While it is well known that ideologically caused famines exacted an immense toll on lives in China and the former Soviet Union, that free-market fundamentalism took a similar toll in India and elsewhere is, by contrast, very little known—and even when the facts of this horrifying history are acknowledged, they are very rarely bracketed with other similar atrocities. Tharoor's framing of this issue holds an important lesson for that vast cohort of young Indians who are so besotted with free-market ideology that they are at a loss to understand why their forebears were ever critical of it.

The irony is that many, if not most, of Tharoor's social media followers are probably of this very persuasion: this was no doubt one of the reasons why they responded with such surprise at their idol's speech at Oxford. For anyone who believes in modernity as a goal—and this now includes the majority of educated people everywhere—the conflict between a vision of history as a progression towards the redemptive endpoint of 'modernity' and the actual record of empire must necessarily create an almost irreconcilable dissonance, a dilemma that forces a slippage, as it did with Dr Manmohan Singh, in which the imagined endpoint overshadows the historical record. If one truly believes that the trajectory of history, especially after the Enlightenment, represents a forward movement towards ever-greater freedom, justice and economic 'progress', then how does one reconcile that with the fact that for most of its duration the post-Enlightenment period has been an age of empires?

Within the tradition of liberal Indian nationalism—which Tharoor claims as his own—this conundrum was resolved by arguing that the British Raj was an aberration, an exception to the trajectory of the post-Enlightenment period, and that liberal Indians were the true heirs of the Enlightenment and, therefore, better equipped to realize its promise of progress. But this narrative is bedevilled by an inherent problem of credibility: Is it really plausible to suggest that the most powerful European empire of the last few centuries represents an aberration within the historical trajectory of the post-Enlightenment era? If India is at all to be accorded a place within that trajectory, can the Raj be excluded from it?

Tharoor is himself a liberal, progressive and modernist, and his book is inevitably riven by the struggle to reconcile the two axes of the contradiction that it inhabits. This is indeed one of the most interesting questions that the book poses: at a time when most modernist liberals, progressives and those who subscribe to such beliefs have allowed their teleological fantasies to overshadow the historical record, why has Tharoor persisted in holding it up to scrutiny?

Needless to add, these interconnected conclusions and assumptions have nothing whatsoever to do with the actual record of the British empire in India. They derive from metaphysical beliefs about time and history— now generally prevalent amongst most educated people in the West and elsewhere—and their waterproofing is so sound that they would not be breached even by immense floods of empirical evidence to the contrary. A well-delivered compilation of counterarguments and historical data may jolt this vessel, as Tharoor's speech did, but ultimately it will regain its equilibrium and sail on until such time as someone else feels compelled to give it another jolt.

Nor are these the only reasons why so many Indians have chosen to overlook this history. The forgetting of the costs of empire is now so widespread, especially among global political elites, that the real question in a sense is why Tharoor has chosen to stand out as an exception to a pattern that was embraced even by his own political mentor. Does it have something to do with his undergraduate education in India? Or is it perhaps traceable to his years in the United Nations, when he was often at loggerheads with liberal interventionists? What is undeniable is that in this respect he has been completely consistent, even at the cost, possibly, of damaging his career. I remember watching him on American television in the 1990s as he took on neo-conservatives and liberal interventionists of various stripes: other than him, there was no one who had the fluency or the rhetorical nimbleness (not to speak of the accent) that could silence them.

*An Era of Darkness* will not put an end to the debate on the British Raj: the political dynamics in which the discussion is embedded are powerful enough to ensure that. But in clearly outlining the cautionary lessons of the actual—as opposed to the imagined—legacies of empire, Tharoor has rendered the world an important public service.

# TWENTY-THREE

## Priya Satia's *Time's Monster*

How did a family of ardent pacifists become Britain's leading gun manufacturers? How did conscientious British officials convince themselves that they had to stand by and let millions of Indians die of hunger in famines that were largely caused by colonial policies? How did devoutly evangelical opium merchants from Britain and New England come to be convinced that they were doing God's work in selling drugs to the Chinese?

Questions of this kind recur often in the work of Priya Satia. In her seminal 2018 book, *Empire of Guns: The Violent Making of the Industrial Revolution*, Satia, who is a professor of British and international history at Stanford, addressed them by focusing on a single family, the Galtons of Birmingham. Throughout the eighteenth century and a part of the nineteenth, the Galtons were England's most successful gun manufacturers and a major presence not just in Britain's economy but also in the country's intellectual life. But it was the Galtons' connections with the British state that made the family one of the driving forces of the Industrial Revolution.

From the late seventeenth century onwards, Britain was almost continually engaged in wars in North America and Asia, and the government's insatiable appetite for military matériel hugely enriched armaments manufacturers and shipbuilders. The Galton family's lucrative government contracts, and the pressure to improve their weaponry, led them to invest heavily in innovation. Some of the crucial innovations of the Industrial Revolution were pioneered in their workshops, and they also funded inventors like James Watt and Matthew Boulton.

Colonial warfare was, therefore, a critical factor in Britain's industrialization. In effect, what Satia shows in *Empire of Guns* is that: 'Violence committed abroad, in service of imperial expansion, was central to the making of capitalist modernity.' While she is by no means the first, or only, historian to make this argument, the sharpness of her focus on the Galtons, and the astounding extent of their circle's influence on British financial, scientific and intellectual life, enables her to present the argument with exceptional force and clarity.

But this story has another twist to it: the Galtons, like many in their circle, were Quakers, which meant that they belonged to a sect that rejected war and even the bearing of arms: these were indeed the core principles on which the sect was founded. Yet the Galtons' involvement in the manufacture of guns went without criticism from their fellow Quakers for many decades. It was not until the 1790s that objections to their trade began to be voiced, leading to formal charges in 1795.

Those charges were answered by Samuel Galton Jr., who was not only an extremely able businessman but also a member of the Royal Society and a formidable intellectual in his own right. Turning the tables on his accusers, many of whom were also successful in business, he asked: 'Do you not *all,* in many ways *contribute* to the War by supplying the Government directly, or indirectly with *Money*, which is so necessary, that it is called proverbially the *Sinews* of War?'

The implication, as Satia points out, is that warfare was so fundamental to the country's life that no one who participated in Britain's economy could claim to be exempt from wars and violence. Galton thus directed the charge of hypocrisy back towards the Quakers by pointing out that they were victims of 'another kind of false consciousness, which endures today: avoiding the truth that modern life is founded, intrinsically, on militarism …'

Samuel Galton Jr. was thus making the same argument that Satia offers in relation to the Industrial Revolution, and were she an economic historian, she might have been content to leave it at that. But economics is by no means Satia's primary concern. The reason that Galton's self-defence is of interest to her is that she is also a historian of what might be called the moral, or ethical, life. It is this that makes her ask questions that professional historians generally avoid.

Satia returns to those concerns, even more directly, in her new book, *Time's Monster: How History Makes History*. Right at the outset, she makes it clear that the book hinges on a single query: 'How did … avowedly "good" people live with doing bad things?' (5)

This question, which has tormented thinkers since antiquity, makes it evident that *Time's Monster* is not a conventional history but a philosophical and ethical inquiry. It is for this reason that, unlike conventional historical studies, the book is not based on a particular archive or a specific set of documentary materials (what conceivable archive could provide an answer to her question?). Inasmuch as Satia addresses primary sources, it is by revisiting the archives on which her two earlier books, *Spies in Arabia* and *Empire of Guns*, are based. This makes *Time's Monster* somewhat disjointed in structure, with whole chapters being devoted to material from the earlier books. Other than that, *Time's Monster* deals mainly with scholarly and theoretical works, and with the writings of a small number of poets and novelists: the fact that a few names recur often may make the book appear self-referential to some professional historians, and I am sure much will be said about this.

But these problems, such as they are, arise, I think, out of a desire to ask questions that are so big and so difficult that they are generally dodged by professional historians. Nor is this surprising, for the answer that Satia arrives at ultimately is that it was the discipline of history itself, ever since its emergence as a field of academic inquiry in nineteenth-century Europe, that provided well-intentioned, highly educated Western liberals with a set of ethical tools for the management of their consciences as they unleashed murderous violence on 'backward' peoples across the planet. 'The story of empire,' she writes, 'is one in which the villains of history, if there are any, are historians themselves ...'

Crucial to the functioning of 'history' as an ethical toolbox is a linear conception of time, which allows present-day suffering to be justified as being necessary for the realization of a better future. This, of course, is none other than the doctrine of 'progress' that lies embedded in the foundations of the discipline: it is this doctrine that, in its many guises, provided the charter for Western imperialism, and continues to do so to this day. 'Modern imperialism promised progress,' writes Satia. 'It was grounded in a vision of history understood as necessarily progress-oriented.' It is in this sense that *Time's Monster* 'is a book about how the historical discipline helped make empire—by making it ethically thinkable—and how empire made and remade the historical discipline'.

Within a few pages of the last sentence, I came upon references to a book of my own: *The Great Derangement: Climate Change and the Unthinkable* (2016). Since I have myself made many references to Satia's *Empire of Guns* in a forthcoming book, it was a pleasant surprise to discover that Satia and I—two people who do not know each other personally and have never exchanged so much as a word—have nonetheless been in each other's heads for a while, conducting an extended conversation that includes many other interlocutors. This being the case, I feel that I have been relieved of the burden of writing a conventional review and might more fruitfully speculate about how these conversations began and where they might lead.

In many ways, the most notable—and the most uncanny—feature of these conversations is that they were not initiated by debates within history or philosophy or literature. They were sparked off, rather, by the interventions of actors and agents who have never before been included in such exchanges simply because they are not human. The historian Dipesh Chakrabarty, who is an important interlocutor for both Satia and me, has described how his awareness of the world, and of his discipline, were radically altered by his experiences of climatic disruptions. I have done something similar in relation to fiction in *The Great Derangement*.

It seems to me that *Time's Monster* proceeds from a similar starting point, for it is climate change, above all, that has upended our expectations of the future, thereby exposing the fundamental fallacies that underlie the idea that history is a linear chronicle of progress. In that sense, it could be said that these conversations were instigated by a range of perspectives and voices that were not attended to in the past merely because they were other-than-human. At the same time, vast numbers of marginalized human voices have also entered conversations of which they were not previously a part because they were thought to be voiceless and lacking in historicity.

Decolonization is crucial to both these developments—the rising clamour of other-than-human voices *and* the broadening of conversations about history. Just as decolonization made it possible for post-colonial states to accelerate the climate crisis by expanding their carbon footprints, it also created an upheaval within the discipline of history by bringing in voices and perspectives that can no longer be easily silenced or marginalized. This is a story that Satia tells at some length in the latter chapters of *Time's Monster*: 'Through these shifts in writing history during the era of anticolonialism emerged the popular twentieth-century understanding of the historian as critic of government ... History set out to expose the scandal of empire.'

In this sense, history has itself provided the tools for the upending of long-dominant narratives. And such is the explosive power of the counter-narratives that they can no longer be contained within ivory towers. They have burst forth and spilled out into the streets, overthrowing statues and entering the pages of the *New York Times* with features like the '1619 Project', which use the scholarly apparatus of academic history to better effect than do many established scholars.

Yet, ironically, even as the old narratives are being upended, the doctrine of 'progress' based on a unidirectional, linear conception of time is becoming even more entrenched. Thus, calls for justice and reparations are themselves often articulated in terms of 'progress', and frequently claim the vindication of being 'on the right side of history'. An even greater irony is that it is the left that clings most determinedly to these conceptions, to the point where its political aspirations have become synonymous with the word 'progressive'.

Is it possible to conceive of historical time in a fashion that is not linear and unidirectional? Satia devotes many pages to this question, teasing different conceptions of time out of Urdu poetry and the work of certain writers and thinkers, most of them from the Indian subcontinent. This geographical focus is due, no doubt, to Satia's position within her discipline, as a historian of the British empire and South Asia.

This, in itself, is illustrative of the difficulties that arise in approaching expansive issues from within the regional specializations of academic history. Because answers to the questions that Satia asks are not by any means best sought for in the colonial history of the Indian subcontinent. The material that is perhaps most relevant to those questions dates back to the earliest and most brutal period of European colonization: the sixteenth and seventeenth centuries. The principal theatres of that history lay in the Americas and the East Indies; the colonization of India was a relatively late chapter in that story, and as a result, many of the conceptions that the British brought with them to India had already been prefigured elsewhere. The doctrine of 'progress', for instance, was explicitly articulated only in 1752 by the French political economist A.R.J. Turgot. Yet the essence of the idea was already contained in the notion of 'improvement', which English colonists used to justify the seizure of Native American lands.

That Satia would be reluctant to address these materials is perfectly understandable in light of the regional specializations of academic history. And it is for that very reason perhaps that Satia does not allow her search for alternative conceptions of historical time to bring her closer to home, meaning North America. For some of the most powerful critiques of Western conceptions of linear time and history have come from precisely those who have historically faced the full fury of those ideas in their most savagely destructive forms—the Indigenous peoples of the Americas.

For the Lakota thinker Vine Deloria Jr., for instance, the most significant alternative to Western conceptions of linear time lies in the Native American relationship with space, with meaningful narratives being anchored by particular places rather than dates. Temporal narratives, Deloria argues, anticipating Satia's position, can defer ethical choices by reference to abstract, future endpoints; spatial thinking allows no such evasion, since it is insistently focused on the world as it is.

The Pueblo writer Leslie Marmon Silko uses the same idea to suggest another possibility: 'In the case of many of the Pueblo narratives,' she writes, 'it is impossible to determine which came first: the incident or the geographical feature which begs to be brought alive in a story ...' (270). What this suggests is that Pueblo oral narratives, in being centred on particular places, and the geological and botanical features that are emplaced in them, accord a significant degree of agency to non-human elements of the landscape.

This brings us to the brink of a chasm that Satia gestures at, even as she backs away from it: What happens when we suddenly wake to the realization that the planet itself as well as a vast range of other beings are all actors, fully capable of inserting themselves forcefully into human narratives? How would historical narratives have to change to include the voices of these protagonists? What would be the sources on which such stories would be based?

It is at this juncture that it becomes apparent why history, in the modern, disciplinary sense, took shape among a tiny group of elite Europeans. These men, and their class, wielded so much power that they were able to convince themselves that they, and only they, were true historical agents: all other beings, animals, landscapes, plants and, of course, the vast majority of humans were, in their view, brutishly wedded to 'Nature' and were, therefore, incapable of historical agency. In other words, built into the foundations of history and, indeed, many other disciplines in the humanities is the repression of some of the most difficult questions about human existence on this planet. These questions have long eluded the modern gaze but were self-evident to those who did not wear the blinders of 'humanism': that is why their stories are filled with non-human voices and other-than-human protagonists.

Priya Satia's fearlessness in tackling big questions, even to the point of indicting the very discipline that has raised her to a position of not-inconsiderable eminence, suggests that she might well be the historian who could summon the courage to leap into this chasm.

(First published in Scroll, 26 June 2021)

# 6

# PRESENTATIONS

Many of the pieces in this collection were originally conceived as blogposts or as presentations, accompanied by a succession of images. In a sense, it is a misnomer for them to be described as 'essays' because blogposts and presentations are, in my view, entirely different genres. This is because the role that images play in posts and presentations is not that of mere 'illustration'. Rather, it is the reverse that is true: often the text serves largely as an appendage to the pictorial elements. It was indeed out of a desire to find genres of expression that were not purely logocentric that I turned to blogposts and visual presentations.

The difference between essays and presentations is analogous to the distinction that linguists make between context-sensitive and context-neutral utterances (for more on this see my piece on A.K. Ramanujan, in this section). An essay falls on the context-neutral side of this divide because it can be read by anyone, anywhere, regardless of who they are and where they are. A presentation, on the other hand, is necessarily sensitive to context because it is addressed to a particular group of people, in a particular place, and is intended to be heard and watched rather than read.

For me, presentations belong more to an oral than a textual tradition (which is why I prefer the term 'presentation' to 'lecture', because the latter, being derived from the Latin *legere* [to read], invokes reading rather than listening or watching). In that sense the texts that accompany my presentations are scripts for performances rather than essays as such.

The blogpost and the presentation are both new forms, brought into being by recent changes in communications technologies. Although they are distinct genres, they both permit the merging of texts and images in a fashion that is near impossible to reproduce in print, simply because it would be prohibitively expensive. Such pairings are not without precedent, however: perhaps the most beautiful form ever invented for the merging of text and image is the art of Chinese scroll painting (scrolls even had the equivalent of a 'comments' feature, with interpolations and seal marks being added over the centuries).

In any event, posts and presentations have now become a major part of my practice as a writer, and thanks to internet video-sharing apps, I probably reach more people through them than I do through print. Inevitably, as in a translation, when a post or presentation becomes a part of a printed book like this one, something is lost in the transition. Yet, something is also gained when a transitory act of expression acquires a certain stability and permanence.

# TWENTY-FOUR

## The Making of *In an Antique Land*: India, Egypt and the Cairo Geniza

When Mark Cohen suggested that I discuss the writing of *In an Antique Land* (published 1992), I thought it would be a simple matter of digging up a few notes. But the book was written so long ago that I'd forgotten how extensive those notes were: my travel journals alone make up some fifteen closely written volumes. Looking over them in preparation for tonight, it occurred to me that this talk could quite easily be a book in its own right—and some day, when I have a great deal of time on my hands, perhaps that is what it will become.

Meanwhile, here is an abbreviated version: The story starts in 1979 at Oxford, when I was a twenty-three-year-old graduate student—a somewhat reluctant one, I might add, for I had opted for higher study principally as a means of seeing the world. My dream was of writing fiction, but like many an aspiring novelist, I felt I lacked the necessary richness of experience. The writers I admired—V.S. Naipaul, James

Baldwin and others—had gone out into the world and watched it go by: I wanted no less for myself. The year I turned twenty, in the searing heat of the Delhi summer, I visited the embassies of Laos, Ghana, Fiji, Tunisia, Cameroon, Côte d'Ivoire and some thirty other countries, delivering a letter that offered my services as a teacher. My hopes were pinned, I remember, on Malawi and Lesotho, but alas I never heard back from them. The few responses I received said—sometimes in terms of no little indignation—that the nation in question had plenty of teachers, thank you, and quite enough Indians besides: they were aware of no pressing need for any more.

What I had not taken into account was that the word 'travel', when applied to young men from poor countries, has the connotation not of mind-broadening but rather of illegal immigration. For us there were no Peace Corps, no gap years and no hard currency; our best hope of emulating the First Worlders who passed through Delhi sporting bead necklaces and long hair lay in finding our way to some hospitable foreign university. So I put in an application for a scholarship offered by a family of wealthy Indian expatriates and was fortunate to get it. There I was, in 1979, studying for a diploma in social anthropology, a subject I had chosen because it seemed to offer the richest possibilities of travel.

Oxford was enormously exciting but not in the ways I had expected—socially it was the most fun place I had ever been, but intellectually it was far less stimulating than my old university in Delhi. On the other hand, Oxford offered something that Delhi didn't, something that was eminently to my taste—which was an approach to anthropology that was more literary than social-scientific. I was particularly fortunate in entering the orbit of the brothers Godfrey and Peter Lienhardt, who had been disciples of the critic F.R. Leavis and saw themselves primarily as writers. It was Peter Lienhardt who suggested that I do a DPhil in anthropology and even took it upon himself to find me the funding. I was fortunate also in that I had become fast friends with my neighbour in my student house: an Australian by the name of James Simpson. He is today the Loker Professor of English at Harvard and one of the world's leading mediaevalists. It was James's influence, I suspect, that stimulated my interest in the Middle Ages, and it was this that led me to the work of the great Islamicist Ignaz Goldziher. It was through Goldziher that I learnt of the existence of the extraordinary treasure trove of materials known as the Geniza documents; it was Goldziher too who revealed to me that many of these documents were related to India and were being compiled into a book by Prof. S.D. Goitein of Princeton University. Thus it happened one day that in the fine eggshell light of one of Oxford's great domed libraries, I found myself reading Prof. Goitein's translation of a letter by a twelfth-century Jewish merchant, Abraham Ben Yiju: the document mentions an Indian slave whose name is spelled with the characters B-M-H. The letter caught my attention at once: not, I might add, because of the religious affiliations of the protagonists but because of its resonance with my own experience. Here I was, delighting in the discovery of a world that was new to me—Oxford—as if no one from my part of the world had ever been abroad before; and here was a letter that attested to the experience of a compatriot who had vanished into a much stranger universe 800 years before.

It was at about this time, so far as I remember, that I was faced with the problem of choosing a place to do fieldwork. In those days, the expectation in anthropology was that if you were Indian—or, for that matter, African or Arab or Southeast Asian—you went back to your own country and became a somewhat elevated species of native informant. This held no interest for me because travel, as I understood it, meant to go somewhere where you had not already been. But on the other hand, the matter could not be decided by flipping a coin between Baffin Island and Easter Island either: I wanted to go to a place where I would be able to find deep and textured connections with my own world. Was it only because of Prof. Goitein's translated letter that I chose to go to Egypt? No. I had grown up in the India of the Non-Aligned Movement, when Cairo and New Delhi were thought of as sister capitals. Egypt seemed like a country that would not cavil at giving a visa to an Indian and might even accord him a friendly reception. But the letter was not unimportant either, for it removed some of the arbitrariness from my decision—it was proof that my journey was part of a cycle of travel that stretched back hundreds, if not thousands, of years.

Thus it happened that in late April 1980, at a time when my proficiency in Arabic did not extend beyond the stringing together of a few words, I went to Egypt and, through the good offices of the eminent anthropologist Dr Aly Issa, was soon installed in a small village near the town of Damanhour: in *Antique Land*, I gave this village the name Lataifa.

In the book, I describe at some length the family I lived with, in particular my loathsome landlord, to whom I gave the name Abu-'Ali. Here are excerpts from three successive diary entries, written in late May 1980, when my Arabic had somewhat improved by total immersion:

> Ustad Hamdy [Abu-'Ali cousin] is short and plump, with a little half-moustache and a white cap; he is forever snatching anxious glances at his watch to make sure that he hasn't missed the hour of prayer. He spends much of his time rushing in and out, to and from his devotions. He's a pleasant, welcoming kind of man, full of smiles and little jokes. He speaks some English and obviously wants to improve, so often speaks it to me. Or else he speaks a very grandiose and high-sounding Arabic—so high-sounding that I think even he has trouble with it. He asked many questions about 'Hinduki' as he puts it—about the customs of dealing with the dead, whether suttee is practised nowadays or not. And finally, of course, there was

> the Big One—what was our God 'like'. This, I must confess, I found myself completely unable to deal with and took refuge in stuttering inarticulacy. But neither Ustad Hamdy nor his nephew Mamdooh were about to pass this one up; they both leaned forward, all eagerness to hear my answer. Luckily the call to prayer intervened. I spent the break trying to think up an answer. Illumination was not forthcoming, however, and I was greatly relieved to find that they'd forgotten all about it by the time they came back.

The next day:

> Ustad Hamdy came up here at about six o' clock. As always he spent his time glancing at his watch, waiting for the hour of prayer. When the time came, he tried, with eager hopefulness shining in his eyes, to persuade me to come with him to the mosque—to watch, he said, not to take part in the prayers. He added in English that he wanted me to 'understand and learn about Islam, so that you can decide whether you want to stay in your religion or to know God'. This seemed to me a good opportunity to make myself clear, so I said I could not convert and he must not think of it. Whereupon he looked very abashed and embarrassed and said something about cultural exchange. Later, it struck me that I'm the fanatical one—all I care to talk about is kinship and agriculture.

A couple of days later,

> Hamdy came in again at about five with Mamdooh. It wasn't long before he got on to the subject of religion. I think he really is hoping for a conversion. Asked what my father would think if I converted. When I said the question would never arise,

but in any case he would be livid, this seemed to carry some weight. Then, lecturing me, he said that if a man truly believes something else is better, he should not hesitate to convert; he, Hamdy, would himself gladly convert if he thought this 'Hinduki' business was better than Islam. Yes, indeed! Keeps asking me if my father has ever read the holy books of Islam. In an absurd way, this touches me, for I know how his mind is working—here, he says to himself, is a nice, well-educated man, with a nice, well-intentioned father: surely, surely, if they had but read some books about Islam, they would have converted?

But then Ustad Hamdy's questions soon grew more pointed. Was I a Marxist who didn't believe in God? No, no, that wasn't it. Who made the world, then? Who was the first man and the first woman if not Aadam and Hawa? I tried to explain that in Hinduism, people believe that God made the world, but do not think specifically of any first man or woman. He misunderstood this, I think, for he asked: 'So they live for the present only?' I said, yes, whereupon he turned away with infinite sorrow at the thought of such folly. Then he tried to make me go with him to the grave of his father to listen to him reading from the Koran. I told him, as on every such occasion—later. Afterwards I went for a walk with Mamdooh and some others to the fields. Someone asked how many Muslims there were in India and I said, a lot. And what kind of people are they, they asked, good or bad? I said, they're like all people, which was well taken. Someone asked whether cows were divine in India and I said, people don't eat them because they give milk and many other things. They weren't taken in by this kind of foolish cultural ecology and said immediately—no, that can't be the only reason. Whereupon I gave in. Later a cow was pointed out to me, with what expectation I do not know—all this, I must add, in the most good-humoured way.

I should note here that although I was brought up in an observant Hindu family, I am not a follower of any organized religion. In fact, this is a persuasion to which I am growing ever more firmly attached the more I look around at the havoc that has been wrought upon the world by the various fundamentalisms that have taken root in the Indian subcontinent, northern America and the Middle East.

In Lataifa in 1980, there were already some signs that the religious life of the villagers was taking a new turn. On Fridays, the mosques would resound with sermons that urged people to make sacrifices for the war in Afghanistan (the old one); many boys and young men were growing beards and joining the Muslim Brotherhood; zealots were busy stamping out customs deemed to be 'heathen', most of which had to do with the autonomy of women. But the questions Ustad Hamdy posed to me that day were not, I think, a reflection of this movement's growing strength: like almost everyone I met in Lataifa, he asked these questions out of a genuine concern for my well-being.

I happen to be from a part of the world where sectarian tensions are so palpable that people learn very early that there are certain consequences to the stirring of this particular pot. The same is true, I am sure, in those parts of the Arab world where different communities and religious groups live in close proximity—places such as Lebanon and even those parts of Upper Egypt where there are substantial numbers of Coptic Christians. But there were very few non-Muslims in the area around Lataifa, and the people of the village had no reason to tiptoe around the subject of religion. The questions came at me in thick, steady volleys; several times each day, I would be asked: Why don't you convert? Can't you see that Islam is the best and most rational of religions? Rarely, if ever, were these questions asked in a spirit of hostility; what they represented most often was a kind of puzzlement, of the sort that nineteenth-century scientists are said to have exhibited when they came upon the duck-billed platypus. I was a creature out of place—an apparently reasonable man who would not embrace a set of beliefs that appeared to them to be self-evidently valid.

I must admit that in time these interrogations became deeply, profoundly wearisome. On bad days, I would long to get the hell out of there; on good days, I would tell myself that there was something very admirable about the straightforwardness with which people expressed what was in their minds. I would remind myself that every society has its ways of telling outsiders about their alienness. In Oxford, for example, scarcely a week went by without some ugly manifestation of racism. Of this affliction, at least, Egypt—in my experience the most colour-blind of countries—was mercifully free.

Yet the cumulative weight of the questions I had to face became in time almost unbearably oppressive, amounting finally to a kind of trauma. This feeling will be familiar to anyone who has done fieldwork the old-fashioned way—and let me add here that the pressure to convert is not by any means the only factor that can cause it; it was merely the most pressing aspect of my own experience of it. When I left Egypt in 1981, I wanted to be done with my thesis as soon as possible so that I would never again have to think about Lataifa and its environs. I wrote the thesis at breakneck speed, finishing it in a few months, and upon receiving my degree, I returned to India and launched immediately upon my first novel, *The Circle of Reason*, which was published in 1986. This was followed in 1988 by another novel: *The Shadow Lines*.

I was by this time well launched on my career as a writer, so my years of being an accidental anthropologist should have been well behind me. Yet Lataifa would not go away: I was haunted by it; there were times when I would wake up at night sweating, imagining myself back in the village. And then there was my ten-volume diary, the keeping of which, I realized in retrospect, had been formative to my development as a writer. It was on my first visit to the US, in 1988, that I came to understand that I would have to write about Lataifa if I were to make peace with it. But why had I gone there at all? Did I really know? Where might I look for others who had lived through a similar experience? The slave of Ben Yiju's letter was the obvious answer, and I decided that he would be my avatar in aloneness, my point of departure. Ben Yiju's own story, as a North African in India, would make, I thought, an interesting weft to the warp of the time I had spent in Egypt; and the tale of the slave's life in Cairo would provide a further overlay of depth and colour.

I should stress that when I launched upon the project, I was of the belief that Prof. Goitein had already published his 'India Book'. I fully expected that Abraham Ben Yiju's letters would be available in translation and that I would be able to reconstruct his life from them. Imagine my shock when I learnt that Prof. Goitein had died in 1985 without ever publishing the 'India Book'. What was I to do now? There was no turning back, because a publisher, Bill Buford of Granta [Books], had already bought my proposal, which was for a book to be titled 'An Infidel in Egypt'.

Hoping to find some way ahead, I came to Princeton to see Mark Cohen, who was then the custodian of the Goitein papers. Mark had little comfort to offer: Prof. Goitein had indeed transcribed and translated many of Ben Yiju's letters, he said, but he could not make them available to me because they were being prepared for publication by another scholar. So there was Mark, in his chair, with the letters no more than a few feet away—but for me, they might as well have been buried in a vault in Antarctica. I begged and pleaded but he was unyielding. If you want them so much, he said at last, why don't you translate them yourself?

My mouth fell open. But I don't know Judaeo-Arabic, I said. How can I translate them when I don't know the language they're written in?

You can speak Arabic, can't you, said Mark. Judaeo-Arabic is just spoken Arabic written in Hebrew characters. All you have to do is familiarize yourself with the script. You'll find that written Hebrew is much simpler than written Arabic. You'll see—it's easy.

Right, I thought—mediaeval Arabic written in the Hebrew script. What could it be but easy?

I went away thinking he was making fun of me, but he had planted a seed that would not be easily uprooted. A few months later, I went to Cairo to take a first-hand look at the neighbourhoods that Ben Yiju and his slave would have inhabited. By the time of this visit—17 December 1988—the city had acquired a sleek new subway system, and all one had to do was step off at the Mar Girgis station and walk through the sunken lanes of the old Roman township of Bab al Yun. This was then one of the most picturesque, as well as the most historically interesting, settlements in Egypt. Here is how I described it in my notebook:

> … dust-blown, crumbling houses crowded along narrow alleys. Went into an old house where two old women, lying on string beds, were guarding the doorway to a small chapel. It reminded me of Benares. The synagogue of Ben Ezra is approached by a narrow dirt track; everything on either side of it is crumbling; there are great heaps of rocks and bricks; on one side there is a Coptic graveyard, derelict but inhabited. The synagogue is at the end of the lane: it is neither large nor imposing; there is a high wall around it, with a gate, topped by a wrought-iron grille, with a Star of David emblazoned on it. The building looks as though it is near collapse; the small yard around it is piled high with debris. The gate was shut but there were a couple of stalls outside—desks spread with tourist-ware—manned by two cheerful Egyptians in jallabeyyas: when they saw that I wanted to go in, they pointed me to an

> elderly caretaker. The old man grinned with pleasure as he led the way in. He seems to be of a quite advanced age—possibly seventy-five—and he is also perhaps a little simple in the head. He is very thin—his face looks as though all the flesh has been sucked out of it; his cheeks have collapsed upon the bones and his skin is like old paper. He was wearing Egyptian clothes—a jallabeyya and a cap like a taqeyya. He began to tell me about the synagogue in French, but he has very few teeth and I could make no sense of what he was saying, so I asked him to switch to Arabic, which he did with some relief. The interior of the synagogue is in ruins, but in a beautifully picturesque way—with shafts of light shining through the dust, filtering in through broken windows. Debris was piled high along the walls—bricks, slabs of stone and tiles. It is a rectangular structure with a central aisle and benches arranged in straight lines. Along three sides of it is a raised gallery—this is the women's section. At the far end of the gallery, on the left hand side, is a rectangular hole in the wall—quite high, about six feet up in the wall. This was the opening into the Geniza, the old man said.

As is well known, the Geniza was, in fact, an antechamber of the synagogue: it was a depository where pieces of writing that bore the name of God were placed to await proper disposal. Fortunately, the depository of the Ben Ezra synagogue was not disturbed until the late nineteenth century, when the structure was renovated: it was the rebuilding of the synagogue that led to the documents' discovery and dispersal.

'Can I go up there?' I asked the caretaker, and he said at once: 'No, no. The stairway to the gallery is broken, and once you get up there, you won't be able to look in because the hole is too high up above the floor. And in any case, there is nothing to see—everything is gone.'

Later he told me that he was born in Egypt and his family has been here 'for too many generations to remember'. But his brothers have long been gone—they are in Europe, America and Israel.

'What is it like for you here?' I asked. 'Do you have any problems?'

'No, no,' he said emphatically. 'We have no problems at all. Everything is fine. The government protects us. This is Egypt, you understand. It's not like Jordan or Syria or places like that. People here understand (*biyifhamu*); they know what it's all about.'

I asked him his name and he said: 'In Hebrew or Arabic? (*bi'l hibri walla arabi*?)' Then he gave me both: 'In Hebrew, it is Nathan Abraham Moshe; in Arabic, it is Shahata Ibrahim Musa.' (But most people call him 'Amm Shahata.) I was to discover later that 'Amm Shahata was himself something of a character in Geniza studies and that some scholars suspected him of being an informer for the secret police.

A few years later, the synagogue was restored, meticulously and at great expense, by a team headed by Phyllis Lambert of Montreal. Today it looks much as it probably did after its nineteenth-century renovation—which is to say it has the appearance of a modest municipal schoolhouse. The restoration was necessary, of course, and I'm glad it was done—but I am glad also that I saw it at a time when it was still possible to imagine it as a place that Ben Yiju might have visited.

From Egypt I returned to the US, where I had a temporary teaching assignment, and in early 1989, I went to the British consulate in New York and applied for a visa so that I would be able to spend a few months in Cambridge, deciding whether I was up to translating Ben Yiju's letters. Of course, my application was promptly denied: the clerk at the counter had heard every kind of excuse and she thought my reason for wanting to go to England was just about the most hilariously transparent ruse any aspiring illegal alien had ever come up with.

I remember vividly the rage and despair that gripped me as I stumbled out of that consulate. Here were these documents that recorded the lives of Egyptians, North Africans, Indians—yet somehow they had been assimilated into a European archive that was beyond my reach. Who then would read these papers with the care, attention and background knowledge that I, as an Indian, could bring to them? The question seemed all the more pressing because I had an inkling by this time of the reason why Prof. Goitein had been so slow and hesitant in publishing the India papers: my sense was that as a Mediterraneanist, he was not at ease with the Indian references in the letters. Indeed, he had actually published an article in India, appealing to Indian scholars to give these papers the attention they deserved. Here I was, trying to do just that, only to be thwarted by a visa clerk who could not see why an Indian should be interested in the letters of a Jewish trader from North Africa. This was deeply ironic: Ben Yiju's stay in India, which would have seemed perfectly normal in the Middle Ages, had captured my interest because it was anomalous in relation to my own experience, in which trade and travel were usually between a Western metropolis and an eastern or southern periphery. But now, just as I was striving to reimagine that originary normalcy, the material possession of the archive intruded to disrupt that attempt: it was as if the history of imperialism were intervening once again to obscure the world it had replaced.

This was not my only brush with the issue of access to the materials of history. Later, when I was well advanced in my work, I had a disturbing encounter with a prominent Geniza scholar. He told me that Prof. Goitein had published the catalogue numbers of the India documents in order to keep other scholars away from them; what was more, he declared in unmistakably threatening terms that he would make it his business to ruin my career if I continued with what I was doing. 'I will ruin your career' is not a phrase one hears very often, so it certainly caught my attention. I remember to this day, with the deepest gratitude, the support I received from Mark Cohen at this juncture. He suggested that I write a letter to Prof. Goitein's son, Elon, in Tel Aviv, explaining my position. Here is an excerpt from that letter, written in December 1989:

> I do not think Prof. Goitein's memory is well served by the suggestion that he published the catalogue numbers of the 'India Book' documents in order to warn off other scholars, rather than in the interests of better research. I cannot believe that this was your father's intention, for you must know that he published an article in India, trying to interest Indian scholars in the subject. I consider it a privilege that I am the first Indian who has availed himself of this invitation ... The documents themselves are part of the heritage of Egypt, India and the whole world. They are part of my own history, in that they record the life of one of my countrymen, and it is for this reason that they are of interest to me ... [In conclusion, I] repeat that I have nothing but respect for your father's memory and [his] work.

It will be evident from this that the question of access to these materials rankled greatly with me, and this raises a further question: If I, as a native of a country that is, after all, peripheral to the Geniza, should feel such chagrin, then what might an Egyptian or a Tunisian feel in a similar situation?

Those who are familiar with the history of the Geniza documents will know that they were taken out of Egypt in the late nineteenth century, when Lord Curzon was the chief representative of British rule in that country. Today not one of these documents, so far as I know, remains in the country where they were produced. That the documents are well preserved and well looked-after is certainly a cause for celebration. But a great archive is not just a record of history—it is history itself, a crystallization of lived experience. To destroy its connections with the broader society that created it is to redefine the collective experience—it is, in effect, to partition the past. It is commonplace to lament the loss of the cosmopolitan, composite character of such cities as Cairo, Alexandria and Tunis; it is equally common to lay the blame for this on post-war developments. Yet the history of the Geniza reminds us that the project of partitioning this shared experience started before the twentieth century and that the initiative for it did not come from the Arab side. It is worth remembering also that it is the future that will pay the price for the vivisection of the past.

What can be done to redress this now? It seems to me that at the very least there should be a functioning Geniza museum in Cairo, with extensive digital archives and even a few real documents. The mere physical existence of such an archive, in providing a reminder of a composite past, would point, I think, to productive ways of imagining the present and the future.

To return to my narrative: I did not, of course, tamely reconcile myself to the denial of a visa. I protested, I wrote letters and generally made a nuisance of myself until Her Majesty's Government relented and granted me one. In the summer of 1989, I went to Cambridge and introduced myself to the custodians of the Geniza collection; in marked contrast to my experience at the consulate, I was met with nothing but goodwill and encouragement, both from the keepers of the documents, such as Stefan Reif and Geoffrey Khan, and the scholars who were working there—most notably Menahem Ben-Sasson. Within days of my arrival, armed with a copy of Joshua Blau's handbook of Judaeo-Arabic, I walked into the sepulchral quiet of the reading room, where the bulk of the Geniza documents are preserved.

At first, nothing made any sense, but slowly, after many days of sitting, staring and fidgeting, the script began to acquire recognizable shapes and contours. I still remember the day when a string of words suddenly became a sentence: it was miraculous, magical—as if I were listening to an echo from a mineshaft that stretched 800 years into the past. What Mark had told me was the exact truth: behind the arcana and esoterica, there lay something very simple: the voice of an ordinary merchant who was writing in the language of his everyday speech—and it so happened that this dialect was uncannily similar to the colloquial Arabic I had learnt in Lataifa.

Not the least part of the magic lay in the very texture of the paper on which Ben Yiju wrote. In those days, if you called up a Geniza document at the Bodleian in Oxford, it was sent to you in a folder that was tied with string. You could actually touch the paper, feel it, see where Ben Yiju's nib had dripped; on the obverse side, you could see his beautiful, neat handwriting turning into a scrawl as he jotted down a shopping list. Was Ashu yelling down the corridor? Were his children bouncing on his knees? They were more than papers, those letters: they were devices that gave you a mastery of time such as Einstein would have envied.

Later, when I went to Mangalore—a city I had never visited before—my greatest regret was that I had approached the city not by ship, from the sea, as Ben Yiju would have, but from the opposite direction, by bus. On 15 June 1990, I wrote:

> [The landscape is] densely wooded, thickly populated, with long rows of stalls bordering the road, paddy cultivation in hillside terraces, thick stands of areca palms, snatches of music blaring out of shops with bright signs, long-horned cattle ambling by. In the background are the mountains, green, densely wooded, monsoon clouds hanging low and grey over them, touching the tops. It is very beautiful—I keep wondering what Ben Yiju would have made of it—what impression would the profusion of greenery make on

> someone who was accustomed to the dun colours of Tunisia and Egypt. Did he like it? Or did its lavishness frighten him?

The city was a disappointment: it was a working market town, with no frills, and there was nothing to be seen of its mediaeval glory. On visiting the remnants of the old port, I wrote:

> There is a breathtaking impudence in the thought that this sleepy little place might once have been one of the principal centres of world trade. It is nothing but a long cement wharf with a few flimsy moorings. There were some men fishing, a few boys gossiping, a few small riverboats drifting by. The frontage was a line of narrow, two-storeyed warehouses with tiled roofs and small doors; they didn't look like they could store much.

One thing that remains unchanged about Mangalore from Ben Yiju's time is that it has a richly varied population. The region around it teems with languages, dialects, cultures, religions and, of course, castes: it is home, for example, to a great number of Catholics, many of whom trace their roots back to the sixteenth and seventeenth centuries, when their ancestors fled the Portuguese Inquisition in Goa. The region is also relatively prosperous, as is much of India's west coast, and the standards of living, levels of education and so on are far higher than in the hinterland. One result of this is that there is an intense interest in local history and folklore, much of it fuelled by identity politics and competition between castes and communities. For me, the parochialism of the local interest in the past was a great help in some ways. Ben Yiju's letters afforded very few clues to the identities of the people who figured in them: not much more, in fact, than a few names—Ashu, Bomma, Nair and so on. But in India, names are frequently imbued with great significance, and the folklorists and local historians of Mangalore were able to spin entire identities out of a few syllables (as I describe in *In an Antique Land*). Yet those very scholars were sometimes amazed by the wider contours of the story: some were astonished, for example, to know that Ben Yiju—and presumably Ashu and Bomma as well—had travelled regularly along the Malabar coast, visiting small towns and ports. So wedded were they to a vision in which their ancestors were rooted in their native soil that they could scarcely credit the thought that some of them had occasionally ventured outside their own region. In my journal, I noted: 'Ben Yiju's letters give us a picture of this region that is much richer and more detailed than anything that is known of them from currently available sources. Being mainly inscriptions, these tend to give a very formalistic picture, devoid of colour and texture.'

The most pleasurable part of the journey came when I followed Ben Yiju's footsteps along the Malabar coast—a region that truly deserves to be known as India Felix. I visited the little towns and villages that he and his correspondents knew as Dahfattan, Jurbattan and the like. Most of them are now sleepy little hamlets, for India's coastal shipping trade, which flourished until the 1940s, is now all but extinct.

My journey, or at least my journal, ended, as Ben Yiju's may also have, at the famous synagogue of Cochin, which is in the old Jewish part of the town. On 26 June 1990, I wrote:

> The area looks crowded, but not in an Indian way—it looks curiously European, like a mediaeval village in Italy or England. There's a square which looks distinctively Dutch or Flemish—all it lacks are cobblestones. It has low houses with tiled, gabled roofs huddled around it. The road to the synagogue leads off from the square. It is a small, free-standing structure, built in the fifteenth century. It has a spacious interior dominated by a pulpit. The floor is paved with rather crudely painted blue-

and-white Chinese tiles. An elderly man was showing tourists around: he was lounging around in his shorts, looking rather disgruntled. He opened a cabinet and showed the tourists the Torah scrolls. The bemused tourists—mainly Punjabis from Delhi—argued over whether they should take pictures of each other or the scrolls. Afterwards, talked to the caretaker a little. He said there were only twenty-four Jews left in Cochin—seven families. All the rest had gone to Israel. The youngest person there is a young girl—and she will have to go to Israel too, for she will not be able to find anyone of her religion to marry in Cochin. He said that the congregation had never had a rabbi—'never needed one'. They had spoken Malayalam as a first language, but each family had taught Hebrew to its children.

And what of Lataifa and its sister village, Nashawy? I visited several times, during and after the writing of *In an Antique Land*. The most memorable and most moving of these visits was in 1988, when I returned after a gap of seven years. I was received with unreserved warmth and affection: friends and acquaintances came pouring out of their houses and off their fields, eager to hear about and tell of all that had happened during my absence. The strange thing was that there were no young men to be seen—it was as if one whole layer of the demography had fallen out of the pyramid. Most of them were in Iraq, but there were many also in Saudi Arabia and the sheikdoms of the Gulf. The village itself and the countryside around it had changed almost beyond recognition: almost every house had an electrical connection; the creaky old water wheels had been replaced by diesel pumps; many, if not most, households had acquired refrigerators, TVs and washing machines; and everywhere one looked, new houses built of solid brick were sprouting from the ground. It was as if an epidemic of prosperity had broken out.

Today there is a tendency in the US to write about Egypt and the Arab world in general as if they had experienced nothing but a decades-long downward spiral. This is simply not true. The late '80s were a time of great hope and optimism in many parts of rural Egypt. In fact, the expanding economies of the Gulf had effected a redistribution of wealth such as no government initiative or aid programme could possibly have done. It was disproportionately the poor, the landless and the educated unemployed who had taken jobs abroad, and the funds they sent their families had created a minor social revolution back home, putting money in the hands of people who had never had it before.

It was the aftermath of the First Gulf War that put an end to this. Let me stress here that I am not questioning the merits of the war itself but rather the management of its aftermath. The lesson that the oil sheiks drew from the First Gulf War was that workers from other Arab countries could present a political threat in times of crisis. After the war, they altered the balance of their workforces to favour Indians, Pakistanis, Thais, Filipinos and other Asians over Arabs from neighbouring nations. Egyptian workers found their avenues of employment abroad closed, not just in Iraq but also in the other countries of the Gulf. Of the many species of folly and viciousness of which these potentates are guilty, this is perhaps one of the most egregious; the US, whose client regimes these are, shares their culpability, for it could easily have prevailed on them to provide avenues of employment for the millions of Egyptians and others who had lost their jobs in Iraq and elsewhere.

This I can attest to, in any event, that for the area around Lataifa and Nashawy, the First Gulf War and its aftermath were a catastrophe: in the mid-'90s I returned a couple of times to find the villages littered with the shells of unfinished houses, their lanes swarming with idle and angry young men. It is often said that there is no better recipe for social upheaval than the thwarting of rising expectations: I suspect that this had a great deal to do with the global turn of the Egyptian fundamentalist movement in the late '90s.

It took no great prescience to know, even then, that something terrible was going to grow out of this toxic brew. Yet it was with a sickening jolt of horror that I learnt soon after 9/11—at a time when the fumes of the World Trade Center could still be smelt in the Brooklyn air—that Mohamed Atta, the leader of the attacks, had family links with an area near Lataifa, and that he had been radicalized in the period after the First Gulf War.

It was in the shadow of the First Gulf War that I finished working on *In an Antique Land*, but it was by no means the only conflict that informed its writing. In India, the Babri Masjid had been torn down by Hindu fundamentalists in 1991, leading to one of the worst outbreaks of violence since the country's independence. In Israel, the intifada was raging, and there was a ghastly massacre of Muslim pilgrims in Hebron. The literary world too was in the grip of a crisis such as it had never known before: *The Satanic Verses* was beset by controversy and Salman Rushdie was still in hiding.

And in the midst of all this, there I was, writing a book about Hindus, Muslims and Jews.

The last thing I wanted was for my book to disappear into a maelstrom of controversy: I wanted it to live, to survive, to be read. I had come to be convinced that behind the conflicts of South Asia and the Middle East there lay not just a failure of the imagination but also an inadequacy of narrative. To me, one of the most admirable aspects of the work of such Geniza scholars as S.D. Goitein, Mark Cohen and others was that they were attempting to re-narrate and reimagine these histories. I wanted to do no less: the challenge, as I conceived it, was to be able to tell the story in such a way that the characters and their communities would be able to recover some of the unemphatic accommodations that grow out of common endeavours and shared space. If writers could not do this in their imaginations, I asked myself, then how could one blame politicians for their failures in the real world?

One of the most difficult steps was to abandon the catchy title I had thought of—'An Infidel in Egypt'—which I felt to be inappropriate by the time I had finished the book. In this, I met with bitter resistance from my publisher, who knew the word 'infidel' was likely to cause controversy and sell copies. We were both adamant, but since the book was mine, in the end I prevailed. When *In an Antique Land* was published, it appeared that my attempt to protect its integrity had been all too successful: it attracted hardly any attention, sinking, as booksellers say, without a trace. Yet decades later, here I am, speaking about its writing, so it would seem that it continues to find readers to this day. A still greater source of pride for me is that it is one of the few books about the Middle East that has made a place for itself in both Egypt and Israel. It is as if it had borrowed a leaf from its characters and learnt how to survive in a world of contending beliefs, unyielding borders and unattainable visas.

(Delivered as part of the Annual Carolyn L. Drucker '80 Memorial Lecture, 29 March 2008)

# TWENTY-FIVE
# Computers and Spinning Wheels

I would like to start by saying that it is a pleasure to be here in IIT Kharagpur, an institution that has done more perhaps than any other to change India's standing in the world. As an Indian, I cannot tell you how much pride and pleasure it gives me when I read in the American media that many young students are now turning down offers from Harvard and MIT for the IITs. The great poet after whom this lecture is named often wrote of how he dreamt of the restoration of India's once-vaunted intellectual prowess. He too, I think, would have been proud to see what I see in front of me today.

Yet it is precisely because our pride in our present accomplishments is very great that we need sometimes to be reminded of the historical circumstances that have made them possible. This is important above all because it prepares us for the future—not just as a nation or as an institution, or indeed as any kind of collectivity, but also as individuals, as thinking and sentient human beings.

So let us think back for a moment to the intellectual and historical context that led to the foundation of such institutions as the IITs, the

IIMs and the outstanding medical institutions of contemporary India. One important element of this context was a set of beliefs that we might broadly call 'progressivist'—let me add that I use this term here to describe rather than applaud these ideas. However, I do think they deserve a respectful elucidation, if for no other reason than simply because they underlie the foundations of this remarkable institution.

One important aspect of this set of beliefs is the notion that technological and scientific advancement will have certain beneficial social consequences, such as greater equality and the erasure of historical prejudices. In short, it could be said that the progressives of the Nehruvian era believed that the advancement of science would bring about greater social justice. This idea is so widely accepted, especially in India, that it often passes without questioning. This is why I would like to spend a little time interrogating it—through the eyes, as it were, of someone who spends a good deal of time in the US.

Now, if it were the case that scientific and technological development were truly the engines of social justice, then it would follow that the US, which is the most technologically advanced country in the world, would also be the most just society not only in the contemporary world but also in all history. Is this actually the case? I don't think it takes much reflection to see that it is not. Indeed it could well be said that—from a progressivist point of view—the technological leadership of the US has led to a pronounced regression in human affairs. Let me recount for you some of the ways in which the US of the present day, despite the unprecedented affluence of some of its population, is coming more and more to resemble the societies of the pre-modern world.

One very striking instance of this is in income distribution. The aggregate statistics show that the gap between rich and poor in America is now roughly of the same order as in the nineteenth century. This gap, which had narrowed markedly over the middle years of the twentieth century, widened sharply in the 1990s and is increasing even more rapidly today under the tax policies of the current US administration. The late 1990s were, of course, the years of the dot-com boom, in which the graduates of India's IITs played a justly celebrated part. Let it be said without reservation that the world of the internet is wonderful in many ways. The trouble with it is that it has an implacable gatekeeper—literacy. Not only is this universe closed to the illiterate, but it is also structured around a very strict hierarchy of educational skills. This means that it is inevitably closed to many. I spent a great deal of time in the US in the 1990s, and I lived not in Palo Alto or Cambridge but in a part of Brooklyn that was still largely an African American neighbourhood: I saw at first hand the consequences of the rise of the dot.com economy on people whose literacy was nominal and whose skill levels were low. They became more and more marginalized, losing access to good health care and secure jobs of the kind they had held in the old industrial economy. I know that many of you believe the dot.com economy will be India's salvation. But just take a moment to think of what it will mean when a literacy-based economy takes control of a country where the majority of the population is illiterate: the same phenomenon that empowers one segment of the population will effectively cause the economic disenfranchisement of half a billion people. I am sure all of you will enter the IT world in its higher reaches: that is why you are here. But reflect for a minute on what it took to get here: many of you are from families that made great sacrifices to make it possible for you to study at an IIT. Think of your brothers, sisters and cousins who didn't make it and what lies ahead for them. Isn't there something to be said for a world in which you could pursue your unique and extraordinary talents without having to exclude those less gifted than yourselves?

This is not to suggest that we should turn our backs on the IT economy—far from it. One of the truly remarkable aspects of the IT revolution, Indian-style, is that it appears to have heightened many successful engineers' awareness of social issues. But I do want to point out that this is an instance that illustrates the fallacy of technologically based progressivism: the truth is that we cannot depend on machines alone to provide the solution to our social problems.

In the US in the 1990s, there was only one sector of the economy that kept pace with the development of the internet, and unlike the IT economy, it is still growing rapidly. This is the economy of incarceration—in other words, the prison sector. As a proportion of the population, the number of people in American jails today far exceeds the Soviet Gulag at its worst. Among certain sections of the population—African American males, for instance—a quarter have either been in jail or are in jail. The prison economy is increasingly a privatized economy and, needless to say, has proven to be a very good investment for many. This economy is large enough to generate satellite industries—the development of new forms of 'restraint', such as stun guns, sprays and such like, is already a major field of research and development.

There are certain counties in America where 30 per cent of the population is involved in the prison economy—they are either prisoners themselves or they are employees of the prison system. Try and apply this number to Kharagpur district and think of what it would be like to live here under those circumstances. This might indeed happen if we end up with an economy that excludes 50 per cent of the population. Think of the division of labour that would result from this: a small percentage of highly skilled people would make a lot of money. But a much larger number of people would be employed in what might be called the coercion sector: they would make their living by exercising control over the rest of the population, making sure that they toiled at low-paying jobs without offering too much resistance. This may sound like a fantasy, but it is already a reality in some parts of the world.

Is there a causal connection between the dot.com economy and the prison economy? I hesitate to adduce one, although common sense suggests that crime may indeed have been the recourse of many of those who were impoverished by the IT economy. What I do want to point out is that this is another instance in which contemporary America resembles European societies of the seventeenth and eighteenth centuries. In seventeenth-century Britain, many millions lost their livelihood because of the process known as 'enclosure'—whereby lands that had once been held in common were given over to private ownership. This process was accompanied by a rapid growth in the prison system—houses of correction, almshouses, etc. Then too the system was largely privatized: many bishops and clergymen ran their own prisons, and these became a major source of revenue for the church and for local civic authorities.

For the upper classes who controlled the British economy and government, there were distinct advantages to the surge in the prison population, not the least of which was that it enormously increased the number of potential military recruits, not just for the government but also for privately owned firms like the East India Company. Convicts were also a pool of transportable labour that could be drawn upon for the settling of new territories like Australia. There was thus a direct connection between early British imperialism and the growth of the prison population.

There are many uncanny parallels between this and the present-day US. As in eighteenth-century Britain, for the poor and unskilled, the choice of a livelihood often boils down to picking between prison and the army. In recent months, there have been several illuminating articles on the ways in which the US Army targets poor and minority youths for recruitment. I learnt of this at first hand while teaching at the City University of New York's Queens College campus, an institution that provides education to many immigrants and underprivileged people: many students told hair-raising stories about the tricks and chicanery employed to lure them into the armed forces. This too is reminiscent of eighteenth-century Britain, when men were regularly kidnapped, tricked and shanghaied into joining the army and navy.

There is no more vivid illustration of the nexus between the prison system and military services in America than the photographs of abuse that came out of the Abu Ghraib prison in Iraq. Let it be noted in passing that one of the most astounding aspects of the war is that the American forces, on entering Iraq, established direct control over only two sets of facilities: oil installations and prisons. That they did so amidst the widespread looting of museums, ministries, hospitals and so on is a sign of the part these industries play in today's America. No matter that the invasion was justified on the grounds of bringing 'freedom to Iraq'. The vision of freedom that is being exported here is clearly one that will result in Iraq becoming second only to the US in the proportion of its population that is in jail.

As for Abu Ghraib, it is known now that one of the ringleaders of the unit accused of abuse was actually trained as a prison guard—and he was not the only one in the unit who had close connections with the US prison system. Given that many of these men and women come from the poor rural districts that are most directly linked with prisons, this is hardly surprising.

It is well known, of course, that life in American prisons is so brutal, so inhuman that the mere threat of entry into it is often enough to force confessions out of criminals. In America, prison guards don't need to torture inmates: they know that to put a newcomer in the company of hardened prisoners will result automatically in rape, sexual humiliation and so on; the inmates will do the job for them. Evidently the members of the unit in charge believed that the same would be true of Abu Ghraib: that handing over their prisoners would result in their being brutalized by the others. But this didn't happen: it is clear from the photographs that the prisoners were supporting each other in their terror, not perpetrating it. Thus the frustration of the guards: they had been assigned the job of giving their prisoners a crash course in techniques of brutality that are the product of a society that is socially atomized and technologically very highly developed. In this lies the peculiar horror of those photographs: these guards—like the leaders who sent them there—see themselves not as being part of a process of violence but as instructors who are part of a process of education. A close look at the pictures will show that the guards' efforts were directed at making the Iraqis brutalize each other; they themselves tend to stand apart, like spectators at a sports event. In effect, the American prison guards had to hold guns to the heads of the Iraqis to make them reproduce the kind of behaviour that is considered normal in an American prison.

It is not just in the manner of recruiting that postmodern warfare is coming to look more and more pre-modern: there are other disturbing congruences. One of these is the use of mercenaries. One of the historic developments of eighteenth- and nineteenth-century Europe was that conducting war became a function of the state. The armies of the pre-modern world were raised by feudal lords, merchants and associations; with the development of the nation-state, it came to be accepted that the state had the monopoly on violence and that private actors would not be allowed to engage in war. Armies would be recruited and paid for by the state with funds raised through taxation. This conception has been turned on its head by the US war machine: as is well known, there are tens of thousands of American mercenaries in Iraq today. These fighters, whose real status is disguised by the euphemism of 'contractor', are recruited by private firms whose involvement in the conflict is explicitly based on considerations of profit. War, thus, is being re-privatized on the model of pre-modern armies.

This in turn creates other disturbing parallels with the pre-modern world. One of the foundation stones of the modern world lay in the idea that laws are based on universal principles rather than, say, on the will of a monarch or the expediency of an oligarchy of rich people. In the pre-modern world, on the other hand, it was common for laws to be restrictively based so that they applied only to certain groups or within certain territories. Thus there could be one law for Brahmins and another for Dalits, or similarly for white, black and brown people. Laws relating to slavery provide a good example of this. In the eighteenth century, it was legal for an English slave trader to enslave an African, transport him to the New World and sell him there. But suppose the slave trader stopped over in London on his way to the New World: his slaves, if they managed to go ashore, could technically reclaim their liberty, for it was illegal to take slaves inside Britain.

The abolition of slavery in the nineteenth century was significant not just for its immediate effects but also because it was a step towards the establishment of the principle that law must be universal if it is to have any meaning: it is intellectually and morally unacceptable to say that something that is wrong in Kharagpur is okay in Kanpur.

However, the principle of the universality of the law has been quietly subverted over the last few decades. Thus, in countries that have a large American military presence, US personnel are not subject to local laws even in such civil matters as rape and theft. This is exactly like the notorious 'Capitulations' system of the eighteenth and nineteenth centuries, whereby Europeans were not subject to Turkish law even on Ottoman territory. For us in India, it is a reminder of the legal system of the British Raj, which worked in markedly different ways for white and non-white people.

Despite its gradual subversion, it was not until the so-called 'war on terror' that the principle of the equality of the law came explicitly to be reversed. Thus in Guantanamo Bay, prisoners are being held by Americans—indeed by an arm of the American government—but are not subject to American law. In other words, it is recreating the situation of the eighteenth-century slave trader who was allowed to practise his trade anywhere other than at home. Similarly, the American government, which is restricted in the practice of torture by law, has acted to extradite prisoners to certain countries for the explicit purpose of subjecting them to torture: in other words, it is subcontracting the use of torture.

These are profoundly dangerous precedents, not only because of what they condone but also because they seek to overturn the hard-won universality of law and re-establish the idea that power is a law unto itself.

It is this last idea that provides what is perhaps the single most disturbing throwback to the world as it was in centuries past. In the build-up to the war in Iraq, President George Bush and other American policymakers took the position that the benefits to be gained from the judicious application of American power were so great as to outweigh any concerns about international law. This is not a new argument: British and French imperialists took the same position in the eighteenth and nineteenth centuries. Britain in particular always justified its expansion in terms of bringing the idea of 'freedom' to the world. Joseph Conrad describes this in the following words in his novel *Heart of Darkness*: 'The conquest of the earth, which mostly means the taking it away from those who have a different complexion or slightly flatter noses than ourselves, is not a pretty thing when you look into it too much. What redeems it is the idea only.'

But who is to judge whether the idea is worth the price of the conquest? The answer is no one: in the end, the value of the idea was only as good as the army that backed it. In other words, this vision of ordering the affairs of humankind is nothing more than a recipe for endless war. And after three centuries of war, we have a clear winner: to put it briefly, it consists of Britain's settler colonies around the world—the US, Australia and, of course, Britain itself. The establishment of Anglo-American hegemony is no mere accident; it has been planned and pursued over several centuries, and after the fall of the Soviet Union, it has become an undisputed reality. While this may be distasteful to some, we should recognize that it need not necessarily be a bad thing for the world at large: if the writ of these powers were to be benevolently applied, it is quite conceivable that a period of great tranquillity might ensue. But that has not happened: instead we find ourselves in a period of extraordinary instability and upheaval. The most puzzling part of this is that it need not have been so. By their own admission, the Anglo-American powers instigated the war in Iraq as a matter of choice rather than necessity, justifying it only, as Conrad puts it, as 'an unselfish belief in [an] idea—something you can set up, and bow down before and offer a sacrifice to'. The reason why the war in Iraq is significant is that it shows that the ultimate sacrifice to this idea is peace itself.

What is clear now is that the mere achievement of hegemony is not enough to set the Anglo-American powers at rest: their mission is to remake every element of the world in their own image. And since no copy can ever completely replicate the original, it means that the task they have set themselves approximates the mathematical notion of an infinite regress. No matter how much others may try—or be forced—to recast themselves in the image of the master culture, there will always be some shortcoming, some essential but insurmountable element of difference.

If the task is to remake the world in the image of Anglo-America, then clearly this is a job that has no horizon and can never reach a conclusion. This war in Iraq is thus a beginning, not an end: we are entering a period of history where war is going to be an end in itself.

To return once more to Conrad and his conception that the conquest of the Earth is redeemed by an idea alone—'not a sentimental pretence but an idea; and an unselfish belief in the idea ...'—if there is a new empire at large in the world, could it really be said that it approximates this ideal? Does it indeed unselfishly and unsentimentally believe that the world can be remade in its image? Or is this so-called idea just a mask for domination by force of arms?

Let us set aside grand ideologies for a moment; let us think of the details. Let us think, for example, of the two-car family. How many cars would there be in India if we were indeed to remake ourselves in the image of Australia, America or Britain? My elementary mathematical skills yield an answer in the range of about 250 million cars. Think about this for a minute: What would become of our cities, our roads? Remember that if we were to fully adopt the Anglo-American model, many of these cars would be SUVs: What would this imply for emissions? For our environment? Now add to our 250 million cars another 250 million in China and perhaps another 100 million in our neighbouring countries. To look at the numbers is to know that the notion that America can be a model to the world is just a hoax: not because American life is not rewarding or enviable, but because the world would asphyxiate.

It is not hard to work this out—even a child can do it. We can be sure that the people who produce the propaganda of empire are perfectly aware that a world remade in the model of Anglo-America is simply not feasible; it would destroy the globe. We can only conclude that they propagate this idea in bad faith—as a mask for a reality that is too ugly to be named. And the reality is this: the world at large must pay the cost for Anglo-America to be what it is. No one has a choice in this matter; those who resist will be put down by force of arms.

Here lies the strange contradiction that must now be enacted by the new empire: it must make war under the pretence of recreating the world in its own image. And if any part of the world were actually to be thus remade, it would have to wage war to undo what it had achieved. War would repeat itself in an endless, perfect circle.

When the history of the second half of the twentieth century comes to be written, it will be seen, I think, as a brief interregnum between empires: a time when the Anglosphere was temporarily confined by the Cold War. This period opened a window of opportunity that is quickly swinging shut again. In that short space of time, a few countries were able to slip through to create institutions of some resilience. Many others, perhaps most, failed in that attempt. We in India happen to be among the lucky ones (although the benefits extend very unevenly through the country), and we should never forget the enormous debt we owe to the brief moment in time that is known as the period of decolonization.

Let me remind you of some of the reasons for this gratitude. In the first place, this institution would not exist and none of us would be here today if it were not for the fact of India's independence. I spoke earlier of the progressivist ideals that underlie this institution. But there was another, more urgent reason for its founding. You will see what that was if you ask yourselves why institutes of scientific and technological education were so few during the 200 years of British rule. It was because empires always kept close control over the right to knowledge, especially the kind of technical knowledge that was instrumental to the creation of empires. When Satyen Bose—of the Bose-Einstein statistics—travelled to Europe, he was constantly followed by British intelligence agents. In the artillery regiments of the old British Indian Army, native sepoys were needed to load guns—but these same Indian soldiers were not allowed to fire the guns they had loaded for fear that they might use this knowledge against their masters. Restricting the flow of knowledge is one of the ways in which empires have always sought to defend themselves, and some of these prohibitions are gradually returning with the advent of the new empire: some of you will have felt their sting in the sanctions imposed on India in 1998. While those have been removed, other, more wide-ranging sanctions have been put in place over the last couple of years: as you may know, in the US, there are many fields of the sciences now that foreign students are either forbidden to study or for which they must get special clearance.

I have said that you—and we Indians as a nation—were lucky that we were able to make use of the period of decolonization. We are indeed fortunate that despite our poverty and our many difficulties and discontents, our nation has not only held together but also produced a vibrant civil society as well as centres of undoubted excellence, such as this one. There are those who draw from this the lesson that India must now seek to become one of the world's master nations—a great power with a small empire of its own.

This idea is to my mind a betrayal of everything that is of value in our past. We must never forget that ours is a nation that entered the modern era through a history of defeat and subjection. There are those who would say that this is a matter of shame, something unmentionable that should be forgotten as quickly as possible; to me, this is our single greatest source of strength. If there is any one lesson to be learnt from the Anglo-American empire, it is that people who have never suffered defeat, who have never learnt the limits of their power, are a danger to themselves and to the world at large.

It was Mahatma Gandhi who made India's weakness into the source of its strength, and it is to him that we must turn for the lessons to be drawn from a history of defeat. To me, the most instructive element of Gandhi's thought is the idea that the means and the ends are inseparable—they are the same thing. Thus for Gandhi, non-violence was not just a means to an end: it was the end itself. In terms of justice for the world, this means that as a nation we must commit ourselves not to goals or ambitions or any particular design; rather our commitment must be to a process. If this process is just, then it will, of itself, lead to a desirable end.

(Delivered as the Rabindranath Tagore Lecture at IIT Kharagpur, 2005)

# TWENTY-SIX

# The Way of A.K. Ramanujan

In my view, A.K. Ramanujan was one of the foremost writers and intellectuals of the twentieth century. His genius was so multifaceted that it is difficult to know which aspect of it to address first, so I will start with his translations, which were the first works of his that I read.

It was in the early '80s, while I was teaching at Delhi University, that I read *The Interior Landscape: Love Poems from a Classical Tamil Anthology*. This is Ramanujan's translation of the *Kuṟuntokai*, a collection of Tamil poems from the Sangam era. I vividly remember the impression the poems made on me. I was electrified; it was as though a bolt of lightning had shot through the centuries to forge a connection so powerful that two entirely different sensibilities, separated by 1,600 years, had fused together to create something utterly new and ravishingly beautiful.

Here is the most famous poem from the collection:

*What could my mother be to yours?*
*What kin is my father to yours anyway?*
*And how did you and I meet ever?*
*But in love our hearts are as red earth and pouring rain:*
*mingled beyond parting.*

The image of 'red earth' mingling with 'pouring rain' will instantly pierce the heart of anyone who has witnessed the breaking of the monsoon over the iron-reddened soils of the part of peninsular India that was once a fragment of the ancient supercontinent of Gondwanaland: it evokes the mounting thirst of a parched landscape; it evokes an almost unbearable desire; it evokes seasons and moods of music; it evokes the renewal brought about by that elemental mating of earth and sky that makes life possible on a region of the planet that is, perhaps more than any other, dependent on the cyclical rhythms of the atmosphere. It is one of those rare images that replicates what it represents: the words fall on the earth, like rain, to create a unity that is 'mingled beyond parting'.

I know of no more evocative or powerful line of poetry: it came as no surprise to me when the words 'Red Earth and Pouring Rain' became the title of a novel, Vikram Chandra's first, nor when they became the title of an album by the British folk-rock band Bear's Den.

As will be evident from this poem, Ramanujan's genius lay in his ability to use words in such a way that they seem to be compacted together, under great pressure, much as diamonds are formed by the accumulated weight of deep time. Everything he wrote was illuminated by his profoundly lyrical poetic sensibility, his subtle wit, his deep classical learning, his extraordinary linguistic range and his rigorous scholarship. *The Interior Landscape*, for instance, is invaluable not only for the unmatched quality of Ramanujan's translations but also for his introduction to the text, wherein he provides a marvellously lucid account of the ways in which metaphors and allusions work in classical Tamil verse. This genre of poetry, he tells us,

> depends on a taxonomy of landscapes, flora and fauna, and of emotions—an ecosystem of which a man's activities and feelings are a part. To describe the exterior landscape is also to inscribe the interior landscape. What the man has, he is: the landscape which he owns, in which he lives ... (50) Neither in the Tamil poem nor in ... upanishadic passages ... does the opposition of nature-culture make sense; we see that the opposition itself is culture-bound. There is another alternative to a culture vs. nature view: in the Tamil poems, culture is enclosed in nature, nature is reworked in culture, so that we cannot tell the difference. (50)

I was working on my first novel, *The Circle of Reason*, when I read this introduction, and it had a huge impact on my writing: the ideas that Ramanujan presented made me grapple with the question of whether it was at all possible to create formal structures of allusion in a contemporary work of fiction.

For me, one of the most important aspects of Ramanujan's work is the context from which it emerged. He hailed from a family of Tamil Brahmins settled in Karnataka, and was fluent in Tamil, Kannada, English and, I am sure, several other languages as well. He wrote poetry in Kannada as well as in English, and apart from translating classical Tamil poetry, he also translated from mediaeval and modern Kannada. It was he who translated U.R. Ananthamurthy's *Samskara*, and this had much to do with making it one of the most influential Indian novels of the last few decades. Given this context, it is hardly surprising that Ramanujan was a scholar of linguistics, for the formal study of languages has been a foundational element of the Indian intellectual tradition for millennia.

In other words, the mingling of languages and the fusion of identities were central to Ramanujan's work: he was, to use his own phrase, a 'multiple diglossic', not just linguistically but also culturally. Neither he nor his work can be reduced to any one language, tradition or identity; and in this, he embodies the systematic, inescapable pluralism of Indian life-worlds. This is a cultural universe in which language, identity and meaning are always dependent on context; they are never simply 'givens' as they might be in other, more homogeneous cultures.

Ramanujan himself addressed this question with his usual wit in one of his most brilliant essays: 'Is There an Indian Way of Thinking?', which was published in 1989. I can't resist quoting a few paragraphs from it.

> The problem [of whether there is an Indian way of thinking] was posed for me personally at the age of 20 in the image of my father. I had never taken a good look at him till then. Didn't Mark Twain say, 'At 17, I thought my father was ignorant; at 20, I wondered how he learned so much in three years'? Indeed, this essay was inspired by contemplation of him over the years, and is dedicated to him. My father's clothes represented his inner life very well. He was a south Indian Brahmin gentleman. He wore neat white turbans, a Sri Vaishnava caste mark (in his earlier pictures, a diamond earring), yet wore Tootal ties, Kromentz buttons and collar studs, and donned English serge jackets over his muslin dhotis which he wore draped in traditional Brahmin style. He often wore tartan-patterned socks and silent well-polished leather shoes when he went to the university, but he carefully took them off before he entered the inner quarters of the house.
>
> He was a mathematician, an astronomer. But he was also a Sanskrit scholar, an expert astrologer. He had two kinds

> of exotic visitors: American and English mathematicians who called on him when they were on a visit to India, and local astrologers, orthodox pundits who wore splendid gold-embroidered shawls dowered by the Maharajah. I had just been converted by Russell to the 'scientific attitude'. I (and my generation) was troubled by his holding together in one brain both astronomy and astrology; I looked for consistency in him, a consistency he didn't seem to care about, or even think about. When I asked him what the discovery of Pluto and Neptune did to his archaic nine-planet astrology, he said, 'You make the necessary corrections, that's all.' Or, in answer to how he could read the Gita religiously having bathed and painted on his forehead the red and white feet of Visnu, and later talk appreciatively about Bertrand Russell and even Ingersoll, he said, 'The Gita is part of one's hygiene. Besides, don't you know, the brain has two lobes?' (42-43)

The richness of this essay is such that it is hard to sum it up. Suffice it to say that Ramanujan's argument proceeds by analogy: 'The grammarian sees grammar in all things,' he writes. 'I shall be true to my bias and borrow a notion from linguistics and try it for size.' (47)

'There are ... two kinds of grammatical rules,' he continues, 'the context-free and the context-sensitive.' The former are general rules that apply irrespective of context; the latter are dependent on circumstances and situations. A parallel situation, Ramanujan argues, can be observed in cultures: some are governed by 'tendencies to *idealise* and think in terms of either the context-free or the context-sensitive kind of rules ... In cultures like India's, the context-sensitive kind of rule is the preferred formulation.'

Ramanujan cites a study by a cognitive anthropologist that compares evaluations of people by American and Odia adults. The study shows that 'Oriya and American adults ... describe persons very differently: Americans characterised them with generic words like "good", "nice", Oriyas with concrete contextual descriptions like "he brings sweets".'(52)

Perhaps the most telling examples of Ramanujan's idea of context-specificity come from Indian literature.

> No Indian text comes without a context till the nineteenth century. Works are framed by *phalasruti* verses—these verses tell the reader, reciter or listener all the good that will result from his act of reading, reciting or listening. They relate the text, of whatever antiquity, to the present reader—that is, they contextualise it ... Texts may be historically dateless, anonymous; but their contexts, uses, efficacies, are explicit. The Ramayana and Mahabharata open with episodes that tell you why and under what circumstances they were composed. Every such story is encased in a metastory. And within the text, one tale is the context for another within it; not only does the outer frame-story motivate the inner sub-story; the inner story illuminates the outer as well. It often acts as a microcosmic replica for the whole text. (48)

Similarly: '[T]he *ragas* of both north and south Indian classical music have their prescribed appropriate times. Like the Tamil poems, the genres and moods are associated with, placed in, hours of the day and times of the season.' (52)

An example that occurs to me of context-free rules is that of the blanket bans on carrying weapons that exist in some European countries. In India, such a law would have to make contextual exceptions—for example, for trishuls carried by certain Hindu religious figures and kirpans carried by Sikhs in certain situations. Such examples could be multiplied indefinitely.

Ramanujan is careful not to essentialize. 'My purpose,' he writes, 'is not to evaluate but to grope toward a description of the two kinds of emphases.' He notes that even the most rigorously universal laws are sometimes forced to make exceptions, and even context-specific rules must accommodate certain universals. 'All societies have context-sensitive behaviour and rules,' he writes, 'but the dominant ideal may not be the "context-sensitive" but the "context-free"... In predominantly "context-free" societies, the counter-movements tend to be towards the context-sensitive ... In "traditional" cultures like India, where context-sensitivity rules and binds, the dream is to be free of context.' (54) Not only are these two imperatives joined in a relationship of tension, but also the balance between them is constantly evolving.

In the final section of the article, Ramanujan cites India's modernization as an instance of a movement

> from the context-sensitive to the context-free in all realms: an erosion of contexts, at least in principle. Gandhi's watch (with its uniform autonomous time, governing his punctuality) replaced the almanac. Yet Gandhi quoted Emerson, that consistency was the hobgoblin of foolish minds. Print replaced palm-leaf manuscripts, making possible an open and egalitarian access to knowledge irrespective of caste. The Indian Constitution made the contexts of birth, region, sex and creed irrelevant, overthrowing Manu, though the battle is joined again and again ... In music, the ragas can now be heard at all hours and seasons. Once the Venkatesasuprabhatam, the wake-up chant for the Lord of Tirupati, could be heard only in Tirupati at a certain hour in the morning. Since M.S. Subbulakshmi in her devotion cut a record of the chants, it wakes up not only the Lord, but anyone who tunes in to All India Radio in faraway places. (55-56)

The work of Ramanujan's that is perhaps best known in India today is his essay 'Three Hundred Ramayanas', which was written for a conference at the University of Pittsburgh in 1986, three years before 'Is There an Indian Way of Thinking?' was published. But given the long lag between submission and publication in academic journals, I suspect that he might have been working on the two essays at about the same time. Certainly, the argument of 'Three Hundred Ramayanas' is, in a sense, an extension of the contextualist view that he expounds in 'Is There an Indian Way of Thinking?' In 'Three Hundred Ramayanas', Ramanujan is making the argument that people's experiences of the great epics are always shaped by the contexts in which they are read and translated, recited and remembered.

What then would Ramanujan have made of the controversy that erupted around his essay on multiple Ramayanas in 2011, and its subsequent removal from the Delhi University syllabus? I should note here, in parentheses, that I am not one of those who believes that the removal of a text from a curriculum is equivalent to a 'ban' or suppression of the text itself. My own work has been periodically prescribed and removed from various syllabuses, including that of this university. I feel grateful to those who advocated for the retention of my book *The Shadow Lines*, but at the same time, I do not believe that any work has a permanent claim on any academic course. To me, it seems only natural, even desirable, for a university's curriculum to change from time to time. But it goes without saying that in an institution of learning, such changes should be dictated by educational imperatives and not by political parties, as was the case with 'Three Hundred Ramayanas'.

But to return to the question: What would Ramanujan have made of the 2011 controversy? I suspect that in his characteristically quizzical way, he would have seen it as an instance of the tension between context-free and context-sensitive rules that he describes in 'Is There an Indian Way of Thinking?'. In other words, he would have seen the controversy as yet another step in the attempt to impose a singular, 'modernizing' generality upon a culture whose sensitivity to context made it systematically pluralist. And he would also, I think, have been mildly amused by the sheer futility of this impulse—for at the very moment at which his plural vision of the epics was being violently opposed, hundreds of new retellings of the epics in which gods and heroes are presented in distinctly contemporary guises were rising to the top of the bestseller charts.

It is through this prism too that I think Ramanujan would have viewed the current divisions around citizenship in India today: in a sense, these conflicts too are instances of a homogenizing, reductive impulse ultimately running up against the contextualizing, pluralizing dynamic that is so deeply rooted in India's soil. The truths of Assam and Tripura are simply not the same as those of Uttar Pradesh or Gujarat: they are completely dependent on context.

One of the great regrets of my life is that I never met A.K. Ramanujan. We did, however, have many friends and acquaintances in common, including my long-time editor and publisher Ravi Dayal. Shortly before the publication of my second novel, *The Shadow Lines*, Ravi sent a proof copy to Ramanujan. I could hardly believe it when Ravi wrote to me to say that Ramanujan had written a few lines in praise of the book. His words were prominently featured on the cover, and I glory in them to this day.

(Delivered as the fourth A.K. Ramanujan Memorial Lecture at Ramjas College, Delhi University, 2020)

# Afterword

In the introduction to this collection, I wrote that we are now in a time between the ending of one epoch and the birth of another—'a time of monsters', in the words of Antonio Gramsci. The strange thing about this interstitial era, however, is that it could also be described as a 'time of benedictions', in that it has suddenly become possible to contemplate, and even embrace, potentialities—that were denied or rejected during the age of high modernity—such as the idea that plants might possess something akin to intelligence; that rocks might be sentient; that rivers might be regarded as persons; or that certain topographical features might possess qualities and attributes that cannot be reduced to their geological composition.

Such vitalist conceptions have been widely prevalent in human cultures since the infancy of our species, and they continue to exist in many different forms across the world. It was only after the beginning of the early modern era, when a tiny group of elite European men invented a philosophy in which sentience, thought, reason and historical agency were ascribed solely to human beings, that vitalist beliefs came to be contested, denied and suppressed. Over the following centuries, with the Western conquest of most of the world, this kind of human-centredness eventually became a core component of elite ideologies everywhere.

Today, as the planet hurtles towards environmental and social collapse brought about by the interlinked vectors of global warming, biodiversity loss, species extinctions and the spread of new pathogens, it has become evident that modernity was founded on a profoundly mistaken understanding of the world and that it is the elevation of humans above all other species, indeed above the Earth itself, that is largely responsible for our current planetary crisis. The discrediting of modernity's anthropocentrism is itself a part of the ongoing collapse that we are now witnessing.

Just as it dawns on us that there is much to be learnt from premodern ideas and understandings, the Earth seems to teem with sentience; everything seems to have a spirit, a soul, not just trees and plants but also leaves, blades of grass and so on. This is where we step back in alarm. Would it be at all possible to exist in a world where everything is sentient? Would I be able to get out of bed in the morning if I thought that my houseplants were talking about me?

This is why it is important to remember that vitalist understandings of the Earth are not incompatible with doubt and scepticism: indeed—and there should be no mistake about this—the default position of humanity in relation to the vital qualities of the more-than-human world is not belief, or credulity or 'superstition'; it is doubt.

I noted earlier that most human beings throughout history were open to the possibility of non-human vitality. This does not mean, however, that people uncritically accepted every story they were told about trees that talk and birds that communicate. As Nils Bubandt has shown in his fine study of witchcraft on the Malukan island of Halmahera, even though the islanders allow for the possibility that certain kinds of actions can be effected by supernatural means, each particular instance of such an action is subjected to critical scrutiny.[1]

The critical faculty is by no means specific to modernity; it is the conceptual prism through which people make their peace with a world that teems with sentience. This is a necessary condition of human existence because if we did not regard the non-human world with a certain degree of disbelief, we might well lose our minds. Humans have never, for instance, wanted farmers to tell them about their conversations with their trees, nor have they wanted goatherds to talk about their communications with their animals. And if those people did talk about such things, they were met with derision, dubiety and laughter; no one took them seriously.

The only domains of human culture where doubt is held in suspension are poetry and fiction. If someone tells a story or recites a poem about ghosts, aliens, or talking trees, we may not believe in the literal truth of their tales, but we listen anyway. This is because stories and poems unfold within the realm of the subjunctive, where certain otherworldly potentialities might be said to exist, even if they cannot be verified. That is why there is no better way of imagining the possibility of non-human sentience than through stories and poems.

This was something that Jagadish Chandra Bose, the first scientist to study plant sentience, understood. As is well known, J.C. Bose was a Bengali physicist who did pioneering work on electricity and magnetism that led to the development of the coherer, a highly sensitive instrument that played a crucial role in Guglielmo Marconi's invention of wireless telegraphy. Bose's contributions to wireless communication were widely recognized, and he was awarded the Royal Society's Medal in 1900. However, Bose's true passion lay in the study of plant life. He believed that plants possess a form of sentience and can respond to stimuli much like animals do. To investigate this hypothesis, he devised ingenious experiments that measured the electrical responses of plants to various stimuli, such as light, touch and sound. Using innovative devices of his own invention, like the crescograph, Bose showed that plants emit electrical impulses that are strikingly similar to those of animals. He demonstrated also that plants can experience stress and fatigue, and that they can even die from shock.

Bose was, of course, doing this work at the start of the twentieth century, when high modernity was in the ascendant. His findings ran so much against the grain of the prevalent materialist dogmas that they were met with shock and astonishment in Europe. Though they initially occasioned a flurry of interest and even acclaim, eventually 'the dominant style of science in the modern West with its positivist emphasis on manipulation, control, prediction and power' took its revenge, and Bose's findings came to be dismissed as the work of a charlatan.[2] In India, however, he continued to be revered, perhaps because to most Indians the idea that plants were sentient seemed like simple common sense.

Today Bose stands vindicated, and the subject of plant sentience is now a burgeoning field of study among scientists. A significant number of botanists have even come to be convinced that trees possess the ability to communicate with each other in a fashion that is akin to talking.[3] Although Bose never went quite that far, he did write a short piece in Bengali called 'Gachher Kotha', which could be translated as 'Tree Talk'.[4] This is how it begins:

> Do trees say anything? Many will say, what sort of question is that? Have trees ever had anything to say?
>
> But do humans always express everything they want to say? And that which they do not express, is that not worth speaking of? We have a boy who cannot express everything he wants to say; and the few things he does say are said in such a broken and incomplete way that those who don't know him cannot understand what he means. But we, on the other hand, can understand everything he says. And not just that. There are

many things that our boy doesn't express verbally, but does so instead through movements of his eyes, mouth and hands, or by gesturing and shaking his head—and we who know him can understand all of this while others can't. One day a pigeon from our neighbour's house flew over and perched on our house; then it began to sing with all its might. This was our boy's first meeting with the pigeon, and he began to imitate its song. Why does a pigeon sing? It sings when it wants, when it's happy or sad; and even sometimes in its own mind, silently. Learning this new skill gave the boy no end of joy.

One day I came home and found the boy very ill; his head was aching and he was lying in bed with his eyes closed. The playful child who would disturb the whole household with his antics, could not even open his eyes today. I seated myself beside his bed and started to stroke his head. The boy recognized my touch and with great difficulty, opened his eyes and looked at me. Then he sang the pigeon's song. I heard many things in this song. I understood that he was saying: 'Have you come to see your son? He loves you very much.' I understood many other things too that I cannot express in words.

You might ask: How could you have heard so many things in the song of a pigeon? The answer is—because I love the boy. You will have seen for yourselves, that by looking at a boy's face his mother understands what he wants. Often there is no need for words. Where there is love many possibilities can be seen, many things can be heard.

High modernity taught us that the Earth was inert and existed to be exploited by human beings for their own purposes. In this time of angels, we are slowly beginning to understand that in order to hear the Earth, we must first learn to love it.

# Notes

## Climate Change and the Environment

1 The term is Naomi Klein's. *The Shock Doctrine: The Rise of Disaster Capitalism* (New York: Knopf, 2007).

2 See Pankaj Sekhsaria, ed., *The Great Nicobar Betrayal: Pushing a Vulnerable Island Knowingly Into Disaster* (Chennai: THG Publishing Group, 2020); and Madhusree Mukherjee, 'Great Nicobar Island is a Paradise in Danger', *Scientific American*, 21 June 2024.

## 1: The Great Uprooting: Migration and Displacement in an Age of Planetary Crisis

1 This includes both the Indian state of West Bengal and the nation of Bangladesh.

2 I use the terms 'migrants' and 'refugees' almost interchangeably because, as Assefaw Bariagaber observes, 'the conceptual distinction between a refugee and a migrant has become increasingly blurred'. ('Globalization, Imitation

Behavior, and Refugees from Eritrea', p. 15, *Africa Today* 60, no. 2, Special Issue: Postliberation Eritrea (Winter 2013), pp. 3–18.) For a discussion of the history of the terms 'refugee' and 'migrant', see Katerina Kondova, 'The Smartphone as a Lifeline: The Impact of Digital Communications Technologies and Services on Refugees' Experiences during Their Flight' (master's thesis, Erasmus School of History, Culture and Communication, Erasmus University Rotterdam, 2016), pp. 10-11.

3 'US officials have described Bangladesh, the seventh most populous country in the world, as "a voice of moderation among developing countries, in the Islamic world and in South Asia."' Paul J. Smith, 'Climate Change, Mass Migration and the Military Response', *Orbis* (2007): 631.

4 Kaushik Basu, 'Bangladesh at 50', Project Syndicate, 5 March 2021.

5 See, for example, the 2017 publication by the UNHCR: 'ITALY Sea arrivals dashboard'. Bangladesh was second on the list of the migrants' countries of origin at that time. That is still the case in 2021: Cf. 'Most common nationalities of Mediterranean sea and land arrivals from January 2021'.

6 See, for example, 'Bangladesh Prepares for a Changing Climate,' *IMF Country Focus*, 18 September 2019; and Grammenos Mastrojeni and Antonello Pasini, 'Effetto Serra, effetto Guerra', (Milan: Chiarelettere, 2017), loc. 919.

7 Innumerable corporations use 'a better life' as a slogan. See, for example: 'Panasonic Establishes "A Better Life, A Better World" as Its New Brand Slogan', 4 September 2013.

8 For their help in Italy, and for sharing their insights, I would like to thank Luca Ciabarri, Mauro Van Aken, Roberto Beneduce, Shail Jha, Stefano Liberti, Sara Scarafia, Antonio Fraschilla, Mara Matta, Fausto Melluso, Gianfranco Benello, Alessandro Triulzi, Paola Splendore and Hasnahena Dalia Mamataz.

9 See, for instance, Sanjay Chaturvedi and Timothy Doyle, 'Geopolitics of fear and the emergence of "climate refugees": imaginative geographies of climate change and displacements in Bangladesh', *Journal of the Indian Ocean Region*, 6:2, 206–222; and Rafael Reuveny, 'Climate change-induced migration and violent conflict', *Political Geography* 26 (2007): 656–673.

10 Camelia Dewan, 'Misreading the Bengal Delta: Climate Change, Development and Livelihoods in Coastal Bangladesh' (Seattle: University of Washington Press, 2021), p. 106.

11 Camelia Dewan, 'Climate Refugees or Labour Migrants? Climate Reductive Translations of Women's Migration from Coastal Bangladesh', *The Journal of Peasant Studies* 50, no. 6 (2023): 2340.

12 Jason Cons, 'Staging Climate Security: Resilience and Heterodystopia in the Bangladesh Borderlands', *Cultural Anthropology* 33, no. 2 (2018): 273.

13 Mike Hulme, 'Reducing the Future to Climate: A Story of Climate Determinism and Reductionism', *Osiris* 26 (2011): 245–266.

14 Camelia Dewan notes, similarly: 'Among my interlocutors, climate or environmental reasons were never given as a cause of migration to the Gulf', 'Climate Refugees or Labour Migrants? Climate Reductive Translations of Women's Migration from Coastal Bangladesh', *The Journal of Peasant Studies* 50, no. 6 (2023): 2352.

15 In the words of Assefaw Bariagaber, 'imitation minimizes costs, maximizes benefits, and reduces anxiety because possible outcomes are more predictable'. Bariagaber, 'Globalization, Imitation Behavior, and Refugees', p. 5.

16 See, for example, Rozina Visram's *Ayahs, Lascars and Princes: Indians in Britain, 1700–1947* (London: Pluto Press, 1986) and *Asians in Britain: 400 Years of History* (London: Pluto Press, 2002); Michael H. Fisher's *Counterflows to Colonialism: Indian Travellers and Settlers in Britain, 1600–1857* (Ranikhet: Permanent Black, 2004); Claire Alexander, Joya Chatterji and Annu Jalais, *The Bengal Diaspora; Rethinking Muslim Migration* (New York: Routledge, 2016); and my article 'Of Fanás and Forecastles: The Indian Ocean and Some Lost Languages of the Age of Sail,' *Economic and Political Weekly*, 21 June 2008. For lascar journeys to the United States, see Vivek Bald's excellent book *Bengali Harlem and the Lost Histories of South Asian America* (Cambridge, MA: Harvard University Press, 2013).

17 'In 2012, Gallup reported that 8 million Bangladeshis expressed a desire to migrate to the United States (as compared to 10 million Indians and 5 million Mexicans), and it is evident that emigration is the ambition of ever more Bangladeshis, from all segments of society.' Ellen Bal, 'Yearning for Faraway Places: The Construction of Migration Desires among Young and Educated Bangladeshis in Dhaka' *Identities* 21, no. 3 (2014): 279.

18 Geoff Shullenberger, 'Mimesis, Violence and Facebook: Peter Thiel's French Connection', The Society Pages, 13 August 2016. In another essay, Shullenberger writes: 'Social media platforms, a Girardian analysis suggests, are machines for producing desire. Their equalizing structure—what is most widely celebrated about them—converts all users into each other's potential models, doubles, and rivals, locked in a perpetual game of competition for the intangible objects of desire of the attention economy. By embedding users in a standardized format, social media renders all individuals instantly comparable in simple, quantitative terms.

Enabling instantaneous comparison creates the conditions for a universal proliferation of horizontal rivalry. In this situation of universalized mimetic antagonism, conditions are ripe for scapegoating. Tensions may be redirected onto (innocent) victims in episodes of bullying that form communities enabled by tools of mimesis: sharing, retweeting, hashtags, and so on.' 'The Scapegoating Machine', The New Inquiry, 15 December 2016.

19 For a detailed account of the penetration of cellphones in India, see Ravi Agrawal's *India Connected: How the Smartphone Is Transforming the World's Largest Democracy* (New Delhi: Oxford University Press, 2018).

20 My argument here owes a great deal to N. Katherine Hayles and her articles: 'Cognitive Assemblages: Technical Agency and Human Interactions', *Critical Inquiry* 43 (Autumn 2016): 32–55; and 'The Cognitive Nonconscious: Enlarging the Mind of the Humanities', *Critical Inquiry* 42 (2016): 783–807. I am grateful to Debjani Ganguly for bringing these articles to my attention.

21 For examples, see Madhav Gadgil, 'Ecosystem People, Biosphere People, Ecological Refugees', *Social Change* 53, no. 1 (2003): 20–26.

22 This a circumstance in which, as Hayles notes: 'both humans and technics share moral agency and, implicitly, moral responsibility …' 'The Cognitive Nonconscious', p. 804.

23 See, for example, P.W. Singer, 'The Ethics of Killer Applications: Why Is It So Hard to Talk About Morality When It Comes to New Military Technology?', *Journal of Military Ethics* 9, no. 4 (2010): 299–312.

24 'Computational media,' writes Hayles, 'are not just another technology. They are the quintessentially *cognitive* technology, and for this reason they have special relationships with the quintessentially cognitive species, Homo sapiens.' 'The Cognitive Nonconscious', p. 803.

25 'The emergence of new technologies, leading to reduced communication costs and "rich" communication content (in conjunction with decreased travel costs), is changing migration processes and structures. New technologies made snowball migration easier by increasing the number of friends and relations abroad who can be found and might be willing to provide assistance.' Lee Komito, 'Social Media and Migration: Virtual Community 2.0', *Journal of the American Society for Information Science and Technology* 62, no. 6 (2011): 1077.

26 'Social media has become critically important to smuggling operations, as they allow for faster communication between the different actors, which has contributed to networks being able to operate more flexibly and to easily adapt to new circumstances.' Peter Tinti and Tuesday Reitano,

*Migrant, Refugee, Smuggler, Savior* (New York: Oxford University Press, 2017), p. 62.

27 Quoted by Andrea Di Nicola and Giampaolo Musumeci in their study *Confessioni di un trafficante di uomini* (Milan: Chiaralettere, 2014), loc. 1620 (my translation).

28 Cf. Matthew Brunwasser, 'A 21st-Century Migrant's Essentials: Food, Shelter, Smartphone', *The New York Times*, 25 August 2015.

29 As Bruno Latour remarks: 'It is a characteristic of these technical mediators that they ultimately require invisibility.' 'Morality and Technology; the End of the Means', Bruno Latour, trans. Couze Venn, *Theory, Culture and Society* 19, no. 5/6 (2002): 247–260.

30 Di Nicola and Musumeci, *Confessioni*, locs. 1888–1901 (my translation).

31 As Tinti and Reitano point out, 'Those most likely to move are rarely the poorest of the poor … Migrating, even illegally, costs money the poorest seldom have.' *Migrant, Refugee*, p. 27.

32 Tinti and Reitano, *Migrant, Refugee*, p. 51.

33 In the words of a Syrian refugee: 'Most people go in families or groups or something. It's very rare to have someone alone. Even if he's alone, during the journey he'll meet someone who will be a friend or something.' Kondova, 'The Smartphone as a Lifeline', p. 40.

34 Tinti and Reitano, *Migrant, Refugee*, p. 5.

35 Cf. Muhammad Irshad et al., 'Flood Severity Assessment in Jhelum Watershed of Punjab Province, Pakistan', *Journal of Biodiversity and Environmental Sciences* 16, no. 2 (202): 39–49.

36 For a detailed account of migration as stage-in-life cycles, see Mauro Van Aken, 'The Experience and Hierarchy of Migration: Egyptian Labourers in the Jordan Valley', 2006, pp. 231–236.

37 The Italian anthropologist and ethno-psychiatrist Roberto Beneduce and his associates at the Frantz Fanon Center in Turin have been pioneers in investigating the relationship between migration and traditional rituals and spiritual beliefs. See, for instance, his article 'Traumatic Pasts and the Historical Imagination: Symptoms of Loss, Postcolonial Suffering, and Counter-memories among African Migrants', *Transcultural Psychiatry* 53, no. 3 (2016): 261–285. The work of the anthropologist Cristiana Giordano, who has worked with Beneduce and the Fanon Center, is also a major contribution to these subjects, especially her book *Migrants in Translation: Caring and the Logics of Difference in Contemporary Italy* (University of California Press, 2014). Matteo Garrone's *Io Capitano* is a rare film that captures these elements of migrant journeys.

38 David Kestenbaum, 'Just Another Kind of Outdoor Game', This American Life, 16 March 2018.

39 Roberto Benduce has analysed in detail the forms of complicity that arise 'between humanitarian workers, lawyers and asylum-seekers to construct credible stories'. 'The Moral Economy of Lying: Subjectcraft, Narrative Capital, and Uncertainty in the Politics of Asylum', *Medical Anthropology* 34, no. 6 (2015): 563. Similarly, Giordano observes, 'Through conceptual acts of translation, a complex interplay of therapeutic, bureaucratic, and religious apparatuses transforms foreign others into political categories—the "migrant", "refugee", and "victim"—that the state can recognize and use to legitimize their difference.' *Migrants in Translation*, p. 10.

40 'Those whom the Italian press has re-baptized as the new slaves, are regarded, in their countries, as little heroes.' From Gabriele del Grande's *Il Mare di Mezzo; Ai Tempi dei Respingimenti*, 4th ed. (Rome: Infinito Edizioni, 2012), p. 212 (my translation).

41 My 2008 novel, *Sea of Poppies*, is about some such journeys. See also Clare Anderson, 'Convicts and Coolies: Rethinking Indentured Labour in the Nineteenth Century', *Slavery and Abolition* 30, no. 1 (2009): 93–109; Surendra Bhana, ed., *Essays on Indentured Indians in Natal* (Leeds: Peepal Tree, 1991); Marina Carter, *Servants, Sirdars and Settlers: Indians in Mauritius 1834–1874* (New Delhi: Oxford University Press, 1995) and *Voices from Indenture: Experiences of Indian Migrants in the British Empire* (London: Leicester University Press, 1996); and Brij V. Lal, *Girmitiyas: The Origins of Fiji Indians* (Canberra, 1983; reprint, Lautoka: Fiji Institute of Applied Studies, 2004.)

42 Cf. Brij V. Lal, *Fiji Yatra: Aadhi Raat Se Aage* (New Delhi: National Book Trust, 2005); Vijaya Teelock, *Bitter Sugar: Sugar and Slavery in 19th Century Mauritius* (Moka: Mahatma Gandhi Institute, 1998); and Hugh Tinker, *A New System of Slavery: The Export of Indian Labour Overseas 1830–1920* (London, 1974).

43 Tinti and Reitano note that smuggling networks 'have become a vector for global migration, quick to identify loopholes, exploit new areas of insecurity, and target vulnerable populations whom they see as prospective clients. They no longer simply respond to demand for smuggler services: they actively generate it.' *Migrant, Regugee*, p. 6.

44 Tinti and Reitano, *Migrant, Regugee*, p. 71.

45 Beneduce notes that the EU's asylum policy 'produces ignorance': it is 'a system that systematically deletes identity while at the very same time demanding 'performances of identity'. 'Moral Economy', p. 563.

46 Kondova, 'The Smartphone as a Lifeline', p. 36.

47 Cf. James O'Malley, 'Surprised that Syrian refugees have smartphones? Sorry to break this to you, but you're an idiot', *The Independent*, 7 September 2015.

48 See 'Denmark, under fire, ups limit of valuables that refugees can keep', Reuters, 8 January 2016; and Bethany Bell, 'Europe migrants: Austria to seize migrants' phones in asylum clampdown', BBC, 20 April 2018.

49 Ed Brayton, 'Trump and the Syrian Refugees with Cell Phones', Patheos, 18 December 2015. See also Kondova, 'The Smartphone as a Lifeline', p. 5.

50 See, for instance, 'Phones are now indispensable for refugees', *The Economist*, 11 February 2017.

51 See, for instance, 'National Security Implications of Climate-Related Risks and a Changing Climate; Response to Congressional Inquiry on National Security Implications of Climate-related Risks and a Changing Climate', p. 4.

52 The late Alessandro Leogrande, a well-known journalist, noted: 'Young Afghans and Pakistanis, like Syrians fleeing from war, know all of Europe from Facebook and international telephones ...' From Leogrande's *La Frontiera* (Milan: Feltrinelli Editore, 2015), loc. 3336 (my translation). Similarly Katerina Kondova observes, '... in the last few years Facebook turned into the main platform for information exchanges as regards every single aspect of the refugees journey and needs on the road. Facebook groups created by and for refugees turn into meeting points for former, current and future refugees where all kind of valuable insights about the journey circulate ...' 'The Smartphone as a Lifeline', p. 23.

53 Ellen Bal, 'Yearning for Faraway Places', p. 286.

54 Cf. Dipesh Chakrabarty, 'The Climate of History: Four Theses', *Critical Inquiry* 35, no. 2 (Winter 2009): 197–222.

## 2: Storm of Consequences

1 Sunil S. Amrith, *Crossing the Bay of Bengal: The Furies of Nature and the Fortunes of Migrants* (Cambridge, MA: Harvard University Press, 2013).

2 'Results and Achievements of the BOBLME Project' (Bay of Bengal Large Marine Ecosystem Project, 2015).

3 P.S. Swathi Lekshmi and B. Johnson, 'Migrant Labourers in the Primary Sector of Marine Fisheries: A Case Study in Karnataka'. 38 (Central Marine Fisheries Research Institute, 2013).

4 E. Vivekanandan, M. Srinath and Somy Kuriakose, 'Fishing the Marine Food Web along the Indian Coast', *Fisheries Research* 72 (2005): 241–52.

5 Brajgeet Bhathal and Daniel Pauly, '"Fishing Down Marine Food Webs" and Spatial Expansion of Coastal Fisheries in India, 1950–2000', *Fisheries Research* 91 (2008): 26–34.

6 Aaron Savio Lobo et al., 'Commercializing Bycatch Can Push a Fishery Beyond Economic Extinction', *Conservation Letters* 3 (2010): 277–85.

7 Robert S. Pomeroy et al., 'Coping with Disaster: Rehabilitating Coastal Livelihoods and Communities', *Marine Policy* 30 (2006): 786–93.

8 Joeri Scholtens, 'Fishing in the Margins: North Sri Lankan Fishers' Struggle for Access in Transboundary Waters' (PhD diss., University of Amsterdam, 2016).

9 V. Suryanarayan and R. Swaminathan, *Fishing in Palk Bay: Contested Territory or Common Heritage?: Thinking Out of the Box*. (Chennai: Ganesh and Co., 2009).

10 San Yamin Aung, 'Myanmar Bans Foreign Fishing from Its Waters', *Asia Sentinel*, 3 April 2014.

11 Ei Cherry Aung, 'As Catch and Sales Fall, Burma's Fishermen Sink into Debt', *The Irrawaddy*, 10 January 2017.

12 Sara Schonhardt, 'What's the One Thing in Thailand Visible from Space?', blogpost on *The Wall Street Journal* (2014).

13 Sam Jones, 'Trafficked into Slavery on a Thai Fishing Boat: "I Thought I'd Die There"', *The Guardian*, 16 December 2015.

14 Ursula L. Kaly, 'Review of Land-Based Sources of Pollution to the Coastal and Marine Environments in the BOBLME Region', (FAO-BOBLME Programme, 2004): p. 100.

15 Laura A. Bristow et al., 'N2 Production Rates Limited by Nitrite Availability in the Bay of Bengal Oxygen Minimum Zone', *Nature Geoscience* 10 (2017): 24–29.

16 K.S. Jayaraman, '"Dead zone" found in Bay of Bengal', *Nature India*, 12 December 2016.

## 6: A Tragic Predicament

1 Quoted in Matthew Schneider-Mayerson, 'Some Islands Will Rise; Singapore in the Anthropocene', *Resilience,* vol. 4, nos. 2–3, p. 169. The quote is taken from Chua Beng Huat, 'Singapore as Model: Planning Innovations, Knowledge Experts', in *Worlding Cities: Asian Experiments and the Art of Being Global*, eds Ananya Roy and Aihwa Ong (Malden, MA: WileyBlackwell, 2011), pp. 29– 54.

## 7: Santanu Das and the First World War

1 Santanu Das. *Touch and Intimacy in First World War Literature* (Cambridge: Cambridge University Press, 2005).
2 Santanu Das, ed., *Race, Empire and First World War Writing* (Cambridge: Cambridge University Press, 2011).
3 Paul J. Bailey, '"An Army of Workers": Chinese Indentured Labour in First World War France', in *Race*, ed. Das.
4 Kimloan Hill, 'Sacrifices, Sex, Race: Vietnamese Experiences in the First World War', in *Race*, ed. Das.
5 Santanu Das, 'Indians at Home, Mesopotamia and France, 1914–1918: Towards an Intimate History', in *Race*, ed. Das.
6 Joe Lunn, 'France's Legacy to Demba Mboup? A Senegalese Griot and His Descendants Remember His Service during the First World War', in *Race*, ed. Das.
7 In *Race*, ed. Das.

## 8: *Abhi Le Baghdad*

1 The page references are to *Abhi Le Baghdad* ('On to Baghdad') by Sisir Sarbadhikari (Calcutta, 1958). The excerpted passages are my own translations of this text.
2 Bengalis, like most Indians, were not classified as a 'martial race', hence were not eligible for recruitment into the armed services; they were thus shut out of one of the country's most lucrative job markets.
3 Author's introduction.
4 Mokkhoda Debi, *Kalyan-Pradeep: Captain Kalyan Kumar Mukhopadhyay, I.M.S.-er Jiboni* ['Kalyan-Pradeep: The Life of Captain Kalyan Kumar Mukherji, I.M.S.'] (1928), pp 324-25.
5 Sarbadhikari took the title of his book from this episode.
6 A *ghara*, or earthen water pot.
7 As I was writing this, I discovered, to my astonishment, that I have a personal connection with Sisir Sarbadhikari, of the six-degrees-of-separation kind. The reference here is to Ranada Prasad Saha, who would go on to make a fortune in what is now Bangladesh. He would also become a legendary philanthropist. It so happens that he and his family were friends of my parents, and I visited his house in Narayanganj several times as a child. I was very young then and had no idea that he had served in Mesopotamia.

Saha and his son were taken away by the Pakistani Army during the 1971 war of liberation. They were never seen again.

8 'Siege of Kut', Wikipedia.

## 9: At 'Home and the World' in Iraq, 1915–17

1 Mokkhoda Debi, *Kalyan-Pradeep: Captain Kalyan Kumar Mukhopadhyay, I.M.S.-er Jiboni* [Kalyan Pradeep: The Life of Captain Kalyan Kumar Mukherji, I.M.S.] (1928).

2 All translations from *Kalyan-Pradeep* are my own.

3 Santanu Das, 'Indians at Home, Mesopotamia and France, 1914–1918: Towards an Intimate History', in *Race, Empire and First World War Writing*, ed. Santanu Das (Cambridge: Cambridge University Press, 2011), p. 78.

4 Kalyan Mukherji's choice of words when he is writing about the British Indian force is revealing. He usually writes of 'the English' or 'this side'—not 'our side'.

5 This is a literal transcription of the Bengali spelling. I haven't been able to identify the town.

6 *edik-kar dol*—note, not 'our side'

7 Capt. Mukherji's words are: '*Swadesh-premer mukhe jhata*': lit. 'a *jharu* (broom) in the face of loving your own country'; *Kalyan-Pradeep*, p. 334.

8 Ten million

9 From 'Nationalism in Japan', in *Nationalism* (San Francisco, 1917), pp. 111-12.

10 From 'Nationalism in India', in *Nationalism* (San Francisco, 1917), p. 147.

11 Another battle between the dominant European and Asian powers of the day had been fought at Ctesiphon more than fifteen centuries earlier, on 29 May 363 CE. The protagonists were the Sassanid king Shapur II and the Roman emperor Julian (who is the subject of a wonderful novel by the recently deceased and greatly lamented Gore Vidal).

12 He was probably referring to typhoid, which also devastated the Armenian camps.

## 10: Shared Sorrows: Indians and Armenians in the Prison Camps of Ras Al-'Ain, 1916–18

1 Cf. Mesrov Jacob Seth, *Armenians in India: From the Earliest Times to the Present Day* (Calcutta: 1937; reprint, New Delhi: Asian Educational Services, 2005), chapter 1.

2 The school was originally known as the Armenian Philanthropic Academy. The building, at 39 Free School Street, was purchased in 1883 for Rs 48,000. W.M. Thackeray was born there on 18 July 1811. Ibid.

3 Santanu Das, 'Indians at Home, Mesopotamia and France, 1914–1918: Towards an Intimate History', in *Race, Empire and First World War Writing*, ed. Santanu Das (Cambridge: Cambridge University Press, 2011), which prompted me to seek it out.

4 I owe many thanks to Dr Swapan Chakravorty and Sri Ashim Mukhopadhyay of the National Library of India, Kolkata, for their help in this regard. The page references (in parentheses) are to this copy of *Abhi Le Baghdad*.

5 Cf. Pradeep P. Barua, 'Inventing Race: The British and India's Martial Races', *Historian* 58, no. 1 (1995): 107–16; and Kaushik Roy, 'Recruitment Doctrines of the Colonial Indian Army: 1859–1913', *Indian Economic and Social History Review* 34, no. 3 (1997): 322–54.

6 The precise numbers remain undetermined, but it is estimated that about 3,000 British and 10,000 Indian soldiers went into captivity after the surrender. Cf. Heather Jones, 'Imperial Captivities: Colonial Prisoners of War in Germany and the Ottoman Empire, 1914–1918', in *Race, Empire and First World War Writing*, ed. Santanu Das (Cambridge: Cambridge University Press, 2011), p. 24.

7 Quoted in Heather Jones, 'Imperial Captivities'.

8 Santanu Das, 'Indians at Home'.

9 Murali Ranganathan has very recently unearthed another First World War memoir, written in Gujarati by a Parsi, Nariman Karkaria. This is how he describes it: 'This book was published in 1922 by D.A. Karkaria from the Manek Printing Press in Mumbai. It is deceptively titled *Rangbhumi Par Rakhad*, which I would translate as "Sorties on Stage". It was perhaps intended as a pun for *jangbhumi*, a word he uses often in the text.' (The book was published as *The First World War Adventures of Nariman* Karkaria by HarperCollins Publishers India, 2022.) For more on this, see my blog post of 15 October 2012 (www.amitavghosh.com/blog/). I am convinced that other such accounts were written in languages like Marathi, Punjabi, Pahari and Gorkhali. But as of the time of writing, I do not know of any.

10 Cf. Santanu Das, 'Indians at Home'. For a more complete account of the making of *Abhi Le Baghdad* and for a fuller picture of the wider contexts of the Mesopotamian campaign, we will have to wait for Santanu's next book, which is, I am told, nearing completion. I eagerly await its publication.

11 Cf. Heather Jones, 'Imperial Captivities', suggests that the separation of prisoners happened at Ras al-'Ain: 'Non-Muslim other rank Indian

prisoners were eventually segregated at Ras-el-Ain to work on the railway line; Muslim and British other rank prisoners were transported on from Ras-el-Ain by train to separate camps in Turkey proper.' But Sarbadhikari's account suggests that it happened earlier.

12 The term 'Hindu' was perhaps more relevant to the British Army's administrative practices than to the conceptions of the soldiers themselves. In dividing the Indian soldiers by religion, the Turks were possibly following British practices.

13 It is generally agreed that Indian Muslim troops were better treated by the Ottomans; whether this was true of British troops is not clear. For a full discussion of this issue, see Heather Jones, 'Imperial Captivities'.

14 Vedica Kant, an Indian research scholar in Turkey, suggests that this was probably a small town to the north of Mosul. I am very grateful to Vedica for looking up place names and for providing translations of some of the Turkish words that occur in the text.

15 The English traveller J.S. Buckingham also remarks on the distinctiveness of this general region and its inhabitants, *Travels in Mesopotamia* (London: 1827), pp. 204-05.

16 Sisir uses the English word.

17 This town, now on the border of Syria and Turkey, is currently known as Nusaybin. But Buckingham refers to it as Nisibeen, and argues that it was the ancient 'Nisibir': 'The first foundation of Nisibeen is of an antiquity beyond even the reach of records; since it is thought, by some learned divines, to be one of the places enumerated in the Scriptures, as built by Nimrod, "the mighty hunter before the Lord ... Its name is more frequently written "Nesibis", on the medals which are preserved of it. It is found to be written "Nisibis" in Greek authors, while the present pronunciation of the name, "Nisibeen", or "Nesbin", is said, by D'Anville, to be in conformity to Abulfeda, the Arabian geographer.' *Travels*, pp. 242-43.

18 E.A. Walker, as quoted by Heather Jones, 'Imperial Captivities', describes the Indians' accommodation at Ras al-'Ain in the following words: 'They had "no shelter; only their own blankets, bare Turkish ration to live".' Although there is no disagreement in the two accounts, I am struck by the marked contrast in tone; here, as in other parts of the narrative, Sisir's description is remarkably matter-of-fact, his attitude stoical. Perhaps this was because his account was written long after the events, when the raw edges of the experience had been smoothed by the passage of time. Or was it because, as a private and an Indian, he expected less and was more accustomed to difficult conditions?

19 Sisir generally uses the Arabic words Halbe or Halab for Aleppo.

20 Santanu Das writes: 'According to a British eye-witness account, [the Hindu prisoners were like] "animated skeletons hung about with filthy rags".' Cf. Das, 'Indians at Home'.

21 Quoted in Heather Jones, 'Imperial Captivities'.

22 Racial issues recur constantly in both British and Indian writing about the colonial army, irrespective of class and rank. Writing about the diaries of Amar Singh, a Rajput nobleman, Santanu Das observes: '"Slur" is a recurrent word and emotion in the diaries; a constant oscillation between class privilege and racial discrimination forms their emotional core. Experiences of "slight" range from the refusal of the English soldiers to salute him (though he was King's Commissioned Officer) to being teased for not eating beef to being "very rudely" asked to leave the room 25 when important military details are discussed. The personal and the racial are interlinked.' Das, 'Indians at Home'. Elsewhere, in the same article, Santanu points to the British insistence on maintaining racial boundaries: 'In *In Kut and Captivity* (1919), Major Sandes writes that on reaching Baghdad, "our first business was naturally to get separate accommodation for the Indian officers": "we explained also that Indian officers ... were always of inferior ranks to British officers." Even in captivity, the colonial, racist hierarchy is put forward as "natural".'

23 In this passage, as elsewhere, Sisir consistently uses the Bengali word 'gora' to refer to 'white' soldiers. He uses 'kalo' (black) to refer to himself and other Indians.

24 Vedica Kant suggests that this term was: '*kardeş* (pronounced "kardesh"), which is the term for brother'. I have followed her suggestion here, although Sisir's spelling of it would properly be transcribed as 'kardash'.

25 Mardin has long had a large Armenian population. J.S. Buckingham, in describing Mardin, writes: 'The population is thought to amount to twenty thousand, of which, two-thirds at least are Mohammedas, the remainder are composed of Christians and Jews. Of the Syrians, there are reckoned two thousand houses, of the Armenians five hundred, and of the Jews four hundred.' *Travels in Mesopotamia* (London: 1827), pp. 191-92.

26 The word 'genocide' had not, of course, yet been invented, nor its Bengali counterpart.

27 Chronologically speaking, Sisir was once again able to rely on his journal from this point on, for his notes resume from April 1918 (the gap dates back to April the year before).

28 The poem is 'Hatobhagyer Gaan', written in 1899 (1305 by the Bengali reckoning); it is included in Tagore's *Gitobitan*. I am grateful to my sister, Dr Chaitali Basu, and Dr Swachhatoya Banerjee for tracing the poem.
29 It isn't clear whether Sisir wrote this episode from memory or had notes to rely on. Chronologically, the episode occurred after the resumption of his journal. But in the book, he tells the story out of chronological sequence.
30 In the text, this story is told out of chronological sequence.
31 Heather Jones, 'Imperial Captivities'. I am very grateful to Santanu Das for bringing this reference to my attention.
32 In the British Indian Army, by long tradition, fifers and drummers were recruited from orphanages for Eurasians. The recruits were often children.

## 11: Of Fanás and Forecastles: The Indian Ocean and Some Lost Languages of the Age of Sail

1 New South Wales Maritime Records, 'Passenger List of the William Wilson, November 1854', New South Wales Government Archives, November 1854.
2 See, for example: Albert Barrère and Charles G. Leland, *A Dictionary of Slang, Jargon & Cant* (London: Ballantyne Press, 1889); and Sir Henry Yule and A.C. Burnell, *Hobson-Jobson: A Glossary of Colloquial Anglo-Indian Words and Phrases, and of Kindred Terms, Etymological, Historical, Geographical and Discursive*, new ed., ed. William Crooke (London: J Murray, 1903). The Persian lashkar in turn is often traced to the Arabic ʻaskari, meaning 'soldier'. The often-adduced link between the Persian and Arabic terms seems suspect to me for many reasons. The Arabic word to start with: ʻaskar/ʻaskari is an unusual term in that it has four root consonants: ʻ-s-k-r. Of these, the first, the guttural ʻain (usually represented in English by an inverted comma) is a consonant that is almost always retained in the orthography of words that have travelled from Arabic to languages that are written in the Arabic script: it does not, however, figure in the spelling of the Urdu/Persian term lashkar. Secondly, the derivation of 'lascar' from ʻaskar presumes that it was adapted into Urdu/Persian with one part of the definite article al- attached (i.e., it went from al-ʻaskar to 'lascar'): this would be an unusual and uncharacteristic procedure, to say the least. The other possibility is that it is the Arabic ʻaskar/ʻaskari that derives from the Persian lashkar (such indeed was the opinion of no less a philologist than the great Henry Yule of *Hobson-Jobson*). But this seems even more unlikely to me, for if this were so, then there would have to be some accounting

for the fact that the Arabic word had, in the course of its travels, lost one consonant—'l'—and acquired another, the guttural. There would have to be an accounting also for the plural of the Arabic word 'askar/'askari, which is asâkir (while lashkar can be used as a collective).

3 Cf. *The Oxford English Dictionary*.

4 Some subcontinental dictionaries do not even list the nautical meaning of the word. See, for instance, Dr Shaikh Ghulam Maqsud Hilali's *Perso-Arabic Elements in Bengali*, ed. Dr Muhammad Enamul Haq (Dhaka: Central Board for Development of Bengali, 1967).

5 Cf. David A. Chappell, *Double Ghosts: Oceanian Voyagers on Euroamerican Ships* (New York: M.E. Sharpe, 1994).

6 On this subject, see also, Isaac Land: 'Many of the naval victories and lucrative seaborne enterprises of the early nineteenth century were made possible by the labour of foreign, colonial, or "minority" seamen whose contributions are largely forgotten today. Britain continued to rule the waves, but only by relying on Lascars (sailors from South Asia and neighbouring regions) to make up for its own manpower shortages in the merchant fleet. At Trafalgar, about 15 per cent of Nelson's "British" sailors were in fact from overseas, largely from other European countries but also from Africa, Asia, and the Americas.' 'Bread and Arsenic: Citizenship from the Bottom Up in Georgian London', *Journal of Social History* 39, no. 1 (Fall 2005): 89–110.

7 Herman Melville, *Moby Dick* (London: Penguin Popular Classics, 1994), p. 176.

8 Herman Melville, *Redburn: His First Voyage, Being the Sailor Boy Confessions and Reminiscences of the Son-of-a-Gentleman in the Merchant Service* (New York: Anchor Books, 1957), p. 165.

9 Ibid., p. 164.

10 See Anne Bulley's *The Bombay Country Ships, 1790–1833* (Richmond: Curzon Press, 2000), pp. 207–10.

11 Melville, *Redburn*, p. 165.

12 Ibid., p. 166.

13 B.R. Burg, *Sodomy and the Pirate Tradition: English Sea Rovers in the Seventeenth-Century Caribbean* (New York: New York University Press, 1995), pp. 146-47.

14 See Isaac Land, 'Customs of the Sea: Flogging, Empire, and the 'True British Seaman' 1770 To 1870', *Interventions* 3, no. 2 (2001): 169–85.

15 For more on the curtailment of the Indian shipping industry, see Anne Bulley's *The Bombay Country Ships, 1790–1833* (Richmond: Curzon Press, 2000), p. 239; Asiya Siddiqi's 'The Business World of Jamsetjee Jeejeebhoy',

*Indian Economic and Social History Review* 19, nos. 3-4 (July–December 1982): 301–24; and Amalendu Guha's 'Parsi Seths as Entrepreneurs: 1750–1850', *Economic and Political Weekly*, no. 35 (1970): pp. 107–15.

16 See, for example: Rozina Visram's *Ayahs, Lascars and Princes: Indians in Britain, 1700–1947* (London: Pluto Press, 1986) and *Asians in Britain: 400 Years of History* (London: Pluto Press, 2002); Michael H. Fisher's *Counterflows to Colonialism: Indian Travellers and Settlers in Britain, 1600–1857* (Ranikhet: Permanent Black, 2004); and Isaac Land's 'Customs of the Sea: Flogging, Empire, and the 'True British Seaman' 1770 To 1870', *Interventions* 3, no. 2 (2001): 169–85, 'Sinful Propensities: Piracy, Sodomy, and Empire in the Rhetoric of Naval Reform in Britain and the United States, 1770–1870' (forthcoming as a chapter in *Discipline and the Other Body*, Duke University Press) and 'Bread and Arsenic: Citizenship from the Bottom Up in Georgian London', *Journal of Social History* 39, no. 1 (Fall 2005): pp. 89–110.

17 Lt Thomas Roebuck, *An English and Hindostanee Naval Dictionary of Technical Terms and Sea Phrases: To Which Is Prefixed a Short Grammar of the Hindostanee Language* (Calcutta: Printed; reprinted for Black, Parry & Co., Booksellers to the Hon. East India Company, Leadenhall Street, 1813).

18 Capt. Thomas Roebuck, *A Laskari Dictionary or Anglo-Indian Vocabulary of Nautical Terms and Phrases in English and Hindustani*, revised and corrected by George Small (London: W.H. Allen & Co., 1882).

19 Cf. Albert Barrère & Charles G. Leland, *A Dictionary of Slang*.

20 Of these common swear words, Roebuck provides no translation, which can be forgiven, considering that his is a technical glossary. The same cannot be said, however, of the *OED*, which, while providing definitions for scores of obscure and archaic Hindi/Urdu words, is unaccountably silent on these, which were probably the first learnt by most Englishmen on arriving in India. *Hobson-Jobson* does indeed list 'banchoot' and 'beteechoot', but only to offer a coy evasion: 'terms of abuse which we should hesitate to print if their odious meaning were not obscure "to the general". If it were known to the Englishmen who sometimes use the words, we believe there are few who would not shrink from such brutality'.

21 Roebuck, ibid., lxvi.

22 This silence is not reducible merely to a lack of familiarity with written English: it extends even to the written corpus of the languages of the Indian subcontinent. In Bengali, for example, Ghulam Murshid was able to find few traces of lascar history that predate the twentieth century. See Ghulam Murshid, *Kâlâpânir Hâthchâni: Bilete Bângalir Itihâs* (Dhaka: Abosar, 2008). I would like to thank Ashraf Hossain of Dhaka University for bringing this work to my notice.

23 Catalogue number: JOD 5, Caird Library, National Maritime Museum, Greenwich. The text of this journal has not, to my knowledge, ever been published. This transcription is mine and I have retained the original spellings, punctuation, etc. I would like to thank the museum and its staff for their courtesy and cooperation.

24 Ocington (1690), quoted in *Hobson-Jobson*, p. 65 ('Sir G. Birdwood tells us that this is a phrase still current in Bombay').

## 12: Wordless Pasts: The Indian Exodus from Burma and the Writing of *The Glass Palace*

1 Leslie Glass, *The Changing of Kings: Memories of Burma, 1934–1949* (London: Peter Owen, 1985).

2 Hugh Tinker, 'A Forgotten Long March: The Indian Exodus from Burma, 1942', *Journal of Southeast Asian Studies* 6, no. 1 (1975): 1–15.

3 Ibid.

## 13: Confessions of a Xenophile

1 I owe the concept of 'xenophilia' to Leela Gandhi, who explored it brilliantly in her seminal work *Affective Communities: Anticolonial Thought, Fin-De-Siecle Radicalism, and the Politics of Friendship* (Durham: Duke University Press, 2006).

## 15: The Spice Islands

1 Bartolomé Leonardo de Argensola, *The Discovery and Conquest of the Molucco and Philippine Islands*, trans. John Stevens (London: J. Knapton et al., 1708).

2 Cf. Willard A. Hanna, *Indonesian Banda: Colonialism and its Aftermath in the Nutmeg Islands* (Philadelphia: Institute for the Study of Human Issues, 1978; reprint, Banda Neira: Yayasan Warisan dan Budaya Banda Naira, 1991), p. 29.

3 Quoted in ibid., p. 56.

## 18: Wild Fictions

1 See Jason Wilson's introduction to *Journey to Mauritius* by Jacques-Henri Bernardin de Saint-Pierre (New York: Interlink Books, 2003), p. 11.

2 Cf. Bernardin de Saint-Pierre, 'La Chaumière Indienne', in *Œuvres choisies de Bernardin de Saint-Pierre, contenant Paul et Virginie, La Chaumière Indienne, Le Café de Surate, Voyage en Silésie, à bÎle de France, L›Arcadie, De la Nature de la Morale, Vœux d›un Solitaire* (Paris: Librairie de Firmin Didot Frères, 1843).The passages in quotation marks are my translations, from the above edition.

3 'le berceau de tous les arts et de toutes les sciences', ibid., p. 128.

4 'l'Athènes des Indes', p. 129.

5 'Partout, répondit le paria: ma pagode, c'est la nature', ibid., p. 143.

6 Saint-Pierre's love of nature is said to have revealed itself very early in his life. The story goes that as a child, his first response to the Cathedral of Rouen was to cry: 'My God, they're flying so high!' He had not seen the spires at all, only the blackbirds that were nesting on them. The works of man made no impression on him, Saint-Beuve tells us; he had eyes only for nature.

7 *The Voyage* was first translated and published in English in 1775 as *A Voyage to the Island of Mauritius*. The references here are to the 2003 edition edited by Jason Wilson and published under the title *Journey to Mauritius* (New York: Interlink Books, 2003).

8 For an account of Saint-Pierre's complex relationship with Poivre, see Jason Wilson's introduction to *Journey to Mauritius* by Jacques-Henri Bernardin de Saint-Pierre (New York: Interlink Books, 2003), pp. 7-8.

9 For a comprehensive account, see P.J. Moree, *A Concise History of Dutch Mauritius 1598–1710: A Fruitful and Healthy Land* (London: Kegan Paul, 1998).

10 Cf. Richard H. Grove, *Green Imperialism: Colonial Expanision, Tropical Island Edens and the Origins of Environmentalism, 1600–1860* (Cambridge: Cambridge University Press, 1995), chap. 5, 'Protecting the Climate of Paradise: Pierre Poivre and the Conservation of Mauritius under the Ancien Régime', p. 235.

> The island ... became the central motif of a new discourse about nature which we can safely characterise as environmentalist rather than simply conservationist. This insular discourse became so strong in the Romantic tradition that it allows us to trace many of the central features of early Western environmentalism back to the pattern established by the French on Mauritius ... Indeed one could even say that environmentalism was, to a great extent, born out of a marriage between physiocracy and the mid-18th century French obsession with the island as the speculative and Utopian location of ... idyllic societies.

11 My narrative of this event is based on Blyth's account in his 1859 article 'On the Great Rorqual of the Indian Ocean, with Notices of other Cetals, and of the Syrenia or Marine Pachyderms', *Journal of the Asiatic Society of Bengal* 28, nos. 1–5, pp. 481–498. See particularly the footnotes on pp. 482, 483 and 490-91. See also Blyth's report on the carcass of a young globicephalus that was 'killed in the Hugly near Serampore', *Journal of the Asiatic Society* 21 (1852): 358; and also, John Anderson, *Anatomical and Zoological Researches: Comprising an Account of the Zoological Results of the Two Expeditions to Western Yunnan in 1868 and 1875; and a Monograph of the Two Cetacean Genera, Platanista and Orcella* (London: Bernard Quaritch, 1878), p. 369.

12 Cf. Loren Eiseley, *Darwin and the Mysterious Mr. X* (New York: E.P. Dutton, 1979).

13 Charles Darwin, letter to J.D. Hooker, 10 May 1848, in *The Correspondence of Charles Darwin*, vol. 4, 1847–1850 (Cambridge: Cambridge University Press, 1991), p. 139: 'Did you see Mr Blyth in Calcutta; he would be a capital man to tell you what is known about Indian zoology, at least in the Vertebrata; he is a very clever, odd, wild fellow who will never do, what he could do, from not sticking to any one subject. By the way, if you should see him at any time, try not to forget to remember me very kindly to him: I liked all I saw of him—' I am grateful to John Matthew for bringing this exchange to my notice.

14 Blyth implies in his article that the villages ('natives') had set only the dead animals adrift, but the text suggests that they had applied themselves to also freeing the live animals.

15 Alfred Russell Wallace, *The Malay Archipelago*, pp. 97-98.

16 At least one of Blyth's contemporary fellow-naturalists, Alfred Russell Wallace, might well have asked such a question.

17 Buell defines the concept as a 'residual capacity (of individual humans, authors, texts, readers, communities) to awake to fuller apprehension of physical environment and one's interdependence with it', in his book *Writing for an Endangered World: Literature, Culture and Environment in the US and Beyond* (Cambridge, MA: Belknap Press of Harvard University Press, 2001), p. 22.

18 There is now extensive literature on this subject. For other accounts of some similar belief systems, see Ole Bruun and Arne Kalland, eds., *Asian Perceptions of Nature: A Critical Approach* (Richmond: Curzon Press, 1995); Arne Kalland, *Nature Across Cultures: Views of Nature and Environment in Non-Western Cultures* (Dordrecht and Boston: Kluwer Academic Publishers,

2003); and Anna Tsing, *In the Realm of the Diamond Queen: Marginality in an Out-of-the-Way Place* (Princeton: Princeton University Press, 1993).

19 Cf. Ravi Rajan, 'Imperial Environmentalism or Environmental Imperialism? European Forestry, Colonial Foresters and the Agendas of Forest Management in British India 1800–1900', in *Nature and the Orient: The Environmental History of South and Southeast Asia*, eds. Richard H. Grove, Vinita Damodaran and Satpal Sangwan (Delhi: Oxford University Press, 1998), pp. 324–71. Rajan writes: 'A critical element of the attitude of colonial foresters to local populations was the perception that their claims were illegitimate because of their ostensible scientific and technological backwardness ...' (359) But he points out that this tendency began in Europe long before it came to colonial India. See also Mahesh Rangarajan, 'Production, Desiccation and Forest Management in the Central Provinces 1850–1930', pp. 575–89, in the same volume.

20 This case and the one that follows are described in 'That Hunted Feeling' by Pramila N. Phatarphekar, *Outlook*, 11 July 2005, vol. 45, no. 27.

21 Ramachandra Guha and Madhav Gadgil have been pioneers in the critique of exclusivist governmental forest management in India and, more generally, of what might be called 'forest fundamentalism'. This essay is indebted particularly to the following works: Ramachandra Guha and Juan Martinez-Allier, *Varieties of Environmentalism* (London: Earthscan Publishers, 1997); and Madhav Gadgil and Ramachandra Guha, *Ecology and Equity: The Use and Abuse of Nature in Contemporary India* (New Delhi: Penguin, 1995). For another valuable critique, see Smitu Kothari and Pramod Parajuli, 'No Nature Without Social Justice: A Plea for Cultural and Ecological Pluralism in India', in *Global Ecology: A New Arena of Political Conflict*, ed. Wolfgang Sachs (London: Zed Books, 1993), pp. 224–41. The recently published collection *Nature in the Global South: Environmental Projects in South and South-East Asia*, eds. Paul Greenough and Anna L. Tsing (Hyderabad: Orient Longman, 2003) also contains several important contributions to this subject.

22 India's Forest Conservation Act of 1980 significantly augmented the powers of Forest Department officials, and the aborted Forest Bill of 1982 would have increased these further still, granting them rights to arrest without trial and so on. But the Bill was vigorously resisted by activist groups and the government was forced to drop it (see Ramachandra Guha, *The Unquiet Woods: Ecological Change and Peasant Resistance in the Himalaya* (New Delhi: Oxford University Press, 1989), p. 212.

23 My account of the Khunjerab Park's founding and history is based upon Are Knudsen's analysis in his article 'State Intervention and Community

Protest: Nature Conservation in Hunza, North Pakistan', in *Asian Perceptions of Nature: A Critical Approach*, eds. Ole Bruun and Arne Kalland (Richmond: Curzon Press, 1995).

24 The interested reader is referred to Paul Greenough's excellent summation of the early history of Project Tiger in his article 'Pathogens, Pugmarks and Political "Emergency": The 1970s South Asian Debate on Nature', in *Nature in the Global South: Environmental Projects in South and South-East Asia*, eds. Paul Greenough and Anna L. Tsing (Hyderabad: Orient Longman, 2003).

25 In a recent article (*Hindustan Times*, 16 June 2005), Ramachandra Guha has ascribed the relative success of the Sundarbans project to the implementation of Joint Management techniques. However, in my experience, the Forest Department's presence weighs no less heavily on the lives of people in the Sundarbans than anywhere else.

26 The full title of the measure is Scheduled Tribes and Forest Dwellers (Recognition of Forest Rights) Bill. The Bill was announced on 1 February 2005. See the *Hindustan Times*, 2 February 2005.

27 The figures cited in this paragraph are quoted by the economist Mihir Shah in his article 'Governance Reform for India's Forests', *The Hindu*, 20 May 2005.

28 It has been alleged in the press that the sudden breaking of the 'news' of the decline in the tiger population is 'a planned attempt by a lobby comprising senior forest officers to scuttle' the Forest Rights Bill (*Hindustan Times*, 4 May 2005). Or as another writer puts it: 'Tigers versus Tribals: this is how the debate on the [Forest Rights Bill] has been framed.' *The Indian Express*, 20 June 2005.

29 For an account of the failure of exclusivist conservation policies in Africa and their subsequent revision, see Raymond Bonner's *At the Hand of Man: Peril and Hope for Africa's Wildlife* (New York: Knopf, 1993).

30 Thus Piers Vitebsky writes, in discussing the collapse of traditional religion among the Sora, 'Local knowledge, however mythological the idiom in which it is cast, is at the same time intensely practical. It is a form of action by the intellect on the environment and gives to its knowers the conviction of commanding a certain area of experience. This remains "knowledge" for as long as it continues to satisfy that conviction. Yet under certain circumstances experience itself can move away from the certainty of knowledge, defy it, slip out of its grasp. An entire system of knowledge or parts of it, become ineffectual in the face of reality.' 'A Farewell to Ancestors: Deforestation and the Changing Spiritual Environment of the Sora', in *Nature and the Orient: The Environmental History of South and Southeast Asia*, eds. Richard H. Grove, Vinita Damodaran and Satpal Sangwan (Delhi: Oxford University Press, 1998), p. 981-82.

31 I would like to thank Mihir Shah, Ramachandra Guha and Rahul Srivastava for reading and commenting on this article; I am deeply grateful also to Cecil Pinto for his help in tracking down certain details.

## 19: *Provincializing Europe*: A Correspondence

1 'The centre of gravity of the *adda* lay in a direction away from the telos of productivity or development (in this case that of a purposeful discussion). Hirankumar Sanyal recalls how food (and, I might add, a gendered division of labour) were once used in a meeting of the Monday Club to defeat Prasantachandra Mahalanobis's plans to inject into the proceedings a sense of purpose. Sanyal writes:

> Every ... [meeting] included a feast. But one day, Prasantachandra turned obstinate [and said], "Eating makes discussion impossible. Why do you waste so much time just eating? I will serve you only tea and cheap biscuits." The meeting was at his place that day. There were some tiny little biscuits available those days called "gem" biscuits—usually offered to pet cats and dogs. Everybody raised a hue and cry. Tatada [Sukumar Ray] realized protesting would not achieve anything, for Prasanta would not listen. He whispered to me, "Go inside [the house] and tell Prasanta's sister that Prasanta has invited a group of people for tea but has not arranged for any food. Just say this and come back." After about fifteen or twenty minutes a variety of food appeared ... Prasanta said: "What is this? Who got all this?" Tatada replied, "How does that concern you? The food is here and we will eat it."' (*Provincializing Europe*, 204-05)

2 *Provincializing Europe* (p.215) cites Tanika Sarkar's argument that nineteenth-century Bengali writings on domestic arrangements simply reflected the fact of European domination of public life in colonial Bengal as an instance of such a reading.

3 'In pursuing the history of the Santal rebellion of 1855, Guha unsurprisingly came across a phenomenon common in the lives of the peasants; the agency of supernatural beings. Santal leaders explained the rebellion in supernatural terms, as an act carried out at the behest of the Santal god Thakur. Guha draws our attention to the evidence and underscores how important this understanding was to the rebels themselves (103) ... But in spite of Guha's desire to listen to the rebel voice seriously, his analysis cannot offer the Thakur the same place of agency in the story of the rebellion that

the Santals' statements had given him. A narrative strategy that is rationally defensible in the modern understanding of what constitutes public life—and the historians speak in the public sphere—cannot be based on a relationship that allows the divine or the supernatural a direct hand in the affairs of the world. The Santal leaders' own understanding of the rebellion does not directly serve the historical cause of democracy or citizenship or socialism. It needs to be reinterpreted. Historians will grant the supernatural a place in somebody's belief system or ritual practices, but to ascribe to it any real agency in historical events will be go [sic] against the rules of evidence that gives historical discourse procedures for settling disputes about the past.' (*Provincializing Europe*, 104)

4 'Historicism—and even the modern, European idea of history—one might say, came to non-European peoples in the nineteenth century as somebody's way of saying "not yet" to somebody else.' (*Provincializing Europe*, 8)

5 'A.K. Ramanujan … once wrote about his astronomer father who had no difficulty being an astrologer as well:

> He was a mathematician, an astronomer. But he was also a Sanskrit scholar, an expert astrologer. He had two kinds of exotic visitors: American and English mathematicians who called on him when they were on a visit to India, and local astrologers, orthodox pundits who wore splendid gold-embroidered shawls dowered by the Maharajah. I had just been converted by Russell to the "scientific attitude". I … was troubled by his holding together in one brain both astronomy and astrology; I looked for consistency in him, a consistency he did not seem to care about, or even think about…' (*Provincializing Europe*, 253)

## 20: Imperial Denial

1 Dipesh Chakrabarty, 'The Climate of History: Four Theses', *Critical Inquiry* 35, no. 2 (Winter 2009): 197–222.

2 See Julie Cruikshank's *Do Glaciers Listen? Local Knowledge, Colonial Encounters, and Social Imagination* (Vancouver: University of British Columbia Press, 2005).

3 Humanity reels blindly through a labyrinth that we call history, whose entrance, exit, and shape nobody knows.' Carl Schmitt, *Political Theology: Four Chapters on the Concept of Sovereignty*, trans. George Schwab (Cambridge, MA: MIT Press, 1985), p. 59.

4 This phrase is borrowed from Clive Hamilton, *Growth Fetish* (Sydney: Allen & Unwin, 2003).

5 Interview, *Der Spiegel*, 1966.

## 21: Storytelling and the Spectrum of the Past

1 Claire Anderson, *Legible Bodies: Race, Criminality and Colonialism in South Asia* (Oxford: Berg, 2004).

2 In this effort, I drew extensively on works such as Radhika Singha, *A Despotism of Law: Crime and Criminal Justice in Colonial India* (New Delhi: Oxford University Press, 1998); James H. Mills, *Madness, Cannabis and Colonialism: The 'Native Only' Lunatic Asylums of British India, 1857 to 1900* (Basingstoke: Macmillan, 2000); Elizabeth Kolsky, *Colonial Justice in British India: White Violence and the Rule of Law* (Cambridge: Cambridge University Press, 2010); Alessandro Stanziani, *Sailors, Slaves and Immigrants: Bondage in the Indian Ocean World, 1750–1914* (Basingstoke: Macmillan, 2014); and David Arnold, 'The Colonial Prison: Power, Knowledge and Penology in Nineteenth-Century India', in *Subaltern Studies*, vol. 8, eds. David Arnold and David Hardiman (New Delhi: Oxford University Press, 1994), pp. 148–187.

3 There is a vast body of work on Canton's role in international trade. See, for instance: Hosea Ballou Morse, *The Chronicles of the East India Company, Trading to China, 1635–1834*, 5 vols. (Oxford: Clarendon Press, 1926); Michael Greenberg, *British Trade and the Opening of China 1800–42* (Cambridge: Cambridge University Press, 1951); Louis Dermigny, *La Chine et l'Occident: Le commerce a Canton au XVIIIe siecle, 1719–1833* (Paris: S.E.V.P.E.N, 1964); Tan Chung, 'The British-China-India Trade Triangle, 1771–1840', *Indian Economic and Social History Review* (1974); Jacques M. Downs, 'American Merchants and the China Opium Trade, 1800–1840', *Business History Review* 42, no. 4 (1968): 418–442; Thomas N. Layton, *The Voyage of the* Frolic*: New England Merchants and the Opium Trade* (Stanford: Stanford University Press, 1997); Hunt Janin, *The India-China Opium Trade in the Nineteenth Century* (Jefferson: McFarland, 1999); Joyce A. Madancy, *The Troublesome Legacy of Commissioner Lin: The Opium Trade and Opium Suppression in Fujian Province, 1820s to 1920s* (Cambridge, MA: Harvard University Press, 2003); Carl A. Trocki, *Opium, Empire and the Global Political Economy: A Study of the Asian Opium Trade 1750–1950* (London: Routledge, 1999); Paul A. Van Dyke, *The Canton Trade: Life and Enterprise on the China Coast, 1700–1845* (Hong Kong:

Hong Kong University Press, 2007); and Frederic Wakeman Jr., 'The Canton Trade and the Opium War', in *The Cambridge History of China*, vol. 10, ed. John K. Fairbank (Cambridge: Cambridge University Press, 1978), pp. 163–212. A recent article by Kate Boehme opens up very interesting new perspectives on the trade between China and India under the British Raj: 'Capitalism and Inter-Asian Linkages: The Impact of China on Developing Business Networks in Western India, 1750–1850)'. The version I read had not yet been published; Kate Boehme was kind enough to send me a copy of the version she had presented at a conference:

a. The political situation in Canton and its hinterland around the time of the first Opium War has been analysed and described by many historians and writers, for example: Göran Aijmer and Virgil K.Y. Ho, *Cantonese Society in a Time of Change* (Hong Kong: Hong Kong University Press, 2000); Dilip Basu, 'Chinese Xenology and the Opium War: Reflections on Sinocentricism', *Journal of Asian Studies* 73, no. 4 (2014): 927–940; Hsin-Pao Chang, 'Lin Tse-Hsu and the Coming of the Opium War', (PhD diss., Harvard University, 1958); and *Commissioner Lin and the Opium War* (Cambridge, MA: Harvard University Press, 1964); Peter Ward Fay, *The Opium War: 1840–42* (Chapel Hill: University of North Carolina Press, 1975); P.C. Kuo, *A Critical Study of the First Anglo-Chinese War, with Documents* (Shanghai: Kelly & Walsh, 1935); Julia Lovell, *The Opium War: Drugs, Dreams and the Making of China* (London: Picador, 2011); Jonathan Spence, 'Opium Smoking in Ch'ing China', in *Conflict and Control in Late Imperial China*, eds. Frederic Wakeman Jr. and Carolyn Grant (Berkeley: University of California Press, 1975), pp. 143–173 (reprinted in Jonathan Spence, *Chinese Roundabout: Essays in History and Culture* [New York: W.W. Norton, 1992], pp. 228–256); Tan Chung, *China and the Brave New World: A Study of the Origins of the Opium War (1840–42)* (New Delhi: Allied Publishers, 1978); Frederic Wakeman Jr., *Strangers at the Gate: Social Disorders in South China, 1839–1861* (Berkeley: University of California Press, 1966); and Maurice Collis, *Foreign Mud: Being an Account of the Opium Imbroglio at Canton and the Anglo-Chinese War that Followed* (London: Faber and Faber, 1946).
b. On the art and material life of eighteenth- and nineteenth-century Canton, see Carl L. Crossman, *The Decorative Arts of the China Trade: Paintings, Furnishings and Exotic Curiosities* (Suffolk: Antique Collectors' Club, 1991); Craig Clunas, *Superfluous Things: Material Culture and Social Status in Early Modern China* (Honolulu: University

of Hawai'i Press, 2004); H.A. Crosby Forbes, *Shopping in China: The Artisan Community at Canton, 1825–1830* (Washington, DC: Smithsonian Institution Press, 1979); Patrick Conner, *George Chinnery 1744–1852; Artist of India and the China Coast* (Suffolk: Antique Collectors' Club, 1993); intro., *Chinese Views, Western Perspectives: 1770–1870 (The Sze Yuan Tung Collection of China Coast Paintings and the Wallem Collection of China Coast Ship Portraits)* (Hong Kong: Hong Kong Maritime Museum, 1996); and *The Hongs of Canton: Western Merchants in South China 1700–1900, as Seen in Chinese Export Paintings* (London: Martyn Gregory Gallery, 2009); Martyn Gregory, *Canton and the China Trade: An Exhibition of Early Pictures Relating to the Far East*, Catalog 43 (London: Martyn Gregory Gallery, 1990); G.H.R. Tillotson, *Fan Kwae Pictures: Paintings and Drawings by George Chinnery and Other Artists in the Collection of the Hongkong and Shanghai Banking Corporation* (London: Spink & Son, 1987); and James Cahill, *Pictures for Use and Pleasure: Vernacular Painting in High Qing China* (Berkeley: University of California Press, 2010). A fine selection of Canton export art can be viewed at MIT's Visualizing Cultures website.

c. On the subject of botany and gardening in Canton, Fa-ti Fan, *British Naturalists in Qing China: Science, Empire, and Cultural Encounter* (Cambridge, MA: Harvard University Press, 2004) is a seminal study of the botanical and zoological exchanges that occurred in eighteenth- and nineteenth-century Canton. The city also figures prominently in eighteenth- and nineteenth-century European literature on Chinese gardens. For more on this, see Yu Liu, *Seeds of a Different Eden: Chinese Gardening Ideas and a New English Aesthetic Ideal* (Columbia: University of South Carolina Press, 2008).

d. Among nineteenth-century scholarly works on pidgin, the most notable are S. Wells Williams, 'Jargon Spoken at Canton', *Chinese Repository* 4 (1836): 429–435; Sir John F. Davis, *A Commercial Vocabulary Containing Chinese Words and Phrases Peculiar to Canton and Macao and to the Trade of those Places; Together with the Titles and Addresses of all the Officers of Government, Hong Merchants, &c. &c. Alphabetically Arranged and Intended as an Aid to Correspondence and Conversation in the Native Language* (Macao: 1824); William Lobscheid, *Select Phrases in the Canton Dialect, Collected by Dr Kerr and Prepared for the Press by the Revd. William Lobscheid* (Hong Kong: 1867); and 'Pidgin English', *Scribner's Monthly* 15 (1878): 372–376. In 1920, A.P. Hill and C.B. Weisz published a lexicon of pidgin called *Broken China: A Vocabulary of Pidgin English* (Shanghai). The most important contemporary scholarly works on pidgin are Dingxu Shi, 'Chinese Pidgin English: Its Origin and Linguistic Features', *Journal of Chinese Linguistics* 19 (1991): 1-41; Kingsley Bolton, 'Language and Hybridization: Pidgin Tales from the China Coast', *Interventions* 2, no. 1 (2000): 35–52; and *Chinese Englishes: A Sociolinguistic History* (Cambridge: Cambridge University Press, 2003).

4 Many of the merchants, missionaries, travelers and officials, foreign and Chinese, who were in Canton or its vicinity around the time of the First Opium War kept journals, wrote letters and penned first-hand accounts of the city, describing people and events. Here are some: David Abeel, *Journal of a Residence in China and the Neighbouring Countries from 1830–33* (New York: D. Appleton, 1835); Elijah C. Bridgman, *Description of the City of Canton* (Canton, 1834; repr., 1996); Sir John F. Davis, *Sketches of China: Partly during an inland journey of four months between Peking, Nanking, and Canton; with notices and observations relative to the present war* (London: Charles Knight, 1836); and *China, During the War and Since the Peace* (London: John Murray, 1852); C. Toogood Downing, *The Fan-qui in China in 1836-37*, 3 vols. (London: Henry Colburn, 1838); Robert Bennet Forbes, *Letters from China: The Canton-Boston Correspondence of Robert Bennet Forbes, 1838–1840*, ed. Phyllis Forbes Kerr (Mystic: Mystic Seaport Museum, 1996); Charles Gutzlaff, *Journal of Three Voyages Along the Coast of China* (London: Westley & Davis, 1834); William C. Hunter, *The Fan-Kwae at Canton before Treaty Days, 1825–1844* (Shanghai: Kelly & Walsh, 1882); Daniel Irving Larkin, ed., *Dear Will: Letters from the China Trade 1833–36* (Amherst: University of Massachusetts Press, 1987); Sir Andrew Ljungstedt, *An Historical Sketch of the Portuguese Settlements in China; And of the Roman Catholic Mission in China* (Boston: James Munroe and Company, 1836); Gideon Nye, *The Morning of My Life in China: Comprising an outline of the history of foreign intercourse from the last year of the regime of honorable East India Company, 1833, to the imprisonment of the foreign community in 1839* (Canton: 1873); E.H. Parker, *Chinese Account of the Opium War* (Shanghai: Kelly & Walsh, 1888); James Duncan Phillips, ed., *The Canton Letters 1839–1841 of William Henry Low* (Salem: Essex Institute, 1948); Samuel Shaw, *The Journals of Major Samuel Shaw, the First American Consul at Canton, with a Life of the Author by Josiah Quincy* (Boston: 1847); and Julian Sturgis, *From Books and Papers of Russell Sturgis* (Oxford: Clarendon Press 1893). In addition, many of the traders, merchants and officials who were active in Guangzhou at this time have been written about in individual biographies and in studies

of mercantile groups and associations: Weng Eang Cheong, *Mandarins and Merchants: Jardine Matheson & Co., A China Agency of the Early Nineteenth Century* (London: Curzon Press, 1979); and *The Hong Merchants of Canton: Chinese Merchants in Sino-Western Trade, 1684–1798* (Surrey: Curzon Press, 1997); Jacques M. Downs, *The Golden Ghetto: The American Commercial Community at Canton and the Shaping of American China Policy, 1784–1844* (Bethlehem: Lehigh University Press, 1997); Richard J. Grace, *Opium and Empire: The Lives and Careers of William Jardine and James Matheson* (Quebec: McGill-Queen's University Press, 2014); Amalendu Guha, 'Parsi Seths as Entrepreneurs, 1750–1850', *Economic and Political Weekly* 5, no. 35 (1970): 107–15; and 'The Comprador Role of Parsi Seths, 1750–1850', *Economic and Political Weekly* 5, no. 48 (1970): 1933–36; Guo Deyan, 'The Dutch and the Parsees in Canton during the Qing Dynasty', in *Sailing to the Pearl River: Dutch Enterprise in South China, 1600–2000*, eds. Cai Hong Sheng and Leonard Blussé et al, (Guangzhou: Sun Yat-sen University Press, 2004); Nan Powell Hodges and A.W. Hummel, eds., *Lights and Shadows of a Macao Life: The Journal of Harriet Low, Travelling Spinster, Pt 1: 1829–1832* (Redmond: Writers Club Press, 2002); Susanna Hoe and Derek Roebuck, *The Taking of Hong Kong: Charles and Clara Elliot in China Waters* (Surrey: Curzon Press, 1999); C.P. Liang, *The Hong Merchants of Canton* (Taiwan: Academia Sinica, 1960); Denys Lombard and Jean Aubin, eds., *Asian Merchants and Businessmen in the Indian Ocean and the China Sea* (New Delhi: Manohar Publishers, 2000); Steven B. Miles, *The Sea of Learning: Mobility and Identity in Nineteenth-Century Guangzhou* (Cambridge, MA: Harvard University Press, 2006); Betty Peh-T'i Wei, *Ruan Yuan, 1764–1849: The Life and Work of a Major Scholar Official in Nineteenth-Century China before the Opium War* (Hong Kong: Hong Kong University Press, 2006); Asiya Siddiqi, 'The Business World of Jamsetjee Jeejeebhoy', *Indian Economic and Social History Review* 19, nos. 3-4 (1982): 301–324; Lawrence Wang-chi Wong, 'Translators and Interpreters During the Opium War between Britain and China (1839–1842)', in *Translating and Interpreting Conflict*, ed. Myriam Salama-Carr (New York: Rodopi, 2007). Individual merchants, traders and officials, European and Chinese, are also referred to in many unpublished letters and journals. The library of the National Maritime Museum, Greenwich, London, has many such writings in its collection. Among those I consulted were the following: *Journal kept by William Kershaw, 1814–16*, Log/C/12; *Journal kept by Colin Campbell, passenger on HCS General Hewitt*, Log/C/19; *Journal of Thomas Gardiner kept on 3 voyages to Bengal and China on the EIC's ships, 1830*, JOD/159; and *Diary of events kept by Capt H. Giffard, HMS Volage and Cruiser, 1840*, [JOD/38].

5 The English journals published from Canton's foreign enclave, the *Canton Press*, the *Chinese Repository*, edited by Elijah C. Bridgman, and the *Canton Register*, edited by John Slade, provide detailed chronicles of day-to-day events in the city. The *Chinese Repository* had a section called 'Journal of Occurrences' that is particularly rich in this regard. John Slade later published a journal of this period entitled *Narrative of the Late Proceedings and Events in China* (Macao: 1839). Others who were in the foreign enclave at that time would also publish accounts of these events later, among them William C. Hunter, 'Journal of the Occurrences at Canton During the Cessation of Trade, 1839', reprinted in the *Journal of Royal Asiatic Society* 4 (1964). There is every reason to believe that a good number of first-hand narratives of the same events also exist in Chinese, but sadly very few have been translated into English. The most notable among them are Parker, *Chinese Account of the Opium War* and Arthur Waley, *The Opium War through Chinese Eyes* (Stanford: Standford University Press, 1968).

6 Substandard provisions and irregularities in the procurement process were responsible for the deaths of many sepoys and soldiers during the British expeditionary force's occupation of Chusan in 1840-41. This is implied in several dispatches and official records. One official letter, after noting that the spread of disease among the men was aggravated by bad provisions, makes the following recommendation: 'We think the Committee which sat at Calcutta should have called before them the Commissary General and the Executive Commissariat Officer at the Presidency to ascertain the means which were taken to procure the best supplies, and the care used in inspecting and packing them. In the absence of such enquiry we are unable to relieve our minds from the impression given by the Evidence that to a very great extent the supplies were defective.' ('Reply to Letter dated 14th October 1841 (No. 135)', India and Bengal Despatches 12 Jan to 30 March 1842, IOR E/4/769, p. 811, British Library. See also 'Answer to letter No. 95', Bengal Military Letters Received, 1842, IOR L/MIL/3, p. 48; British Library.)

   a. Similarly, some of the troop ships for the sepoy contingents were unseaworthy, a fact that was well known within the British community in India at the time. In 1840, after the *Golconda*, which was hired to transport one wing of the 37th Madras Native Infantry Regiment, went down in a storm with hundreds of men, the *Bengal Catholic Herald* commented: 'The vessel was unseaworthy; and was known to be such before she was engaged. No conscientious man would ever have risked the lives of others in her.' (Vol. 1, no. XXVII,

11 September 1841, p. 53.) Accusations of financial irregularity were not uncommon in the British military establishment: in 1841, one Major Davidson accused his subordinate Captain Smith of having embezzled Rs 11,756. Smith was acquitted, but Major Davidson (who may have embezzled the money himself) was not prosecuted as this would have required the re-trial of Capt. Smith. (India and Bengal Despatches 13 July to 1 Sept 1841, IOR E/4/769 & Bengal Military Letters Received 1841 IOR L/MIL/3/47; British Library.) None of this is surprising since fraud and corruption were common in British merchants' dealings with the East India Company. The enormous costs of building the new Fort William in Calcutta, for example, were largely 'attributable to fraud and over-charging' by private traders. (P.J. Marshall, 'The White Town of Calcutta under the Rule of the East India Company', *Modern Asian Studies* 34, no. 2 (2000): 307–331, here 314.

7 See, for example, Chang, *Commissioner Lin and the Opium War*, p. 46.

8 In 1830, a well-traveled Englishman, Thomas Gardiner, wrote in his journal, soon after arriving in Canton: 'About 4 pm we neared Canton, and the novel scene which now presented itself was Extraordinary. Vast numbers, I may say, I think thousands of native boats of all sorts and sizes, from the Junk to the sampan, were here collected together as far as the Eye could Reach, and as we passed along the City of "Canton" presents a Vast mass of one Storey houses, of Extraordinary architectural design and of most fantastic decoration. The Factories of the East India Company, the French, American and Dutch factories, appear large and of modern construction, but as far as I can judge, of very substantial importance! The colours of the different countries are flying during the day and here may be seen men of all Nations crowding together to this celebrated focus of Eastern Commerce.' (Thomas Gardiner, *Journal of Thomas Gardiner on board HEIC Ships DUKE OF YORK and ASIA, 1829–1833* [National Maritime Museum, Greenwich, London, JOD/159.]) An earlier visitor, James Johnson, wrote of his first impressions of the city that they 'all combine to form a scene so novel and striking that the impression which it leaves on one's memory can hardly ever be erased'. [James Johnson, *The Oriental Voyager or, Descriptive Sketches and Cursory Remarks on a Voyage to India and China in His Majesty's Ship* Caroline, *performed in the years 1803-4-5-6* [London: 1807], p. 173.)

9 Apart from George Chinnery and the innumerable Chinese artists who lived and worked in Guangzhou, many European travelers and artists also painted or sketched the city, among them William and Thomas Daniell;

Captain Robert Elliot (*Views in the East; Comprising India, Canton and the Shores of the Red Sea, with Historical and Descriptive Illustrations* [London, 1833]); Robert Burford (*Description of a View of Canton … Painted by Robert Burford* [London: 1838; repr., Zug: 1986]); and Émile D. Forgues (*La Chine Ouverte; Aventures d'un Fan-Kouei dans le Pays de Tsin, par Old Nick, ouvrage illustré par Auguste Borget* [Paris: 1845]).

10 The journals that were published in Canton in these years are a particularly rich source of information on the city, especially the *Chinese Repository*. Its editor, Elijah C. Bridgman, also wrote a book entitled *Description of the City of Canton*, which is one of many nineteenth-century works that describe the city in detail. James Johnson's *The Oriental Voyager* is another.

11 Valery M. Garrett's fine book on Canton is called *Heaven Is High, the Emperor Far Away: Merchants and Mandarins in Old Canton* (Oxford: Oxford University Press, 2002). Other books have been cited above in notes 4 and 5.

12 Many sources suggest that British colonial officials largely shared their Chinese counterparts' views on the deleterious effects of opium. These views also informed their administrative practices. Consider these passages in a letter written by L.C. Reid, a district official in the Bombay Presidency, to the Revenue Commissioner in 1839: 'I am happy in being able to shew almost a complete cessation in the cultivation of opium in the past year … This favourable result is caused by my having myself and through the Agency of the several Mamlutdars of the zilla explained fully to the Patells and Riots the intention of the Govt of India contained in Mr Secy Prinsep's letter of the 7th Aug 1839 … to prohibit the Cultivation of Opium under the Bombay Presidency except by license … I strongly urged them to revert to the Cultivation of the Products they formerly had previous to the introduction of the Opium Culture in this zilla in A.D. 1821/22 for which their lands were so well suited and which always yielded them a remunerating returns (if not better) than the drug. The Land therefore which was formerly occupied with opium is now sown with Tobacco, Jeera, Ginger, [and] Garlic … It may therefore be inferred the Culture is at an end in this zilla, and it is sincerely to be desired that with the disappearance of the poppy from the zilla they will themselves gradually forget its use and not feel the want of the stimulating and insinuating drug a habit which has extended itself 100 fold since the first introduction of its growth in these parts.' [IOR Board's Collections 83888 to 84180, 1841-42, vol. 1938; F/4/1938; British Library]

a. The records are strewn with passages that demonstrate that Chinese and British officials did not, in fact, see opium in a vastly different light. Needless to add, the governmental practices of the Anglosphere continue, to this day, to be largely informed by such views, as evidenced by American attempts to deal with the current epidemic of opiate use in the USA.

13 The books I have in mind are: Multatuli, *Max Havelaar: Or the Coffee Auctions of the Dutch Trading Company*, trans. Roy Edwards (London: Penguin Books, 1995); Leonard Woolf, *The Village in the Jungle* (London: Edward Arnold, 1913); J.R. Ackerley, *Hindoo Holiday: An Indian Journal* (London: Chatto & Windus, 1932); Louis Couperus, *The Hidden Force*, trans. Alexander Texeira de Mattos (New York: Dodd, Mead & Co., 1921); Maurice Collis, *Into Hidden Burma; An Autobiography* (London: Faber and Faber, 1953); Victor Segalen, *René Leys*, trans. J.A. Underwood (New York: New Directions, 1988); and Han Suyin, *The Crippled Tree* (London: Jonathan Cape, 1965) and *A Mortal Flower* (London: Jonathan Cape,1966).

14 The works that helped me think about these issues were by no means all explicitly focused on questions of affect and emotion. Among them are Clare Anderson, *Convicts in the Indian Ocean: Transportation from South Asia to Mauritius, 1815–53* (London: Macmillan, 2000); Robert J. Antony, *Like Froth Floating on the Sea: The World of Pirates and Seafarers in Late Imperial South China* (Berkeley: University of California Press, 2003); Kenneth A. Ballhatchet, *Race, Sex and Class under the Raj: Imperial Attitudes and Policies and Their Critics,1793–1905* (London: Weidenfeld and Nicolson, 1980); B.R. Burg, *An American Seafarer in the Age of Sail: The Erotic Diaries of Philip C. Van Buskirk, 1851–1870* (New Haven: Yale University Press, 1994); Antoinette Burton, 'Fearful Bodies into Disciplined Subjects: Pleasure, Romance and the Family Drama of Colonial Reform in Mary Carpenter's *Six Months in India*', *Signs* 20, no. 3 (1995): 545–574; Marina Carter, *Voices from Indenture: Experiences of Indian Migrants in the British Empire* (London: Leicester University Press, 1996) and *Lakshmi's Legacy: The Testimonies of Indian Women in 19th Century Mauritius* (Mauritius: Mahatma Gandhi Institute, 1996); Michael H. Fisher, *A Clash of Cultures: Awadh, the British and the Mughals* (Maryland: The Riverdale Co., 1987); Harald Fischer-Tiné, 'Flotsam and Jetsam of the Empire? European Seamen and Spaces of Disease and Disorder in Mid-Nineteenth Century Calcutta' in *The Limits of British Colonial Control in South Asia: Spaces of Disorder in the Indian Ocean Region*, ed. Ashwini Tambe and Harald Fischer-Tiné (London: Routledge, 2006), pp. 121–54; Durba Ghosh, *Sex and the Family in Colonial India: The Making of Empire* (Cambridge: Cambridge University Press, 2006); James Hevia, *English Lessons: The Pedagogy of Imperialism in Nineteenth-Century*

*China* (Durham: Duke University Press, 2003); Bret Hinsch, *Passions of the Cut Sleeve: The Male Homosexual Tradition in China* (Oakland: University of California Press, 1990); Toni Huber, *The Holy Land Reborn: Pilgrimage and the Tibetan Reinvention of Buddhist India* (Chicago: University of Chicago Press, 2008); Ronald Hyam, *Empire and Sexuality: The British Experience* (Manchester: Manchester University Press, 1990); Isaac Land, 'Customs of the Sea: Flogging, Empire, and the "True British Seaman", 1770 to 1870', *Interventions* 3, no. 2 (2001): 169–185; and '"Sinful Propensities": Piracy, Sodomy, and Empire in the Rhetoric of Naval Reform in Britain and the United States, 1770–1870', in *Discipline and the Other Body: Correction, Corporeality, Colonialism*, ed. Anupama Rao and Steven Pierce (Durham: Duke University Press, 2006); Thomas W. Laqueur and Catherine Gallagher, eds., *The Making of the Modern Body: Sexuality and Society in the Nineteenth Century* (Berkeley: University of California Press, 1987); Philippa Levine, *Prostitution, Race and Politics: Policing Venereal Disease in the British Empire* (London: Routledge, 2003); Keith McMahon, *The Fall of the God of Money: Opium Smoking in Nineteenth-Century China* (Maryland: Rowman & Littlefield, 2002); James H. Mills, *Madness, Cannabis and Colonialism: The 'Native Only' Lunatic Asylums of British India, 1857–1900* (Basingstoke: Macmillan, 2000); Rudrangshu Mukherjee, 'The Sepoy Mutinies Revisited', in *War and Society in Colonial India, 1807–1945*, ed. Kaushik Roy (New Delhi: Oxford University Press, 2006); Douglas M. Peers, '"The Habitual Nobility of Being": British Officers and the Social Construction of the Bengal Army in the Early Nineteenth Century', *Modern Asian Studies* 25, no. 3 (1991): 545–569; 'Sepoys, Soldiers and the Lash: Race, Caste and Army Discipline in India, 1820-50', *Journal of Imperial and Commonwealth History* 23, no. 2 (1995): 212–247; *Between Mars and Mammon: Colonial Armies and the Garrison State in Early Nineteenth-century India* (London/New York: Tauris Academic Studies, 1995); 'Privates off Parade: Regimenting Sexuality in the Nineteenth-Century Indian Empire', *The International History Review* 20, no. 4 (1998): 823–854; and 'Imperial Vice: Sex, drink and the health of British troops in North Indian cantonments, 1800–1858', in *Guardians of Empire: The Armed Forces of the Colonial Powers c. 1700–1964*, ed. David Killingray and David Omissi (Manchester/New York: Manchester University Press, 1999); Kaushik Roy, *1857 Uprising: A Tale of an Indian Warrior* (Gurgaon: Penguin Random House, 2008); Heather Streets, *Martial Races: The Military, Race and Masculinity in British Imperial Culture, 1857–1914* (Manchester/New York: Manchester University Press, 2004); and Yangwen Zheng, *The Social Life of Opium in China* (Cambridge: Cambridge University Press, 2005).

15 D.H.A Kolff, 'Sanyasi Trader–Soldiers', *Indian Economic and Social History Review* 8, no. 2 (1971): 213–220; Nile Green, 'Jack Sepoy and the Dervishes: Islam and the Indian Soldier in Princely India', *Journal of the Royal Asiatic Society of Great Britain and Ireland* 18, no. 1 (2008): 31–46; and *Islam and the Army in Colonial India: Sepoy Religion and the Service of Empire* (Cambridge: Cambridge University Press, 2009); William R. Pinch, 'Soldier Monks and Militant Sadhus', in *Contesting the Nation: Religion, Community and the Politics of Democracy in India*, ed. D. Ludden (Philadelphia: University of Pennsylvania Press, 1996), pp. 140–61; and *Warrior Ascetics and Indian Empires* (Cambridge: Cambridge University Press, 2006). See also D.N. Lorenzen, 'Warrior Ascetics in Indian History', *Journal of the American Oriental Society* 98, no. 1 (1978): 61–75.

a. D.H.A. Kolff, *Naukar, Rajput and Sepoy: The Ethnohistory of the Military Labour Market in Hindustan, 1450–1850* (Cambridge: Cambridge University Press, 2002) is indispensable reading for a general understanding of pre-modern Indian soldiering. Amiya Barat, *The Bengal Native Infantry, Its Organisation and Discipline, 1796–1852* (Calcutta: Firma K.L. Mukhopadhyay, 1962); Seema Alavi, *The Sepoys and the Company: Tradition and Transition in Northern India, 1770–1830* (New Delhi: Oxford University Press, 1995); Pradeep Barua, *The State at War in South Asia* (Lincoln: University of Nebraska Press, 2005); and Tan Tai Yong, *The Garrison State: The Military, Government and Society in Colonial Punjab, 1849–1947* (New Delhi: Sage Publications, 2005) were all hugely valuable in establishing the nineteenth-century context.

16 Ultimately the greatest obstacle to understanding the affective and emotional worlds of Indian soldiers in the early nineteenth century is the near complete absence of any extended trace of the sepoy's own voice: this is a silence so resounding that it must be counted as a form of resistance to history. The one first-hand account that exists from this period—the memoirs of Seetaram Subedar (*From Sepoy to Subedar*, trans., James Thomas Norgate [London: 1873; Calcutta: 1911])—may well be apocryphal: it is said to have been dictated in Awadhi (a dialect of Hindi), to a British officer, but the original text has never been found and it exists only in translation. Fortunately the English text has been rendered into Awadhi by a major Hindi writer, Madhukar Upadhyaya, (*Kissa Pande Sitaram Subedar* [Delhi: 1999]). This wonderfully evocative text was hugely useful to me in trying to imagine the life-world of the sepoys who fought in the First Opium War. Other than this, traces of the nineteenth-century sepoy's voice are so few

that I was forced to resort to records from later periods, ranging as far afield as the First World War (which was, in some ways, a nineteenth-century war, especially for the million and a half sepoys who fought in it). Franziska Roy, Heike Liebau and Ravi Ahuja's collection of letters, drawings, photographs and recordings from German prisoner-of-war camps for sepoys and lascars (Roy, Liebau and Ahuja, eds., *When the War Began We Heard of Several Kings: South Asian Prisoners in World War I Germany* [New Delhi: 2011], including a CD ROM) is an extraordinary resource, complete with recordings of songs and stories. A remarkable article by the literary scholar Santanu Das ('Indians at Home, Mesopotamia and France 1914–1918: Towards an Intimate History', in *Race, Empire and First World War Writing*, ed. Santanu Das [Cambridge: Cambridge University Press, 2011], pp. 70–89) led me to two real treasures from the Mesopotamian campaign of 1915-16, both in Bengali: Mokkhoda Debi, *Kalyan-Pradeep: Captain Kalyan Kumar Mukhopadhyay, I.M.S.-er Jiboni* ['Kalyan-Pradeep: The Life of Captain Kalyan Kumar Mukherji, I.M.S.'] (Calcutta: 1928); and Sisir Sarbadhikari, *Abhi Le Baghdad* ['On to Baghdad'] (Calcutta: 1958). In my view, these two books rank among the finest literary works to come out of the First World War. Unfortunately no complete translations exist as yet.

17 Indeed I have been taken to task on this score by the historian Ravi Ahuja, who writes: 'In Ghosh's account there is little attempt to explore the contradiction between the seafarer's quotidian, painful experience of confinement and monotony on the one hand, and of their unusual spatial mobility, on the other.' (Ravi Ahuja, 'Capital at Sea, Shaitan Below Decks? A Note on Global Narratives, Narrow Spaces, and the Limits of Experience', in *History of the Present* 2, no. 1 (2012): 78–85; here 82]. In this and his other writings on lascars, Ahuja provides graphic examples of the extraordinary everyday violence and oppression that lascars had to live with. See also: Marcus Rediker, *Between the Devil and the Deep Blue Sea: Merchant Seamen, Pirates and the Anglo-American Maritime World, 1700-1750* (Cambridge: Cambridge University Press, 1987); Michael Sokolow, '"What A Miserable Life A Sea Fareing Life Is": The Life and Experiences of a Nineteenth-Century Mariner of Color' (PhD diss., Boston University, 1997); and Anonymous, *Voyage and Venture, Or the Perils of a Sailor's Life* (Philadelphia: Lindsay & Blakiston, 1858). B.R. Burg, *An American Seafarer in the Age of Sail: The Erotic Diaries of Philip C. Van Buskirk, 1851–1870* (New Haven: Yale University Press, 1994) is based on a uniquely frank diary and it chronicles in extraordinary detail the tensions that are reflected in Melville's nautical stories and novels.

18 Consider for example, a case brought against one Lt. Charles Mann, of the 11th Madras Native Infantry Regiment for 'having at the Village of Pannaghur near Jubbulpore, on the 10th of March 1840 … made an assault upon Serroop, his servant, and then and there, struck with a Spear, the said Serroop in and upon the right side and thereby inflicted a mortal wound, whereof he, the said Serroop, died on the road, as he was being conveyed into Jubbulpore on the same day'. The Court found Lt. Mann guilty of manslaughter and gave him a sentence of two years imprisonment 'in such place, and commencing from such time as the Major General Commanding the Army in Chief may be pleased to direct'. British Library: IOR Madras Despatches 1 Jan to 2 July 1841 E/4/955. Many similar cases are described in Kolsky, *Colonial Justice in British India*.

19 Herbert Marcuse, *One-Dimensional Man: Studies in the Ideology of Advanced Industrial Society* (London: Routledge and Kegan Paul, 1964), pp. 76-77.

20 Ibid., p. 79.

21 This terrain has been explored at length by Peter Gay (*The Bourgeois Experience: Victoria to Freud*, 5 vols. [New York: Oxford University Press, 1984–98]) and Franco Moretti (*The Bourgeois: Between History and Literature* [New York: Verso, 2013]).

22 Thomas W. Laqueur, *Solitary Sex: A Cultural History of Masturbation* (New York: Zone Books, 2003).

23 Jean Stengers and Anne van Neck, *Masturbation: The History of a Great Terror*, trans. Kathryn Hoffman (New York: Palgrave, 2001); on hysteria, see Rachel P. Maines, *The Technology of Orgasm: 'Hysteria', the Vibrator and Women's Sexual Satisfaction* (Baltimore: Johns Hopkins University Press, 1999).

24 Tansen Sen, *Buddhism, Diplomacy and Trade: The Realignment of Sino-Indian Relations, 600–1400* (Honolulu: University of Hawai'i Press, 2003).

25 Among Thampi's publications are *Indians in China, 1800–1949* (New Delhi: Manohar Publishers, 2010) and *China and the Making of Bombay* (with Shalini Saksena, Mumbai: K.R. Cama Oriental Institute, 2009).

26 Prasenjit Duara, *The Crisis of Global Modernity: Asian Traditions and a Sustainable Future* (Cambridge: Cambridge University Press, 2015).

27 Matthew W. Mosca, *From Frontier Policy to Foreign Policy: The Question of India and the Transformation of Geopolitics in Qing China* (Stanford: Stanford University Press, 2013).

28 Anand Yang, 'Travel Matters: An Indian Subaltern's Passage to China in 1900', *Education About Asia* 11, no. 3 (2006): 12–15; and '(A) Subaltern('s) Boxers: An Indian Soldier's Account of China and the World in 1900-1901',

in *The Boxers, China, and the World*, ed. Robert Bickers and R.G. Tiedemann (Lanham: Rowman & Littlefield, 2007), pp. 43–64.; and 'China and India Are One: A Subaltern's Vision of "Hindu China" during the Boxer Expedition of 1900-1901' in *Asia Inside Out: Changing Times*, ed. Eric Tagliacozzo and Helen F. Siu (Cambridge, MA: Harvard University Press, 2015), pp. 207–225. The memoir on which these articles are based is Thakur Gadadhar Singh's *Chin meh Terah Mas: (Chin Sangram)* (Lucknow: 1902).

29 Published in 1992 by Ravi Dayal Publisher (New Delhi), Granta Publications (London) and in 1993 by A.A. Knopf (New York).

30 I am deeply grateful to Shatarupa Ghoshal for copy-editing this article and for some very helpful comments. I would also like to thank Julia Adeney Thomas and Sir Christopher Clark for reading and commenting on this paper.

## Afterword

1 Nils Bubandt, *The Empty Seashell: Witchcraft and Doubt on an Indonesian Island* (Ithaca: Cornell University Press, 2014), p. 5.

2 The words are Ashis Nandy's, in *Alternative Sciences: Creativity and Authenticity in Two Indian Scientists* (New Delhi: Oxford University Press, 1995), p. 119.

3 See, for instance, Suzanne Simard, 'The Wood Wide Web: How Trees Talk to Each Other'. TED video, filmed June 2016; and ' Monica Gagliano, John C. Ryan and Patrícia Vieira, eds. *The Language of Plants: Science, Philosophy, Literature* (Minneapolis: University of Minnesota Press, 2017).

4 Jagadish Chandra Bose, *Abyakta* (Calcutta: Shatabdi Press Pvt. Ltd, 1921), pp. 30–35.

# About the Author

AMITAV GHOSH was born in Calcutta, and grew up in India, Bangladesh and Sri Lanka; he studied in Delhi, Oxford and Alexandria. He is the author of several acclaimed works of fiction and non-fiction including *The Shadow Lines*, *The Glass Palace*, *The Hungry Tide*, the Ibis Trilogy (comprising the novels *Sea of Poppies*, *River of Smoke* and *Flood of Fire*), *The Great Derangement*, *Gun Island*, *The Nutmeg's Curse*, *Jungle Nama*, *The Living Mountain* and *Smoke and Ashes*.

Amitav Ghosh's work has been translated into more than thirty languages. He has been awarded and felicitated across the world. In 2019 Foreign Policy magazine named him one of the most important global thinkers of the past decade. The same year, the Jnanpith Award, India's highest literary honour, was conferred on him: he was the first English-language writer to receive it. In 2024, he was awarded the prestigious Erasmus Prize for his writings on the planetary crisis and climate change.

# HarperCollins *Publishers* India

At HarperCollins India, we believe in telling the best stories and finding the widest readership for our books in every format possible. We started publishing in 1992; a great deal has changed since then, but what has remained constant is the passion with which our authors write their books, the love with which readers receive them, and the sheer joy and excitement that we as publishers feel in being a part of the publishing process.

Over the years, we've had the pleasure of publishing some of the finest writing from the subcontinent and around the world, including several award-winning titles and some of the biggest bestsellers in India's publishing history. But nothing has meant more to us than the fact that millions of people have read the books we published, and that somewhere, a book of ours might have made a difference.

As we look to the future, we go back to that one word—a word which has been a driving force for us all these years.

Read.

Harper Collins · 4th · HARPER FICTION · HARPER NON-FICTION · HARPER BUSINESS · HCCB HARPERCOLLINS CHILDREN'S BOOKS

HARPER DESIGN · Harper Sport · HARPER PERENNIAL · HARPER VANTAGE · हार्पर हिन्दी